ITALIAN VENICE

Venice will not be worthy of the twentieth century until the Grand Canal is transformed into the most beautiful road in the world, with a footpath on each side, two lines of trees and two steam-driven *tramways*, and a paved road in the middle. [The old Venice could perhaps be] transported piece by piece and re-erected in some English park or between a coal mine and a tanning shop in Chicago. With the Grand Canal buried, the area will be more beautiful, with five-storey housing adorned with iron-clad attics and concrete frames, steel balconies, plastered light yellow and with pinkish shutters. We shall have Piazza San Marco covered in glass. The two columns of the Piazzetta will be removed and replaced by a sign that recalls their removal. At the museum, a life-size model of a gondola will be preserved. It will be made of ebony or silver or gilded copper or black velvet.

Archaeologist nightmare of 1887, as recounted in Giacomo Boni, *Il cosidetto sventramento: appunti di un veneziano* (Rome: Stabilmento Tipografico Italiano, 1887), 5–7

For a Venetian a bridge is a necessary structure for passage across a city built on water, which you normally cross by foot. For a tourist . . . a bridge is something else. Every bridge and not just the Rialto. It is a lookout where you stop to admire the view, and to take 'unforgettable' photographs from one side and then the other, assuming automatically that anyone who wants to pass will stop and wait. It is also a place where you can stop and exchange impressions with friends or, especially if you are young, sit on the steps. . . . Such tourists simply do not see the urban purpose of the bridge, and neither do the great majority of other tourists who throng around. They only see a place of beauty, leisure and socialisation.

Enrico Tantucci, *A che ora chiude Venezia? Breve guida alla disneylandizzazione della città* (Venice: Corte del Fontego, 2011), 6–7

R.J.B. BOSWORTH

ITALIAN VENICE

A HISTORY

YALE UNIVERSITY PRESS
NEW HAVEN AND LONDON

For Giovanni Minelli

For information about this and other Yale University Press publications, please contact:
U.S. Office: sales.press@yale.edu   www.yalebooks.com
Europe Office: sales@yaleup.co.uk   www.yalebooks.co.uk

Set in Minion Pro Pro by IDSUK (DataConnection) Ltd
Printed in Great Britain by TJ International Ltd, Padstow, Cornwall

Library of Congress Cataloging-in-Publication Data

Bosworth, R. J. B.
   Italian Venice : a history / R.J.B. Bosworth.
      pages cm
   Includes bibliographical references and index.
   ISBN 978-0-300-19387-9 (cloth : alkaline paper)
1. Venice (Italy)—History—1797–1866.   2. Venice (Italy)—History—1866–
3. Venice (Italy)—Social conditions.   4. Social change—Italy—Venice—History.
5. Venice (Italy)—Politics and government.   I. Title.
   DG678.5.B67 2014
   945'.31109—dc23

2014018999

A catalogue record for this book is available from the British Library.

10 9 8 7 6 5 4 3 2 1

Contents

Illustrations and Maps

Illustrations

Maps

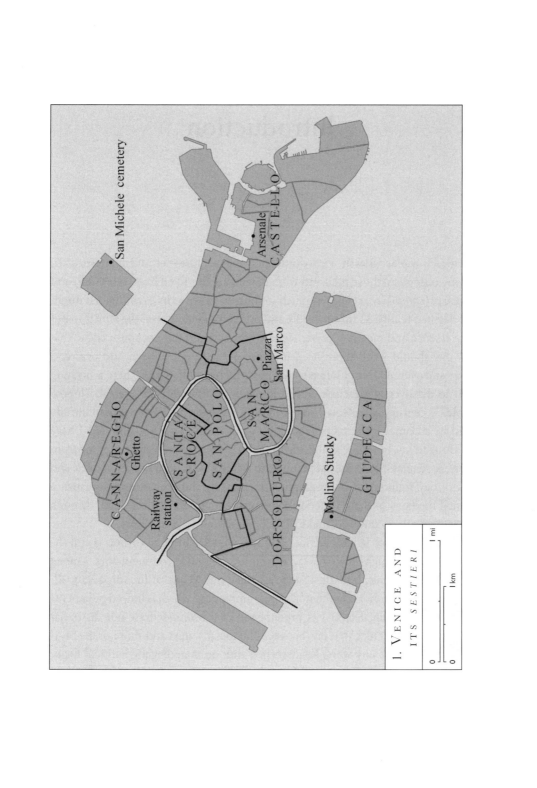

San Michele cemetery

Arsenale
CASTELLO

CANNAREGIO
Ghetto

Railway
station

SANTA
CROCE

SAN POLO

Piazza
San Marco

SAN
MARCO

DORSODURO

Molino Stucky

GIUDECCA

1. VENICE AND
ITS SESTIERI

0   1km

0   1 mi

Introduction

Venice is a place awash with words and images, histories and memories. To many observers, those men and women who are found on its streets (*calli*) and squares (*campi*) live at least as much in the mind's eye as in anything that might be deemed reality. So innumerable and unrelenting have been the efforts to put the essence and meaning of Venice into words that it has become a cliché that no one should write about it again, since everything has been said over and over and over. As Henry James stated more than a century ago, 'there is nothing left to discover or describe, and originality of attitude is completely impossible'.[1] A century later, Gore Vidal, candidly assessing his TV portrait of the city and its accompanying picture booklet, confessed wryly, 'Not only did I have nothing to say, but there *is* nothing to say.'[2] Yet accounts of Venice ranging from austere scholarship to tourist manuals to crime novels pour off the presses, and every day millions of photographs are taken by those anxious to burnish a visual memory of their Venetian moments, convinced that they can, through the images they conserve, make Venice, somehow defined, theirs.

Despite Henry James's advice, 'attitude', whether original or not, is still the quest, often the high-flown quest, of the more celebrated commentators. Among French intellectuals, Jean-Paul Sartre affirmed that Venice is 'the surpassing-all-or-nothing embodiment of that "absolute ambiguity" which is indeed radiant life containing certain death'.[3] His predecessor Paul Morand drew not dissimilar lessons from a Venice that lay 'between the foetal waters and those of the Styx'. The canals of the city were, he discerned with an unapologetic national focus, 'black as ink; it is the ink of Jean-Jacques, of Chateaubriand, of Barrès, of Proust; to dip one's pen into it is more than a Frenchman's duty, it is a duty pure and simple'.[4] Two generations later, *Annales* historian Fernand Braudel, lauded as a theorist of the nature of time, deemed Venice a place where the 'present annuls itself by itself'. By contrast, the past lapped everywhere and in every detail; the *calli* and *campi* brimmed with it. Its seeping over the place was threatened only by the tourists who, Braudel complained, arrived in 'swarms . . . lacking provision and knowledge'; 'they can be compared to the infantry of an army engaged in a permanent, covert and dangerous war that Venice fights in order to live'.[5] A generation later, Régis Debray, the youthful revolutionary turned French government official, was still harsher about the present, damning Venice as dragging an entire continent into becoming no more than 'a wholly museumised Europe'. Venice, he judged, was 'the most vulgar resort frequented by people of taste'. Nothing was 'genuine' there. 'Venice plays at being a town and we play at discovering it.' The tourists constituted no more than 'faceless extras'; yet without them Venice 'would decline and collapse in a week, its text dissolving, lost, haggard, like a great star forced to play nightly to an empty house'.[6]

It is not unusual for French intellectuals to win gold medals in portentousness. But when it comes to Venice they have many challengers. Australian historian Manning Clark knew from a brief visit that the city was threaded by 'that something else, beyond what we can see, touch, smell and hear'; it was where we know 'we are alone'.[7] Another seeking to catch the special ticking of Venetian time, F. Marion Crawford, a *belle époque* American novelist, maintained that Venice was 'the most personal of all cities in the world, the most feminine, the most comparable to a woman, the least dependent, for her individuality, upon her inhabitants, ancient and modern. The imagination can hardly picture a Venice different from her present self at any time in her history. . . . In the still canals, the gorgeous palaces continually gaze down upon their own reflected images with placid satisfaction, and look with calm indifference upon the changing generations of men and women that glide upon the waters. The mists gather upon the mysterious lagoons and sink away again before the devouring light, day after day, year after year, century after century; and Venice is always there herself, sleeping or waking, laughing, weeping, dreaming, singing or sighing, living her own life through the ages, with an intensely vital personality which time has hardly modified, and is altogether powerless to destroy. Somehow it would not surprise those who know her, to come suddenly upon her and find that all human life was extinct within her, while her own went on, as strong as ever.'[8]

Special parts of the city have also been portrayed more or less evocatively. For one crime novelist, Piazza San Marco looked like 'a giraffe – absurd, impossible, and beautiful beyond computation, as if Michelangelo, Christopher Wren, Walt Disney and God had sat on a committee to build it'.[9] For another, the city in 1867 was the epitome of decay, a place that did not generate capital as modernity required.[10] Less euphoniously, an American writer reckoned that 'the Stazione Santa Lucia is like a gleaming syringe, connected to the industrial mainland by its long trailing railway lines and inserted into the rear end of Venice's Grand Canal, into which it pumps a steady provender and daily pumps off the waste'. As such it amounted to 'that tender spot where the ubiquitous technocratic circuit of the World Metropolis physically impinges upon the last outpost of the self-enclosed Renaissance *Urbs*'.[11]

But the palm in recent commentary should be awarded to Peter Ackroyd for a book that aims to display today's Venice to the world. In its pages, Ackroyd asserts that Venice and Venetians are radically cut off from other Italians, a mobile prey to water, tides and the sea, floating like Ophelia, naturally double and duplicitous, pure, dream-like, artificial, quintessentially touristic, devoted to retailing their pastness, expressive of rank rather than the individual, corrupt, psychopathic, anxious, unstable and unpredictable, self-obsessed, fearful, vivacious, gay, radiant, extravagant, energetic, buoyant, spontaneous, urgent, facile, exuberant and impetuous, and so like all cities and their peoples.[12] Enough to be going on with, it might be concluded.

Ackroyd's book is unusual in that it purports to deal with Venice's story in modern times, whereas most accounts chronicle the Republic from its (alleged) foundation near the Rialto at the stroke of noon on 25 March 421 to its destruction by Napoleon, whose troops occupied Venice on 12 May 1797. (A few weeks earlier, the general of the revolution had picked St Mark's Day, 25 April, brutally to inform appeasing Venetian negotiators that he intended to be a new 'Attila' to the city.) Somewhere in the background to this dogged focus on the Republic and the implicit or explicit deprecation of history after 1797 lies the enormously influential figure of John Ruskin and his meticulous depiction of a version of the city in *The Stones of Venice* (1851–3).[13] It was Ruskin, another to imagine a city that was very much his own, who stipulated to a receptive audience in Victorian Britain and to his many admirers in Venice, Italy and Europe that the Doge's Palace was 'the central building of the world' and San Marco 'a great Book of Common Prayer'.[14]

Through labours that extended from the 1840s to the 1880s and included eleven stays in the city, the most productive of which were those through the winters of 1849–50 and 1851–2, Ruskin pioneered the view that a comprehension of the passage of time, and so of history, was the key Venetian message to the world. In that regard, he urged that time and history split into good and bad phases. Everything in the city had once been wonderful and transcendent; God had all but taken human form in the artistic triumphs of the early Republic. But the Renaissance marked 'the knell of architecture, and of Venice itself'.[15] By the mid nineteenth century, the contemporary city lay dead or gasping its last breath; as he put it in 1846 in a homely metaphor, 'the rate at which Venice is going is about that of a lump of sugar in hot tea'.[16]

At San Donato on Murano, Ruskin was appalled by the Venetians whom he encountered: 'woful [sic] groups of aged men and women, wasted and fever-struck, fixed in paralytic supplication, half-kneeling, half-couched upon the pavement; bowed down, partly in feebleness, partly in fearful devotion, with their grey clothes cast far over their faces, ghastly and settled into a gloomy animal misery, all but the glittering eyes and muttering lips'.[17] They and their fellows were the epitome of degeneracy, once brilliantly able to erect a paradise on the waters, but now renouncing knowledge for superstition and work for begging. Fickle and wan, present-day Venetians had no political merits and ideals just as they had no aesthetics. It was meet, right and proper that they be ruled by the alien Austrians. Despite the revolution and siege of 1848–9, they offered no resolute opposition to their political enslavement (although that was probably too grand a word for it). Such half-men could not rise above 'general grumbling and vague discontent'.[18] All Italians were the same: 'slothful – ignorant – incapable of *conceiving* such a thing as Truth or Honesty – Blasphemous – Murderous – Sensual – Cowardly – . . . Governed severely because they can be no other wise governed'.[19] In their disgraceful torpor, they and their contemporary history could no longer provide humankind with useful lessons. Venice, and Italy, were dead beyond repair.

During and after the mid nineteenth century, most Venetians did their best to ignore Ruskin's derisive view of what, in the 1850s, was the rapidly approaching Risorgimento, devoted to the unification of Italy into a Liberal nation state that would proclaim itself as committed to delivering to its people an 'age of improvement' as was Victorian Britain. Venice was to join Italy in very specific circumstances in 1866, five years after the new kingdom had come into existence and four years before it made Rome its capital (thereby beginning the complex task of finding a use for the many imperial and other histories of that place, while ensuring recurrent mathematical complications in the framing of national anniversaries). But for quite a few Venetians, the message that mattered in Ruskin's depiction of their town was to be found not in his lucubrations on its present decay but in a lapidary phrase destined to be deeply inscribed into the city over the succeeding years: 'com'era e dov'era' (how and where it was).

This formula counselled Venetians not so much to harness values expressed in the past for present or future use but rather to stem the flux of time. Since, under the Republic, Venice had been the best and most beautiful, nothing that was left over from that past should be disturbed or changed. Doubtless, the passage of the years demanded watchfulness always and repair sometimes. But the latter must entail exact and literal reconstruction. The Venice of the twentieth or twenty-first centuries must keep intact the Venice of the Republic and its glories 'to be a light to lighten the Gentiles' – that is, to allow the world, still and for ever, to mark, learn from and inwardly digest its grandeur. So, for almost half a century, until his death in 1928, the lawyer, journalist and politician Pompeo Molmenti bore aloft the torch that Ruskin had lit, while naturally rejecting the Englishman's contempt for modern Italy and campaigning loudly against any who sought to chart a 'black legend' about the Republic as a political system devoted to secret murder and putrid corruption.[20] As he told the wider world in a work intended for international consumption, written just before his death and so expressing his last thoughts on the subject, 'No government was less despotic [than that of the Republic]. No people knew such serenity and happiness.'[21]

For a generation, Molmenti led with stubborn consistency those who objected to change and strove to turn back the attempts of engineers and medical experts to bring improvement to the city through demolition of the old and construction of the new.[22] The eventual intrusion of 'modernising' Fascism into the city and the continued meddling of modernising capitalism there complicated matters after his death. But Molmenti's attitudes, with their certainty that the treasures of the past must be preserved at any cost, retained, and still retain, a major place in discourse about the city. As he urged expansively, 'The characteristics of Venice have never been altered. The earliest plans of the city – and one goes back to the XIIth century – show it just as it appears today.'[23] In recent decades, the plea to 'save Venice' (analysed in greater detail in chapters 8 and 9) has been at the centre of much commentary and labour, almost always carrying the unspoken belief that salvation must leave the place 'com'era e dov'era'.[24]

A determination to focus on (certain aspects of) distant Venetian history ensured that the spur to Molmenti and his friends was a regretful nostalgia, and the more sophisticated and richer foreign visitors to Venice are equally likely to remain wistful in their approach. As the historian John Julius Norwich, son of Diana Cooper, has recently meditated, 'Venice is by far the most beautiful city in the world, but she is also one of the saddest: never, never would I recommend a Venetian honeymoon.'[25]

Norwich is scarcely alone in his deep pessimism about Venice's current situation and his all but certain expectation that the city's death is at hand. Thomas Mann's novella *Der Tod in Venedig* may have been written for specific purposes and at a specific time, as shall be noted in chapter 3.[26] But his title has since become deeply branded, both consciously and unconsciously, into efforts to comprehend the city. Death is never far away in thoughts about Venice. Ruskin and Mann therefore act as a sort of two-headed Cerberus, jointly guarding local, Italian and global approaches to Venice and directing commentators down one path to meaning rather than another.

Many an introduction to the city thus stops short at 1866 (or 1797), dismissing in a few words or sentences Venice's fate since it became part of the Italian state. Even the guide to the place produced by the Comune at the high point of Fascism in 1938 restricted itself to noting that the events of 1848–9 had inscribed a 'page of glory which redeemed the sorrow of '97', before hurrying on to conclude that 'in 1866 Venice was finally joined to Italy'. This end, it implied, dissipated any further historical impulse or interest.[27]

Today, too, artistic and architectural guides are rich in detail about the achievements of Palladio and Sansovino, Palma il Giovane, Tiepolo, Tintoretto, Titian, the Bellinis and the rest.[28] But more modern aspects of the city are mostly overlooked or dismissed with asperity as having infringed the rule 'com'era e dov'era'. It is true that the Australian art historian Margaret Plant has produced a fine, lengthy account of the cultural history of the place since 1797.[29] More humdrum aspects of social and political history, however, pass her and almost all other commentators by. Again Peter Ackroyd offers a template. His account of Venice through time nowhere mentions Giuseppe Volpi, entrepreneur of the Marghera industrial site, initiator of the film and music festivals, recognised even by Benito Mussolini, the Fascist dictator and Duce, as the doge of interwar Venice, a man whose widow and children continued to play a major role in the battles over what the city should mean throughout the post-1945 era. Ackroyd, in portraying the modern city to his readers, omits the most important and influential Venetian of the twentieth century.

Somewhere in such a fuzzy response to the Venice subjected to Italian rule lurks another grand binary opposite. Experts, devotees, those attuned to aesthetics and high culture, comprehend much about Venice before 1797 while happily conceding that a more perfect comprehension of the Republic's past needs still further research. In their skills, devotion to scholarship, worthiness and individuality, they sharply distinguish themselves from the tourist clutter, those who do not really know the city at all but exploit it as though it were but another 'Disneyland'[30] – that is, a dumbed-down place of brittle show, shame-lessly selling a concocted but not a real history. Intellectuals, yes, tourists, no, often seems to be the formula with which the current city should be approached.

The common lesson is that 'ordinary' tourists are not real people and have no claim to inclusion in Venetian history. Their 'pilgrimages' to Venice, or at least to certain parts of it, are not pious but sordidly unholy.[31] Like locusts, they consume the city and its native inhabitants. 'Nothing', becomes the continuous cry, 'would be more melancholy and negative than to have a Venice without Venetians.'[32] Sadly, this discourse runs on, the populace flee to Mestre on the mainland, however 'hideous it may be'. A fatal destiny drags 'the world's loveliest city . . . to become nothing more than a waterlogged museum, the thinking man's Disneyland'.[33] In the interim, the best people gather to 'save Venice' and certainly favour the costly employment of modern science (not to be paid for by themselves, however) to stop the place from becoming the new Atlantis and disappearing beneath the waves of the Adriatic.

This book is written to challenge the legacy of Ruskin, Molmenti and Mann, as well as more contemporary superciliousness. My view is that Venice is washed by many pasts, some old, some new, each of interest to a historian and many worth drawing to the attention of the city's visitors, learned or not, who themselves have histories that are also part of Venice. I write on the assumption that, over the last hundred and fifty years, and in fact well before that, Venetian history was not merely made or owned or used by those born in the city. I shall remain highly sceptical therefore when James (Jan) Morris assures me that Venetians under the Republic possessed a 'peculiar national history [that] lasted a millennium', and that, throughout time, the city's inhabitants are best understood as 'a race *sui generis*'.[34] Rather, throughout time, the peoples of many nations and many non-national loyalties left an imprint on Venice and in turn had its imprint engraved upon their souls.

My purpose will therefore be to depict the multiple Venices that have pasts that can still be represented. But my focus will be on the modern histories of a territory that was absorbed into Italy on 19 October 1866, technically a gift from the French emperor, Napoleon III, who had been handed it by the Austrian emperor, Franz Josef, a gift that was formally approved in a referendum held two days later.[35] I shall analyse how the city reacted to the prospect and the reality of Italian ownership and review how the nation and its aspirations to be liberal at home and a Great Power – ideally a Great Imperial Power – abroad impacted on Venetians, rich and poor, male and female, old and young, Catholic and anti-clerical, resident or in transit, and on through the other divisions and disagreements of modernising societies.

By chapter 3, I shall have reached the *belle époque*, a time of splendour and misery in the city, going on to examine what the First World War, entered belatedly by Italy on 24 May 1915, did to a Venice that lay near the frontline – indeed, after the heavy defeat at Caporetto in October 1917, very near. For many reasons, this conflict wracked the city and its inhabitants in a way that would not be fully replicated during the Second World War – or Nazi-Fascist war – of 1940–5. In that later war, despite Fascist claims to have militarised all Italians into devoted legionaries awaiting the call of Mussolini, their Duce, Venice slipped back into its vocation of providing rest and recuperation, and, contrary to Fascist swank about at last having fully nationalised Italians, retained a local and a cosmopolitan purpose as much as a national one. What

Fascism did to Venice and what Venice did to Fascism is thus another natural topic of this book.

Venice survived the violent depredations of Nazi-fascism with relatively little loss and barbarity, and sleekly enough moved into a post-war era, soon characterised by the national 'economic miracle', with its resultant lights and shadows for Venetians, while the city further reinforced its tourist appeal both to glamorous international high society and to the masses. Now, too, Catholic Venice took a leading role, Giuseppe Roncalli being patriarch of the diocese of Venice from 1953 until his election as Pope John XXIII on 28 October 1958 (ironically the thirty-sixth anniversary of the Fascist 'March on Rome'). Roncalli followed a path that had already been trodden by Pius X (1903–14), who, as Giuseppe Sarto, had been patriarch for almost a decade from 1894. In turn, Albino Luciani, patriarch of Venice from 1969 when he was promoted from the junior Venetian see of Vittorio Veneto, became the short-lived Pope John Paul I on 26 August 1978, dying barely a month later on 28 September.

At a basic political level, then, Venice was, until 1966, another part of that Italy in which a battle for economic and social control was fought between communist Peppones and Christian Democrat Don Camillos, as so cheerfully described by the novelist Giovannino Guareschi.[36] Then came the Great Flood, the highest and worst *acqua alta*, an event occurring with deep historical irony on 4 November 1966 – that is, Vittorio Veneto Day, the forty-eighth anniversary of the battle through which, as far as patriots were concerned, Italy had won the First World War. The waves – those that swept over the island of Sant'Erasmo were said to have been thirteen feet high, while in Venice the waters were 194 centimetres above normal – carried a simple and disastrous message, 'Venice is dying', like Shakespeare's Earl of Suffolk, dying by water, that water from which it had long lived.

The result was once again to underline the fact that Venice was not merely an Italian city, all the more when governments in Rome, who seemed to delay, confuse and corrupt the process of restoration and of defence against further, perhaps still worse floods, became the object of international criticism. The last chapter of my book will therefore examine the nature and meaning of the 'salvation of Venice', notably through the much-debated construction of the MOSE (Modulo Sperimentale Elettromeccanico, Experimental Electromechanical Module), the completion of which is said to be imminent.

Notably complex was the relationship between such projects, with their protective and protectionist ideals, and the neo-liberalism that began to assume hegemony over the world from the 1980s. In Venice, the disadvantages of too untrammelled a belief in the market and the freedom of the individual were made obvious by the Pink Floyd concert staged on a floating platform off the

Piazzetta on 15 July 1989, the date suggesting that any commemoration of the French Revolution was indeed over. As a local commented bitterly, the concert was the ultimate example of a 'throwaway society', in which the real audience was constituted not by the 200,000 fans who, in his view, were trashing the city but rather by TV viewers across the world. 'It was all just a long ad, celebrating the rock group. Venice's part was merely to be the backdrop to it,' he lamented.[37] The Pink Floyd visit thus became a trigger for an ongoing discussion of how many tourists Venice should, and can, accommodate and whether the operation of the market in this particular arena needs to be controlled and circumscribed. Although its usage may have been ironical, a line from one of the Pink Floyd songs – 'Money, it's a gas' – was seen by determinedly hostile critics as proof that Mammon should not be allowed to roam totally free in Venice.[38]

There are histories enough worth remarking, then, of that Venice which has been governed by Italy since 1866. One of my tasks in this book will be to nudge readers into viewing the memory sites of these pasts that survive in the city and that might demand attention and thought at least as much as the Tintorettos. Each of my chapters will begin with portraits of such places. I shall perforce have to omit many; one tabulation estimates that 126 memorial plaques are affixed to city walls, and this calculation omits most that refer to twentieth-century events.[39] Plainly there are plenty of triggers for those who tramp the city in search no less of modern than of early modern or medieval memory.

A good place to start is the building first erected in 1869 that now houses the 'two-star' Hotel San Fantin. It stands in Campiello della Fenice, just round the corner from the Fenice opera house, opened in 1792 and since 2004 back in the music business 'com'era e dov'era' (but with updated technology), following the controversial and devastating fire of 29 January 1996 (see map 9). The hotel's website, justifying itself with a more abbreviated past, claims, in uneasy translation into English, that it has been run by the same family since 1957, 'who always keeps his passion for the hospitality and welcome'.[40] For those in search of grander histories, more significant is the entrance, a pink structure, surmounted by the Winged Lion of the city, with the open book signifying peace, and with a plaque set in place in 1869 commemorating the determination of the Venetian Republic on 11 April 1849 to resist the Austrians 'at any cost'. Serving as a sort of frieze to the rectangular edifice is a line of cannon balls, another six of which circle two bull's-eye windows on the front of the building, while the doorway is guarded by a pair of cannon set vertically into the wall. There is similar ornamentation on the building's side. At the left of the entrance, a seated female embodiment of the city is portrayed in a round plaque. She is bearing a sword and a flag, armed with an apposite quotation from Dante, so frequently presented as the Great Italian National Poet.

The weaponry at the site is said to have been salvaged from the Austrian bombardment of the city, which ended in the fall of the Republic headed by Daniel Manin on 28 August 1849, an event that, after 1866, was made to symbolise the national Risorgimento and became proof of the unfailing and

1 Hotel San Fantin today

universal desire of Venetians to be Italians. The Hotel San Fantin is therefore an instructive spot from which to commence reflection on how the city and its territories on the mainland became part of the Italian nation state.

One final point as I prepare to unroll Venice's modern histories. I have already established that my definition of who finds a place in these pasts and who therefore might be claimed to be Venetian is a flexible one. To those who lived and died in the city I am willing to add visitors, whether long-term residents or day-trippers, intellectuals equipped with many telling words or tourists armed only with a camera or a bag in which to tote their souvenirs. After all, the population of the city was never unchanging; the inhabitants were never themselves 'com'erano e dov'erano'. A fine study of the area around Campo Santa Margherita has demonstrated that, in 1881, less than a quarter of the population resided in the same place as in 1869, while by 1931 92 per cent had lived there for only one or two generations. In a paradox that will lie at the heart of my book, the student of Santa Margherita nonetheless avers that, well into the twentieth century, each *campo* rejoiced in its own identity and definition, and Venice as a whole was therefore equipped with 'lots of little cities within the city'.[41]

Certainly, any geographical definition of Venice is almost as complicated as the historical. In 1866 the Comune of Venice simply meant the old city, extending from the railway station and Santa Marta to the island of Sant'Elena, and consisting of the six *sestieri* of San Marco, San Polo, Santa Croce, Dorsoduro (including the Giudecca), Castello and Cannaregio (see map 1). In 1883 the urban administration annexed the still sparsely populated Lido and Malamocco (see map 4). The First World War and its aftermath brought further expansion, with 'Venezia' now including Marghera (from 1917), Pellestrina (1923), Murano, Burano and Ca' Savio (1924), and the villages of Chirignago, Zelarino, Malcontenta and Favaro, as well as what was to become the city of Mestre, from 1926 (see map 8). At the present time, the Comune is subdivided into six municipalities (Venice–Murano–Burano; Lido–Pellestrina; Favaro–Veneto; Mestre–Carpenedo or central Mestre; Chirignago–Zelarino or west Mestre; and Marghera). The first has 69,679 inhabitants, while the two Mestres and Marghera total 154,095 – that is, more than twice as many.

It is impossible to write the modern history of Venice without some reference to Mestre and Marghera. My focus, however, will be on the old Venice, the 'centro storico', to use a term that gained prominence from the 1960s.[42] But even there geography is anything but certain. The various *sestieri* and the parishes within them have had different fates since 1866. To make one obvious point, the tourist experience of Venice rarely covers the whole historic centre, Strada Nova or Piazza San Marco pullulating, for example, while the 1920s new model suburb of Sant'Elena remains exempt, unless crossed by football crowds heading for the stadium where Il Venezia Foot-Ball Club plays in notoriously erratic fashion, or by studious visitors wanting to examine the eleventh-century church of Sant'Elena (radically restored between 1927 and 1930). It would be a mistake, therefore, to be too precise in answering the question, where is the Venice whose stories are here to be recounted? Just like its pasts, Venice's physical lineaments, its 'place' or places, are to quite a degree in the mind and subject to change, debate and disagreement. In our own day, as in the past, there are many Venices and not just one, the infinite variety of whose fates can entertain and instruct in their stories of change as well as of continuity.

CHAPTER ONE

Awaiting an Italian destiny

Venice to 1866

The architecture of the Hotel San Fantin may broadcast a patriotic history to passers-by; its cannon balls may blazon a claim that Venetians heroically brought themselves into union with the nation, Italy, and urge that the Risorgimento was a popular movement backed by a people who unanimously knew themselves to be Italian and longed to be free of alien rule. On the other side of the Rialto bridge, however, another square carries a more complex message in its very name, 'Campo Cesare Battisti già della Bella Vienna' (the square of Cesare Battisti, formerly that of fine Vienna; see map 2). It is a place coursed by histories rather than a single past.

At first sight, all might seem straightforward. Vienna is doubtless a nice place, but it was the capital of that Habsburg Empire whose rule over Venice Italy dislodged in 1866. Moreover, Cesare Battisti was a martyr-hero to the nation in its First World War, an 'irredentist' (that is, someone committed to the 'return' of Italy's 'terra irredenta', or 'unredeemed', Italian-speaking lands) and nationalist (although ready to leave the German-speaking parts of the Tyrol outside Italian control, while also trying to remain some form of social democrat). Despite having been born in Trento and therefore being an Austrian citizen, he volunteered to fight for Italy in 1915. He was captured by his enemies, court-martialled and then garrotted and hanged with studied humiliation, not in Italian uniform but in dirty civilian clothes, by the Austrian army on 11 July 1916.

He was not, however, a Venetian. Although he orated in the city during the so-called 'intervento' – the period that separated the start of war between the Great Powers in August 1914 and Italian entry into the conflict, at least against Austria-Hungary, nine months later on 24 May 1915 – his concerns were not particularly Venetian. Even his war-front, contested in the high country above Trento, was not as near to Venice's fate as that conducted lower down on the

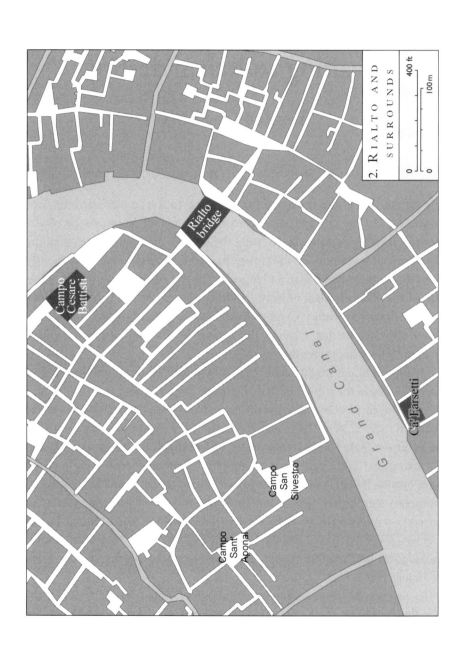

2. RIALTO AND
SURROUNDS

0 _____ 400 ft
0 _____ 100m

Rialto
bridge

Campo
Cesare
Battisti

Grand Canal

Ca' Farsetti

Campo San
Silvestro

Campo
Sant
Aponal

2 Campo Cesare Battisti: multiple histories in a Venetian square

Venetian plain, across the river Isonzo until the Italian defeat at Caporetto (Kobarid) in October 1917 and thereafter beside the river Piave, some forty kilometres to the east. When Fascism took Italian nationalism to an extreme and made memory of the 'total' effort in the First World War the historical justification for its own 'totalitarianism', Battisti's widow by no means fully or automatically endorsed the dictatorship. It was thus telling that the opening of a strikingly modernist memorial to Battisti above Trento in June 1935 was attended by King Victor Emmanuel III but not by the Duce, Benito Mussolini.[1] The ghost of Cesare Battisti therefore carries into the *calli* of Venice not so much a 'divided memory'[2] as a multiplicity of histories. His name is not a simple patriotic counter to the 'bella Vienna' of a defeated *ancien régime*.

In any case, how should foreign rule over Venice from 1797 to 1866, whether French or Austrian, be judged? The standard nationalist Italian line, endorsed by English historians with romantic inclinations, such as G. M. Trevelyan early in the twentieth century[3] and Jonathan Keates in our own times,[4] is one of hated misrule and oppression. Such accounts will explain that the Napoleonic extinction of the Republic meant disaster for Venice, the most obvious proof being that the population of the city tumbled from 136,000 in 1799 to 125,000 in 1812 and 100,000 in the 1820s[5] (by 1871 it had risen back to 141,000, plus 26,000 on the islands, then administered from Murano, and 23,000 in and around what was still the village of Mestre).[6]

In 1797 the French revolutionary forces had time to pull down the wooden doors of the ghetto, which had confined the two thousand Jews of the city within their part of the *sestiere* of Cannaregio.[7] On 12 July these religious and social barriers were ceremoniously burned in the centre of the ghetto square, where a Liberty Tree was planted in demonstration that liberty, equality and fraternity must now take root in Venice.[8] This promise of revolutionary change and the practice of fraternity proved fleeting, however. By the end of the year the Republic's territory, reduced to a pawn in diplomatic dealing, had been handed over to Austrian control by the terms of the Treaty of Campo Formio, Habsburg forces establishing themselves in the city in January 1798.

That solution did not last, either, and seven years later further victories by Napoleon, now French emperor, saw Venice and the Veneto melded into the puppet state of the 'Kingdom of Italy' under the Peace of Pressburg. The change was scarcely beneficent. Telling is the visit that Napoleon made to Venice in 1807, his preoccupations characteristically combining Enlightenment science and revolutionary rapine. The cemetery island of San Michele was modernised at his command, so that the dead could rest in order and efficiency. His agents checked the *murazzi* or sea walls off the Lido for wear and tear, high water or *acqua alta* having lapped into Venice on 3 December while Napoleon was in residence. Within the city's bounds, the emperor commissioned the covering of the main canal that ran into the *sestiere* of Castello, opening in its place the spacious Via Eugenia, named in honour of his stepson and viceroy in Venice and Italy, Eugène de Beauharnais. More than seventeen metres wide, it was planned by its local architect to be 'the most beautiful road in the city', its form illustrating that even Venice's narrow and twisting, congested 'medieval' *calli* could be readjusted to become as rational and spacious as Enlightenment urban vision demanded. Nonetheless, critics soon condemned the Via Eugenia as un-Venetian and leading nowhere.[9] Nearby, Napoleon fostered another Enlightenment urban ideal, a public park, the origin of what was to become the Giardini and from the end of the nineteenth century the site of the Biennale exhibitions. Of similar lasting impact was the reconstruction of the western end of Piazza San Marco, where seven bays of the Procuratie Vecchie and the Sansovino church of San Geminiano[10] were demolished and replaced by the Ala Napoleonica, its name indicating that not even the city's most celebrated square had passed into modernity 'com'era e dov'era'. While French rule prospered, the new wing housed a ballroom and extra office space in Beauharnais's palace and administrative centre; today it is the home of the permanent and special exhibitions of the Museo and Pinacoteca Correr.

At the same time as drastically rebuilding the heart of the city in proof that modern times and scientific planning had taken hold in Venice, the French were ruthlessly stripping the city's churches and galleries of such artworks as Veronese's *Marriage at Cana*, a huge canvas still kept at the Louvre, and numerous beautiful Titians, Tintorettos, Bellinis and Carpaccios. With overweening arrogance, they carried back to Paris the 'Quadriga', the four bronze horses that sit above the grand portal of the Basilica di San Marco, sculptures purloined from Constantinople after its brutal sack in 1204 by Doge Enrico Dandolo, who had diverted the Fourth Crusade there.[11] For this and other reasons, in 2003 particularist elements in Venice, seeking their own usable past with modish reference to the advantage of historical closure, put Napoleon on trial for political and cultural 'war crimes' against Venetians,[12] finding him guilty in December of that year.

In more academic circles, French revolutionary rule in Italy has been subject to equally withering criticism, current interpretations placing less emphasis on modernity and Enlightenment rationality than on pillage and death.[13] Rather than acting as a prompt towards national unification in the Risorgimento, the French are deemed cultural imperialists of the crassest kind, racist in their assumption of Italian inferiority.[14] On occasion, revisionism may go too far, however. Certainly, the two decades following 1797 saw many changes in the city and thereby did much to frame Venice's path to 1866 and beyond. Early modern Venice may not have been wrenched into a new Enlightened shape. But it was jostled, physically and spiritually.

Largely destroyed was the fabric of religious welfare that had helped to salve (and to preserve) the gaps between rich and poor in the early modern city, whether provided by the 337 extant confraternities and Scuole Grandi (all were formally suppressed in 1806, while the city parishes were reduced from seventy to thirty) or by the numerous monasteries and nunneries. The number of religious who lived in the city halved and then halved again by the 1850s, when only 471 priests retained office in Venice.[15] In addition to San Geminiano, tens of other churches were demolished or transferred to lay control. As befitted an age of war, the house of the Benedictine nuns of Santa Maria della Grazia, occupying its own island between the Giudecca and San Clemente, was converted into a barracks. This process of secularisation, once begun, continued under Austrian and national Italian rule. According to Alvise Zorzi's careful reckoning of 1977, only 101 of the 187 churches that had been open under the Republic were still available for worship by that year, 70 having been razed to the ground (45 in Venice itself, 13 in Burano–Mazzorbo–Torcello

and 12 in Murano). Seventeen survived in usage that was not religious, San
Leonardo having become the practice venue for the municipal band, Santa
Marta, Santa Maria Maggiore and San Lorenzo warehouses, Santa Croce alla
Giudecca a prison and Santa Margherita a cinema.[16] Still mouldering is the
Scuola Vecchia della Misercordia in Cannaregio, which no longer serves as a
basketball court and gymnastics stadium (its fate before the First World War,
when modern sport entered the city), but whose more profitable use still
remains unresolved.

Perhaps the most profound alteration in the religious fabric of the city was
the transfer of cathedral status from San Pietro in Castello to San Marco in
1807, an action that sparked discussion whether the latter church needed alteration to permit greater numbers access to religious services. After the Austrians
took over, the new patriarch, Ján Ladislaus Pyrker, pressed in 1822 for the
removal of the fourteenth-century iconostasis, bearing statues of the twelve
apostles, the Virgin and St Mark but also blocking visual and physical access to
the high altar and the celebrated Pala d'Oro (another gorgeous piece filched
from Constantinople, which the guidebooks list as containing 1,927
gemstones).[17] As for the expeditious movement of people – so much a priority
of all government in that era – a local planner, Luigi Casarini, now argued that
only a modern road cut through from Piazza San Marco to the mainland could
save the city from complete ruin.[18] As Alvise Zorzi has ruefully remarked,
Casarini would have many successors anxious to urge that the city had been
'enslaved by its own beauty' and should not remain a medieval relic.[19]

Further repugnant aspects of French rule included conscription for
Napoleon's endless and bloody wars and a harsh but effective taxation system
designed to pay for them and for costly 'benefits' being introduced in Paris and
the rest of the empire. Neither was likely to win immediate popular backing
from Venetians, rich or poor. The opportunity for the French to more permanently implement revolutionary programmes in the territories once governed
by the Republic was quickly thwarted by events, however, the Kingdom of Italy
collapsing early in 1814 after Viceroy Beauharnais had taken 27,000 Italian
troops with him, most of them to their deaths, on the disastrous invasion of
Russia, and after the residue of the imperial French forces had fallen to their
enemies at the Battle of Leipzig, 16–18 October 1813. As a result, Venice and
Venetia were again passed like a parcel back into Austrian hands, a possession
confirmed at the grand peacemaking at Vienna in 1815 by which the revolutionary era was brought to an end.

The Austrian government of Venice has a mixed press. The traditional line
has emphasised the general inability of the Habsburg Empire to adapt to the
new age of the nation and identified a specific failure to grant Venice serious

priority in the plotting of imperial policies. Klemens von Metternich, chief minister of Austrian rule and architect of the Peace of Vienna, accompanied his emperor, Francis I, on an exploratory visit to their new lands in December 1815. Venetians greeted their latest rulers with applause and decorum. But Metternich wrote the city off as 'one great ruin', not therefore, he implied, worth the cost and effort of resurrection.[20]

In the decades that followed, Metternich and his emperor, despite some thought that 'Italy must be Germanised',[21] became preoccupied with stifling the rise of nationalism, both in Austria's extensive Italian territories and elsewhere. Among the victims was Silvio Pellico,[22] a Piedmontese writer and patriot, harshly imprisoned by the Austrians for some months in Venice and then from 1822 to 1830 in the bleak and forbidding Spielberg fortress near Brno in what is now Slovakia. On his release, Pellico wrote *Le mie prigioni*, a book that, whatever its intended or literal meaning, was read by patriots in Italy, before and after the Risorgimento, as a vehement condemnation of Austrian tyranny.[23] A plaque in the *sestiere* of San Marco reminds passers-by of Pellico, his imprisonment in Venice and a visit that he made there while still a free man in September 1820.[24] Its patriotic intent, however, forbears to mention that Pellico had been less than flattering about the Venetians, dismissing them as a people who 'live in idleness, joyously forgetful of any dignity. . . . They do not think, they do not feel.'[25]

As Pellico's words implied, Venice was, in quite a few senses, the least of the Habsburg regime's worries. Although the city was meant to be, with Milan, a twin capital of an imperial province grandly called the Kingdom of Lombardy-Venetia, Milan was the more bustling centre of political and economic activity. More threatening was Venice's increasing subordination to the rapidly growing and notably cosmopolitan port of Trieste, away to the east, where the Venetian plain metamorphosed into the rocky hills of the Balkans, a territory that, unlike the rest of Istria and Dalmatia, had never been subject to the rule of St Mark. The Austrian Lloyd shipping company grew rapidly after its foundation in Trieste in 1836, while the Südbahn railway connected the port with Vienna from 1857, underlining that Trieste rather than Venice was the Habsburgs' preferred transit point for all southern trade. Still grander in its capitalist future was the insurance firm, the Regia Privilegiata Compagnia di Assicurazioni Generali Austro-Italiche, or Assicurazioni Generali, as it was more familiarly known, which opened for business in Trieste in 1831 (Venice became its second base).

An image exists, then, of a Venice groaning under grievously incompetent or tyrannous rule. It has recently been given a special cast by the British historian David Gilmour, who has argued that wiser peacemakers at Vienna in 1815 would have restored Venetian independence, sparking a process that could have turned it into 'another Netherlands'.[26] More common is the nationalist line, which sees Venetians waiting their chance to become patriotic Italians. That image has been challenged most purposefully by David Laven, who maintains that, although the Italians, somehow defined, were the third biggest linguistic group in an empire trying to chart a nationality policy (Italian remaining the language of command in the Habsburg navy until 1848), the Venetians were the fourth largest. Those who lived in the city and its territories, he is willing to concede, did cherish 'a vivid memory of independence'. A paradox lurks, however. Venetians, he contends, 'had good grounds for entertaining a fiercer sense of their own identity than other Habsburg subjects. In fact, . . . quite the opposite was the case: between 1815 and 1846 Venetia was probably the most politically tranquil area of the whole monarchy.' There, Emperor Francis's rule was 'characterized by a bureaucratic and judicial structure that was neither corrupt nor arbitrary, but rigorous, hard-working, fair, and well-meaning, if on occasion annoyingly inflexible and ponderous'.[27] The population, Laven insists, were less interested in lofty chatter about an Italian future than in a reliable administration that gave attention to their current 'needs and aspirations'. By that yardstick, the Austrians 'stood in stark contrast to the rule of Napoleon', which had entailed the 'ruthless exploitation of the region for the benefit of France and its ['Italian'] Lombard collaborators'.[28] For quite a few Venetians, after 1815, the argument is, Vienna was in its way 'bella'; Paris and Milan were not.

Not that tourists minded. They were soon evident in the city again once peace had broken out. In 1818 an English visitor was predictably struck by the beauty of Piazza San Marco. It was, he told his diary, '*unique*; rich, venerable, magnificent'. There, he found 'the congregation of all nations, in their various costumes' (no doubt less skimpy than on a May day now). They 'lounge under the purple awnings of the cafés – smoking, playing at chess, and quaffing coffee – [and] add much to its embellishment'. In their variety, they were 'in character with the buildings; where all orders of architecture seem jumbled together', the Basilica itself being evidently of 'mixed breed'. As for the locals, this visitor observed, they were enduring that destiny which decreed that a Republic 'falls like Lucifer, never to rise again', given that it naturally lacked any 'public spirit'.[29]

From 1820 the Austrians did impose conscription on the populace, if with less rigour than the French,[30] and the 'Quadrilateral' of fortresses – at Mantua, Peschiera, Verona and Legnago – was reinforced so as to overawe any objection in northern Italy to Habsburg control. In the process, the military became a public part of the new system, and in the following decades Piazza San Marco was a setting where German-speaking officers sought relaxation, a good coffee and the sound of music. Austrian education policy was by no means benighted, although it scarcely rescued the peasantry on the mainland, for whom starvation remained a recurrent threat should harvests fail, as they did during the wet 1840s.[31]

The greatest symbol of Habsburg modernisation was the railway bridge borne on a harmonious 222 arches that the government of the Kingdom of Lombardy-Venetia began to finance in 1837 and to construct five years later. It opened on 11 January 1846, reducing to a few minutes what had previously been a tedious transit of some hours from Mestre. The Ferdinandea, as the railway was named in honour of the intellectually handicapped Emperor Ferdinand, who had succeeded to his father's throne in 1835 with debilitating effects on Habsburg administration, connected Venice with Milan, and from there potentially the world. A new terminus was completed in 1852. The message of modern change reaching the city was reinforced by the construction of an iron bridge allowing alighting passengers to cross the Grand Canal by foot from the station to the church of San Simeone Piccolo and the *sestiere* of Santa Croce. The bridge was erected through British finance and technology provided by the Neville company, the same concern constructing a further crossing, also made of iron, outside the Accademia two years later.

To be sure, not everyone was happy. The young John Ruskin, who, with unwonted concession to modernity, had brought a 'cynometer' on his first trip to the city in 1835 so that he could scientifically measure the blissful, un-English, blueness of the sky,[32] now lamented that a Venice with trains resembled 'as nearly as possible Liverpool at the end of the dockyard wall'.[33] Despite his exquisite sensibility, Ruskin preserved the most vulgar tourist habit of regularly comparing the 'foreign' to 'home'. Even today, those who, with or without the Englishman's refinement, fear Venice's imminent environmental death date the city's decline from the opening of the railway connection to the mainland (and bewail the allure and sins of foreign modernity imported from there).[34]

If, in 1846, administrators thought they were permitting Venice to reboard the locomotive of history, the city as always retained both local and cosmopolitan features. Together with the railway and its facilitation of tourism, other modern comforts arrived to make life easier for those viewing the traditional cultural sites. In 1833 the city opened its first organised swimming baths on the lagoon, while two decades later the entrepreneur 'Fisola' (Giovanni Busetto) built the initial bathing huts on the still largely deserted Lido, although the beach was taken over for Austrian military use between 1859 and 1866.[35] From

1843 gas lighting rather than moonlight or torches illuminated Piazza San Marco (Ruskin feared the new-fangled equipment made the square look like Birmingham).[36] By 1846 visitors were serviced by eleven reasonably modern hotels, mostly located in converted, historically redolent *palazzi*.[37] From 1842 the well-connected Venetian architect Giovanni Battista Meduna began increasingly controversial efforts to 'restore' San Marco, acting with the blessing of the celebrated French urbanist and theorist of the Gothic revival Eugène Viollet-le-Duc, who had made a first trip to Venice in 1837. The Frenchman liked the Palazzo Ducale, branding it 'the Parthenon of the Middle Ages'. He deemed the Basilica 'a crude coarse factory', however, badly transformed from its purer origins.[38] Yet another foreigner to have an impact on Venice, he advised that massive reshaping should cleanse its exterior and interior of those excrescences that were hiding the beauty he wanted to see.

Soon after the end of the Napoleonic wars, in 1816, the new administration had established a Commissione Civica per le Case Rovinose to examine and amend hopeless cases of decay in city housing.[39] One result was demolitions, which in 1818 opened a path between the Ponte delle Guglie and Campo dell'Anconetta. The purpose was to raise the depressed economic state of that part of Cannaregio and check the area's insalubrity. Yet poverty lingered. In the city as a whole, in 1827 44,630 citizens out of a total of 100,566 were defined as 'wretchedly poor'.[40] The urgency of the matter increased when a major cholera epidemic struck both the city and the province in 1835 and returned in 1837. Of 43,482 Venetians who caught the disease, 23,123 died.[41]

In 1844 a further widening of city pathways was sanctioned near to what would become the railway station. Running from the Scalzi church to Campo San Geremia, the Lista di Spagna eliminated some tortuous alleyways and dead-end canals. It is a track that today merges into what Venetians call Strada Nova (New Road), at any season crammed with tourists and likely to block altogether at peak times. It is lined with shops selling cheap imported glass, masks and other bric-à-brac directed at satiating visitors' desire for souvenirs and seconded by outlets proffering Coca Cola, pizza and other kinds of fast food with no historic basis in Venetian cuisine. Apart from its guileless customers, it has few fans. In the 1840s, however, a number of locals wanted more, Jacopo Pezzato advocating the construction of a horse-drawn tramway on the other side of the Grand Canal, with a single track but, at its edge, asphalted pavements. The tram could run from the designated station across to Santa Croce and get back to the Grand Canal via Rio San Polo, before again crossing certainly to Campo Santo Stefano and perhaps to San Moisè and Piazza San Marco. With the enthusiasm for mathematical precision and progress that had washed into the nineteenth century from the Enlightenment, Pezzato reckoned that the journey of 1,622 metres could be completed in nine minutes. He was certain that such celerity could only benefit Venice and Venetians.[42]

One part of the city where the contradictions of Austrian rule and its timid offer of an economic revival from the 1830s could be seen was the great naval fortress of the Arsenale that occupied half of the eastern sector of Castello (see maps 1 and 7). Some modernisation had commenced there and in other ship-yards in the *sestiere*, even if the workforce, then and for many decades to come, scarcely apprehended itself as an undifferentiated modern working class. More telling of the future was the decision in 1825 to convert one of the old Sale d'Armi, or armouries, into the first museum on the site, offering a collection of relics both from the Republic and from Austria's more recent naval campaigns. In charge of the initiative, with its message that leisure and tourism rather than high policy should be the city's mission, was the Venetian engineer Giovanni Casoni.[43]

As the mid century approached, however, Casoni's life and attitudes took a different direction, one that prompts consideration of another interpretation of Venetian history. In recent decades, Alberto Banti, though no romantic nation-alist, has revived the thesis that the Risorgimento had a popular base. In his account, words especially mattered. Those who wanted political change in Italy as if by osmosis expressed ancient ideas in modern phrasing, the ancient perhaps having more influence here, at least in the short term, than any comprehension that the future was inexorably leading to a nation. National 'prophet' Giuseppe Mazzini and his comrades drew a response from the people when they talked about a national family in which all were 'brothers', or when they condemned the corruption and injustice of the present rule by compar-ison with some lost golden age and suggested that past innocent happiness could be revived.[44] Banti underlines the role and power of a sense of history in this process, the poet Ugo Foscolo (1778–1827), who acquired a national repu-tation but sprang from an impoverished Venetian patrician family, urging that 'a decadent people like the Italians has a special need to reflect on the glories and examples of their fathers'.[45] Equally powerful in Banti's view was the trust still placed in religion (with its own powerful and enduring historic sense), transmuted by Mazzini and others into words about national martyrdom and resurrection, as exemplified by the term 'Risorgimento'. This implied amalgam of religion and the nation derived additional impetus from the accession to the papal throne of Giovanni Maria Mastai Ferretti as Pius IX in June 1846, a pontiff deemed by some to be a liberal and friendly to the national cause. In Venice and its diocese, though firm in its piety, quite a few priests could now bless the prospect of political change.[46]

Significant therefore in Venice's history was the convening in September 1847 of the ninth in a series of 'scientific congresses' that had for some years been engaging in conversation men of ideas from throughout the peninsula. More than eight hundred showed up in a city that would never thereafter lose its appeal as a congenial setting for intellectual conferencing and diplomatic parleying. Among the locals present was Casoni, who urged in a lavish three-volume work, *Venezia e le sue lagune*, launched at the event, that the Arsenale be revived to match the Venetian military glories it had once armed, while more generally he bewailed the errors and inadequacies of 'alien' Austrian rule.[47] Present, too, were Daniele Manin and Niccolò Tommaseo, destined to be rival leaders of the Venetian revolution of 1848–9.[48]

This is not the place to narrate the stirring and violent events of the Venetian revolution, a task that Jonathan Keates graphically fulfilled in 2006.[49] But it is important to discount exaggerated readings of what the inhabitants of the city thought they were doing in mounting an attack on Austrian rule and sustaining their resistance with great bravery and suffering until overthrown by a pitiless combination of cholera and Austrian bombardment of the city centre in July–August 1849. Modern scholarship is clear that metanarratives are out of place in summation of this 'revolution'. Whatever Marx and Engels perceived to be happening in Paris that year, the mass of the Venetian population showed little sense of initiating a class struggle. In January 1849 the spokesmen of the city's assembled gondoliers stated that they had no captious desire to grab what was not theirs: 'The rich should remain rich so that they can give us work, and we will always have respect for our masters.'[50] Neither Manin nor Tommaseo (who was soon sent off to Paris to negotiate ineffectually there rather than pursue his conflicts with Manin in Venice) nor any of the other leaders favoured class conflict. Rather, they believed 'the classes had been divided by a mere *misunderstanding*' (and did little to salve or even admit the desperate needs of peasants on the mainland).[51]

Perhaps another Italian future may be glimpsed in Manin's readiness to assume the title of 'dictator' (as Garibaldi wanted to do in Rome). But rather than dreaming of a Mussolinian regime, Manin was recalling 'history' as narrated by Livy in regard to the classical Roman Republic (thereby providing an early example of the fusion of the Roman and Venetian pasts by city spokespersons). Before the tyranny of the Caesars, Manin knew, a heroic Cincinnatus or Fabius Maximus had accepted the responsibility of supreme rule in an emergency in order to give greater thrust to present decision making, but always with the assumption that, when victory came, he would renounce his immediate authority and return to a humble life.

Most problematic was the national issue, exemplified in the Venetian Republic's use of the 'Italian' green, white and red *tricolore* but with the Lion of St Mark from the old pennon of the Republic at the corner. David Laven is

3 Luigi Querena, *Explosion of a Mine at San Giuliano* (1849)

convinced that, in March 1848, 'Italy' to most Venetians meant the French puppet Kingdom of Italy and the cruelties and exploitation of that time. Venetians, he says, rose for Venice, as was proven by the lukewarm nationalism of most when Austrian rule returned from 1849.[52] It is certainly a relief that nothing came of Tommaseo's hankering for a final act, in which the revolutionaries would fight from monument to monument to win immortality through their deaths and to ensure that the urban ruins gave better counsel to a new generation than had their earlier existence.[53] Manin had always been more tractable in his views, to some extent reflecting the fact that his Jewish grandfather had changed the family surname from Medina when converting to Christianity under the last doge, Lodovico Manin. After 1849, when he fled from Austrian troops to Paris, Daniele Manin became if anything more moderate. By the time he died in 1857, he was a monarchist and an organiser of the Società Nazionale Italiana (Italian National Society), pledged to a liberal but not radical nation and particularly averse to the social intransigence and national religiosity or fundamentalism of Mazzini.[54]

Given the desperation with which the revolutionaries had defended Venice and the use by the Austrians of modern military means in their prolonged assault,[55] it is surprising how quickly normal life resumed, even though an estimated 4,500 Venetians fled the city to fight elsewhere for the national cause.[56] Observers admittedly noted that the number of beggars in the place had risen, and the Austrians set up a government committee to review Venice's 'decadence' in 1850, while instituting a free port of a limited kind to act as an economic stimulus a year later.[57] They also ignored the blithely reactionary view of Ruskin's wife Effie – who, in the winter of 1849, was enjoying dancing her nights away with uniformed Austrian officers – that it would be best to demolish the railway bridge and return Venice to being insulated from modern transport, its cost and its ugliness.[58] The locals she found content if feckless people, with no real politics:

> Many of the Italians here appear to have no homes at all and to be perfectly happy. At eight o'clock in the evening when we return from hearing the Band we see them all lying packed together at the edge of the bridges, wrapped in their immense brown coats and large hoods as warm as friars. Then in the morning there are little stands on all parts of the Quay where they can eat hot fish, rice, soup, hot elder wine, all kinds of fruit, cigars, and this eating al fresco goes on the whole day, with the occasional interruption of Punch or a Juggler or a storyteller when immediately an immense crowd is collected.[59]

Effie Ruskin was scarcely the most discerning of observers. It is nevertheless true that disputes over modern ideologies had again sunk beneath the surface of city life. City merchants saw little to regret in revived Austrian rule, the Salviati family choosing 1859 (the beginning of the Franco-Piedmontese war that led to the Risorgimento) to initiate a new system of glass making on Murano with an international clientele, formalising their governing company in 1866. The poorer segments of society went back to managing their own lives and social relations, while being ever willing to participate in any *feste* organised by richer Venetians.[60] A state visit by the new young emperor, Franz Josef, in the winter of 1856–7 went off well, and he courteously gave imperial support to the restoration fund for San Marco, a project still in Meduna's hands.[61]

The emperor was accompanied by his wife, Elizabeth ('Sissi'), who had just given birth to the first of their children to survive, a daughter. Sissi returned to Venice for seven months in 1861–2 when the marriage was beginning to fail, shortly after momentous events had culminated elsewhere in Italy – a romantic troubled empress in a romantic troubled city, living alone in the imperial rooms of the Ala Napoleonica.[62] 'Love', very frequently love in anguish, would never cease to be part of Venice's attractions, and the highest society as well as more ordinary mortals joined Sissi in contemplating its meaning there.

During the summer of 1859, after bloody victories at Magenta and Solferino, the combined forces of Piedmont and Napoleon III's France had driven Austrian armies back to the Quadrilateral, and by March 1860 the Kingdom of Sardinia of Victor Emmanuel II and his able and ruthless chief minister Camillo Benso di Cavour had taken over the whole of northern Italy except Venetia. In May Garibaldi led his '1000' volunteers against Sicily, which fell during the summer, while the Hero reached Naples in September. Soon afterwards, this 'dictator' surrendered his powers to King Victor Emmanuel and returned to an ostentatiously humble dwelling on an island off the Sardinian coast. In February–March 1861 a national parliament met in Turin, the new country's temporary capital, and Victor Emmanuel accepted nomination as king of a liberal nation.

This 'making of Italy' on the surface and in the short term largely passed Venice and Venetians by, hemmed in or cocooned as they were by the still powerful Quadrilateral. War and high politics did little to discourage foreign visitors from taking residence in the place, two of the more prominent being the Comte de Chambord, the Bourbon Pretender to the throne of France as 'Henri V', and his mother, the Duchesse de Berry, in origin a Neapolitan princess. Despite his exile, 'Henri V' maintained a formal court at Palazzo Cavalli-Gussoni beside the Grand Canal, his mother taking pains to rise and then sit every time he entered a room where she was.[63] The Pretender commissioned the construction of a garden and other major alterations to his palace, untroubled by the demolition of existing structures that it required and utilising the architectural services of the ubiquitous Giambattista Meduna.

The French royals would soon by joined by Don Juan, the brother of the Carlist candidate to the crown of Spain, after his followers' defeat in sporadic civil war against Queen Isabella in that country. With her controversial second husband, the Duchesse de Berry had in 1844 bought Palazzo Vendramin Calergi on the Grand Canal from a decayed local patrician family, and it was to remain a place of social significance into the next century. In 1959 it became the venue of the city casino, and from 1995 it has also housed a major Wagner museum (the German composer died there in rental accommodation in February 1883). For less elevated if still respectable visitors, the number of elite hotels in the city grew to sixteen in 1855.[64]

Yet with Italy made and its aggressive intention to round out its territories with Venetia and Rome obvious and unappeasable, life during the first half of the 1860s became ever more sombre in a Venice whose economy stuttered and whose population had declined by 10,000 since 1848.[65] Even tourists, now reckoned at 20,000 per year,[66] had reason to be gloomy, since the Fenice opera house had closed in 1859 and did not reopen until Venice became Italian.[67] 'Carnevale', or Carnival, which had never regained its eighteenth-century glories, also languished. As the local historian of Austrian rule has put it, Venice was waiting out time in expectation of an event that now finally seemed inevitable.[68]

The foreigner who has provided the deftest portrait of the lights and shadows of Venice during these years is William Dean Howells, an aspiring

American writer who managed to get himself appointed to the sinecure of consul in Venice in 1860 and did not return to the USA until after the end of its Civil War in 1865. Howells wrote evocatively about economics, social life, religion and politics. 'Commercial decay', he reckoned, had sapped the city for at least 'four hundred years'; in his time, he joked, the 'most active branch of industry' was 'plucking fowls'. True, on Murano, improved glass making was being attempted but it did little to salve the inhabited area of that island, where the population amounted to one-sixth of what it had been in its grandeur under the Republic; it was now 'a poor, dreary little town, with an inexplicable charm in its decay'.[69]

Venice itself had scarcely been updated into a vibrant modern metropolis; rather, the habits of early modern times lingered. Perhaps Venetians were not even properly thought such. 'Each campo in Venice', Howells mused, was 'a little city, self-contained and independent. Each has its church of which it was in the earliest times the burial ground; and each within its limits compasses an apothecary's shop, a mercer's and draper's shop, a blacksmith's and shoemaker's shop, a caffè, more or less brilliant, a green-grocer's and fruiterer's, a family grocery – nay, there is also a second-hand merchant's shop where you buy and sell every kind of worn-out thing at the lowest rates. Of course there is a coppersmith's and a watchmaker's, and pretty certainly a woodcarver's and gilder's, while without a barber's shop no campo could preserve its integrity or inform itself of the social and political news of the day'.[70] Modern homogeneity was, in sum, absent. The dialect that people used in Castello or Cannaregio was different from that to be heard in Piazza San Marco, the 'heart' of the city, '[whose] ground-level, under the Procuratie, is belted with a glittering line of shops and caffè', perhaps 'the most tasteful and brilliant in the world', but not quite the emporia of London, Paris or New York.[71] Moreover, despite efforts at mondanity, the quality of restaurants throughout the city was poor.[72] There were always boundaries that were better not crossed; the Giudecca, Howells warned, 'produces a variety of beggar, the most truculent and tenacious in all Venice, and it has a convent of lazy Capuchin friars, who are likewise beggars'.[73]

Gender difference was also massive: 'it is still quite impossible that any young lady should go out alone. Indeed, she would scarcely be secure from insult in broad day if she did so.' Throughout the city, 'a woman has to encounter upon the public street a rude license of glance, from men of all ages and conditions, that falls little short of outrage'. Even austere greybeards offer 'a gross and knowing leer'.[74] With such work as there was done 'patiently' but with no sense of purpose, locals occupied themselves in gossip, all the more since the standards of 'sincerity', 'honesty' and 'morality' throughout Italy scarcely reached the heights expected in English-speaking countries. 'There is no parallel to the prying, tattling, backbiting littleness of the place, elsewhere in the world.'[75] Blasphemy was habitual and no Venetian would dream of sleeping with a window open to be braced by nature's breeze.[76] Few joined Howells in his athletic walks around the *campi* at 4.30 a.m., when, in his view, Venice looked at its best, with its mystery preserved.[77]

In Howells' mind, Catholicism was much to blame for these venal sins. Younger Venetians, he believed, were abandoning Mass, properly so given the tyranny of Church administration. Priests were 'enslaved to their superiors and to each other. No priest can leave the city of Venice without permission of the Patriarch. He is [thereby] cut off as much as possible from his own kins-people, and subjected to the constant surveillance of his class.'[78] In the Basilica di San Marco, Howells could rejoice at the 'sublimity of the early faith', while disdaining the 'superstition which has succeeded it'. Every church came with 'sleek and portly cats . . . on terms of perfect understanding with the [equally well-fed and lazy] priests.'[79] The indolence had some advantages. 'The Catholic Venetian certainly understands that his Jewish fellow-citizen is destined to some very unpleasant experiences in the next world, but *Corpo di Bacco!* that is no reason why he should not be friends with him in this.' Such tolerance, Howells mused with a hint of anti-Semitism of his own, meant that 'the Jew is gathering into his own hands a great part of the trade of the city, and has the power that belongs to wealth', a situation given special slant since the Jews were 'educated, liberal and enlightened'. 'The Jew's political sympathies are invari-ably patriotic, and he calls himself, not Ebreo, but Veneziano,' Howells observed.[80]

Though the American consul may have thought he was describing the entire city, his words often indicate that he saw what his background and assumptions made it likely he would perceive in Venetian society, scarcely penetrating the lives of the very poor. So, too, his account of politics must be treated with scepticism when it depicts a city in which 'all classes', since 1859, had grown 'marvellously unanimous and bitter' in opposing the survival of Austrian rule. Venetians, he argued, detested their rulers 'with a rancour which no concession short of absolute relinquishment of dominion would appease'. Any local woman who married an Austrian was at once rejected by her friends, 'as they cast off every body who associates with the dominant race'. The Venetians were 'a nation in mourning', he concluded (with still innocent choice of noun), a situation demonstrated at every coffee shop every day. 'In regard to the caffè, there is a perfectly understood system by which the Austrians go to one, and the Italians to another', Florian's being the only exception. 'This is because it is thronged with foreigners of all nations, and to go there is not thought a demonstration of any kind.' Foreigners were nonetheless 'obliged to take sides for or against' the national cause, English speakers perforce being split into 'Austriacanti' and 'Italianissimi'. Venetians were 'content to wait for ever in their present gloom' for liberation, Howells declared, but they possessed 'indomitable perseverance'.[81]

In 1866 their waiting ended, if in the event it was scarcely with operatic fanfare. By the summer, a deep crisis was brewing between the Habsburg Empire and its allied nationalist challengers, Italy and, in its Germanic territories, Prussia, led by the adaptable and ruthless Junker Otto von Bismarck. The Italian government, making no bones about its aggressive intent, was the first to attack on 20 June, the day when the then prime minister, General Alfonso Ferrero La Marmora, escorted King Victor Emmanuel II to the front, to be technically replaced as governmental chief by the moderate civilian Bettino Ricasoli. All educated opinion, it was said, favoured the war, viewing it as a mandatory trial for the young nation, testing the truth of period rhetoric about a stalwart inheritance from the Roman and perhaps Venetian empires.[82]

Alas for such illusions. In practice, Austrian forces, although outnumbered, won on the Italian front, by land at the Battle of Custoza (24 June) and by sea at the Battle of Lissa (20 July). Between the two, however, Prussia and its German allies routed their opponents, notably at the Battle of Sadowa (Königgrätz) on 3 July, and in a rapid seven weeks Austria was forced to the peace table. Even though a military historian has judged the Italian effort at Custoza, where their army had a marked numerical superiority, to have been 'as artless and ineffectual a battle as was ever fought on the north Italian plain',[83] the fruits of victory fell into Italy's lap. By the terms of the Treaty of Vienna, signed on 12 October, the Austrians agreed to hand over Venetia to Napoleon III in the knowledge that he would pass the territories on to Victor Emmanuel II and his government.

On 20 October the Austrian commandant withdrew his garrison from Venice, the departure carefully timed to allow the Habsburg soldiers to be replaced in the short term by an armed municipal guard, pledged to preserve order. On 21–2 October the population voted overwhelmingly to accept unification with Italy, the evening of the 21st marked by 'a file of citizens, carrying gigantic "Yes!" signs on their hats, passing across Piazza San Marco and acclaiming the king and the army'.[84] By 7 November, when Victor Emmanuel arrived for a week-long official visit, Venice had at last, for the first time in its history, become Italian, if by that term was meant a nation state that ran from the Alps to Sicily.

How had Venetians responded to the cascade of events since war had been declared? Was the plebiscite proof of official claims that the novel merging into

Italy was greeted with unanimous local joy? It is hard to be certain, although critical accounts of the Risorgimento have long been sceptical about the plebiscites that had similarly endorsed the political changes of 1859–61 and soon would again after Rome fell to Italian invaders on 20 September 1870. Certainly the correspondent of what was then the world's most authoritative newspaper, the London *Times*, noticed the 'gentleness' with which the populace treated the departing Austrians, praising Venetians as thereby showing that 'their long submission to the yoke of Austria has neither uncivilised nor unmanned them'.[85]

A more significant portrayal of the spirit of 1866 can be found in the diary of Letizia, the teenage daughter of the patriotic Jewish economist Isacco Pesaro Maurogonato, who was accorded a celebratory plaque in the city just behind Piazza San Marco in 1894 for having assisted Venice when it 'resisted an empire alone'.[86] In April Letizia had already noted her pleasure that 'what we have longed for is occurring. War is about to start.'[87] Two months later, she recalled the happy anniversaries of the victorious battles of 1859. 'God, how my heart is beating,' she wrote as she waited for news of what was in fact the disaster of Custoza, and then what 'universal desolation' she and her city endured as the calamity there became apparent, an outcome, she knew, that was all the more serious since Italy needed 'glories to become stronger, more redoubtable' and honoured.[88] A month later, the news from Lissa provoked 'universal consternation', as she noted on 27 July, a situation that was only exacerbated when encomia to the victorious Admiral Wilhelm von Tegetthoff appeared in the pro-Austrian local paper, *La Gazzetta di Venezia*, sarcastically damning the Italians as 'a slave people'.[89]

Gradually, however, it emerged that these defeats were not the end of the story, even if Letizia hoped for a more potent national army in the future and pledged herself and her city never to reconcile themselves with the Austrians.[90] When September arrived, she was growing impatient for the Austrians to leave. The city, she said, was joyously preparing to celebrate that event, tickets for a reopened Fenice selling like hot cakes, and portraits of Victor Emmanuel being distributed everywhere, even among the humblest classes, who were buying cheap photos for two *soldi*. Her wealthy father had set up a 'grand and magnificent portrait' of the king in their home, standing above 'the Savoy coat of arms supported by the Lion of St Mark'.[91] The bourgeoises of the city loved to wear national emblems as they strolled through a Venice about to be liberated, while on a Saturday the *banda municipale* performed a patriotic repertoire that embraced the Bersaglieri fanfare, the March for Prince Umberto, extracts from the opera *Alzira* (an early and less than successful work by Giuseppe Verdi) and the Garibaldi march. When such tunes resounded, Letizia claimed, people leapt to their feet and cheered 'all our liberators, all our martyrs, all our dead', while also exulting in Prussia and the Prussian alliance. The only small cloud she noticed was that fake Garibaldini were circulating in the city and trying to rob people even as they celebrated, although it was also true that Venetians were well enough informed not to cheer La Marmora or Napoleon III, reserving their salutes for the king and Ricasoli and such dead heroes as Charles-Albert (Victor Emmanuel's father), Cavour and Manin.[92]

Yet the final act had not yet played out. Letizia began to be depressed at the inaction and to claim that her own views were shared by all, especially since rumours spread that cholera had returned (she blamed it on Austrians arriving from Trieste).[93] Finally, however, the moment of apotheosis arrived with 20 October and its plebiscite. Letizia told her diary it was 'the most solemn and blessed day' imaginable. Then everyone rose at dawn and flooded into Piazza San Marco, adorned with their own national symbols and greeted by others in a totally beflagged and brilliantly illuminated city; one standard paraded across the square was the flag of 'Garibaldini veneziani'. Bands played fortissimo, yet their music was often drowned by the cheers and applause of the crowds going to vote or returning from the ballot box.[94] Officially, in the province as a whole 647,246 voted for Italy and 69 against.[95]

All that was now left was the king's visit, an event Letizia judged the culmination of 'the greatest period of modern history and perhaps also the greatest fact of all history', since, of the various Italian peoples, Venetians had suffered the most and sacrificed the most. Not even a persistent fog could dampen the glory of proceedings on the day and evening of 7 November, when a great many foreigners had joined the locals in filling every vantage point, balcony and roof along the Grand Canal and in Piazza San Marco. 'The communal palace, the Rialto bridge, the Foscari palace, the two [iron] bridges of the Neville company, were decorated in such a way as to become jewels of good taste and elegance.'[96]

On the following evening, the beaming king attended a ceremony at the Fenice, accompanied by his family and court, and was greeted with 'delirious' applause, especially from the women there. On the 9th he went to the Arsenale to hail its past and guarantee its future. On the sunny 11th he presented the whole city with a flag recording its valour, and presided over a spectacular regatta conducted 'in the Venetian fashion'.[97] On the 12th it was the turn of the Accademia, the Frari and Murano, while a 'galleggiante' (barge) floated up and down the Grand Canal, stopping now and again so that the orchestra on board could play 'choruses and anthems'. Nothing, Letizia ended her diary account by stating, could have been better than that.[98]

A rival diarist whose observations continued after these exciting events was less euphoric. In October 1866 he too had felt 'delirium' at the thought that Venice was now free in a liberal and united Italy. Four months later, however, he was complaining that all had been seized by 'abject cupidity', and that 'the honest man and the philosopher are forced to live in retirement almost as it was when Austrian spies predominated'; the national financial situation, he feared, was a 'cancer for young Italy'.[99]

The destiny of Venice and Venetians under Italian rule will be the chief topic of this book. For the moment, however, it is worth underlining that the Venice that conjoined itself to the new nation was drenched in histories that did not necessarily fuse into one grand, national, story. All nations seek to maximise the lessons that can be drawn from the past, ideally one of great antiquity and rampant glory. But the actual histories of Venetians, whether those that remained or could be reinvented from before 1797, or those that had been experienced under 'foreign' French or Austrian rule since that time, were scarcely automatically or singularly 'Italian'. Exemplary was the fact that Venice's 'empire' would prove a natural attraction to Italian imperialists, despite the fact that its past was barely Italian. That situation would be rendered more complex by the lingering power of the myth of the Roman Empire, already an often malign influence on Italians and soon to be drastically reinforced by the determination from 1870 to place the national capital in Rome (in ambiguous relationship with the existing capital of a Catholic Church 'eternally' equipped with a spiritual *imperium* on which the sun never set). For very many reasons, then, a historian must ask, would not national and nationalising Italians in Venice prove as 'foreign' as their immediate predecessors? What, too, about liberalism, with its earnest promise of 'improvement' for all, and therefore of the translation of many enlightened ideas about the need to organise space and time mechanically and mathematically, and to build a future based on efficiency, statistical accuracy and good order? How could such a prospect be applied to an urban area that was presently still 'medieval', its people necessarily crammed into buildings blatantly in need of modernisation? How could Venice's timeless beauty and old history adapt to new times?

It was ironical that, during those years in which the Italian flag began to flutter in Piazza San Marco, Napoleon III in Paris and Franz Josef in Vienna were presiding over the massive reconstructions of their capital cities wherein the boulevard would triumph over the lane and ancient walls were bulldozed into nothingness. But Venice was walled in by a sea that not even nineteenth-century science could altogether curb, and the city-space was too confined to be wrenched into providing much room beyond that available in Piazza San Marco and the other grander *campi*. None fitted the military display that was a key part of the design of the Champs-Élysées or the wide Rings in Vienna (or the eventual Via dell'Impero – Empire Street – in Rome). In these circumstances and given these multiple living pasts, in the decades that followed 1866 trying to work out what Venice 'really' was and how it might remain a 'living city' would prove to be a most vexing issue, whether for locals, Italians or the city's many devoted and interfering foreign admirers.

CHAPTER TWO

The lights and shadows of Liberal improvement in Venice, 1866–1900

As we have seen, a slew of memorials to Venice's unification with Italy are scattered around the *campi* and *calli* of the city. The most portentous is the equestrian statue to King Victor Emmanuel II, 'first king of Italy', with its stylistic ambition to be an updated national version of Andrea del Verrocchio's celebrated Renaissance representation of the *condottiere* Bartolomeo Colleoni, located outside San Zanipolo (Santi Giovanni e Paolo). On Victor Emmanuel's death in 1878, Venetian liberals surpassed themselves in grovelling condolence, avowing that for the wider world the dead king had epitomised Italian patriotism to a degree that was historically shared by Michelangelo, Raphael and Dante.[1] Four years later, a prominent intellectual reviewing royal memory sites trusted that they would manage to evoke 'the real Christian, the real Sovereign, the real Gentleman'.[2] Surrounded by such rhetoric, any monument to the king in the city had to be striking.

Victor Emmanuel duly stands in a prime position overlooking the lagoon on the Riva degli Schiavoni, and today surveys a motley crowd of *vaporetto* passengers heading to or from the San Zaccaria stops, and either being tempted by or trying to avoid those who are selling sticky sweets and the other gewgaws of contemporary tourism (see map 7). It is just as well the king is frozen into a monument, since the jostling throng could with difficulty concede room for a monarch depicted as portly but full of energy, spurring a hefty horse headlong towards the Piazzetta. He wears a helmet sprouting the black capercaillie feathers of the crack Piedmontese and Italian cavalry corps, the Bersaglieri, and sports phallic moustaches, while waving aloft in his right hand a militant sword. The sculptor was Ettore Ferrari, and his commemoration of the king was ready for official opening on 1 May 1887 (before May Day had acquired its socialist connotations).[3] The event coincided with the holding of the sixth national art exhibition in Venice, whose success was to pave the way for the Biennali.[4]

Contemporaries saluted the statue's grandeur, although it could scarcely match that of the equestrian memorial to the king that adorns the massive Victor Emmanuel monument in Rome.[5] Later observers, wary of past nationalist and monarchist stone grandiloquence, can agree that today the king looks best when viewed through a thick and sombre autumnal fog, especially since a sceptical historian might be troubled by the geography of his memory site. Victor Emmanuel is riding west, away from the river Piave, Trieste and the national frontier with a 'Slav' world, as though in rapid retreat from another crushing defeat by Italy's 'natural' enemies. But then an optimist might counter that perhaps, pell-mell, he is bringing the good news from Trst (Trieste, Slovene version) to Venice (or Milan or Turin).

Whatever the case, given the political radicalism of Ferrari, who doubled as patriotic sculptor and long-term head of a key national Masonic lodge, perhaps the real message of the statue lies not in its ostentatious evocation of the monarch but at its base. Here are displayed, on one side, an enchained (female) Venice with a bedraggled pennon of St Mark and a sleeping Winged Lion, and on the other again the city's symbolic representation, but here wearing a laurel wreath and accompanied by a roaring lion, its wings spread for instant action. The only problem with the monument's pointedly positive account of Venice's Italianisation might be – as cynics used to remark of the maps of the growing Roman Empire set beside the Fascist Via dell'Impero in Rome in the 1930s – that the message could be read in opposite manner depending on which way a passer-by was walking.[6]

In today's Italian Republic, the charging king and his statue's furniture may be seen as a period piece. More layered is the city's commemoration of Daniele Manin, the 'hero' of 1848–9 and the most obvious and, in the Liberal era, safest candidate for apotheosis into a national hall of memory. More speedily than the king or even Garibaldi, whose monument was erected in 1885 (it stands where the former Via Eugenia, renamed in his honour on popular initiative immediately after unification, abuts the Giardini),[7] Manin acquired a now stained bronze statue in the prosperous *sestiere* of San Marco in March 1875.[8] It is located at the centre of what had been Campo Paternian but was then subjected to major rebuilding (a surviving medieval tower was demolished and other alterations made in what had scarcely proved a 'sacred' historical context for the hero) and renamed Campo Manin (see map 9). In 1880 the local savings bank was permitted to erect its head office on the east side of the square 'in neo-Lombard style';[9] after the Second World War it would be replaced by a more controversial modernist building. In his memorial, the hero of 1848 is portrayed with rumpled hair and clothing, and, although wearing a sash of office, looks eminently bourgeois, even if there must be Napoleonic echoes in the tucking of his right hand into his chest, in the pose made redolent of conquest by the French emperor. Manin has a growling Winged Lion at his feet and his name is engraved in large letters on the plinth, in case he should be forgotten.

4 Campo Manin today, with the modernist Cassa di Risparmio building in the background

Somewhat ironically, only a few steps away in Campo Santo Stefano is a marble statue of Manin's partner and rival, Niccolò Tommaseo, sculpted in 1882 by the Milanese Francesco Barzaghi, an artist who made it in Paris while being best known for various works commemorating the Risorgimento (see map 9). Perhaps because Barzaghi was an outsider, his monument quickly earned the unflattering soubriquet of 'the book-shitter' (*cagalibri*). The thoughtful, bearded and frock-coated bourgeois Tommaseo has his arms folded around a newspaper and is carrying a pen, while his coat rests at the back on an uneven pile of books that might be assumed to have tumbled from his nearest orifice.

Manin's ghost may chuckle at Tommaseo's fate. He too, however, has a more paradoxical place of memory than the statue in Campo Manin. After 1866 it was swiftly decided that the hero's ashes needed repatriation from their foreign burial.[10] Two years later, conveniently the twentieth anniversary of the outbreak of the 1848 revolt, Manin's remains were exhumed in Paris and transported with fanfare by rail to the new station at Venice. Thence, the relics holy to the nation were carried down the Grand Canal on the night of 22 March, borne on a lavishly and patriotically decorated barge, escorted by boats and gondolas, while the scene was lit by flaring torches and guttering candles in a ceremony that had already become habitual in Venice and was destined to be replicated on many further occasions.[11]

The predictable intention, it was said, was to ensure that Manin could eternally lie within the cathedral church of San Marco, therein blending his history with all that had gone before and all that was to come. The Church authorities refused permission, however, and, amid testy and prolonged argument, in 1875 Manin was interred in the mean shelter of a fenced-in external arcade on the northern side of San Marco, hidden from the Piazza, the Piazzetta, the Campanile, the Palazzo Ducale, the lagoon and the sunlight (see map 3). The tomb rather faces the Piazzetta dei Leoncini, best known for its eighteenth-century red marble lions and its more ancient well. This small square is now officially named Piazzetta Giovanni XXIII, in honour of a pope born in territories once ruled by the Republic. In today's Venice, the lions and the well often elicit more admiration than either the pope or the hero of 1848, few bothering to peer through the guarding screen and the enveloping shadow at the grave of the most celebrated architect of the Venetian Risorgimento. In this setting, any message that Manin and his comrades might transmit to the present is muted and may be given darker resonance by the fact that the hero's sarcophagus is surmounted with a threatening fasces and spear.

Perhaps Manin's silent rest is an appropriate fate, given the common view that Liberal Italy of the generation after 1866 was a dull and mediocre country

5 Manin's tomb today, in obscurity at the side of San Marco

of prose, no more than the least of the Great Powers, 'Italietta', a nation of failing grades by comparison with the poetic expectations of heroism, grandeur, modernisation, wealth, power and empire that had stirred the Risorgimento. Certainly the existing forms of Venetian politics did not have to shift much to accommodate the new regime. The first head of local government was the patrician rentier Giobatta Giustinian (technically *podestà* from 28 October 1866 to 13 January 1867, thereafter *sindaco*, or mayor, until he resigned on 4 August 1868; he returned for a second period of office in 1877–8), who boasted descent from the doges. His successors came from similar backgrounds – for example, Lorenzo Tiepolo, who served between 1888 and 1890. Change was delayed until the accession to the mayoral office of the radical writer Riccardo Selvatico (*sindaco* from 21 April 1890 to 3 August 1895), who headed the only leftist giunta to rule the city until after the Second World War. Longest in tenure was Selvatico's successor, 'il sindaco d'oro' (mayor of the golden age), Filippo Grimani (15 November 1895 to 25 October 1919), a landowner and lawyer. He boasted ancient patrician roots, with three doges in his lineage, welcoming elevation after 1900 to the Italian nobility. The first worker elected to the Comune was Cinildo Bellemo in 1889.[12] He had few successors.

In its public administration, Italy inherited from Piedmont a centralised 'Jacobin' system, where local authority fell to the prefect, appointed by and responsible to the Ministry of the Interior. Prefects were less reliably aristocratic than the city mayors, although they always belonged to the national Establishment, often being lawyers and expecting membership of the Chamber of Deputies or Senate. Their terms of service in Venice were not long; the city welcomed seventeen new prefects between 1866 and the outbreak of the First World War. Few made an overt mark on a city that did not represent the most senior posting in the country. The more ambitious moved on; others waited out their appointments in expectation of comfortable retirement and with a preference to let sleeping dogs lie rather than interfering messily with the accustomed systems of local power and patronage.[13]

A partial exception was Luigi Torelli, who became the second prefect to serve in Venice on 5 May 1867, remaining there until his retirement for reasons of health on 28 July 1872. He arrived from Palermo expressing the studiously liberal hope that he could 'contribute to the resurrection of the city in the lagoon, whether in its economy or in its hygiene'. The Austrians, he grumbled, had left the place in 'picturesque dirt', a romantic state that might please tourists but was scarcely good for the inhabitants.[14] One major improvement, he advised, could be the construction of an eight-metre-wide road along which carriages could roll from Piazza San Marco to the Giardini and Sant'Elena.[15] After all, there were at present 357 *calli* that were less than a metre and a half wide, 45 of less than a metre, and 187 that went to a dead-end, 'Canaregio' (sic) being the most afflicted.[16] But the first priority was modern education, Torelli rapidly instituting popular libraries and evening courses, open to the public each night and on Sundays.[17]

His dismay at the city's backwardness was communicated to others. Quintino Sella, the major financial expert in the national parliament, wrote in December 1867 that he had not realised that Venice was in 'such a sad condition', having been shocked to hear that 35,000 of its residents lived in desperate poverty.[18] He wished Torelli every success in his task of 'making the Queen of the Adriatic rise again', but the job, he surmised, would be neither 'painless nor rapid'.[19] More paradoxically, a female correspondent objected four years later to the way post-Risorgimento 'freedom' had resulted in 'disorder and a greed for [government] jobs and favours of every kind'. With no acknowledgement of hypocrisy, she then moved on to request support for a local writer, 'our friend, a cultured man'.[20]

These exchanges illustrate the complications arising from the imposition of liberal and national rule in a city where modernisation and the nationalisation of the masses were easier to announce than to achieve and where much

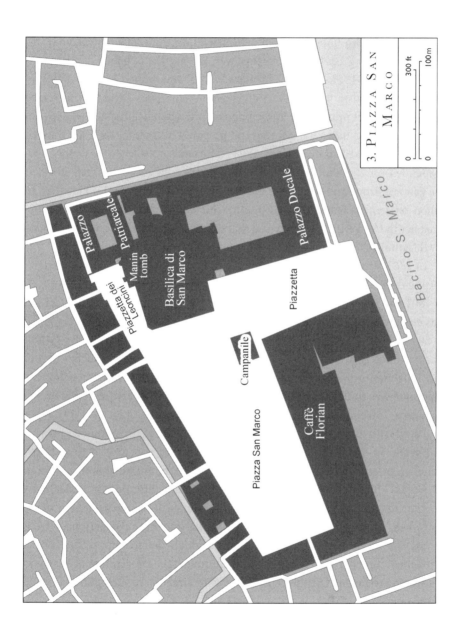

3. PIAZZA SAN MARCO

300 ft

100 m

Palazzo

Patriarcale

Manin
tomb

Piazzetta dei
Leoncini

Basilica di
San Marco

Palazzo Ducale

Piazzetta

Campanile

Piazza San Marco

Caffè
Florian

Bacino S. Marco

'backwardness' and tradition lingered. One problem sprang from the function of Catholicism in Venice and, more especially, in the pious region of the Veneto. The Catholic Church had been a seemingly neutral observer of the fall of Venice into Italian hands. After his own flight from the Roman Republic in 1848–9, Pius IX had terminated what anyway was no more than a confused half-flirtation with liberalism and nationalism. In the 1860s he was preoccupied with shoring up his temporal power, issuing the Syllabus of Errors on 8 December 1864. The Syllabus proffered a root and branch condemnation of 'progress, liberalism and modern civilization'.[21] In 1866–7 the fate of Venice was therefore not uppermost in the pope's mind when he proclaimed a special Jubilee in the still holy city of Rome and prepared himself for the First Vatican Council, convoked on 28 June 1868. The still unfinished assembly was suspended on 20 October 1870, one month after Italian troops had stormed the gates of Rome and converted the city into the Italian capital. Thereafter, in sullen retirement from national politics, Pius announced himself to be 'the Prisoner in the Vatican' and advised that it was inappropriate (*non expedit*) for loyal Catholics to vote in Italian parliamentary elections.

In 1862 Venice had acquired a new patriarch, Giuseppe Luigi Trevisanato, sprung from a poor local family; he had been born on the peripheral Giudecca in 1801 and reigned until his death in 1877. He was emphatic that the Church was everywhere under siege from the wicked, attendance at Mass having fallen to 50 per cent in 1849 and continuing to decline after unification. By 1900 it was reckoned that, in the more socially blighted *calli* of Castello, 85 per cent of the inhabitants no longer took confession, although a reverence for the Madonna was profoundly rooted there.[22] In the parish of Sant'Eufemia on the Giudecca, 750 confessed, 3,750 did not.[23]

Faced with this laxity in religious practice, Trevisanato summoned a provincial synod in 1865, the first to meet for 150 years, and used it to rally the Venetian priesthood behind the Syllabus of Errors, damning liberalism and all its works. He also took occasion to deplore modernity more generically by denouncing a hybrid mix of 'summer swimming, levity in the behaviour of the betrothed, blaspheming, unjust profit making and the profanation of [religious] *feste*'.[24] He was nonetheless realist enough not to oppose the formal implementation of the new nation state, approving the referendum of 1866 and continuing to favour Catholic charitable work aimed at reducing the suffering of the poor.[25]

In the decades after 1866, the leadership of conservative Catholicism in the city and elsewhere in Italy fell to Count Giovanni Battista Paganuzzi, a local lawyer who lived until 1921. In those decades, Paganuzzi headed the Opera dei Congressi, a movement that accepted the *non expedit* but nonetheless mustered

Catholics in what might seem a political manner. Paganuzzi had summoned the Congress in June 1874 at the Madonna dell'Orto in Cannaregio in the presence of Trevisanato. Yet with that fondness for historical reference that was automatic in the Church, and that in this case was perforce drawn from 'Venetian history', he backdated the movement's foundation to 7 October 1871, the three hundredth anniversary of the Battle of Lepanto, when Ottoman Turkey was defeated by a 'Holy League' in which the forces of the Venetian Republic were predominant. Now, Paganuzzi proclaimed, his Opera would summon the virtuous to war against 'modern Muslims', a term that meant those anti-clerical liberals who, he implied, were viciously corrupting Venice and Italy.[26] Curiously, therefore, under Paganuzzi's aegis, provincial and local Venice became for many decades a major national fulcrum of (universal) Catholic reaction.

Following the papal interdiction, Catholics, officially at least, had to withdraw from national political activity but could campaign in Venice. In their eyes, the state was not a legal entity, whereas the city was. There, participation was scarcely 'democratic'. All the males of the region may have been expected to vote in the referendum, but the Liberal system that was now imposed on Venice was far from being based on universal manhood suffrage (Italian women did not get the vote until after 1945). In November 1874 a correspondent of the London *Times* found the conduct of national elections to be quaint by comparison with that in his own country. Only 5,071 citizens out of 140,000 people who lived in the city, the journalist noted, had the right to attend the polls. Of these, 1,826 had done so across the three city electorates.[27] Catholics, by definition, excluded themselves. Moreover, if Venetians wanted to vote, they had to turn up at the municipal office either at 10 a.m. or 1 p.m. and wait patiently until their names were called. Searching for what might interest readers at home, the reporter added that gondoliers ignored such vexations because they preferred not to declare their incomes; besides, most were not literate. Despite such absences, he nonetheless mused, class antagonism was less conspicuous than in London, since 'Venice is so small that its great men, in addition to being on foot like the humblest of their admirers, are constantly in full and easy view', while one gondola looked much like another.[28]

One year later, a communal report added greater detail. 129,676 people lived permanently in Venice, with a further 8,700 being resident. There were 106.7 women to every 100 men. Thirty-nine per cent of men could read (up from 29 per cent in 1868) and 27 per cent of women (up from 18 per cent). There were 4.8 children resulting from every marriage, although the birth rate was falling; mortality was about 30 per 1000 and also in decline. It was still too high among infants aged up to five years, their mothers' poverty and ignorance

6 Everyday life in Liberal Venice

being largely to blame for that social curse. Tuberculosis was not increasing, while scrofula and cancer were declining. The overall situation was, therefore, 'satisfactory', the report concluded.[29]

Despite such complacency and despite an accompanying reluctance to introduce fuller democracy, liberals did focus on urban issues, with the expressed ambition that their governance mean 'improvement', compared with past Habsburg inefficiency and Catholic superstition. 'Science' was the answer. It depended on accurate information and therefore a detailed tabulation of those whose lives needed improving. One blatant issue was housing. A damaging *acqua alta* surged into the city on 15 January 1867 (from 16 to 20 September 1880, followed by a major flood), reminding the authorities of the pervasive poverty and deprivation of poorer Venetians. Infant mortality in Venice remained high; in the early 1890s it was 27.7 per cent; in 1911–13 it had fallen to 14.1 per cent, the latter figure being the same as for the nation as a whole, a sign of relative gain for Venice.[30] Photographic evidence nonetheless shows the children of the poor barefoot, even in winter; adults, too, could not necessarily afford to be shod.[31] When, in the first summer of independence, a deadly outbreak of cholera had struck first the province, then the city, Garibaldi, whose political role in the new nation remained clouded but who could be relied on to be anti-clerical, had turned up in Venice with the graphic advice that 'priests constituted Italy's real *morbus cholera*'.[32]

Before the Austrians left, a commentator had begun what would become a tradition of investigating the inadequacy of popular housing in the city, urging remedy, if also being doubtful whether charity should extend to the undeserving poor. The term 'poverty', he cautioned with liberal rigour, was 'displeasing to the poor themselves'.[33] More generous was a doctor, who commenced his study of living conditions in 1865 fearing that 'the prime school of bad habits among the young is often to be found within domestic walls', where sexual congress was rarely inhibited by 'shame'. New construction, he advised, with the watchwords '*salubriousness, economy* and *morality*', must top administrative priorities, all the more since the condition of a third of current homes was destructive of the physical and spiritual health of their residents.[34]

Faced with this housing crisis, the new Comune established a committee to review the cityscape (Commissione per lo Studio di un Piano di Riforme delle Vie e Canali della Città di Venezia). Predictably, it recommended 'the systematising of urban circulation and the reduction of the number of squalid old houses in preference for commodious and healthy middle-class-style housing'.[35] In 1874 Dr Cesare Musatti, a member of a local family of Jewish origin that was achieving prominence in many sectors of city life, pursued the issue in a talk at the Ateneo Veneto, the most prestigious centre for the exchange of ideas in the city. His attention had been drawn to the matter, he explained, when a thirteen-year-old boy was admitted to hospital with suspected TB. The child was a shoe-maker who worked for many hours every day bent over and unable to breathe freely. To check such ills, Musatti urged, Venice should establish teaching posts in worker medicine. But, he ran on, the greater issue was housing. The home must become a citadel of hygiene, cleanliness and good diet, as well as the place where superstition and prejudice could be routed. At present, neither drains nor water supplies functioned reliably, while tall, dark, damp, narrow, airless buildings needed to be pulled down as Napoleon III had done in Paris (where sufferers from scrofula were now much reduced in number) and as municipal councils in Great Britain were still doing. Once sunlight brightened the domestic hearth, once houses possessed modern toilets and a reliable supply of clean water, 'those idle boys, blighted by rickets or TB, who infest our streets' and who 'crowd the city dives and multiply under our eyes every day like the miraculous loaves and fishes', must vanish. In the process, the quality of life and work would improve, as liberalism pledged. After all, Musatti concluded with flourishing recourse to history as the ultimate judge, the rulers of the city had always solicitously watched over their population's health.[36]

In Venice, housing reform was harder to achieve than in Baron Haussmann's radically reconstructed Paris, even if the new regime was not averse to expending time and money in renewing the drains (not a straightforward matter in Venice) and more generally updating the narrower, darker and more putrid sectors of the city.[37] The ruling liberals and their predecessors and successors covered over at least fifty canals, with an estimated length of six kilometres.[38] Some changes were uncomplicated; others were more arduous. The worst accommodation, then and later, was often on ground level, nearest to the water and most vulnerable to its invasion. The better off lived on the floors above and had little reason to favour alteration of their building stock, especially when it might look or be beautifully historical.

Once again, the issue of 'com'era e dov'era' surfaced to challenge the easier schemes for modern improvement. Prominent among the more bitter critics of Liberal Venice today is environmental historian Pietro Bevilacqua, who sees the creation of a new port, the Stazione Marittima at Santa Marta, from 1869 (it was completed in 1880) as leading inexorably to the massive and polluting development across the lagoon at Marghera. By implication, Bevilacqua has little sympathy with the port's rise to hold second rank in trade behind Genoa, by 1901 giving direct or indirect employment to 20 per cent of the urban work-force.[39] Instead, he bemoans the fate of 'a city pushed into the territory of a nation state and so rendered unable to think for itself and its own economies and their natural connections with the lagoon'. This situation, he avers, ensured that Venice would, in every sense, be a 'place condemned to be admired by outsiders' eyes', no longer, as it had always been, genuinely 'amphibian'.[40]

The implication that it would have been ideal if Venice could have been fenced off from the social, economic and political currents of the time sounds naive, and certainly was not what actually happened. One tradition that could scarcely continue was the rule of the gondola, inefficient and time-consuming in a world where the expeditious was assumed to matter. *Vaporetti*, boats driven by steam rather than oars, by machine rather than manpower, began operating to Chioggia in 1873. In April 1881 they commenced service along the Grand Canal as arranged by the Compagnie des Bateaux de Venise, organised with the aid of foreign finance by the Piedmontese entrepreneur Alessandro Finella. The first vessel was courteously named the *Regina Margherita* after King Umberto I's glamorous queen, and was soon reinforced by eight more ferries. In 1890 extra capital arrived through a takeover by the Società Venezia Lagunare, with thirty new boats whose itineraries spread across the lagoon. In 1903–4 most services were municipalised after a vote to do so of 5,027 citizens for and 1,450 against.[41] The boats were controlled by the Azienda Comunale per la Navigazione Interna, the *vaporetti* running at ten-minute intervals during peak periods and also at night.[42] Somewhat ironically, it was tourism that kept most gondoliers in business. They continued to regard themselves more as a caste than as a union – they founded their own Mutuo Soccorso, or mutual aid society, in 1868[43] – and were quite successful in defending a place for themselves in the city, if one more richly catering to leisure than to business.[44]

The implementation of a transport revolution was a natural accompaniment to the standard view among the new rulers after 1866 that the city must expand its existing enterprises, introduce new industries wherever possible and restore those drastically damaged in the interregnum between 1859 and 1866.[45] As a student of the railways claimed with studied historical reference, the ancient Romans had understood that 'convenient, frequent and rapid communications by land and sea' were the first basis of grandeur, and so, he said, they remained.[46] Shipbuilding was a natural arena for development, even though another observer admitted that present manufacture at the Arsenale or in the smaller yards was mainly in wood and rarely in iron or steel. For all the chatter about its naval inheritance, Venice lagged as a centre of modern naval production and would continue to do so. By 1914, only five modern vessels had been produced for the navy there and none was a battleship.[47]

The Arsenale was scarcely the only area of backwardness, Alberto Errera, a sober statistician, arguing in 1870 that what Venice really needed was educated workers and risk capitalists willing to invest. The current naval workforce, he acknowledged, was separated into the ancient castes of carpenters, caulkers, draftsmen, cabinet makers, metalworkers, blacksmiths, fitters, boiler makers, copper workers, brass workers, turners, lantern makers, craftsmen skilled with barges, oars and lanterns, or with pumps and bronzes, coopers and tackle makers. The most obvious division was not therefore of class but of age. A great many workers were boys (three were under fourteen), who could expect to earn 0.85 lire per day. Adult workers received 2.57 lire.[48]

According to the 1869 census, 65,367 out of a population of 133,037 in the city and its islands were actively employed – that is, just under 50 per cent. At that time, only 899 plied the fisherman's trade; 6,310 were policemen, soldiers or customs officials, 6,297 domestic servants and 5,980 shop or innkeepers or their staff; 5,035 worked as gondoliers or in other forms of transport, and 4,141 as clerks or agents or professionals of some other kind; 6,667 were involved in the clothing industries from tailors to shoemakers, 6,262 worked with wood or metal and 4,120 with pearls, while 2,521 earned a living from their skills with skins or textiles, hemp or tobacco. No fewer than 3,381 of the city's employees were officially deemed under the age of fifteen. For the majority of Venetians, employment was seasonal or otherwise short-term and unemployment was therefore 'recurrent'.[49]

Lingering corporate traditions (sprung originally from the special history of interclass policies under the doges), Errera's account had continued, meant that workers were for the most part 'sober and diligent'. They scarcely yearned for 'strikes, violent work interruptions, secret societies banded against the *padrone*'. Rather, patriarchal structures survived (Errera, who may have read Walter Scott, thought they resembled those seen in the Scottish Highlands). Workers would identify a senior figure in their place of work and revere him. In the city as distinct from the countryside, deference of workers towards bosses may perhaps have diminished, but demagogues and agitators had not fully penetrated Venetian workplaces.[50] Errera was, by implication, happy about that. Description rather than analysis was his purpose and he avoided debate whether modernity might demand a tougher probing of the relationship between the workforce and those who owned the means of production.

Yet it was soon to be plain that talk among the elite about making life better for the people had strict limits. For many liberals what the new regime meant was work, more efficient and more productive work, work for all, work full-time, work that was not to be avoided by the poor, work or else. Typical was a short paper by Angelo Papadopoli, a member of a prominent noble banking family (destined to play a major role in the Marghera development). In 1871 Papadopoli promulgated the liberal version of charity, one, he implied, that must necessarily temper past Catholic softness. During the last years of the Republic and also under the Austrians, the city had been 'afflicted by the plague of a proletariat', he lamented with loose comprehension of a working class. Despite widespread belief that welfare acted as a necessary safety valve, the undeserving poor were multiplying and thereby reinforcing the regrettable pervasive presence in Venice of patron–client networks and 'inertia' in so far as work and productivity were concerned. In despairing reaction, common sense advised that rigid social divisions were incurable, as was human suffering.

But common sense was wrong. Under effective liberalism, society no longer needed to be sundered into classes. Rather, 'wealth has become the goal of whoever knows how to get it and keep it. Industry and commerce are free and are expanding wonderfully.' In these happy post-Risorgimento circumstances, 'poverty' was 'a fault', Papadopoli stated. With its 25 per cent 'poor', Venice was afflicted by a sort of elephantitis, undermining its 'health and strength'.[51] Those claiming to be wretched should therefore be tallied and expelled if recalcitrant. Charity must be secularised, since priests could never bring themselves to exert proper authority and rigour. At the moment 'to be poor in Venice is a profession', Papadopoli charged.[52] Those who thought they could work in good season and carelessly spend the proceeds must be persuaded otherwise or removed. 'Idleness is the father of all vices,' he counselled sententiously.[53] The popular fondness for drink and gambling must end. Whatever they themselves wanted, boys must go to school (even if another observer protested that local craftsmen and artisans had a 'limitless hatred' of any form of modern education, being especially allergic to suggestions that they understand science and the machine).[54] Ragamuffins, Papadopoli demanded, must not wander the streets, as they presently did, 'sweaty and in rags, playing, yelling and cursing'.[55] Perhaps the liberals could augment the doctors in the city, but the medical profession must treat the poor sternly. Most effective would be the introduction of poorhouses on the British model, so long as the government ensured that they entailed punishment and not relief. 'The fact is that the Venetian populace do not want to work' and that was why Lombard immigrants dominated the blacksmith shops and Friulans the building trade. 'To render this town worthy of its name and its ancient fame', Papadopoli concluded in upbeat manner, 'the people must be moralised'.[56]

Less exalted in his family background than the banker-moralist but similarly a liberal anxious to foster work, virtue and deference, notably among the female poor, was the lace entrepreneur Michelangelo Jesurum, whose company won the prize for lace production at the Universal Exhibition in Paris in 1878 and, though no longer a family concern from the interwar period, long remained a major enterprise in Venice. On Pellestrina, Jesurum thriftily paid his female workers less than one lira for a fifteen-hour day.[57] Nonetheless, in 1873, three years after reorganising the ancient art of lace making in the city and its surrounds (ultimately on the island of Burano in particular),[58] the entrepreneur explained worthily that he was being impelled to act by historical memory, given the Republic's dominance of the field before the rise of Flanders, at which point Venice became 'a slave to other nations'.[59] Best employed in the business were the 'wives and daughters of fishermen and sailors', since 'lace making gave them a means to sustain their families during the long and dangerous absences of their men'. Equally valuable was the fact that young women should work at home and not in a factory, where who knew what evil skulked when more than a hundred women gathered. As his employees, girls would never be expected to walk fearfully by themselves at night through the populated parts of the city (Jesurum here confirming Howells' description of male behaviour). 'The girls who work in this business', the entrepreneur maintained with liberal propriety, 'would never go far from maternal eyes', a happy situation given that mothers were 'the securest guardians of [their daughters'] shame'.[60]

Most romantic among female workers were the 'pearl threaders', or *impiraresse*, another job done most readily at home, or, given the fearsome demands that the work made on the eyesight, in the light at its portals. Observers often

7 Lace makers at organised work for the Jesurum 'factory' after 1900

thought this activity traditional and beautiful,[61] and scarcely reckoned with the fact that a day's labour might win a woman or girl less than fifty *centesimi*, the price of a loaf of bread.[62] In 1872 the *impiraresse* were emboldened to strike for better pay and conditions, and in 1904 they formed a union,[63] although the piecework nature of their employment hampered collective action.

A sceptical historian has noted that, like many Venetian workers, they did their best to eke out unofficial gains from their hard and physically damaging labour by hiding some of the pearls that they were given and then disposing of them on their own account. Popular theft, he added, was endemic, involving 'soap, chickens, grain, copper objects, washed clothes, wood' or indeed anything that was not nailed down; gondoliers were notoriously light-fingered.[64] Such traditional behaviour, scoffed at by liberals as backwardness, was one reason why the Comune, under the radical but non-socialist Selvatico, financed the establishment of a Camera del Lavoro (Chamber of Labour) in 1892, enrolling more than four thousand members in the hope of thereby stimulating greater worker solidarity with the urban community. Clause 3 of the Camera's initial constitution forbade any political or religious discussion there, and general pledges followed that the body would bring capital and labour together.[65] Although a section of the International had been founded in the city in 1872, a regular branch of the Italian socialist party with more combative purpose was not properly instituted until 1893.[66]

More modern than the lace making or pearl embroidering industries in its employment of women was the Manifattura Tabacchi, or tobacco factory, which before 1914 already had its own *fondamenta* and *calle* in an area of the city subject to ongoing reconstruction related to the eventual creation of Piazzale Roma as the terminus of the vehicular bridge that would be opened in 1932. Tobacco had been rolled into cigars and cigarettes since 1786, the factory having being taken under the charge of the Italian state as a monopoly in 1884. Working conditions were harsh and there was much unchecked pollution, a critical historian summing up work practices as 'hierarchical and militarised' rather than 'rational and modern' as the bosses promised.[67] The largely female workforce received higher pay than most other employed women, however. From the 1880s they could also rely on some work-injury and old-age protection from the Cassa Nazionale di Previdenza per l'Invalidità e la Vecchiaia, while from 1877 Elisabetta Michiel Giustinian, the charitable wife of the first city *sindaco*, opened a nursery on the Rio Terà dei Pensieri to safeguard (and supervise) the workers' young children, whose suffering and bad behaviour alarmed many liberals.[68] The tobacco workers held a first strike as early as 1884, soon acquiring national fame as a militant workforce in a country where feminism lagged and in a city where the infant socialist movement often found adjusting to female activism taxing.[69]

Not far away was the textile factory, or Cotonificio Veneziano, which began production in 1882 in premises on the Fondamenta Barbarigo near Santa Marta and the new port facilities, its erection involving major alterations to local architecture. The founder was Baron Eugenio Cantoni from Gallarate near Milan. He determined to make his factory an example of 'efficiency, rationality and functionality', utilising the medical prestige of Cesare Musatti to guarantee that dust would do little damage to workers' lungs, and boasting that the factory toilets were the most modern obtainable.[70] In 1884 the concern was duly awarded a gold medal by the Ministry of Industry and Commerce at the Turin National Exhibition. Profits, however, were slow to mount, and a workforce of 927 in 1887 was many fewer than the 3,000 promised. It took another decade and the establishment of better links with other factories on the mainland for the Cotonificio to flourish; in 1911 it produced 25 per cent of national textile exports. By then, much of the workforce was female or juvenile (sixty girls, quite a few taken from a nearby female orphanage, and thirty boys between the ages of twelve and fifteen worked there in 1901). Shifts ran for twelve hours, with one twenty-minute break, and could take place at night. There were many work injuries.[71]

Other industrial concerns that were changing the face of the city and altering its lifestyle could be found on the Giudecca, the Stucky mill being the longest-lived.[72] Giovanni Stucky, born in 1843, was a well-travelled Swiss entrepreneur with a Venetian mother, who from 1867 opened a mill at Treviso using technology imported from Central Europe. In 1880 he moved to Venice, four years later occupying premises at the western end of the Giudecca. His business continued to expand, and in 1890 he constructed an iron bridge over the Rio di San Biagio and further development followed.[73]

With such industrialisation, however partial, proceeding, it was inevitable that some enthusiasts would ask for more. Surely, one councillor urged, a new connection could be made from San Girolamo in Cannaregio, behind the station, across what was often marshland to San Giuliano near Mestre. After all, he added, a modern city could not be 'real' unless it possessed an ample industrial and agricultural hinterland,[74] even if, he conceded, he would be the last to imagine vehicular traffic, cyclists and tramways trundling through Venice's streets. Science must advise how best to ensure that the flow of the lagoon was not altered by any bridge. Perhaps it could have many spans and a new, deeper canal could be dug alongside it?[75]

Debates about transport to or within the city waxed and waned, but the best symbol of the modern political economy, both national and liberal, that was sparking Venice after the Risorgimento was Luigi Luzzatti, a man destined to be briefly prime minister of his country in 1910–11. Luzzatti came from a local Jewish family, and his brother Davide had joined the National Guard in 1848. Luzzatti, who took pains always to underline that he sought to serve the nation rather than the city,[76] trained in law and economics. It was in the latter field that he made a name for himself, assuring students in a phrase that summed up much about Italian liberalism: 'the reactionaries humiliate you, the Socialists flatter you, whereas it is only by honest work and savings that a splendid future can be prepared for you.'[77] Luzzatti became an advocate and organiser of co-operative banks that spread across northern Italy, was elected to the Chamber of Deputies for Oderzo in the hinterland of Treviso, and in 1891 was promoted to Minister of Finance. He maintained his earnest commitment to what he thought was rationality, in 1909 publishing a tract on the freedom of conscience and science. Progress, he was sure, could advance for ever, even if one prefect who served him in Venice unkindly characterised him as 'possessed of a vast culture, a supremely versatile mind, an excellent memory, great imagination, and above all an immense vanity, intimately persuaded that he was a kind of semi-deity, owed complete power without challenge'. His great idea was 'to be pleasing to all, the friend of all, both the protector and the slave of everyone.'[78]

Such may often be the Whiggish mind-set. 'Progress' in Venice was, and is, however, always likely to arouse critics, especially those who want the city to remain 'com'era e dov'era'. One who gave voice to the dilemma whether liberal 'improvement' was positive or negative was the Roman-born engineer, architect, art critic and writer Camillo Boito, who worked on the restoration of the church of Santi Maria e Donato on Murano, and who regularly intervened in Venetian cultural and political debates, endeavouring to fuse the ideas of Ruskin and Viollet-le-Duc, while also advocating compromise between modernisers and their foes.[79] In 1883 he wrote in *Nuova Antologia*, organ of cultivated liberals, about changes reaching the city, notably through the modernisation of the areas around Santa Marta and Sant'Elena, further to the east, where the first plans were being drafted for major new housing. Boito was glad that Venice had acquired its cotton mill and other factories, and did not oppose development. But he feared that, at both ends of the city, 'the mechanical engineer is bossing the place like a despot, mocking and crushing the artist'. The widening of too many city alleyways, he complained, was threatening to make San Marco and the Palazzo Ducale look awry; from 'live things they might become mummies'.

Boito particularly regretted the loss of what he claimed had been the lissom, smiling girls of Santa Marta. He remembered them in bright clothes, with garlands in their hair, dancing and singing with their elders. All had 'lain on the grass or sat in the open air before tables groaning with food'. Other *popolani*, in the company of their wives, children or lovers, . . . also ate and drank and sang', while they 'festively saluted the setting of the sun'. Lest such arcadian scenes be expelled from city life, innovators must not scorn beauty. 'The future is not such a determined enemy of the past as they believe,' he advised sagely.[80] History, beauty and modern greatness were not contradictory.

Given what actual living conditions were like for the Venetian poor, it might be concluded that Boito had been watching too many operettas (his brother Arrigo was a composer, as well as a librettist for Giuseppe Verdi). But Boito was scarcely alone in allowing nostalgia to colour his image of Venice and its purpose in the modern world. Foreigners were especially to the fore in this regard, one example being the English romantic novelist 'Ouida' (Maria Louise Ramé), who in the 1870s had taken up residence near Florence. In 1885 she wrote to *The Times*, urging the cancellation of further concessions to the new motorised ferries in Venice and damning (fledgling) development on the Lido; now, she lamented, 'this lovely island is not much better than Ramsgate or Rosherville'. But her real fear was for the gondolas, whose oarsmen she knew were 'fine, vigorous men, stalwart, though fed scantily on polenta and fish, and "with the right Giorgione colour on their brows and breasts"'. Iron bridges were also a bad idea, as were advertising posters, which must be torn down. Smoking factories and glass works were even more pernicious, ruining, as they evidently were, Venice's 'wonderful colours'.[81]

The most prominent and enduring British interpreter of pre-war Venice was Horatio Brown, a scion of the Scots gentry, who, with his mother, took up residence in Italy from the late 1870s, moving into an apartment on the Grand Canal before setting up at Ca' Torresella on the Zattere in 1889, in a house that he shared with his close friend, a gondolier, and his family. Brown soon became the most active member of the Venetian 'British community', generous in sharing his gondolier's services or proffering English-style sandwiches at his weekly teas to which everyone came.[82] He was proud to be warden of the Anglican St George's, which had opened in the city in 1892, converted from a warehouse at Campo San Vio in Dorsoduro.[83]

Brown did not die until 1926. In 1887 he published a general history, sure that Venice, like Shakepeare's Cleopatra, possessed 'infinite variety'.[84] Seven years later, he amplified his account, being emphatic about 'the distinctive set of customs' to which different Venetians clung in their tenacious devotion to home life and sure therefore that there was more than one Venice. 'One district speaks of another as a separate nation,' he contended. 'There is the nation of San Nicolò, the nation of Castello, the nation of the Giudecca. And the physical peculiarities, and even the dialects of these various quarters, almost justifies this very pronounced distinction.'[85] Bread also varied from one part of the city to the next (although it always tasted good).[86] Brown said that he had met old women at Santa Marta who had never ventured as far as San Marco, while 'a girl who marries out of her own quarter will talk as if she were going to a foreign country'. After all, he had learned, 'the *costume* of the city has always been in favour of a quasi-Oriental treatment of women. The wife's place is in-doors; she has no business to be out at all without her husband or for a very good reason.' Women of the people remained direly ignorant of physical and medical matters and thus contributed to the 'appallingly high' infant mortality rate, typically feeding their babies on 'coffee, sour wine, and raw apple'.[87]

A decade later, Brown's musings had grown grander as he opined that Venice, like Siena, Prague and Oxford, was a 'city of the soul'. 'Venice', he maintained, 'is to be felt not reproduced; to live there is to live a poem, to be daily surfeited with a wealth of beauty enough to madden an artist with despair.' Although the Republic had fallen, he added, a unique 'Venice still remains; Venice, the place and the people'. Warming to his theme he ran on, 'it is in the streets of Venice that one comes to know the people and the manner of life they lead. And it will be strange if one does not like them, in spite of all their faults. There is a gaiety, a laughter and a light-heartedness about these children of the lagoons that is very winning; a disengagement and apparent frankness that captivates, for all their indifference to truth, and that fatal desire to find out what you want to say and to say it.'[88] 'Few crowds are more cheerful or better ordered than a Venetian crowd,' he maintained cosily. 'The people love to congregate; everyone is out on the business of pleasure, and determined to enjoy themselves to the full.'[89]

Given the survival of such deeply inscribed stereotypes, even in one who lived for decades in Venice, it was natural that special attention should be given abroad to the restoration of San Marco. After all, for many foreigners 'Venice' really meant only the most central area of the city. In the Basilica's regard, Ruskin's posture was frequently endorsed; in November 1879, at a crowded meeting of the British Society for the Preservation of Ancient Buildings off the Strand, William Morris (the Hon. Sec.) and Edward Burne-Jones led the condemnation of what they charged was 'the proposed total destruction and rebuilding of the west front' of the church.[90] A week later, at the Sheldonian Theatre in Oxford, Morris, Burne-Jones and the Dean of Christ Church, stiffened by a letter of support from Liberal ex-prime minister W. E. Gladstone, were sure that 'Englishmen have a right to protest against the deformation of what was rendered sacred by Byron's poetry,' voting firmly that 'to "restore" [St Mark's] was an impossibility. The work of an individual genius could in no case be restored.'[91]

Here were some deep waters, but they did not stop Morris from issuing a public letter appealing to Italians 'to forbid for the future all meddling with the matchless mosaics and inlaid work which are the crown of the glories of St Mark's.'[92] A *Times* editorial, expressing views that any government then needed to reckon with, thundered its approval, asserting that 'St Mark's is, in a way, the pride and possession of the whole world.'[93] Just who Venice belonged to remained, and remains, a key issue in any study of the city's identity, but in November 1879 *The Times* won an appeasing response from the Italian Ministry of Education, which assured Venice's foreign admirers that all 'bad work' on the Basilica had stopped, while emphasising that 'whatever may prove to be necessary in the way of restoration or of repair will be done, but with the utmost care and tenderness.'[94]

Tourist claims on Venice were growing; annual numbers estimated at 160,000 in 1883 soared to 3.5 million in 1907.[95] Opponents of modernisation and development could also be found in the city, however, led by Pompeo Molmenti. In 1887 he announced dramatically in *Nuova Antologia*, 'Venezia delenda est,' endorsing Boito's complaints about structural changes occurring at Santa Marta and Sant'Elena and also bewailing the new fish market beyond the Rialto that had opened in 1884. This last, he conceded, might have some hygienic advantages, but architecturally, he moaned, it was 'an insult to art and good taste'. Venice, he added, must not mimic 'boring and monotonous modern cities', especially since, 'more than an Italian city, it is the artistic patrimony of the world'. It must not be stained by the 'shameful constructions, of uniform vulgarity', that were favoured by the council and their friends out of 'presumptuous vanity and a doltish love of the new'. An extra bridge was utterly to be opposed.[96] It would 'svenezianizzare' (de-Venetianise) Venice.[97]

Molmenti had begun his career as a follower of Luzzatti, although his liberalism was tempered by his Catholicism and he was no starry-eyed Whig believer in Progress. Equally, his commitment to the nation took second place to his self-assumed role as the defender of old Venice against its foes, wherever they might be. Molmenti had many international contacts and could rely on his books being translated into other European languages. As a historian he was particularly alert to rebutting any who endorsed stories of tyranny or corruption under the Republic.[98] That regime, he believed, had been 'a model of good government and social peace'. History, he maintained more generally, must be 'the *magistra vitae*, the impulse to any thought about the present'.[99] It (or rather his version of it) was plainly on his side. In Venice, the spirit of the Republic and its artistic and architectural legacies must live into the future. Anything that besmirched that past or made it harder to discern should not be permitted.

Despite Molmenti's pertinacious campaigning and the widespread support he received,[100] the dawn of the last decade of the century seemed to promise novelty in Venice given the installation of a left-leaning giunta under Riccardo Selvatico, a poet and writer best known for his sentimental depictions of popular virtue. Fans today can track his lingering presence in the city through a bronze herm in the Giardini, a portrait in the modern collection at Ca' Pesaro, a Campiello named after him in Cannaregio and a plaque near his birthplace at Ponte Sant'Antonio.

After its installation, Selvatico's council endorsed an ambitious plan for urban improvement, containing twenty-four separate projects for health-based reforms and sixteen for greater viability in the city, while also cutting taxes paid by the poor.[101] In 1894 the hated impost on flour and therefore bread, still the staple for many Venetians, was eliminated.[102] In practice, however, what the radical administration is best remembered for is the 'First Biennale', the international art exhibition, which opened in the presence of King Umberto and his queen on 30 April 1895 (they stayed for five days and visited the displays on four occasions)[103] and was to attract 224,000 visitors.[104] By the eighth staging in 1909 this tally had doubled.

The 'fathers' of what was by then a highly successful venture were Selvatico, Giovanni Bordiga, an academic mathematician in charge of the Comune's

cultural policy, and Antonio Fradeletto, a radical journalist, orator and politician, destined to be the main cultural manager in the city until after the First
World War. Fradeletto's patriotic modernity was well displayed in the fact that,
during the 1890s, he was the leader of the local branch of the Dante Alighieri
society[105] and of the teachers' union, while proselytising the spread of the
gymnastics movement in the city and backing the location of an area devoted
to target shooting. It thus may not surprise to find that the first Biennale was
advertised not only as an art show but as offering 'Venetian festivals, serenades,
regattas, sporting competitions, open-air light shows, concerts, the feast
inspired by the Redentore, an international fencing contest, firework displays,
major theatrical spectacles and other great parties'.[106]

Soon, however, the event narrowed and it became widely accepted that
'Fradeletto is the Biennale and the Biennale is Fradeletto'.[107] In 1900 Fradeletto
was elected to the Chamber of Deputies in Rome for the seat of Venice III,
covering San Marco and Cannaregio. Thereafter, he drifted to the moderate
right to reach ministerial rank by the end of the First World War, by which time
he was also seeking closer relations with the newly organised Associazione
Nazionalista Italiana (ANI, Italian Nationalist Association).

Despite the patriotic gloss, however, the Biennale aimed from its beginning
to be international, 60 per cent of the art displayed there in 1895 originating
outside Italy.[108] The exhibition therefore underlined Venice's claims, separate
from the nation of Italy, to have its own global meaning. As early as 1866 the
Comune had offered translation services in a dozen European languages, and
in the years that followed the city had welcomed people from diverse backgrounds, ranging from Richard Wagner and Friedrich Nietzsche to 'Chief
Black Elk', who brought a 'troupe' of 'Indians' (Native Americans) to Venice in
1889.[109] In 1906, this last's visit was seconded by that of 'Buffalo Bill' (W. F.
Cody), who, with 'two redskins', performed on the Lido.[110] Now, despite warn-
ings, destined to become ever more strident, that tourism did not help Venice
'morally',[111] the city opened itself to what, in the belle époque, would become
ever more numerous visitors, with the result that what Venice meant was at
least partially what its visitors thought it meant.

Yet during the two decades leading to the First World War, the most influential person to inscribe Venice into current thought was Gabriele D'Annunzio,
an outsider who became a city intimate. He had been born at Pescara in the
Abruzzi in 1863, first visiting Venice in 1887 (for the inauguration of the statue
of Victor Emmanuel II). As the local journalist Gino Damerini stated, thereafter Venice would lie at the base of D'Annunzio's 'entire attitude to poetry,
politics and war'.[112] In many senses, the poet fused into Venice (or rather a
special Venetian history), and Venice (or rather a version of Venice) fused into

D'Annunzio, who loved to boast that 'the world must see that I am capable of everything'. His lush (and well-publicised) literary concentration on 'murder, eroticism, cruelty, and madness, along with hints of incest and necrophilia' was making him into an Italian and international celebrity, even if his writings never sold enough to cover his lavish lifestyle.[113] At one level, then, D'Annunzio embodied the city's black legend, what the French sports journalist and rightist thinker Maurice Barrès[114] and the German liberal writer Thomas Mann would soon summarise as 'death in Venice'.[115]

Each of these writers emphasised corruption and morbidity, a permanent decadence. Barrès maintained that ordinary Venetians were so poor that the local pigeons and cats instinctively mistrusted them. D'Annunzio took the allure of pervasive death as far as he could, but, in major and unresolved contradiction, he also imagined a Venice armed with a potent historical message of empire and conquest. With their capital in Rome, the Italian elite could scarcely ignore the myths of Roman conquest in what was already frequently called the 'mare nostrum' of the Mediterranean. To this 'memory', D'Annunzio added that of the Venetian domain, spread across the Adriatic and the lands washed by it, Greece and Asia Minor. As he had put it in a series of papers published in 1888, Italy, under impulsion from its Venetian past, 'either will be a Great Naval Power or it will be nothing'. War, he announced, must come soon; the 'prodigious naval defeat at Lissa' must then be cancelled by 'a prodigious naval victory'.[116] Uniting his public and private lives, in 1887 D'Annunzio named his third child 'Veniero', after the Venetian admiral who commanded the Christian fleet at Lepanto.

It was D'Annunzio, already a celebrity in Italy and beyond, who gave the Biennale its most immediate fame, elevating it beyond a mere art exhibition in a city torn between liberal improvement and historical preservation 'com'era e dov'era'. Sex provided an extra impulse, since in 1894 the married D'Annunzio had met Eleonora Duse, an actress of international fame, herself married and his senior. He became her lover, and by 1896 was living off her money.[117] When D'Annunzio gave the formal concluding oration to the Biennale on 8 November 1895, exulting in a Venice that throbbed with power and pleasure, it sounded as if life was orgasmically imitating art, whether for the poet or for the city and Italy. The electrifying mixture was complete when, in 1900, D'Annunzio published a novel, *Il fuoco* (The Flame), that seemed to be a thinly veiled account of his recent experiences.

Early in the book, the protagonist Stelio Effrena, a poet and orator, asks his woman, Perdita, 'Do you know of any other place in the world like Venice that sometimes has the power to stir great forces in human life and arouses desire to fever pitch?' 'When one is in Venice', Stelio mused, 'one cannot feel except through music or think except through images. They come from everywhere in such profusion, endlessly; they are more real and alive than the people who jostle in a narrow street.'[118] Stelio was given to speechifying from a balcony (in possible premonition of Mussolini), D'Annunzio preaching that 'the spoken word which is directed at a mass of people should have but one aim, that of inspiring action, even violent action'. Stelio's Venice might be 'autumnal and womanly', but it panted for intercourse with the poet as the person who could mystically transmit beauty to the crowd.[119] Venice was not therefore the city of death, readers of *Il fuoco* learned. Like the endless tide, 'she sucks out souls every day and then returns them pure and whole, refreshed with some completely original newness on which tomorrow the traces of things will be impressed with limpid clarity'.[120] Even an *acqua alta*, in D'Annunzio's evocation, was exciting rather than annoying or destructive, and his beauteous Venice bore the future as well as the past.[121]

At the 1895 Biennale, the winning entry, which saw off challenges from Burne-Jones, Whistler and Millais, was Francesco Michetti's *Daughter of Iorio*, a large, dark portrayal of a young girl walking past some male peasants, with snowy peaks behind, perhaps in evocation of Michetti's home region of the Abruzzi. His prize was a rich 10,000 lire. Michetti shared a regional background with D'Annunzio, who was omnipresent at the Biennale, the poet claiming that he was inspired by the painter's vision a few years later to produce his own salacious theatrical version of what Iorio's daughter had been doing. But at the exhibition the more sensational work was the Piedmontese painter Giacomo Grosso's *The Last Gathering*, displaying five auburn-haired naked beauties disporting themselves on and around a bier at a Venetian church funeral, a mingling of life, death and perverse sexuality with a highly D'Annunzian texture. Presumably to Grosso's pleasure (although he was later commissioned to produce a portrait of Pope Benedict XV, 1914–22), the painting brought down anathemas on the whole exhibition from Cardinal Patriarch Giuseppe Melchiorre Sarto, just as Venice's Comune was passing from Selvatico's radicals back to Grimani's Catholic conservatives.

Born in Riese in the peasant hinterland of Treviso in 1835, Sarto had been anointed patriarch immediately after being made cardinal in June 1893. He had not, however, assumed his post for almost a year, having been blocked by the anti-clericals. In 1892, Selvatico's friends had, to flaunt their rationalism, erected a monument meant lastingly to expose Counter-Reformation ignorance and tyranny at Campo Santa Fosca, where, more than two centuries earlier, papal-inspired assassins had sought to kill the independent Venetian priest Paolo Sarpi. Thereafter, squabbling between Church and state continued over whether Sarto's elevation could be recognised, the council ostentatiously refusing to send a formal representative to his installation at San Marco in 1894.

Sarto himself was no conciliator, being driven by what a friendly biographer has described as 'an absolute intransigence' against liberal ideas on science and education, Freemasonry and divorce (only savages, he pronounced, could want it),[122] and was soon working to undermine Selvatico's council.[123] Catholics who tried to be liberal were, he pronounced, the irreconcilable foes of the embattled Church. It was sustained, however, by Christ, the 'King for all eternity', and had always vanquished its enemies, whether they were the Emperors Maximin and Decius, Henry VIII and 'Cromuel' (sic) or the French Jansenists.[124] Its rule would live eternally, and must be obeyed in everyday life as well as during religious worship. Women must know their place and not seek participation in church choirs, for example.

As for workers and artisans, they should consider their labour as penitential in purpose. 'Blessed are you, the poor, who endure a hard and austere life amid deprivation and effort, so long as you bear it with constant Christian resignation and set your sufferings against your sins.'[125] Charity they could hope in; socialism they must eschew. In 1903 Sarto would succeed Leo XIII as Pope Pius X. In the papal office, he would savagely denounce 'modernism', meaning any modish desire to intrude liberalism and democracy into the thought and government of Church or state. Now a saint, he remains a model at the far right of his Church, his followers across the world organising themselves into a society named after him (the Fraternità Sacerdotale San Pio X).[126]

Patriarch Sarto, it is plain, had a grand history awaiting him, one that may have been tinctured with Venetian tones but was also to be universal, would outlast D'Annunzio's fame, and can today mock the period-piece anti-clericalism of Selvatico and the Venetian radicals of the 1890s. Yet what is also evident from Venice's story during the first three decades of Italian ownership is that the city had changed in its urban frame since 1866 and that Venetians had altered in their habits and ideas since becoming 'Italian'. It is equally clear that many different currents ran through the place or had by now washed into it. Liberalism meant 'improvement' and improvement there had been. But its definition was neither simple nor singular, and liberal rule did not affect all in the same way.

After all, the embrace of the nation, Italy, was problematic in Venice, be it because of the enduring localism of many Venetians (who often extracted most meaning from their belonging to a family, a parish or a *sestiere*) or because some observers now began to proclaim that the imperial past of the Venetian Republic must be resurrected under a national flag. As will be seen in the next chapter, quite a few converts to this cause would decide that empire must entail a greater industrialisation of the city and its hinterland, a more ruthless and pervasive modernisation than the liberals had so far provided. Yet for every advocate of factories and speedy transport there was an exponent of the opposing case that Venice must be left 'com'era e dov'era', beautiful beyond compare and timeless in its pasts.

Simultaneously, tourism was ensuring that Venice had an ever more solid universal cast as well as the national and local ones. In quite a few ways, Venice was already set on a course that would lead it to be enshrined as 'historic centre' of the world. Certainly foreigners were not behindhand in expressing the view that they had as much right as those who lived in Venice to define what the city meant.

The best farewell to Risorgimento Venice and its optimism can be found in the pages of a book published in 1898 by a local printer and entitled *Venezia nel 1930* (Venice in 1930). Its author was a journalist named Giorgio Moscarda, who was not destined to win eternal fame. His work has a curious and early place in a genre on 'the shape of wars to come' that would sell well in *belle époque* Europe[127] and acquire historical significance in delineating the 'generation of 1914'. Moscarda focuses less on war than on glorious, wealth-building peace. Moving his city forward three decades, he tells of the return of Angelo Vianello, a humble if not the poorest Venetian, born on the Via Garibaldi. He and his Venetian wife, both trained in medicine, had moved to East Africa (notorious in 1896, given Italy's humiliatingly unavenged defeat by the Ethiopian emperor, Menelik), where their experiences amount to a ripping yarn.

The Vianellos' combination of modernity and humanity leads the local people to elect Angelo their emperor. In this post he moves from triumph to triumph, abolishing taxes and customs duty, while unleashing victorious military force where needed, helped in his success by Menelik's dying after eating too many watermelons on a visit to the Paris Exhibition in 1900. Europeans flock to the new *imperium*, living in racial harmony with the indigenes and prospering in industry, agriculture and commerce. The emperor and his wife Eufemia, however, have not forgotten their native city. Venice becomes the 'landing place and emporium' of African trade, ensuring that the city's riches and population expand mightily from one year to the next.

Under such an impulse, Venice changes. Forcibly expropriated from the selfishly reluctant, the Via Garibaldi area transmogrifies into a garden city that the English acknowledge equal to their own. A train service runs to Sant'Elena and, across a revolving bridge, to the Lido, powered by electricity and needing only two men to work it. A new island is dredged between San Marco and Malamocco for the use of global yachtsmen, who take their ease at a hotel in the Eastern style, with wondrous architecture borrowed from 'Constantinople,

Jerusalem and Cairo etc. On its top stands a navigation light in the form of a star, like the star of Italy, and by night its luminous multi-coloured rays act as a guide to shipping.'[128] Another new bridge connects San Giobbe with San Giuliano, bringing profit and employment, especially given the opening of a massive market near the departure point from Venice, where three new squares have been built. A bicycle factory wins fruitful markets in Dalmatia. Similarly, a vast, modern new shipyard opens near the old Arsenale specialising in trade to the East. As a result, Italy peacefully reinforces its culture and language in an area that had seemed about to 'succumb' to 'Slav barbarism', Moscarda states, with racial venom that contrasts with his views on 'Africans'.[129] Best is the massive demolition of all the rotting buildings between Piazza San Marco and Campo San Luca, where now stands the grandest of *gallerie*, full of luxury shops, cafés and food outlets and thronged by a cosmopolitan public, who are each day sheltered from the sun, snow and rain, and so rejoice (and spend) in the new Venice.

Venice in the *belle époque* was indeed to be the city of many people's dreams (including Freud's), before becoming, in its First World War, a place of nightmare. No dreamer in the happy decade before 1914 would, however, match Moscarda in the guileless expression of what had, in 1866, been the hope of the triumphant liberal elite with regard to the improvement that beneficent modernity under their administration could install in Venice.

CHAPTER THREE

Venice in the *belle époque*

At midnight on 8 May 1997 and through the wee hours of the next day, Venice became the scene of a political event that could hardly have been more photogenic. A dozen armed separatists, representing the Veneto Serenissimo Governo, a purported government of the Venice region, occupied the Campanile in St Mark's Square (see map 3). They unfurled their flag from its upper loggia, proclaiming 'national independence'. The date, however, was wrong. If crusaders for a Venetian Republic were looking for a telling anniversary, the historic Republic had agreed to dissolve itself on 12 May 1797. A second historical curiosity was also involved, one that carried ironical echoes from the city's *belle époque* of before 1914, an era in which, as will be seen, Venice competed with Paris as a world centre of leisure and high culture. The Campanile that was the separatists' target and base, with the implication that it transmitted into the present a timeless history, was not an old structure but a new one (however much masquerading as having existed in the *longue durée*). The medieval Campanile, much altered in the sixteenth century when it had been adorned with Sansovino's beautiful *loggetta*, had crumbled to the ground on 14 July, Bastille Day, 1902. It was rebuilt, amid controversy, debate and rival readings of its historical message, to be inaugurated on 25 April 1912, the Feast of St Mark, bolder commentators claiming that that day marked exactly one thousand years since its first erection. The Campanile of San Marco is therefore not so much a surviving medieval architectural jewel as a central urban memory site for the decade in which Venice began to chart the path it would follow in the twentieth-century world.

The bell-tower's fall echoed mightily, proof if any was needed that 'Venice', or at least Piazza San Marco, held sway in many minds. A first count by local officials reckoned that in July–August 1902 no fewer than 367 publications in prose or verse had painted a word-picture of the Campanile's fate.[1] A later tabulation, covering the period from 1902 to the end of 1911, recorded 178 pieces devoted to the actual collapse, 104 to the causes of and responsibility for it, 94 to issues initially raised in its reconstruction, 242 to rebuilding work and 30 to the effects on the Sansovino *loggetta* (the fragments of which were being lovingly reconstituted), as well as an additional 120 poems varying between the 'serious and facetious',[2] humorous articles and satiric vignettes, and ten collections of the iconography of the site.[3] One of the first to comment in print was the young socialist Benito Mussolini, then an emigrant in Switzerland, who lambasted bourgeois Europeans for the tears spilt over the inanimate Campanile, while they deplorably did nothing to curb current Armenian massacres in the Ottoman Empire. Furthermore, declared the future Duce, striving manfully to cut a figure in what was as yet his small circle, the ancient monument was 'artistically of dubious taste'.[4]

More decorously, *L'Ateneo Veneto*, in its first issue after the fall, published twenty stanzas by a local poet, addressing the edifice as 'tu' (the intimate form of 'you') and pledging that Venice and the world were bent on its resurrection. A discourse multiplied, asserting that high and low could not secure themselves in the cityscape without the framing of the Campanile. Queen Mother Margherita (her husband had been assassinated at Monza in 1900, to be succeeded by their son Victor Emmanuel III) was widely quoted as grieving that, if she could not see its bell-tower, she could no longer 'map Venice in her mind'. D'Annunzio, as ever merging self-dramatisation with the city, was 'prostrated by grief and weeping' at the news, pacing from room to room, unable to work. 'And in the newspapers someone dares to be happy because there were no human victims,' he grumbled captiously.[5] After all, it was true that, even if considerable damage was done to Sansovino's *loggetta*, the only animate casualty of the collapse had been the caretaker's cat.

More ordinary people, it was reported, were measuring their life spans against a Campanile that had always been and must now again be there.[6] After all, it was noted as if the bell-tower had itself been a Venetian citizen, 'the good Campanile, although dying so miserably, had not wanted to kill or offend anyone and had not even damaged its partner, the golden Basilica' (San Marco).[7] Journalist and man about town Gino Damerini recalled being on the Lido when the structure crumpled, watching aghast while a whitish cloud masked the sun and sky and then puzzling over a lost harmony. 'We could no longer find the lines that composed the city,' he recalled wistfully. Everyone piled onto the next ferry to swell a crying, cursing crowd, which scanned the smoking pile of bricks and mortar, discountenanced by the realisation that something primordial had been excised from the city's meaning.[8] With his own reckoning of what was elemental in life, Patriarch Sarto gave thanks for the fact that no one had died in the event, at the same time preaching austerely that what the disintegration of such a famous structure taught was that God held charge of all things, man being a mere 'illusion and lie'.[9] In the days that followed, he endeavoured to salve Venetians with church ceremony, positioning in public view on the cathedral's main altar a 'most sacred image of the Virgin', and holding a full pontifical mass on 23 July and a solemn Vespers with procession and Te Deum two days later, because his Basilica's escape, he was sure, was 'miraculous'.[10]

Foreigners were not behindhand in commentary. The London *Times* reported that the city had been wrenched out of joint by the loss of its Campanile: 'The attitude of the people', a correspondent wrote, 'is most pathetic. Women are weeping in the street, and as hour passes hour and the Campanile bells are silent a void is felt which those who know Venetian life can appreciate.'[11] With its own austere politeness to worthy foreigners, the paper was ready to congratulate the prefect and local police for their supervision of the actual event: visible cracks had begun to scour the building some days before it fell and the civic authorities had warned everyone to stay away from it. The Thunderer's tone could readily turn pessimistic and critical, however. That the Campanile had caved in, it agreed, was 'a terrible misfortune. Venice will never be quite the same again'; hereafter Piazza San Marco would cease to be the most beautiful square in the world and the globe would mourn. But with their carelessness about their heritage, the 'Venetian authorities' and those elsewhere in the country must shoulder the real blame. Owing to official fecklessness, many major buildings in the city were threatened with subsidence, and, in circumstances of general urban crisis, there was little likelihood that the bell-tower could or should rise again. Blatant neglect of Venice's architectural inheritance was 'causing much bad feeling among the citizens'. As indeed it should, the paper charged.[12]

The readiness of foreigners to whip the locals for perceived failings, with the impertinent assumption that they were but caretakers of a cityscape that mattered more to the world than to them, was scarcely new and would not cease with the Campanile's revamping. But a reconstruction there was, Antonio Fradeletto happily recalling a decade later that, on the evening of 14 July, the city leaders had at once agreed that the Campanile must return 'com'era e dov'era'. 'No hesitation, doubt or dissent' had been voiced, he underlined; rather, the Comune had automatically expressed 'a firm collective will ... one of those moral fruits growing from profound sentimental roots – that is, from instinct – ripe in an instant'.[13] Among Venetians, he contended, a 'religious respect for the past branches out of basic culture, constituting a delicate kind of intellectual altruism'. The cost of rebuilding had been high, more than

2.2 million lire. But there had been no hesitation in paying it. After all, some of the material remains were demonstrated to go back to the Roman Empire, and that heritage could steel the Third Italy in this as in many other matters.[14] Pompeo Molmenti agreed with his younger colleague. The new Campanile, he stressed, was 'of the same stone, the same clay', enriched by 'the soul of memory, the life of an immortal people'.[15]

It was certainly true that the architects and engineers involved did their best to identify every stone that had pitched intact from the Campanile or the side of the *loggetta*, even if, over the weeks after 14 July, barge-loads of rubble and dust were dumped into the lagoon. Yet some novelty could not be avoided. In the reconstruction, the foundations of the Campanile were broadened, five steps were added to the entry (amid some wrangling), and modern concrete was deployed where necessary. The biggest bell had remained intact but four new ones were now cast, formally to be blessed before erection on 15 June 1910.[16] When, two years later, they rang for the first time after the reopening, Pope Pius X, with untoward indulgence in modern science, arranged to hear the clangour conveyed by telephone to his apartment at the Vatican.[17]

Every now and again a critic might timidly suggest that Piazza San Marco looked 'more dignified and harmonious *sans* Bell Tower'.[18] Immediately following the fall, an anonymous commentator in *Nuova Antologia*, though realising that 'the voice of the race was weeping' at the loss, had audaciously suggested that a new structure should rise in a different part of the square; that, he argued, was what had been done in classical times when the Romans confronted architectural loss. Such a positioning, he affirmed, might be better at persuading the nation to pursue a modern life.[19] His ideas won backing from the sculptor Davide Calandra, who asserted that a new Campanile could best show that 'ours is an age of revival and renewal', hostile to 'embalming' the nation. Could there not be an international competition for the replacement, he asked innocently?[20]

Such heretical murmuring in favour of what was readily damned as a transgression of history was soon quieted. On 25 April 1912 a distinguished international company assembled for the reopening ceremony, in which Mayor Grimani spoke of the deep ties between city and nation, the past and the present, at a moment when Italian troops were engaged in colonial war in what they called, in Roman style, 'Libya'. Between the national enterprise in Tripoli, he insisted, and the rebuilding of 'this mighty tower that returns to speak with the ancient voice of God and Fatherland . . . there is an intimate moral harmony. Each event affirms in various guises the magnificent rebirth of our race.' James Rennell Rodd, the British ambassador, who was only one among a score of foreign dignitaries (and royals) present at what he remembered as 'one of the most impressively beautiful ceremonies I have ever witnessed', enjoyed the release of two thousand carrier pigeons from the tower's summit to 'bear the announcement of its completion to every city of Italy'.[21] When it came to speeches, Rodd agreed in period phrasing that the restored Campanile must hereafter act as 'a virile symbol of the good blood that belies itself not'.[22] Even before the event, a *Times* editorial had pronounced that 'the Italians are at this minute giving splendid proof of their patriotism towards their country as a whole [in Libya]; but no people in the world have known how to combine this wider feeling with intense local patriotism so completely as they, and nowhere in Italy is local patriotism stronger or more fervent than in Venice'.[23]

Certainly, April 1912 was a month in the *belle époque* when Venice was at its most beguiling, at least to the best people, for whom, frankly speaking, charm and leisure mattered more than the sound of distant battle or rising nationalism. Among key events that spring was a Grand Ball in the style of eighteenth-century Venetian painter Pietro Longhi, held with mayoral permission in Piazza San Marco. It was animated by the Marchesa Luisa Casati, according to her biographers 'possibly the most artistically represented woman in history after the Virgin Mary and Cleopatra'.[24] Married into the Lombard aristocracy, Casati was the sparkily independent wife of the president of the Italian Jockey Club and joint Master of the Staghounds of the Italian capital. Her parties were diligently flashy and cosmopolitan. In the instance of the 'Ballo Longhi', Grimani had courteously or cautiously organised a police squad to guard the square. Once arrived, prosperous and aristocratic guests, decked out in wigs and crinolines, were ushered to their seats at tables scattered across Piazza San Marco by candelabra-bearing black servants in white wigs, red velvet coats and ropes of pearls.

The Marchesa made her own entry by water at the Piazzetta, heralded by a 'gondola-borne orchestra . . . lit by countless Chinese lanterns'. On landing, she was saluted 'by flag bearers, trumpeters and a trio of falcon handlers'. Using material patterned by the celebrated Spanish designer Mariano Fortuny (who had taken up residence in the city and made it his)[25] and woven into a robe by Bakst (of Paris), Casati presented herself as a 'Tiepolo deity' in a hooped gold skirt, with the 'massive train held up by a pair of young footmen adorned with plumes'. 'Led by ropes of turquoise beads', her twin pet cheetahs, the constant companions of her city walks (on which, it was rumoured, she was often nude beneath her fur coat), trailed behind. When she entered the Piazza, there was loud and prolonged applause.[26] Not for nothing did D'Annunzio, ever present in Venice, confess that Casati 'was the only woman who ever astonished me'.[27]

Despite her magnetism, Casati was scarcely the most blithe of beings, as her exaggerated persona might suggest, being destined to die in reduced circumstances in 1950s London. She was not alone in her unhappiness. The history of love in Venice was stained by suicide, be it of eminent foreigners or inconsolable locals. In spring 1880 the young husband of English writer George Eliot leapt from their hotel balcony into the Grand Canal to his intended death, apparently when he discovered during his Venetian honeymoon that his matrimonial arrangement with his wife entailed sex. In January 1894 American Constance Fennimore Wilson succeeded in drowning herself in the Grand Canal, perhaps out of frustrated love for Henry James, who was well-manneredly saddened at the act.[28] The suicide with the most political ramifications was that of Guido Fusinato, prominent in Liberal educational policies and the framing of national foreign policy, who took his life on the mainland on 22 September 1914, in desolation at Italy's retreat from its membership of the Triple Alliance. Even after Fascism evinced a stern dislike of the 'self-indulgence' of suicide, commentators continued to be alarmed by its elevated rate in Venice. It was estimated as the third highest in the country, having increased from an average of four per annum in 1861–5 to twenty-three between 1876 and 1880, and thereafter remaining high, mainly provoked by despair among the poor, whether male or female and whether occasioned by love or the cost of living.[29]

Yet during those glittering last springs and summers before the European lamps went out, such sadness could be ignored as prosperous sectors of the city gave ever fuller proof of progress, an advance enjoyed by both the locals and the accelerating number of visiting foreigners. Among them was Diana Manners (in marriage to become Diana Cooper), thought by the British to be the most beautiful young woman in society. A debutante in 1911 she spent Easter 1912 in Venice, where, also dressed by Fortuny, she attended the inauguration of the bell-tower (she saw no *lèse-majesté* in donning a Bersagliere cloak and feathered hat) and the Casati party (and remembered not minding the jostling that offended some of her elders). In spring 1913 she was back, this time in the company of the family of Liberal British prime minister H. H. Asquith. Occasionally stroking her arm yearningly, the older man took her around the city armed with his Baedeker, an activity, she recalled, that was followed by 'the gruelling questioning of an evening on the day's learning', when they also read Ruskin together.[30]

For every commoner attracted to the city, there often seemed to be an equal number of aristocrats and royals. Among the latter was the heir to the Habsburg throne, Archduke Franz Ferdinand, who, with his morganatic wife Sophie, Duchess of Hohenberg, took a holiday there. He was photographed, with minimal guard, feeding pigeons outside San Marco on a mild summer day in 1910. Although celebrated as an insatiate hunter, with a lifetime tally surpassing

8 Archduke Franz Ferdinand in Venice 1910, not Sarajevo 1914

300,000 birds and animals, Franz Ferdinand presumably did not know that a local expert had warned sententiously of the danger that Venice's pigeons, resident in the city for 'very many centuries', were being increasingly cross-bred with a less 'elegant and pure' foreign bird. Could the problem, he asked, be provoked by the pigeon-shoot now established on the Lido? Aerial refugees from there were, he feared, permanently corrupting Venetian traditions, and he cited Darwin in proof (together with an impressive array of 'scientific' measurement).[31]

Germany's Kaiser Wilhelm II was a more frequent royal visitor, using Venice as the starting point for cruises on his yacht *Hohenzollern* to his palace on Corfu or in the Adriatic and Mediterranean, even if a British consular official rumoured maliciously that the real reason was the Kaiser's fondness for 'a lovely Italian countess'.[32] With more proper devotion to business, Wilhelm generally stopped for brief confabulation with German and Italian officials to signal the loyalish membership of each nation in the Triple Alliance.[33] According to *The Times*, when the emperor arrived in October 1898 his comfort was guaranteed by luggage that filled eleven train coaches and weighed a hefty 384 tons. Wilhelm was met by Umberto I and his prime minister, Luigi Pelloux, and rowed to the royal yacht on what is likely to have been a groaning gondola.[34] The emperor made his last visit to the city in spring 1914, another

9 The Kaiser visits Venice (again)

occasion on which the Italian king, now Victor Emmanuel III, came north to greet him.[35]

The regular arrival of British queen (after 1910, queen mother) Alexandra provoked fewer political tremors; even if the catty whispered that she was deaf, dull and dowdy, she added presence to the expatriate community and was especially fond of the rose garden established by the gentlemanly Frederic Eden in a backwater on the Giudecca, which he had begun planting in 1884. Alexandra could be relied on for a charitable visit to the Ospedale Cosmopolitano there, which, under the command of a brisk English matron at a site near the Redentore, cared for sick foreigners anxious to avoid Italian medical systems.[36]

In his account of the Elysian field that he rejoiced in on his island, Eden boasted of growing gooseberries as well as new rose stock. He conceded that 'to the natives of the Giudecca, all are foreigners who are not Giudecchite'; yet ordinary life was merry in his perception. 'A huge melon, an excellent supper for four people with bread, sells for 10 centimes. Thus a Venetian, be he Gondolier or Conte, may, and often does in summer time, eat healthily at small cost.' At any season, he added, 'for twopence, too, you may make a beggar happy. Fifteen to twenty figs at five centimes, fifteen centimes of bread, and a generous penny more will bring him free from a glass to a pint of wine, or, what he will like better, a glass of *graspa* [sic], the spirit they distil here from the wine lees, and love.'[37]

Among other visitors to Eden's demi-paradise were the King of Siam (and family), the tsarina mother, the Dukes of Connaught and Edinburgh, the Duchess of Hesse, the king of Montenegro, the aged Empress Eugénie, widow of Napoleon III, and Queen Mother Margherita. D'Annunzio and Eleonora Duse could be relied on to appear, exuding their own celebrity.[38] Other notables to enliven the parties of the British community included the First Sea Lord Jackie Fisher and Lord Kitchener, the latter to become Britain's Secretary of State for War in 1914.[39] But despite the fame of Eden's rose garden, increasingly the most bewitching sector of the city, at least while the sun shone, was the Lido, where both visitors and locals could enjoy what its propagandists strenuously proclaimed had been forged into the 'most elegant beach resort in the world'. For any who today review its past, it is a site of memory of the city's *belle époque* that surpasses the historical imprint even of the Campanile. Yet it reflects a new and twentieth-century history, from the viewpoint of 'com'era e dov'era' almost an anti-history, certainly not an old and 'timeless' one.

On the beach, five hundred metres' stroll from the ferry stop, still stands the Hotel Excelsior. Its first stone laid in February 1907, it was feverishly erected in seventeen months, 'in the Moorish style' mixed with period neo-Lombard and neo-Gothic; in 1914 part of the hotel was furnished in the 'Louis Quinze manner', while a pavilion in the sea was described as 'artistically Chinese'. No wonder the hotel complex could be hailed as the 'grandest and most artistic of tourist haunts'.[40] One commentator, seeking obsequiously to smuggle in a connection with the past, likened Nicolò Spada, its first sponsor, to Michelangelo, swearing that the 'genius of the race' and its 'millennial commitment to the highest forms of beauty' shone through the building and the rest of the Lido.[41] In fact in 1908 the ownership of the Excelsior fell into the hands of the rising entrepreneur Giuseppe Volpi, who, using ready finance from the Banca Commericale Italiana, had just floated the Compagnia Italiana Grandi Alberghi (CIGA, Italian Company of Grand Hotels) to manage the best accommodation in Venice and elsewhere.[42] As we will see, Volpi proved a man of many parts in his city.

The hotel's inauguration on the balmy night of 21–2 July 1908 was fittingly lavish. The building and its canal were ablaze with light. A new fountain gushed. Fireworks burst over the scene. More than 3,000 guests danced away the hours to the enchanting sounds of four orchestras – singing did not cease until 6 a.m. – and all were fed in one part or other of the hotel garden. A further 30,000 onlookers arrived by boat from the city to gawk at the plush scene.[43] Four years later, the American banker J. Pierpont Morgan stated with a rich

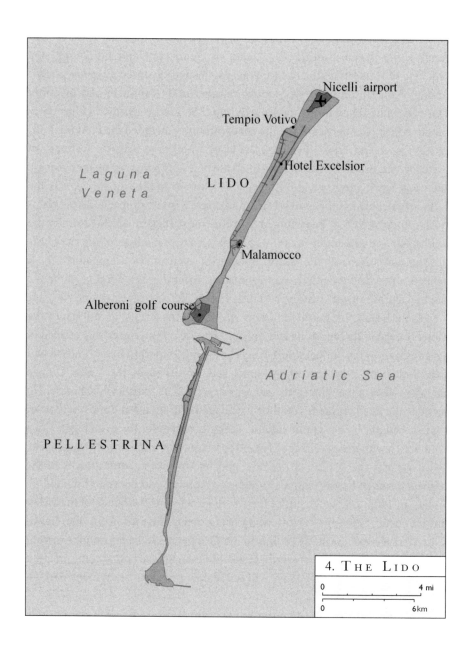

Nicelli airport

Tempio Votivo

Hotel Excelsior

Laguna Veneta

LIDO

Malamocco

Alberoni golf course

Adriatic Sea

PELLESTRINA

4. THE LIDO

0   4 mi

0   6 km

10 Ambitious plans for the Lido, 1914

man's quip, 'In America, those who have visited Europe talk more of your Excelsior Palace than they do of the Doge's Palace.'[44] At the Excelsior and the Lido's other grand hotels, Venice, in unstated competition with French resorts, was making serious claims to be the most captivating place on earth for those who lived, or aspired to live, the high life. After all, the titillating appeal of its dance floor is likely to have been enhanced by Patriarch Aristide Cavallari, who, at the commencement of Carnival in 1914, issued a warning to his parish priests that the 'tango is the shame of our time; it is the most brazen expression of sensual lust and you cannot do it without sin'.[45]

The Lido's was a rapid rise, because it was an area without a history, or with a decidedly humble one, even if puff pieces always mentioned that Byron had ridden there. The Jewish cemetery that spread from near the modern ferry stop was girded with a longer past,[46] although a target-shooting club began to eat into its terrain from 1881.[47] During the first years of Italian occupation, the most celebrated development across the largely deserted sands was a hospice designed to treat scrofulous and rachitic boys and girls from the city, backed by Prefect Torelli and Princess Margherita among other worthies.[48] After her succession, Queen Margherita brought her stunted son Victor Emmanuel to the shore for each of the summers from 1879 to 1883, in the hope that bracing sea baths would encourage him to grow in a more regal manner.[49] At that stage a dusty path was all that connected the beach and the landing stage. It was not until 1900 that the area was joined to the city water supplies (which would be municipalised two years later). Traditionally, the few local inhabitants had slaked their thirst with 'rain water filtrated by the dunes'.[50] Perhaps it brought benefit, since a doctor remarked in the 1880s that, of the three hundred who lived on the Lido, nineteen were more than seventy years old and six were above eighty – elevated life spans at that time.[51]

The year that water arrived saw the opening of the Grand Hotel des Bains, which was to be the Excelsior's partner and rival. Soon a town sprang to life, its street names modishly recalling Venetian power and implying that the city could be resurrected in an empire of leisure: Via Dandolo, Via Lepanto, Via Candia, Via Zara and many more. In the summer of 1913, 97,000 were recorded as sunbathing on the public beach as distinct from those sands reserved for hotel customers, while a co-operative for national civil servants delineated its own sector, where 30,000 disported themselves.[52] From 1907 the Grande Albergo Ausonia e Hungaria rose alongside the spacious Gran Viale Santa Maria Elisabetta. It was built to be a jewel of the Liberty style (to the predictable disgust of Pompeo Molmenti, who inveighed against the overly cosmopolitan appearance of the Lido, especially in its numerous new Liberty villas).[53] From 1913 the hotel acquired a many-hued mosaic façade composed by the Milanese sculptor Luigi Fabris, in which it still glories. A modern tram now bumped visitors past such impressive sights from lagoon to beach, and Spada dreamed of an extension of its track to the Excelsior or even to the Alberoni, kilometres to the south-west, as well as a double lane tunnelled under water to the Giudecca, San Giorgio, San Marco and Sant'Elena, speeding the vehicle along at fifty kilometres per hour.[54] Modern in many matters, his hotel by then offered overweight or gouty customers cures of water, sun and the 'Zander method', advertised as 'utilising equipment brought in specially from Norway, radio-therapy of the most scientific form'. Skills acquired from contact with Cuba and Egypt were said effectively to control local mosquito attacks.[55]

From 1911 a Teatro Kursaal staged the best plays and opera, the latter with the backing of composers Pietro Mascagni and Ruggero Leoncavallo and tenor Tito Ruffo. Destined to be still more popular, Spada hoped, was a public amuse-ment area or 'Luna Park', opened with fanfare on 1 June 1914 and selling 117,000 lire's worth of 30-*centesimi* tickets in its first month of operation.[56] In the interim, entertainment might come from watching an intrepid airman, Umberto Cagno, a friend of D'Annunzio, who, despite a light fog during Carnival in February 1911, flew for an hour and a half above the beach and the sea in a Farman II French-made biplane, to the joyful wonderment of thou-sands of spectators, the wealthiest of whom had grouped on the Excelsior's balconies.[57] Even more exhilaratingly, Cagno took select passengers with him a couple of weeks later, the trip lasting a brief two or three minutes while the plane soared only fifty metres into the air. When not thus occupied in show-biz (even though described as a 'man of few words'), on 5 March 1911, camera at the ready, Cagno became the first person ever to fly over Venice itself, the triumph countering in some patriotic minds the sad fifteenth anniversary of the battle of Adua, disgracefully lost against the Ethiopians in 1896.[58]

Yet, somewhere beneath the frivolity and pleasure, was there a lurking adder of pain, disease and death? A holidaymaker who had intimations of that kind was Sigmund Freud, who kept a record of a disturbing Venetian dream. The inspiration for it was pleasurable: a sunny day during which he and his wife delighted in the ceremonies of an English naval visit – the rich decorations, the sleek modern vessels. But his psychic digestion of the event brought trauma. A nightmare ushered into his mind the 'arrival of enemy warships since we were in a state of war'. The parading boats had been exhibiting the mighty power of the British Empire, by now enrolled in the Triple Entente and arrayed against Austria, Italy and Germany in the Triple Alliance. Freud's troubling imagining of European massacre was fleeting. Soon, since Venice was a holiday town, the horror vanished, and the steel-grey cruisers transmogrified into a floating black tray bearing the cheerful sustenance of breakfast.[59] Unknown to Freud, war was approaching, and fast, but not while the *belle époque* lasted.

Death there was in Venice, nonetheless, and it could not be denied, despite the gaudy nights. The fiftieth anniversary of Italian unification fell in 1911 (only the forty-fifth of the annexation of Venice, although *Il Gazzettino* effusively heralded the Cinquantennio in the biblical vocabulary of the nation as 'the miracle of redemption').[60] Naturally much celebration was planned, headed by the opening of the grandiose Victor Emmanuel monument in the capital, Rome. Other galas took place in Turin, once the capital of Piedmont and, for a few initial years, of the nation. In these circumstances, Venice was relegated to a relatively minor role, with the rhythm of its Biennali disrupted (the eighth was held in 1909, the ninth in 1910[61] and the tenth in 1912).[62] Yet even without an art festival, 1911 promised a full tourist round. By late May *Il Gazzettino* was reporting jubilantly that the summer season was bursting into life on the Lido, where visitors listened to the concerts, watched the bathers or joined in the roller-skating: 'ever more numerous are the elegant couples who abandon themselves to the sensuousness of a sport that is so *de mode*'.[63]

The promise was false. Cholera, it began to be rumoured, had struck the city, just as it had done so often before 1900. Despite doughty efforts by local newspapers and politicians, endorsed by successive prime ministers Luzzatti and, from March 1911, Giovanni Giolitti, Foreign Minister Antonino Di San Giuliano and official national diplomacy, to hide what was happening

(*Il Gazzettino* issued a 'total' denial on 1 June),[64] the season stuttered. In July it was suddenly announced that the traditional festival of the Redentore, in which the church on the Giudecca was joined to the Zattere by a bridge of boats, had been cancelled.[65] In September came the news that Tito Ruffo's debut at the Kursaal on the Lido was postponed until further notice.[66]

The return of cholera in the summer of 1911 was given lasting significance through being inscribed into the plot of Thomas Mann's novella *Der Tod in Venedig*. Mann and his wife had been holidaying at the Hotel des Bains and much of the ominous atmospherics of the story reflected their 'actual experience', as Katia Mann would recall.[67] Although the novel's focus was more on bourgeois sexuality than on the poor Venetians who perished in the epidemic, the fame won by *Death in Venice* left a memory of the shameless lies of government announcements about the outbreak, the USA, whose citizens now arrived in Venice in considerable numbers, and other nations colluding 'with the Italian policy of concealment'.[68] James Long, the American consul, was one among many to pledge to his citizens his 'absolute assurance' that nothing unmannerly was happening in Venice.[69] Not everyone was convinced, however, and a rapid exodus began, the Manns being informed by 'the honest English clerk in the [Cook's] travel bureau' that the spread of cholera was being 'hushed up'.[70]

Count Amedeo Nasalli Rocca, the strong-minded Catholic conservative prefect of the city from October 1907 until his retirement on 15 August 1911 (officially on grounds of health and with a week's notice),[71] provided a caustic account of the cholera outbreak. The government had become aware of coming troubles in 1910, when Luzzatti absurdly tried to put the blame on 'gypsies', demanding that prefects throughout the land arrest and expel them, with no indication of who would bear the cost of their incarceration or of where they might be sent. He soon backed down, Nasalli Rocca observing acerbically that 'Luzzatti, a threatening and brave lion with the weak and undefended, became a rabbit with the strong and violent'.[72]

By late May 1911 Nasalli Rocca was aware of the disease penetrating Venice, forty-one cases being counted between 22 May and 9 June. The majority of the victims were poor and female, but the illness was widespread across the city, with victims in Castello, Cannaregio, Murano, Burano and Pellestrina. A modicum of comfort could be drawn from the fact that the death rate was limited to 26 per cent, below that of past outbreaks. Certainly a 'docile' population was putting up with the epidemic and not contesting Nasalli Rocca's plan that sufferers be isolated at Sacca-Sessola, even though that sanctuary was poorly supplied with electricity and fresh water.[73] However active he was in designing practical means to limit the disease, the prefect simultaneously sought to muzzle the foreign press campaign about it, run, he complained,

from Berlin and Vienna by interests hostile to the city's prosperity. A key step
was to avoid public panic, and Nasalli Rocca found all local newspapers duti-
fully ready to keep mum about the crisis. He did, however, report the details of
victims to the new prime minister, Giolitti, only to be charged with 'impru-
dence and tactlessness' in raising the matter in Rome. The government, he
decided, was adding itself to the enemies of his cautious but serious line. In its
determination to deny everything, Rome simply made things worse, eventually
ensuring that the 1911 season gave 'disastrous results' economically.[74] He was
shocked, for example, when local doctors who asked Giolitti for extra support
were denied and charged with being engaged in 'criminal agitation'.[75] Nasalli
Rocca did concede wryly, however, that the prime minister was willing to back
every specific action the prefecture took against the 'non-existent' epidemic.[76]

Few who lolled at the Excelsior or, fingers elegantly crooked, sipped coffee
at Florian's in Piazza San Marco, and indeed few readers of Mann's novella, paid
much attention to the implications of Nasalli Rocca's reports on the depth of
poverty that still afflicted many Venetians; it was the poor and not the tourists
whom cholera struck (the final death tally for 1911 was reckoned at 103).[77] If
anything, the greater prominence of elite pleasure in the city widened class
difference and incomprehension. Yet, for any who sought it, evidence of indi-
gence there was in the public domain, notably in regard to housing conditions,
an issue of continuing prominence given the conversion of Sant'Elena into a
new city suburb (Molmenti campaigned as usual against the resulting alteration to the cityscape).[78]

In 1909 Raffaele Vivante, the Comune's health officer, commenced what
would be a lifelong devotion to the scrupulous charting of Venetian homes and
their deficiencies.[79] At this time, he reported, almost half had no running water,
more than 15 per cent lacked electricity or any other form of modern lighting,
49.5 per cent placed their toilet facilities in the kitchen where the modern
system of water closets was rare, 159 dwelling places were equipped with no
toilets at all, while 149 did not contain a kitchen. The majority of houses were
damp, dark and dirty; Vivante estimated that 3,524 out of the 23,325 subjected
to his review were uninhabitable by any measure. Almost 50,000 Venetians
made do in one system or other of sub-renting, entailing a deplorable 'promis-
cuity of life among the popular classes', in Vivante's opinion.[80] Gross social divisions separated one part of the city from another. In the prosperous *contrada* of
Santa Maria del Giglio only 13.7 per cent of housing had not been connected to
urban water supplies, a figure that rose to 74 per cent in San Pietro di Castello
and 73.4 per cent at Sant'Eufemia on the Giudecca. As for those slums where
the proper policy was demolition, Castello and Dorsoduro were the worst.[81]
The ideal solution, Vivante advised, was massive building, both through private

initiative and through the Comune. Sant'Elena was a start, and perhaps more could be done on Murano or the Giudecca. But what was really required was 'to make rise on our lagoon a new Venice; either that or we must send part of our population to the nearby mainland,' he counselled presciently.[82]

Venice was scarcely alone in the affliction of its poor. In counter, the Europe that was approaching the First World War seemed to many to be experiencing the unstoppable rise of socialism, with its promise to marry liberty to equality, its easy explanation of how history passed from one stage to another, rather as a locomotive did on its iron tracks, and its commitment to a fair division of wealth. It is no surprise that such ideas took root in Venice, even if the local workforce scarcely fitted vulgar Marxist categorisation as a class. In the pre-war era, strikes grew more and more pervasive, *Il Gazzettino* adopting the bourgeois line in January 1911 in deploring rumours it had heard of a general strike, allegedly to be called in Venice in retribution for owners' infraction of laws curbing child and female labour. Back in 1904, the paper remembered sourly, such action had been provoked by hateful, criminal elements, 'entailing not a general voluntary cessation of work but an imposition on others, forcing them not to work no matter what the violence or damage.'[83]

At that time, a more militantly bourgeois paper, *L'Adriatico*, had denounced the 'violent tyranny and organised hoodlumism' of the strikers.[84] Shortly there-after, a local priest, Don Agostino Catullo of San Pantalon, despite Catholicism's ongoing suspicion of 'Mammon', endorsed such criticisms, excoriating union-ists as 'children of the shadows, emissaries of Satan, perverse and diseased people, agents of sin'. In response, the local socialist newspaper, *Secolo Nuovo*, took evident pleasure in portraying a prelate with 'a reddish blue, lumpy, apoplectic face . . . an angry mouth that stretched from ear to ear, the fleshiest of lips that resembled two buttocks in embryo, ears like curtains, a flattened nose with a pig's nostrils, tiny, lustful eyes', a personage whom it summed up as 'a case study for a psychiatrist'.[85] Such bitter exchanges and the sensational murder in 1910 of the founder of the Stucky mill by one of his workers – he had his throat cut beside the newspaper stand near the steps of the railway station – seemed to Venetian property owners demonstration of the fearsome threat they were facing from below.[86] Urgent action of some kind, many were beginning to argue, would be needed to dispel it.

Much about the Venetian socialist movement manifested itself on May Day 1911, when the third regional congress of its youth wing opened at Palazzo Faccanon, with an attendance of a hundred, including, *Il Gazzettino* noted disapprovingly, at least one young woman. The socialist youth began their day with an anthem, but it was not the official 'Marcia reale' (Royal March). Rather, the members of the Fascio Giovanile 'Carlo Marx' di Venezia (Venetian Karl

Marx Youth Group) led the delegates in a rendition of the 'Internazionale'. Singing led on to speeches. Elia Musatti, a local socialist deputy, transmitted the good wishes of senior party members to the congress, while also drawing scathing attention to a sports day that the leisured were holding on the Lido. 'Sporting activity', he pronounced with socialist propriety, 'is a disguised form of nationalism and irredentism. It is a war cry, a snare and delusion for those committed to the brotherhood of the peoples. It should be opposed and rejected by workers whose labour does not match the pathetic little self-interest of the bourgeoisie, but rather defends the greater interest of the proletariat.' In response, Elvira Pillor urged congress members to take special pains to inform women about this and other matters, and to organise them politically. Another speaker demanded war against the clergy, 'not as ministers of Catholicism but as instruments of class'. When the speeches were over, motions were voted on, one duly condemning nationalism and irredentism and, by implication, sport.[87]

May Day itself was officially a working day, and even though the printers and the metalworkers of the city withdrew their labour, and absentee rates at the Arsenale (by now one of Musatti's electoral strongholds) and the tobacco factory reached 50 per cent, the shops, hotels and businesses of the city stood open. Undaunted by such behaviour, Venetian socialists took the occasion to march across town, assembling eventually in Campo San Geremia, where there was time for more speeches, some being factional in character, as purist social- ists attacked that 'reformism' which had recently led the moderate chiefs Leonida Bissolati and Claudio Treves to contemplate joining the Liberal government in Rome. A comradely dinner ended proceedings.

On this and other occasions, a major issue for critics in regard to the rise of city socialism was the prominence in the movement of Musatti, damned by his enemies as the 'millionaire socialist', the son of a wealthy industrialist of Jewish ancestry and a cousin of Alberto Musatti, an eminent figure in local liberal politics and culture and a foe of Marxists of any kind. Elia Musatti, who in 1909 won a Venice seat to the Chamber of Deputies, led what would be called the 'maximalist' faction in his party, those intransigent in their call for social revo- lution. He had unapologetically backed Venetian participation in a national general strike on 18–19 September 1904 (according to *The Times*, it 'completely paralysed life' in the city; 'even the gondoliers, who reap such a rich harvest from strangers at this season, refuse to work').[88]

In 1911–12 Musatti assumed a high profile in his party's opposition to what he called the 'mad' colonial invasion of Libya, being mocked in the patriotic press as 'Elia Bey' (a traitorous friend of Turks and Arabs).[89] To prove his base in Venice despite the failure of a general strike called against the war, he resigned his seat in late September 1911 and then won it back in a supplementary election.[90] His continued castigation of the Libyan campaign as a bourgeois venture fought with proletarian blood provoked tumult in the city. In November 'students' and socialists brawled outside a café in Campo San Bartolomeo, and there were other stoushes near where Musatti lived in ritzy Santa Maria del Giglio.[91]

Soon thereafter, Musatti was seconded in his work in the city and in his national profile by Giacinto Menotti Serrati, a major figure in the Italian socialist movement from its foundation in 1892, who now became chief organiser of Venice's Camera del Lavoro. Another, younger activist was the Sicilian Girolamo Li Causi, who arrived to study political economy at the university but did not share the enthusiasms of his more gilded fellow students, the great majority of whom preferred new nationalism to socialism. In 1913 he took a socialist ticket and, with encouragement from Serrati, engaged in propagandising the Marxist cause. In his memoirs, Li Causi remembered heated debates between socialist factions arrayed in two rival co-operatives, one favouring radical action, the other accommodation with the bosses. At the Camera del Lavoro, Sunday morning meetings were always crowded and discussion grew lively, even if Li Causi was sometimes put at a loss by the 'incomprehensible' Venetian dialect. A tougher struggle lay outside the socialist headquarters, since the city bourgeoisie stood firm against the workers. When, one afternoon, he disembarked at Burano to make party propaganda, he was driven back onto the ferry with sticks and a hail of stones organised by Jesurum.[92] Not dissimilar evidence of efforts to prevent modern prying into exploitative traditional work practices was even provided by *Il Gazzettino*, which admitted that the arrival of inspectors at the glass factories in Murano produced a 'fuggi fuggi generale' as child workers rushed off to hide, the paper maintaining that two hundred were illegally employed.[93]

The more localist and appeasing side of Venetian worker activism looked to the leadership of Angelo Vianello, the host at Capon in Campo Santa Margherita and known to all as 'Pastassuta' (Spaghetti Man). This square was a part of the city with its own rhythms and traditions, but from 1906 to 1910 it was the home of the Camera del Lavoro (occupying premises that, since 1882, to the scandal of pious Catholics, had housed an evangelical temple of the Chiesa Cristiana Libera, or Free Christian Church, claiming 140 city members).[94] Vianello had presided over a co-operative optimistically named Miglioramento (Improvement) since 1901, enrolling many dockers in it. Three years later, the city could count fourteen rival such organisations, and negotiations began for their fraternal unification. For a while unity seemed near, but in 1909 Vianello stubbornly refused to merge Miglioramento into a federation of port workers' co-operatives. Worse, vulnerable to populist patriotism, in March 1912 he attacked those comrades who wanted to ally themselves with 'Turks' in regard to the Libyan War. By 1914 he and Serrati were again able to parlay, but unity on the political left remained fragile.[95] As was true throughout Europe, *belle époque* Venice was seeing the arrival in its streets not so much of socialism as of socialisms.

The more fundamental split among city radicals may have been the gender one. With unabashed sexism, workers at the Arsenale in 1904 protested when a pay rise was extended to women.[96] With an appearance of greater modernity, bourgeois worthies may have favoured improved female schooling, but with a less than egalitarian focus on 'women's work, reckoning, domestic economy, hygiene and morality . . . that is, everything necessary for the good functioning of the family'.[97] Despite such lingering prejudice among both their friends and their foes, women workers at the state-run tobacco factory were discovering how to be activist on their own account. When in June 1913 a protest parade resulted in arrests, one woman, charged with assaulting a policeman, was reported to have expostulated (in expression of a northern belief that the state bureaucracy was surfeited with southerners), 'You Neapolitans . . . should try working, as we do.'[98]

So relatively successful were the tobacco workers in winning improved pay that the resentful bourgeois catchword that the state was employing 'female workers in silk stockings' soon spread, a charge that was redoubled in wartime with the addition that they were thereby 'betraying our boys'.[99] Before 1914, by contrast, the factory earned visits and praise from no less a feminist notable than Margherita Sarfatti, a wealthy Venetian Jewish intellectual who had married a lawyer and, in 1902, moved to Milan, eventually to become the lover, cultural teacher and patroness of Mussolini.[100] More restrictive in their aim were local Catholics who had some success in attracting women to their anti-socialist welfare and union systems, although it may be surmised that 'a solemn rite' held by Catholic social organisations at Piazza San Marco in 'the presence of the authorities', blessed by Patriarch Cavallari and saluting a banner given by Princess Letizia of Savoy, may not have won over more radical elements.[101] Yet it was true that, by 1911, the Unione Donne Cattoliche (Catholic Women's Association) in the city counted 2,200 members.[102]

Within the women's workforce, one emerging leader was Anita Mezzalira, born in 1886 into a poorish family with, as her first name indicated, Garibaldinian memories. In March 1913 she took a major role in the creation of a female tobacco workers' union, independent though linked to the Camera del Lavoro, charging publicly that the present boss treated all his workers like 'blacks and slaves' and demanding that they must instead be 'respected'. She campaigned energetically for a reduced working day, after resisting a lockout in a sixty-day strike in 1914, with some success.[103]

Just before Franz Ferdinand went to Sarajevo, the Italian left, in Venice as elsewhere, stirred up a wave of strikes known as 'Red Week', which in Ancona included the armed seizure of the Municipio. At such moments, Italy seemed a country where class conflict radically divided workers and bourgeoisie. Certainly, by then, evidence proliferated that propertied Venetians were marking themselves out politically and socially in new and tougher ways. As Elia Musatti had so rudely charged, for some decades better-off youths in the city were engaging in modern sports, target-shooting, gymnastics, basketball, cycling, rowing and football being evident examples. Il Venezia Foot-Ball Club, its foreign name indicating the debt that modern sporting devotion owed to Britain, was constituted on 14 December 1907, generously financed by a Jewish wholesale magnate, Davide Fano. By 1913 Il Venezia had established a ground in what had been a pine forest on Sant'Elena that it was destined to keep, although its hopes of sporting glory were only erratically fulfilled. Fano revealed something about the nature of *belle époque* sport by also belonging to the target-shooting club and, in 1914, being deputy to Senator Alberto Treves in the Volontari Ciclisti e Automobilisti (Cyclist and Automobilist Volunteers), readying to peddle to the front after Italy intervened in the First World War.[104] A more traditional form of paramilitary sporting endeavour was recorded on the Lido in March 1911, when two artillery officers fought a duel over a question of discipline, one being lightly wounded, but with a reconciliation thereafter reached.[105]

Venice had been a pioneer in importing 'German-style' gymnastics into Italy, the country's first sporting paper, *La ginnastica*, being published there from 1868, and, in the following year, a national gymnasts' conference was held in the city. In 1880 a women's section opened. Thereafter progress slowed amid personal wrangles and money problems, until in 1901 the emerging local nationalist politician Piero Foscari proffered financial backing. In 1907 the Seventh National Italian Gymnastics Meeting took place in Venice, which would also host the Tenth Meeting in 1920, when the sportsmen took time off to mount a patriotic demonstration in favour of Italian gains in Dalmatia.[106]

Of the sports that were entering city life, rowing could most readily engage in the invention of tradition, with talk that would not be fully institutionalised until after 1945 of a 'Regata storica', to be contested on the first Sunday in September. Its origins were claimed to go back to 1315, with solemn suggestion that the initial inspiration for it had occurred in 942, when, in a reverse of the rape of the Sabine women prominent in the myth of Rome, local boys had rescued city girls being carried off by pirates to their lair by out-rowing them.[107] Whatever may have occurred in the misty past, some aquatic contest had begun in 1841, only to be suspended after 1849. The institution of a welfare organisation for gondoliers in 1868 did lead to the holding in 1895 of 'a tradi-tional gondoliers' race'. But the real initiative for modern Venetian regattas came from two rival modern sports clubs, the Società Canottieri Bucintoro (Bucintoro Rowing Association), formed in 1882 (evoking history through the name 'Bucintoro', the state galley of the doges, and backed by Jesurum), and the Società di Sport Nautici Francesco Querini (Francesco Querini Nautical Sports Association), formed in 1901.[108] One of its first activities was to sponsor a 'Lord Byron swimming race'. Virile regattas, however, could still readily decay into no more than pleasure cruises down the Grand Canal (with musical accompani-ment). On 30 June 1912 the erection of the new Campanile gave impulse to a more organised race, with a 20,000-lire prize provided by the Cassa di Risparmio di Venezia and the pledge to become an annual event. In practice, however, a second 'historic regatta' was postponed until September 1920.[109]

If sports honed the muscles, overcame fears of racial degeneracy[110] and readied young men for war, a 'generation of 1914' was using Venice as the source of or justification for other ideas. Paris and perhaps Vienna were the meccas of most intellectuals, but Venice also attracted clever young men to its past beauties and present comforts. Marcel Proust,[111] Guillaume Apollinaire (who defined Venice as 'le sexe même de l'Europe'),[112] Hugo von Hofmannstahl and Rainer Maria Rilke (cushioned by the patronage of Princess Marie von Thurn und Taxis and housed in her luxurious palace) drew inspiration from it, while 'Baron Corvo' (Frederick Rolfe) found uncertain sanctuary there. On his death in 1913, Rolfe suffered the posthumous violation of having his 'large collection of incriminating letters and photographs' dropped surreptitiously from a window into the Grand Canal by Gerald Campbell, the British consul, troubled that their evidence of homosexuality could have been 'a haul . . . for a blackmailer'.[113] A little earlier, George Bernard Shaw had remained unim-pressed by two visits to Venice, remarking that being there aroused 'my old iconoclastic idea of destroying the entire show. For it is a show and nothing else. Neither the Italians nor the trippers on whom they sponge have any part or lot in the fine things they see.'[114]

The most extreme rhetorical enemy of old Venice, however, was the Futurist Filippo Tommaso Marinetti, striving in the pre-war era to win recognition even in Paris for the unbridled cleverness of his (bourgeois) determination to skewer the bourgeoisie. It was on 26 April 1910 that Marinetti and his friends caused the greatest commotion in the city by climbing to the top of the clock-tower (Torre dell'Orologio) in Piazza San Marco and flinging to the winds another of their manifestoes, designed to counter any cosy evocation of St Mark the previous day. The Futurists demanded that contemporaries repudiate the old city, 'ravaged by centuries of voluptuousness'. It must renounce its 'crumbling, flea-ridden palaces', its 'stinking little canals' and its gondolas, mere 'rocking chairs for cretins'. Modern electric lighting must free Venice from 'the moonlight of the furnished room'. Only with such drastic change could Venice take on a modern role when Italy moved forward to conquer the Adriatic.[115]

Three months later, Marinetti amplified his attack in a speech at the Fenice that was a prelude to a first exhibition of the work of the Futurist artist Umberto Boccioni at Ca' Pesaro. Now Marinetti demanded that 'we kill the moonlight' and 'free the world from the tyranny of love. We are stuffed with erotic adventures, luxury, sentimentalising, nostalgia.' The Grand Canal, he urged, must be 'widened and excavated so Venice can indeed become a mercantile port'. 'Trams and tramlines' must replace this and other waterways. What was the point of enriching CIGA if Venetians had to grovel to foreign tourists as 'waiters, guides, panders, sellers of second-hand goods, fraudsters, makers of old paintings and plagiarists', mere 'copyists' of the 'new'. Instead of loving the past, he proclaimed, Venice must 'turn itself to the future, so that, together, we can ready a great strong, industrial, commercial and military Venice, projected into the Adriatic and converting it into a great Italian lake'.[116]

Marinetti's studiously insulting words targeted his older rival among Italian writers, Gabriele D'Annunzio, whose lush phrasing and sultry sexuality had continued to fit Venice's meaning in many an imagination. It was not so long ago that D'Annunzio had made a splash of his own with the premiere in Rome in the presence of Victor Emmanuel and his Montenegrin queen, Elena, of his new play, *La nave* (The Ship). Set in 552 in a mythical Venice that was breaking away from the Byzantine Empire, it preached that modern Italy find an imperial future of its own on the sea, and in so doing allow itself to be propelled by the current of history that ran into the present from the Venetian Republic.[117] *The Times* may have reported disparagingly, 'if there is any meaning in d'Annunzio's dramas, apart from their shadowy symbolism and their fantastic reading of history, it is to show how large a part bestiality plays in human conduct'.[118] But few Italians were ready to belittle their national 'Archangel Gabriel' and few prominent Venetians resiled from his reiterated message that the history of the Venetian Empire should shape the modern world.

Within months, the play was being staged in Venice at the invitation of the local branch of the Lega Navale Italiana (LNI, Italian Navy League), then headed by the rising nationalist politician Piero Foscari, a member of what he avowed was a dogal family. (Francesco Foscari, doge in the early fifteenth century, held the office for a record thirty-four years, twelve months into his term erecting Ca' Foscari, 'the most imposing private palace ever to be built on the Grand Canal'.)[119] In 1897 Piero Foscari had married the rich and indubitably patrician Elisabetta Widmann Rezzonico.[120] Thus ornamented with family history, Foscari chose the evening of 25 April to bring *La nave* to Venice. The venue was the Fenice, further proof if it was needed of the habitual fusing of the myths of D'Annunzio, his versions of history and beauty, with those of the city.

In the world beyond literature and its showy bickerings, Foscari was a man who mattered. He pursued policies that expose much about the role of the city bourgeoisie in the approach of the First World War and the hardening attitudes towards class difference. Foscari was born in the city to a faded aristocratic family in 1865 and trained at the Naval Academy in Livorno. As a young officer he served off the coast of East Africa in 1895–6, months that coincided with the humiliating national defeat at Adua, although Foscari's direct experience was of brutal British imperialism in Zanzibar and equally violent Italian action in Mogadishu after an assault on an Italian garrison there. His marriage brought him money and land and, as a result, he left the navy to construct a career in journalism and politics, in 1909 becoming deputy for Mirano on the mainland, after an electoral failure in Venice in 1904.

Foscari was a leading figure in the formalisation of an Italian nationalist movement, which was finding one of its major bases in his city.[121] It was telling that Foscari engaged the leading philosopher of nationalism, Enrico Corradini, to speak at the Fenice on 27 January 1911, his theme being 'Proletarian nations and nationalism'.[122] Foscari and his friends similarly acted as patrons of the academic work of Alfredo Rocco at the University of Padua, helping to finance his weekly, *Il Dovere Nazionale* (National Duty), of which a typical argument ran 'Nationalism believes that races that systematically sacrifice the interests of the group to those of individuals are destined to perish. And we do not want the Italian race to perish.'[123] In Rocco's mind, liberalism had lost its reason for existence and Italy must look elsewhere in the future.

Foscari presided over the second conference of the Associazione Nazionalista Italiana in 1912, after volunteering to return to naval service during the Libyan War, convinced that the plateau above Benghazi had once been the 'Garden of the Hesperides'. Policy-makers, he had urged on more than one occasion, should follow the manifold traces of Italies past and those of present-day emigrants wherever they were, with the clear and dauntless aim of creating a 'greater and more powerful' nation; they could thereby uproot socialism in the way the Kaiser had done in Germany.[124] 'Venice,' he pronounced lustily, 'like Rome, is eternal', and so must ensure that Italy rather than Austria was (re) converting the Adriatic into its 'lake'. The result must be a new 'spiritual Risorgimento' of the nation.[125]

Giolitti, Italy's dominant pre-war liberal politician, did not view Foscari as a friend, particularly disliking his irredentism. Foscari had undertaken the role of city president of the Società Trento e Trieste (Trento and Trieste Society), pressing for the urgent 'return' of these two Austrian cities to the *patria*. According to Nasalli Rocca, the sage Giolitti believed that irredentists were more irresponsible and damaging to the public interest than were anarchists.[126] In 1914–15 Foscari campaigned across the country for Italian intervention in the war, being rewarded between 1916 and 1918 with the post of Under-Secretary for the Colonies. He died in April 1923, shortly after presiding over a meeting at which the Nationalists agreed to fuse themselves into the Partito Nazionale Fascista (PNF, National Fascist Party). Foscari had pioneered the path that many others would take from liberal 'improvement' to Fascist tyranny.

A younger associate of Foscari but with attitudes and purposes of his own was Giovanni Giuriati, who had followed his Mazzinian father, Domenico, a revolutionary in 1848–9, into the law, with some pain, he claimed, as one who sternly refused to join the Freemasons.[127] Giuriati would rise to become a purist secretary of the PNF in 1930–1, attempt to apply his strictures and retire discom-fited. Among his family memories was that his father, possessed of what his son deemed an appropriate 'racial sense', would always hurriedly don gloves if he saw a Jewish colleague approaching along a *calle*, since, respectful of bourgeois form, he knew that gentlemen must shake hands.[128] By late 1913 Giuriati had become the national president of the Società Trento e Trieste, utilising contacts maintained by his father in Trieste and welcoming Italian nationalist refugees from there. Armed with their presence, Giuriati urged, Venice stood out as the national epicentre of irredentism.[129] Tourism, he avowed by contrast, besmirched the city (in 1913 a campaign began to pull down signs in the city in languages other than Italian),[130] and let in too many dubious types from north of the Alps. Rather, he advised, Italians should adopt as their watchword 'habit, order and will' and approach the future with 'an Italian heart and a German method'.[131]

On 28 June 1914 Giuriati was relaxing on the mainland north of Venice when news broke of the assassination of Franz Ferdinand. He later claimed that he had leapt to his feet, crying, 'Viva l'Italia', sure that now 'the longed-for war with Austria' had come. Although his mother was womanishly disconcerted by the prospect, Giuriati broke open a family bottle of 1848 Moscato di Cipro (a celebrated local wine) and drank to a glorious future (linked in his mind with the glorious past of the wine's vintage). Somewhat paradoxically, he then went off on a beach holiday.[132] By 25 July he was on a train to Milan, on which, in a first-class carriage, he met Volpi, the man who with each passing day held greater control over Venetian commerce and industry. With the optimism of a businessman, Volpi disagreed with Giuriati about turmoil in the Balkans. The Serbs, he was sure, would accept the Austrian ultimatum; there would and could never be another European war.[133]

Once Italy had become a dictatorship, Foscari, Corradini, Rocco, Giuriati, the irredentists and nationalists, together with D'Annunzio and Marinetti, were all depicted as worthy men, who, in alliance with Volpi, had, as the First World War approached, brought a new, more virile and positive politics to Venice (and Italy). In reality, in the pre-war era, the alliances had been less firm, as might already have been observed in the Nationalist and Futurist lampooning of tourism and hostility to Volpi's hotel interests and other entrepreneurial deals. This new right's hatred of Giolitti similarly gave it little reason to applaud the use of Volpi as the government's special agent in secret deals with the Turks that paved the way to the Treaty of Ouchy, the formal end of the Libyan War.

The many hints of racism that were surfacing in the phrases of Giuriati and Rocco were also a dilemma, given the make-up of Venetian business groupings and Volpi's friendship with Alberto Musatti and other leading figures in Venice's Jewish community. With a Catholic racism different from that of the Nationalists, Prefect Nasalli Rocca had ironically portrayed what happened when he resisted a certain business deal, the suggested opening of a casino at the Excelsior. City worthies, he remembered, trooped into his office: 'a well-known newspaper editor, an authoritative deputy, various millionaires, bankers and industrialists, the majority from the tribe of Judah, even some clerical moderates and bold democratic radicals ... Each full of good and well-thought-out proposals, each with the name of Venice on their lips, poor Venice, sacrificed through my policy, degraded, blocked in its development, deprived because of me of its chief resource, foreigners.'[134] The business coalition that he depicted and with which Volpi eagerly worked would not survive unaffected by the 1930s, when Fascism went actively anti-Semitic.

Even though tourism, its profits and its discontents remained a hotly debated issue, the greater urban matter in the decade before 1914 was the scheme that was surfacing to build a new port at Bottenighi across the lagoon, the place that was to become known as Porto Marghera.[135] As Foscari, a leading backer, would phrase it, 'wherever the lagoon is, Venice is',[136] and he, Volpi and many others in the city establishment sought thereby to make Venice 'great' again, the capital of a commercial and industrial empire that was already becoming the major provider of the new energy of electricity to the Veneto and beyond, as well as engaging in manifold ventures in the Balkans. In 1903 Volpi and Foscari had joined the board of an Italo-Montenegrin concern that had plans to develop the port of Antivari,[137] helpfully granted linked railway and mining rights and assisted in its financing by a tobacco monopoly in Montenegro (whose ruler was the father of Italian queen Elena). Volpi, then and later, had further hopes for expansion of his companies into Asia Minor, by no means restricting his scheming to a 'restored' Venetian Adriatic. While D'Annunzio orated luxuriantly about past Venetian sea-borne empires, Volpi was doing his best to create what one historian has deemed a military industrial complex, based in Venice and designed to cover the whole Mediterranean.[138] Here, then, was not so much new politics as new economics, certainly a Venice designed to become a world centre of capitalism, a place that could doubtless treasure its accustomed pasts but that would also strenuously advance to the most modern of futures, 'Venezia grande'.

The dreams would fail to match the reality after Porto Marghera won national government approval in 1917. But by the time Franz Ferdinand went to Sarajevo rather than Venice in the summer of 1914, the city did appear to have become a happier place during the *belle époque*, having embraced quite a few currents of modernity that could co-exist in not too troubling a manner with the desire for a Venice of timeless history and unblemished beauty, 'com'era e dov'era'. In developments that seemed hopeful rather than painful, Venice had become awash with more pasts than had eddied through it in 1866.

With its own form of confidence (and naivety), on 4 July 1914 the socialists' paper, *Secolo Nuovo*, reported the Sarajevo murder, adding 'the matter has nothing to do with us', an assessment of the event that, ironically, did not contradict that of the boss Giuseppe Volpi.[139] In their discounting of war, each was tragically wrong. Soon Venetians were to experience a First World War that was their own, a conflict that assaulted liberal compromises and drastically conditioned 'improvement'. In its wartime, Venice, positioned near to and, from October 1917, virtually at the front, was to be made, as it had certainly not been before and after 1919 would never quite be again, Italian and only that. In the city in battle, St Mark's Basilica, the Sansovino *loggetta* and the Campanile (together with other historic treasures) were blockaded against the threat of enemy bombardment, their beauty symbolically obscured from ready sight. Now, too, it was no longer possible for a cosmopolitan crowd to enjoy leisure at the Excelsior or other resorts on the Lido. With war, the easy flow of multiple histories into and around the city was temporarily dammed.

CHAPTER FOUR

Venice and its First World War

An investigation of what the First World War did to Venice and what Venice did to the First World War might suitably begin with an absence – the repercussion of an act of destruction. On a night when the city was lit by a full moon, Austrian planes dropped incendiary bombs targeting the railway station and adjacent iron bridge. Between that canal crossing and the station stood the seventeenth-century church of Santa Maria de Nazaret, known as 'Gli Scalzi' on account of the barefoot Carmelite friars based there (see map 5). Among its artistic glories was a ceiling painted in 1743 by Giambattista Tiepolo; it represented the Madonna's flying house, transported, so the faithful believed, from Nazareth to Loreto in the Marche in 1294 after a stop-over at Rijeka (Fiume), although there are competing stories of its transit and of a rival edifice (located near Ephesus in Turkey).[1] It may well be that, when the fresco was completed in the enlightened eighteenth century, not everyone was convinced that the skies had once been crossed by bricks and mortar. But Tiepolo's image may conveniently stand for a time when no one foresaw that soon thereafter the air would throb to the presence of machines, ones that could bomb and bomb some more, raining ruin and death on what lay below. After the war, such a past was made still more ironical when, in 1920, Pope Benedict XV elevated the Madonna of Loreto into the patron saint of air travellers and pilots.

During two hours of action starting at 10.15 p.m. on 24 October 1915, the Austrian planes hit the church and its ceiling, which was fractured into a thousand pieces.[2] Like so much else in Europe that was afflicted by twentieth-century wars, the edifice was restored, and is there to be visited today. Remarkably, the church reopened for religious services in July 1917, *Il Gazzettino* drawing pious attention to the absent Tiepolo, 'reduced to dust by enemy perfidy'.[3] Tiepolo's *Translation of the Holy House of Loreto* (*Il trasporto della Santa Casa di Loreto*) had vanished forever (although fragments of the

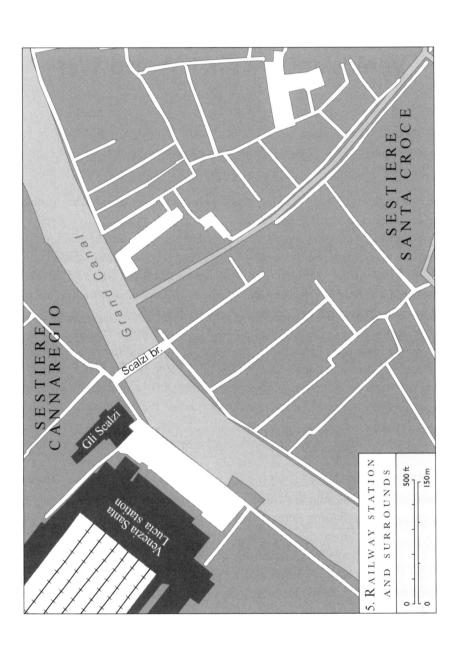

SESTIERE
CANNAREGIO

SESTIERE
SANTA CROCE

Grand Canal

Scalzi br.

Gli Scalzi

Venezia Santa
Lucia station

5. RAILWAY STATION
AND SURROUNDS

500 ft

150 m

0

0

11 The bombed interior of the Scalzi, 25 October 1915

original and a draft sketch by the painter are preserved at the Accademia gallery). According to one nostalgic art historian, the ceiling had been Tiepolo's best, illuminating its surrounds with 'an unequalled sparkle of light and colour'.[4] It was, a contemporary knew, 'a masterpiece of world art'.[5]

The present ceiling bears a replacement work by Ettore Tito (1859–1941), not a great artist, if a sometime prize-winner at the Biennale.[6] Tito completed the substitute fresco between 1929 and 1933, under encouragement from Pietro La Fontaine, the cardinal patriarch of Venice, a prelate who, by then, had earned a reputation for Italian patriotism. In 1915 La Fontaine, who had been installed as patriarch only earlier that year, reached the Scalzi church by 2.15 a.m. on 25 October, remarking with what might seem to be traditional clerical smugness as yet disconnected from national devotion that the smoking ruin represented 'God's summoning of a humanity perverted by sin'.[7] But what Venice was really experiencing in the wreckage of a famous church was the penetration of modern national war into what so recently had seemed its placid destiny to purvey leisure, charm and beauty to its cosmopolitan visitors.

Even today, the story of the shattered Tiepolo in the Scalzi can serve as a sad emblem of cultural loss in the war. Less meek and mild in its message is a memorial to Nazario Sauro that stands beside the Grand Canal beyond the Rialto in a portico of Ca' Farsetti Dandolo, a thirteenth-century edifice that survived through many vicissitudes to house the Municipio, or local government, from 1874 (see map 2). Sauro's story bears parallels with that of Cesare Battisti, related in chapter 1, although it is of more orthodox nationalist vein. Born in Habsburg Capodistria in 1880, Sauro was a politically active irredentist sailor, who, at the outbreak of war, took residence in Venice, campaigning lustily for Italian intervention against Austria-Hungary. Once fighting began, he volunteered for service as a naval officer, and on 30 July 1916 sailed out of Venice in a submarine, intending an attack on Fiume (the possible landing place of the Madonna's house and, from 1919, the site of nationalist poet Gabriele D'Annunzio's 'poetic dictatorship'). But his boat ran aground on a shoal in the gulf of Quarnero. Sauro was captured, tried and hanged by the Habsburg naval authorities on 10 August 1916.[8]

At Ca' Farsetti, the hero is recalled by a rectangular slab of that whitish Istrian limestone which is famed as the chief building material of the city, veined with what almost looks like blood. It is starkly carved with 'Roman lettering': 'SAVRO'. An explanatory plaque reveals, however, that the *romanità* there expressed is post-Fascist, having been hewn into place in 1954, the year when Italy's border with then Yugoslavia was finally confirmed by international treaty.[9] The phrasing

12 Sauro slab

is redolent of an irredentism that had run on regardless into the era after the Second World War. 'These sacred relics of the martyrdom of Nazario Sauro, fugitive here from Pola, Dalmatian and Julian exiles entrust to the maternal piety of Venice, so that they can be preserved until the day of return,' the plaque explains. Battisti's nationalist sacrifice had been justified by Trento's permanent 'restoration' to Italian rule. Sauro's was problematised by the Italian annexation of Istria in 1919 and its loss after 1945. In further demonstration of this deprivation and the hope that it could be reversed, Sauro's physical remains had been moved from his native Istria to the Tempio Votivo (Venice's major war memorial; see map 4) on the Lido in March 1947. This date was one month after Italy had signed, on 10 February, the Peace of Paris, officially accepting the European and colonial territorial cessions that were the consequence of its aggressive participation in the Nazi-fascist war.

The memorial by the Grand Canal and the tomb in the Tempio Votivo are not Sauro's only memory sites in the city, since a *campo* is named after him in the *sestiere* of Santa Croce, ornamented with his bust. The caption affirms grandiloquently, 'Riding the wave set in motion by the dawn of Redeemed Istria, you are Nazario Sauro. Venice welcomes you, captures your heroic spirit and transmits it to Italy.' The date is 22 March 1922 – that is, seven months before the March on Rome and the institution of hyper-nationalist, 'totalitarian' Fascist rule.[10]

But that plaque was not the sole pre-Fascist commemoration of Sauro. One of the more extraordinary documents of Italy's First World War, expressive of the continuity between liberalism and Fascism, is an official account by the Lega Navale Italiana of the elevation of the naval hero to national sainthood, a ceremony replete with a civic religion that has sometimes been regarded as the key to Mussolinian dictatorship. It was held on 21 April 1917, the (alleged) anniversary of the birth of Rome, in the nation's capital, in the hall of the Augusteo, the burial place of the emperor Augustus. Sauro's widow and teenage son (a naval cadet) attended, as did a long list of Liberal worthies.

Among them was Piero Foscari, long a paladin of the Lega Navale, who took the opportunity to urge that Sauro was a 'typical and robust specimen' of the Venetian 'maritime race'. 'Through him', the then Under-Secretary for the Colonies in the national government stated, 'our war acquires . . . a wider breathing space and crosses over the confines [sic]; it points out to us the way to the East, there where his ancestors stamped the land which is awaiting us with a Latin, Italic and Italian character.'[11] Still more strenuous in a rhetoric of empire and a blending of a Roman and Venetian inheritance was the anonymous editor of a booklet commemorating the proceedings, piously made available to Italy's allies, if in evidently hasty translation. Sauro's martyrdom carried a plain lesson, the editor declared. 'The Italian youth [sic] must learn how the hero of Capo d'Istria, Nazario Sauro, died fighting for his Country. They must learn who killed him, and how cruelly: and they must learn to hate Austria.' These wicked foes should be 'punished with the cannon, the bombs from flying machines, [and] the wary [sic] instruments of destruction launched by torpedoboats and submarines'.[12] Sauro's ghost, it was insisted, should drive Italian war-making inexorably and pitilessly forward.

With such extensive and variegated memory sites, Sauro might be thought a man for every patriotic and imperialist season in Italy, whether his ghost be summoned in Venice, in Rome or elsewhere (the navy of the post-war Republic was long equipped with 'Nazario Sauro class' submarines, built at Monfalcone in Venezia Giulia during the 1980s and 1990s).[13] Yet matters are not so simple, at least at Ca' Farsetti, where other memorials and plaques share the sanctuary of the portico.

Indeed, the place is a battleground of rival memories, not so much of the First as of the Second World War. At Ca' Farsetti, the nationalism or xenophobia of the Sauro memorial is checked by plaques hailing the memory of Giovanni Ponti and Giovanni Battista Gianquinto, respectively the first Christian Democrat and first communist mayor of the city after Fascism, each a 'hero' of the Resistance. There is also the sculpted message of General Mark Clark, the American commander of the Allied armies in Rome on 3 May 1945, addressed to the Comitato di Liberazione Nazionale (CLN, Committee of National Liberation), its partisan forces and the Venetian people. Clark conveys his gratitude for an ousting of Nazi-fascism achieved from within, 'with the help and encouragement of the whole population'. The result, he is recorded as saying, had been that, on victory, 'Venice's port and public services were still working and the enemy had not been allowed to damage the many monuments and buildings that express your marvellous tradition of culture and civilisation'. By the time his troops entered the city, Clark maintained, life there had already returned to normal. Venice, he can be construed as affirming, had 'liberated itself'. With these words, Clark endorsed the major theses of the anti-Fascist 'myth of the Resistance', understandings of history that are hard to reconcile with the unrepentant nationalism of the Sauro memorial.

Yet another plaque on the Ca' Farsetti wall deserves attention, all the more because it might seem to offer a historiographical compromise between otherwise incompatible leftist and rightist readings of national and urban history. It is a bronze tablet inscribed with the proclamation of victory not in the Second but in the First World War made by the Italian commander General Armando Diaz on 4 November 1918. (Diaz was made Duca della Vittoria – Duke of

Victory – in 1921, and served as Mussolini's first Minister of War, 1922–5). Diaz's words were incised there, it is explained, by 'the women of Italy', 'in memory of our heroic fighters'. No date is attached. The implication, however, is a 'granitic' interpretation of Italian history that should unite Italians in their nation. Whatever the divisions provoked in the city and elsewhere in the country by the experience between 1922 and 1945 of a generation of Fascist dictatorship and anti-Fascist resistance, the First World War, an observer is meant to learn at Ca' Farsetti, was a good war, fought and won with virtue and determination in a spirit of national sacrifice and unity. It has only one accept-able understanding: as averred by conservative historian Rosario Romeo, it constituted 'the greatest triumph in our history'.[14]

But was that conflict really one in which Venetians were happy to serve and which, whether as locals or Italians, they should be proud to remember? No doubt the national war effort led to formal victory on 4 November 1918. Yet there is reason to count the cost of that triumph and evaluate its malign effect on Venice and its multiple histories.

Back in July 1914, after all, Venetians were distractedly reading ominous reports from north of the Alps, where the leaders of the other five Great Powers were, in the slick rhetoric of later British prime minister David Lloyd George, stumbling 'over the brink into the boiling cauldron of war'.[15] In Venice, by contrast, the sun shone, the hotels overflowed, the lagoon and sea gleamed; it was the peak of another tourist season, one that promised to continue the pattern of recent years of being bigger and better than the last. On 3 July *Il Gazzettino* noted contentedly that the Lido was so full of 'visitors from every nation' that 'you can scarcely breathe there'.[16] Modern business was also detecting advantage, Kodak assuring the paper's readers that 'a holiday without a Kodak camera is a holiday wasted'. King Victor Emmanuel III was known to be an ardent photographer of his family, but in Venice it was Prince Paul of Greece who was expected at any moment.[17] Meanwhile the Redentore festival went off with its usual flair, fireworks bursting gaily over the city. Restaurant seats were being stormed, every space at once occupied, it was reported, 10,000 foreigners having booked into the city for the event.[18] By 26 July Serbian–Austrian relations were deteriorating, but Venetians' immediate worries were jewel thieves operating on the Lido, notably at the Hotel des Bains (a waiter was arrested for the crime on the 30th). Also in the news were further sad cases of suicide among the popular classes.[19] On 2 August *Il Gazzettino* did acknowl-edge that Germanic guests on the Lido were melting away, but, it chirpily believed, their places were immediately reoccupied by Americans, English and non-Venetian Italians.[20]

At a higher cultural level, the 11th Biennale had opened on 15 April, the Russian pavilion having been graciously inaugurated by the visiting Grand Duchess Vladimir, a German-born aunt by marriage to the tsar, admired in royal circles as 'the grandest of the grand duchesses'. Despite its rather negative reviews, the art festival was not scheduled to close until 31 October. Hermenegild Anglada Caramasa from the Balearic Islands was applauded as the best painter on show, although he was scarcely destined to become a household name. Michele De Benedetti, appraising the exhibition in the pages of *Nuova Antologia*, argued that the whole affair needed to be rethought. Too many artworks were displayed, too few being 'of high artistic quality'. 'It is useless', he maintained grouchily, 'every two years to force artists to finish off mediocre productions', just to keep the rhythm of the Biennali going.[21]

Despite the outbreak of war, the 11th Biennale did stay open until October, but Marco Pilo, writing in *L'Ateneo Veneto*, reflected ruefully on its fate now that other Great Powers were contesting their 'bloody match', as he put it feelingly. Europe, he lamented, was for the present no longer enchanted by 'the idyllic green of the Giardini, the tender blue of the Venetian sky, the quiet magic mirror of the Lagoon'. Yet it was not the end, he asserted. 'The immortality of art and knowledge will endure every catastrophe and remain the extreme and supreme comfort, for ever, resisting every anguish, every pang, every torment that politics and diplomacy have always ferociously disseminated across the wide world.' When peace returned, he told himself, Venice's globe-ranging hospitality would again cure all ills.[22]

Such innocent optimism about humankind was, however, growing difficult to sustain in a city that might not yet have been at war but that had nonetheless almost immediately been put in its thrall. At a stroke the city's tourist industry disintegrated, terminating the employment of 12,000 seasonal workers and quite a number of permanent staff, with devastating effect on the urban economy. By mid August many female lace workers had been laid off, while newspapers were appealing plaintively for locals to replace panicked foreigners in the now empty rooms of the Biennale.[23] Shortly thereafter the Excelsior was reported to be less than a quarter full.[24]

By November Mayor Grimani was dolefully portraying a city at the end of its tether, 'workshops closed, shipyards in collapse, shops kept open only for the sake of appearances, market stalls inert, and workers in every category unemployed by the hundreds'.[25] An eighth of the population were making do on less than five lire a day, he feared, their only recourse being to pawn their meagre goods to some rapacious moneylender.[26] Tourists, Grimani noted, had utterly vanished, to be replaced by refugees from across the borders of the Habsburg Empire who had neither jobs nor housing: 270 reached Venice on

16 August, 150 the next day and 250 on the 18th, from Trieste, Dalmatia and other parts of the Empire.[27] They kept coming and, a week later, a committee under Antonio Fradeletto, aiming to sustain 'refugees, unemployed and emigrants', appealed for charity.[28]

Trade through the port rapidly dwindled, by November 1914 being down 75 per cent on a year earlier, with growing anxiety in early autumn that coal supplies would no longer reach the city.[29] So rapid had been the fall from grace that popular demonstrators against living conditions had first gathered on 1 September, when a thousand protested outside Santa Fosca. In ineffective response, charitable ladies opened six soup kitchens, one in each *sestiere*, to be met, it was reported, with suspicion by their expected recipients.[30] Early the following year, the Council, as it strove to avoid bankruptcy, was absorbing rumours that even the bourgeoisie were contemplating social violence to shore up their lifestyles.[31] Was it fair, it was asked by quite a few Venetians of different political persuasions, that their city should pay so drastically for national Italian policy?[32]

The lesson that Venice's real existence was cosmopolitan or nothing was, naturally enough, hard for many Venetians to accept, especially those nationalists and intellectuals who, before 1914, had burnished their anti-tourist vocabulary and who now used the war to enhance it. The city speedily became an epicentre of a more general dispute over what policy the nation should adopt towards the war. Should it remain neutral? By 2 August its government had declared that it was not bound to fight alongside Germany and Austria-Hungary, despite its membership of the Triple Alliance since 1882. Should it enter the conflict? And if so, when, how and on which side?

In the country at large, the two mass movements, socialist and Catholic (the latter still without an organised modern party), tended towards neutrality, although there were defections from the ranks of each, Mussolini's from the socialists in October 1914 being the most notorious in retrospect. The Socialist Party would eventually come up with the weak formula 'neither support nor sabotage' to define their line. In Venice, Elia Musatti had to temper his usual aggressive radicalism by admitting that he, too, saw reason to fight for 'the integrity and freedom of Italy'.[33]

In the city, as in Italy at large, the socialists failed to make themselves the majority, whether in peace or in war. In June 1914 they performed impressively in local elections but scarcely shook the continuing power of Grimani's moderate clerical coalition, which would be stiffened by the rising profile and audacity of the various nationalist groups. The activist socialist women of the Manifattura Tabacchi, who had stubbornly remained on strike for forty-five days over the summer, were distressed to find that war meant the suspension of all work in their factory. Nonetheless, much social protest remained more spontaneous than organised. On 15 March 1915, for example, a coalition of urban women demonstrated until late at night in Campo San Luca against the cost of living, and did so despite the counsel of the local socialist leadership.[34] Two days later, two hundred female activists went to the gates of the Cotonificio Veneziano, which, despite brawls with police stationed there, they took by storm, stopping the machines and demanding that the textile workers join their protest procession.[35]

Leading the anti-socialist 'interventionist' cause were a hybrid and ever noisier group likely to be young, bourgeois and intellectual. They were particularly well represented in Venice, given the pre-war significance of nationalism and irredentism in the city, attitudes that were reinforced by the political stance of many refugees from Austria-Hungary who had found sanctuary after war began. The Liberal elites in Rome were themselves divided, a situation that was complicated by the fact that Giolitti, their leading figure over the previous decade, had left office as prime minister in March 1914, intending soon to return and preserving a majority in parliament. His replacement, Antonio Salandra, more conservative in his social policies than Giolitti, swiftly judged the war to be the chance to end what some critics had damned as the 'Giolittian dictatorship' and was ready to summon the 'nation' in that cause.

Meanwhile, with the menacing imminence of war increasing, in early spring 1915 local worthies had decided that the best of the city's artworks and its archival records – treasured by the population as their household gods, the repositories of their own special, traditional, history, as well as proof of Venice's tourist purpose – should be packed up and moved to some less exposed (but alien) site on the Italian mainland.[36] It was an intimation of what would become the wartime reality that the special features of Venetian life must now be subordinated to the war (and the nation that waged it).

There were thus many reasons why, during the *intervento*, nationalists set the political pace in the city. In their ranks, Foscari and Giuriati naturally took leading positions, the former proclaiming sonorously in September 1914 that the war meant that 'We can save Dalmatia!'[37] As early as 23 August Giuriati had summoned a meeting of the Trento and Trieste Society at which he gave an oration, afterwards shepherding his supporters to Piazza San Marco to demonstrate in favour of intervention against Austria. Giuriati tried to advance the irredentist cause by highlighting the way Venice had become a 'city of exiles', noting his pleasure at meeting Nazario Sauro. Not everyone agreed with this interpretation of the city's purpose, Giuriati recalling that he and his friends were 'watched with diffidence and rancour by neutralists of every gradation, who were scarcely lacking in my City, as well as by people poisoned by socialist preaching'.[38] The first nationalist fracas with their socialist foes broke out in Piazza San Marco, increasingly a patriots' redoubt, on 15 September.[39]

Two months later Cesare Battisti was welcomed as an interventionist advocate. He addressed a crowd estimated to be two thousand strong in the sportive bourgeois surrounds of the Costantino Reyer gymnasium, then occupying the Misericordia abbey in Cannaregio. Following his speech, he and his friends marched to St Mark's Square, grappling with police along the way, and there ceremoniously burned the Habsburg flag. Other visitors sparked similar demonstrations, a notable one occurring on 16 February, when the nationalist journalist Francesco Coppola attacked monarchists and clericals, while 'inveighing against Germanised professors and the pusillanimity of the great mass of the people'. His speech elicited socialist counter protest, the two factions marching from Palazzo Giustinian Faccanon to San Marco, scuffling as they went, fisticuffs willingly being exchanged when the rivals met on the Ponte dei Bareteri.[40]

In the spirit of increasingly violent social conflict, by late 1914 Giuriati was enrolling what he called a paramilitary 'Legion' (with Roman rather than Venetian reference), though he remembered regretfully that he had to do so at Mestre rather than in Venice itself, given the combined opposition there of socialists, the police and what he called 'foreigners'. The plan was to propagandise a 'Christmas among exiles' and the Legion did acquire uniforms and engage in military training. But by February Giuriati had accepted his legionnaires' dissolution; in any case, he had by then left the city to undertake rescue work with his 'Trento and Trieste squad' at the Marsica earthquake that had severely hit that region east of Rome on 13 January 1915.[41]

Soon the final crisis of 'Radiant May' was played out in Venice, while Salandra in Rome pushed Italy into the war on the 24th, not always to his pleasure backed by intemperate urban demonstrators. He was applauded by his country's leading wordsmiths, with D'Annunzio in the van, having returned from a period living in Arcachon in France, where he could avoid his many creditors. In Venice, Giampietro Talamini, the respectable and liberal founder and editor of Il Gazzettino, but an admirer and patron of D'Annunzio, exhibited the vulnerability of his sort of liberal to nationalist excitation by extolling 'national insurrection against traitors to the patria'. Rather forgetting the Venetian Empire, he intoned, 'the moment is grave, but grand and Roman'.[42]

Over the preceding months, Pompeo Molmenti had seemed a sterner defender of liberal or conservative moderation, noting his fastidious disapproval of D'Annunzio's 'horrible verse'. On 23 May, however, even he rallied to the war and to the idea that it should bring Dalmatia home to Italy. For the moment forgetful of Venetian particularity, he relished the thought that battle must ensure that 'Italy will finally be made complete by the virtue of its people, the good sense of its king and the valour of its arms.'[43]

Such patriotic notions had been converted into cruder action on the 15th, when a rumpus broke out between rival bands of interventionists and social-ists, the latter still hopeful that Italy could remain neutral. Partisans fought hand to hand in Piazza San Marco, the victory going to those in favour of inter-vention. The nationalists' slogan had been 'either a beating or out you go'; war, it was becoming evident, was to be an all or nothing, a 'total' matter, in their minds. A socialist attempt the following day to despatch women and children back to the main square to voice hostility to entry was a last desperate gesture of the neutralist cause.[44] By the 21st all shops around the square were decorated with the *tricolore*, and on the 22nd it was reported that crowds there listened in respectful silence while the municipal orchestra played a national repertoire that ran through the 'Va pensiero' chorus from Verdi's *Nabucco*, Rossini's 'Prayer of Moses' and the Mameli anthem.[45]

On 20 May command of the city had passed from civilian hands to the military authorities. Although Grimani, who had steered a cautious path through the altercations of the period, formally remained in mayoral office throughout the conflict, the leading figure in the wartime city was to be Admiral Paolo Emilio Thaon di Revel (who under Fascism was to rejoice in the grandiose title of Duca del Mare, Duke of the Sea). Under his aegis, Venice became the nation's most advanced naval base. Much needed to be forfeited to the waging of war after full-scale military rule imposed controls over most aspects of life, including stern press censorship. Prison numbers rose markedly. On 23 May Venetians were firmly instructed that city electricity supplies would be cut whenever the commander saw fit. The ferries could continue their schedules for the moment but they must not use their lights. All aquatic exits from the lagoon were blocked, as were the entries to some canals within the fortress city, as it now was to be.[46]

In every sense, the local should bow to the national. Characteristically, in November 1917, Thaon di Revel declared that no hesitation could be tolerated, 'when need demanded, in sacrificing Venice's artistic and historic interests to those of national defence'.[47] Back in 1915, at a stroke, 'From a city of art, [Venice] had become just one part of the front.'[48] Now St Mark's, from which the Quadriga had been removed and sent for sanctuary in Rome, and those other city monuments that could not be carried off elsewhere were hemmed in by sandbags and other protective devices. More drastically, on the languishing Lido, the authorities ruthlessly sequestered the wood and metal used to build Luna Park, the sea-based 'Chinese' pavilion and the rink near the Excelsior. In this harsh new world, military uniform ousted the fancy dress that adepts like

13 Aerial defence from the *altane* of the city

the Duke of the Abruzzi had worn when skating was launched there in 1913. Now the raucous sound of war silenced once charming waltz tunes.

The most fertile nationalist propagandist of the city's war experience was Ezio Maria Gray, born in Novara in Piedmont in 1885, a man with a durable and variegated career in extreme right-wing politics that extended beyond 1945. Gray would then shrug off a death penalty that was briefly imposed on him for Fascist activities that varied between violently xenophobic journalism and decorous official employment in the national tourist industry.[49] Like Foscari, Gray was an early member of the Nationalist Association, and in 1912 published a short work extolling the beauty of war.[50] From 1915 he was frequently resident in Venice, where he happily banded with men who camped overnight on the *altane*, or rooftop loggias, that were common in the city and were used in wartime to get clear if mostly ineffectual rifle aim at approaching aircraft.

14 San Marco, without the Quadriga, defended

Gray also beat an insistent propaganda drum of the most paranoid
Germanophobe kind (a generation later, he changed his target but not his
world-view when he led Fascist campaigns against perfidious England). The
Kaiser's repeated visits to Venice and other Italian ports were, he was sure, part
of a gigantic and tightly organised conspiracy by the Germanic world to take
over Italy as once the Germans' ancestors, the barbarians, had done, and with
the same potentially devastating results.[51] 'Attila', he remarked in his sensation-
alist account of German war crimes in Belgium, 'is back and Rome's successors
must again bar his path.'[52] No fewer than 72,000 German agents, he insisted,
were resident in Italy in December 1914, many of them masquerading as Swiss
or cunningly bearing false American passports. German wives, he knew, were
especially perilous, constituting 'a permanent army of German espionage in
Italy'.[53]

Gray's xenophobia was naturally fortified by a long list of traitors within the
gates whom he had fearlessly detected, those who did the Germans' wicked
business for them. Prominent among them were Otto Joel, 'the real German
pro-Consul in Italy', Giuseppe Toeplitz of the Banca Commerciale Italiana and
their client Giuseppe Volpi, 'the wrecker of the Treaty of Ouchy ... the man

who ought to be regarded in Italy as an undesirable alien'.[54] In 1914, Volpi, Gray was sure, had surreptitiously travelled to Vienna on a corrupt neutralist mission, as befitted his subservience to the bidding of German financial interests.[55] Mayor Grimani was another culpable of transgressing the nation, when, in early 1914, he had welcomed the posting of signs in Czech in the city. So was Fradeletto, in parliament 'the member for the [Biennial] Exhibition'.[56] 'Professors', Gray charged, were especially vulnerable to German tricks, and had allowed German historians and archaeologists to seize Italy's imperial past and make its lessons theirs; the German control over geography was yet more sinister, since all German expertise was actually planning for war.[57] Their deplorable racists had the temerity to assert that Dante, Titian and many another national treasure were 'Aryans' – that is, Germans rather than Italians.[58] Socialists were vile by any count, but the 'riots' that had swept over Venice in March 1915 had been sponsored and led by the Germans. The strikers, who acted in spite of local socialist leadership, had been driven to violence by the shouts of a woman near the Rialto with a pronounced foreign accent, Gray attested with classic conspiracy theorist mixing of small-seeming fact and large fiction.[59]

Such evil individuals constituted the outward and visible sign of an inward and spiritual plague afflicting Venice. The 11th Biennale, Gray charged, with a hint of the anti-Semitism that would come to fruition in the 1930s, had attracted a 'cosmopolitan public'. 'And how many! The Lido then looked like a suburb of Budapest.' From there, the visitors 'invaded the city and spent and spent'. As a result, shops had turned into a variety of 'Tunisian souk', while Venice was beset by 'hoteliers' dropsy' and 'philistine commercialism'. People chatted and gossiped in every language except Italian, but all they talked about were 'love affairs, minor scandals, eccentricities, paradoxes'. The arts were dumbed down, with 'that easy gain sometimes resembling begging, throwing the city into the hands of foreigners who did not understand or honour it (with the Kaiser in the lead)'.[60] Moreover, half the hoteliers were Germans, or were acting in the German interest; CIGA was a plain example. From the Lido, it was especially easy for 'waiters or guests to sneak out to the fortified zones' and thence report crucial military detail to Berlin.[61]

Entry to the war must end such disgrace, Gray urged. Venice must no longer be 'a museum, a hang-out for idlers or a convention centre for eccentric art'. It must absolutely renounce tourism, thereby doubtless becoming poorer but also acquiring as a potential reward 'the Adriatic and the Near East',[62] as even Grimani, in 1916, had allegedly agreed. For the present, the urban economy may have been wrecked, but Venice had covered itself with 'Glory' in compensation, Gray urged.[63]

If the pre-war era was sordid, Gray contended in his account of Venice in wartime published in 1917, the city's commitment to battle was exemplary. Even before entry to the war, Foscari and other nationalists had spearheaded a campaign that had culminated in Radiant May, when on 22 May 10,000 had assembled in Piazza San Marco to cry for military action. During the build-up to such exciting days, Nazario Sauro was loved in those cafés where irredentists hung out (especially Florian's). Under his and other inspiration, the whole Veneto had been forged into 'a steel breastplate donned by a people who once were giants and giants again will be'.[64] The special heroes of the moment were pro-war intellectuals; these could include worthy foreigners like the French rightist Maurice Barrès, who reached the city in October 1915 to show that it was not, after all, dead.[65] 'So artists, writers, political thinkers, philosophers . . . came together in [Venice's] defence, forgetful of everything except the duty to save it at any cost,' Gray exulted. 'It really seemed thereby that art and thought were symbolically formed into a Roman cohort [*manipolo*], choosing their battle-post where Italic thought, art and beauty were most directly threatened.'[66]

Peerless among such warriors was Gabriele D'Annunzio, Gray hastened to acknowledge. For the 'people', D'Annunzio was the 'standard-bearer' of the nation, adored because he 'knew every Venetian artistic treasure'. He was thereby both an intellectual and something mysteriously more.[67] D'Annunzio did indeed spend most of the war in residence in Venice, always in richly comfortable surrounds, first at the Hotel Danieli and later at the Casetta Rossa on the Grand Canal, where he typically combined sexual pleasure, writing and dauntless military feats. Afterwards, he produced an account entitled *Notturno*, where death in the fog-bound city earned more attention than heroics, even though they were assumed.

As always, self-obsession ruled as the story of D'Annunzio's lost right eye (his 'favourite' one; it was damaged in an accident resulting from an aerial battle with the Austrians on 15 January 1916) and the suffering that he endured drifted in and out of his narration.[68] Elsewhere, he made it known that the Austrians had dropped fifty-two bombs on the Casetta Rossa, of which he had been the target, though even a friend thought that tally an exaggeration.[69] Still, he was capable of graphic images of a conflict that he memorably called the 'Holocaust' when he painted 'a city, full of ghosts. Men walk about noiselessly, hugged by the fog. The canals smoke. You don't see the bridges, except for the line of white stone at each step. Some drunkard's song, some shouts, some cackling. . . . Cries from the aircraft lookouts made hoarse by the fog. A dream-like city, a city beyond the world, a city bathed by the river Lethe or Avernus . . . [where] the dead stroll this night as they do on the night between All Saints

Day and 2 November.'[70] More predictably, when on a naval raid passing Muggia, once the nearest Venetian outpost to Trieste, his heart recognised that 'all the sea was Dante's' (the medieval religious poet again being conscripted into a prophet of Italian nationalism).[71]

Throughout his war experience, D'Annunzio interwove his own myth as the Poet of the Nation with that of the city, his dashing flights taking off from the Lido and his naval raids sallying out from the lagoon. He achieved an apotheosis in a flight over Vienna on 9 August 1918, when he sardonically dropped red, white and green pamphlets urging Habsburg surrender, thereby making himself the symbol of the victory that was now near.[72] Few in his circle could deny or resist his charisma. One of his (male) admirers jotted into his diary his memory of the poet's 'special and indefinable smell', as further proof that he was irresistible.[73] A French fan judged him the son both of Apollo and of Mars.[74] An English visitor, the later Fascist propagandist J. S. Barnes, was less impressed, recalling a meeting when D'Annunzio had left Venice for a time to be nearer the front. 'His hut was like a coquette's boudoir. There was a safe covered with silk and gay-coloured cushions. The walls were plastered with relics, photographs of actresses and Madonnas, propeller props, sundry souvenirs and statuettes', rendering the surrounds anything but 'severely war-like'. 'It is difficult for a man', Barnes added prissily (or enviously), 'to understand how it is that this little frog, typically half-Jew (and not the handsome kind by any means), with his bald head and hairless face, looking like a skull except for the full lips and staring, bulging eyes, can exert such a physical fascination over women.' Yet when the poet spoke, Barnes conceded, you forgot his appearance, heard only the marvellous words and were buoyed by the emotions that sustained them.[75]

Some of D'Annunzio's colleagues were more direct in grasping the lessons of battle, Manfredi Gravina, a nationalist naval officer from a Sicilian noble family, urging Thaon di Revel to react to the Austrian bombardment that had wrecked Venice's state-owned textile factory by bombing Austrian cities every possible night with more aeroplanes and more bombs (by implication, inflicting more civilian casualties). Such vengeance, Gravina added, dreaming as were many of his sort by 1917 of a Duce, would be better enforced by sterner figures than the dull liberal parliamentarians who commanded the Allied war effort.[76]

The words of writers like Gray and the myth and reality of D'Annunzio merged into what amounted to a spiritual takeover of Venice for the nation and for the Fascist version of it that lay on the horizon. If Gray for one were to be believed, post-war Italian Venice should no longer attract tourists and leisure should not be its delight. Rather, in the rich store of its usable pasts, the artistic 'treasures' were worth preserving not to please the world but because their aura could spark a returned empire. They must therefore be militant and militarised, Venetian perhaps, but above all Italian. Venice must be girded by one history and only one. 'Total war' must continue in peacetime in a total intolerance of alternatives. Thus was the Fascist invention of 'totalitarianism', at least in nationalist intellectuals' minds, 'a fact before it happened' in Venice.

In reality, the people of Venice were enduring a war that was far from being that of the wordsmiths. While battle raged, life was harsh and getting harsher, both for those Venetians conscripted into a national army that scarcely as yet treated ordinary soldiers as citizens equal to each other,[77] and for families surviving in the city, where poverty and deprivation had not dissipated under military governance. Sons of Venice, many of them in the 83rd and 84th infantry regiments, known as 'Venezia', fell for the *patria*, in battles that took more than 600,000 Italian soldiers' lives. Of these, 2,690 from the city and its surrounds found a final resting place at the Tempio Votivo on the Lido, a Fascist structure erected between 1925 and 1930. In June 1928 Cardinal Pietro La Fontaine, who gave a Catholic gloss to the nationalism made concrete there, presided over a patriotic ceremony at which the remains of the 'Venetian soldier who had been the first to perish in the war' were buried.[78] A year later, it was formally agreed that the war memorial should be open to all visitors but that they should pass by a sign declaring, 'This ossuary near the City of Art and the Lido resort, leisure centre for global plutocracy, will show every foreigner that Italy knows how to honour its Dead worthily.'[79] It is not, however, a promise that has been kept into the present, since, today, the Tempio Votivo is mouldering and closed to ordinary inspection. In any case, thousands of Venetian dead lie in Italy's other war cemeteries, there nationalised as Italians whether they wanted to be or not. Their local memory, by contrast, is recorded on lists to be found on the outside walls of most churches in the city.

For those left behind in Venice, even if they did not have to mourn family loss as many did, life was scarcely cushy. By June 1915 meat sales had declined by half since 1914, and in January 1916 the authorities formally banned the sale of meat for two days each week. The fishing catch in 1917 was reckoned to be 10 per cent of that in 1914, and oil and sugar had become notably scarce in city shops. Child mortality rates spiralled disturbingly among the ordinary citizenry.[80] In 1917, 30,000 Venetians, more than a quarter of the population, were classified as wretchedly poor.[81] The Cotonificio was only one local factory to fall into crisis, production rapidly being cut by more than a half. The textile concern was fire-bombed by the Austrians on 16 August 1916 with drastic results, adding nine hundred to the list of unemployed. Despite charitable initiatives both private and from the Comune, there was no solution to urban poverty while the war continued.[82] One memoirist may therefore not merely have been reflecting his leftist politics when he claimed that ordinary Venetians hated the officers and intellectuals who talked big about the nation and its glories in Piazza San Marco, condemning them as class enemies and 'imboscati' (shirkers), whose activities in that part of the city were alien to the rest of its population.[83] Similarly, although Cardinal La Fontaine emerged from the war with the friendship of the nationalists, he found that his efforts in wartime to conduct 'soldiers' Masses' were by no means a complete success, the popular experience of war failing to close the gap between popular religiosity and the hierarchy's comprehension of piety and polite religious practice.[84] The people of Venice, the patriarch would soon complain, were 'ignorant, preoccupied by their own matters, religious and blasphemous, devoted to the Madonna and members of the [socialist] Chamber of Labour'.[85]

From May 1915 to October 1917 Venice was near but not at the front. The eleven battles of the Isonzo and the bitter struggles in the high country of the Trentino meant that the city's main purpose for the military was still the half-touristic one of relief and resuscitation, even while the civilian population dwindled from 159,000 in July 1914 to 113,941 in November 1917. Most of the city's hotels were converted into military hospitals, while the Ospedale Britannico ed Americano on the Giudecca was now opened to all and in practice nationalised,[86] although its legal ownership was still in dispute after the Second World War.[87] In this army and navy town, the Redentore festival of 1917 served as an opportunity to offer for sale in the main *campi* toys crafted by severely wounded soldiers for their benefit. From time to time, the Red Cross organised more exclusive cultural events. In July 1917, for example, they hired Tito Schipa to sing in Bellini's *La sonnambula* at the Teatro Rossini for a heavily uniformed audience. Fine summer days could bring some release from the tensions of war, and, at least according to one aggrieved correspondent to *Il Gazzettino*, gave opportunity for young and aggressive cyclists to charge madly about the Lido with no care for pedestrians.[88]

Much description of the city from these years retains a sentimental gloss, despite emphasis on the stygian gloom of the place under blackout at night (an ironical half-realisation of Marinetti's exhortation to kill the moonlight). Cigars were said to be used as personal anti-collision devices by men traversing the *calli*,[89] while a bitter joke claimed that more, presumably nicotine-free, men and women perished from falling into dark and freezing canals than were killed in the city by enemy action. Daytime was not quite so hazardous, but a correspondent of the London *Times*, granted permission to visit in November 1915, portrayed a place with its monuments, museums and churches sandbagged, its people in most parts absent. Walking from the Arsenale, he noted, 'The houses are all deserted, the blinds closely drawn. I pass no one. Then, suddenly, I come upon the Piazza San Marco. The square is crowded. In the centre a naval band is playing. From three flagpoles, in front of San Marco, faded Italian tricolours – the largest flags in Europe – are flying. Women with their black, long-fringed shawls drawn tightly across their shoulders; soldiers, sailors, officers – all in grey service uniform – stand huddled together, listening to the music. Here and there a flock of grey gluttonous pigeons – grey also – is being fed. The sun is bright, and there is a strong cool breeze. Yet the scene is joyless. Venice is shrouded in a grey pall. The Piazza is grey and black. And so it is throughout the city.' A moral was required to counter what might sound like defeatist talk. So the journalist added that the grey city was still 'the Venice of the Venetians. The true Venice at her post in the front rank of battle. . . . So Venice must have looked when she had manned her galleys to fight the Turk.'[90]

When, eighteen months later, H. G. Wells came on official mission, he noticed the complete absence of waiters and shopkeepers, while near the railway station he remarked almost lyrically that 'a black despondent remnant of the old crowd of gondolas browsed dreamily against the quay'.[91] In more practical mind, a longer-term English resident insisted that the effects of bombing were successfully minimised, since everyone kept their baths at the ready full either of water or of sand (as if the popular classes possessed such facilities).[92]

While the rival armies were slaughtering each other a little way to the north and north-east, naval and aerial warfare directly penetrated Venetian urban space. No doubt, in the main, the Italian and Austro-Hungarian navies avoided conclusive battle in the Adriatic even more timorously than the British and German fleets did in the North Sea. But quite a few naval raids (and not just D'Annunzio's) were planned in Venice and began from there. Partly because of the resultant concentration of shipping in the lagoon, Venice was the first Italian city to endure what contemporaries viewed as serious and continuing bombardment from the air. Planes generally struck on moonlit nights when the Austrian airmen could see their targets, the first being on 24–5 May 1915, to rebuke Italian war entry. One nationalist writer cheerfully described the event as being 'like the Redentore festival. Streets were totally filled just as if it were a traditional party.'[93] But it was the Futurist Marinetti who won the palm for crassness when he wrote that the strong points from which ground retaliation could be launched were 'like *virile members in a state of erection*' (Marinetti's italics).[94]

Forty-two bombing raids on Venice were tabulated after the war by those anxious to proclaim the city's martyrdom in the national cause. An attack at 5 a.m. on 14 August 1917 hit a local hospital, killing seventeen and wounding twenty-eight; one Austrian plane was shot down in retaliation. Overall the aerial

15 Map of the bombed city, 1915–18

bombing resulted in fifty-two deaths and, apart from the lost Tiepolo at the Scalzi, provoked further but rarely grave damage to Venice's artistic patrimony.[95] The raid on the night of 26–7 February 1918 sent a column of the church of San Simeone Piccolo near the railway station flying into the canal, where it sank eleven gondolas and demolished a *traghetto* shed. According to one youthful memory, the boys of the city felt no terror from the bombers, making a game out of collecting shrapnel and other physical remains of the attacks. The chattering of anti-aircraft fire, the memoirist maintained, elicited a frisson of fear and a matching sense of patriotic comfort that Venice was properly safeguarded.[96] Another observer stated that people grew used to sleeping in their work-clothes, adding that they ascribed individual personalities to the unexploded bombs that were always likely to remain a threat after a raid.[97]

Resistance to the aerial assaults earned the city a gold medal for its patriotic contribution in June 1920. On the mainland, peasants, it was noticed, were initially astonished and bewildered by aerial attacks of any sort, although the cooler patriots in the city tried to spread the idea that the bombs should be christened 'Austrian manna', and claimed that they liked to stroll beside the canals carelessly ignoring explosions.[98] Certainly, in retrospect, the assault on the city was contained in its effect; materially, at least, Venice scarcely suffered in the way many European cities (though not Venice) did in the Second World War.

In quite a few ways, 1917 was the decisive year of the war, the time when the USA under President Woodrow Wilson entered it (in April) and when Russia left it (in November, after the Bolshevik revolution). It would also be crucial for

16 Barrage balloons, First World War style

Italy militarily. On 24 October 1917 Habsburg armies, stiffened by German support, swept through Italian defences at Caporetto (Kobarid in present day Slovenia). They were not stopped until the river Piave, some forty kilometres to Venice's east and nearer still to the lagoon's edge. For the next twelve months, anyone sipping a coffee in Piazza San Marco could hear the thunder of guns from the front. During that time, Venetians learned what it meant to be at, or almost at, the front, and therefore to have become a full-fledged garrison and redoubt, in no sense an ordinary city. For very many, evacuation or flight was the immediate result; by April 1918, just over 40,000 people were left.

Yet another matter, occurring a few months before Caporetto, demands notice, since it arguably was to have a more lasting effect on the city than did its First World War. The prime victor in the embattled city, at least in the medium term, was not a soldier, nor a nationalist writer, nor an ordinary citizen, but the adaptable and adroit capitalist Giuseppe Volpi, the man who in July 1914 had believed major international conflict to be impossible and had been damned as an alien by aggressive interventionists.

Volpi, who should be acknowledged as the most important and influential Venetian of the twentieth century, by no means incorrectly labelled the 'last doge', sprang from a family of minor Bergamasque nobility who had taken residence in Venice, where Giuseppe was born on 19 November 1877.[99] His father was an engineer (with alleged connections to Garibaldi)[100] who died in

1897, a loss that drove Volpi to abandon legal studies at the University of Padua (while a student he had already found remuneration as the local representative of a French insurance company) and commence a life in business.

An entrepreneur with a global purview, Volpi turned his attention to the tumultuous Balkans, in a few years achieving a major commercial presence in Serbia, where in 1903 he backed the victorious Karageorgević in their bloody dynastic conflict with the rival Obrenović family (and was awarded the honour of acting as Serb vice-consul in Venice).[101] Volpi quickly expanded his activities into Montenegro, a country with royal connection with Italy.[102] In 1905 Volpi's Antivari company won trade control over what the Montenegrins agreed could be a free port. Volpi also swiftly took out options on forest growth and railway development, while keeping a weather eye on Italian imports to Montenegro. As a Venetian admirer put it, Volpi was a man 'with a profound knowledge of the Balkans, possessed of the highest qualities of ingenuity and action', skills particularly necessary in that part of the world.[103]

Assisted by loyal financial support from the Banca Commericale Italiana, whose deputy director, Giuseppe Toeplitz, was based in Venice between 1900 and 1903, thereafter to retain a deep fondness for the city,[104] Volpi assembled an urban coalition of such Venetians as Foscari, the latest heir of the Papadopoli family, who owned a large palace on the Grand Canal (and, appropriate to a banker, was an expert on the city's early modern coinage),[105] and Achille Gaggia, an ambitious and capable engineer and industrialist, born at Feltre in 1875. A crucial partner was Vittorio Cini, born at Ferrara in February 1885, a man with wide-ranging heavy industrial, agricultural and trade interests as well as, eventually, cultural influence, who, like Volpi, made Venice his home and inscribed his own meaning onto it.

It was natural that Volpi's gaze would extend beyond the Balkans to Asia Minor, the entrepreneur positioning himself in relation to the major current question of the future of the Ottoman Empire. In 1907 Volpi established the Società Commerciale d'Oriente (Eastern Trading Company) to push his own, his bank's and Italy's interests there. It was this last background that explained Giolitti's use of him as his personal negotiator for the Treaty of Ouchy, which, in 1912, brought the Turks to recognise Italian ownership of Libya. Volpi won this position in spite of a public attack from the Nationalist paper *L'Idea Nazionale* (The National Idea), berating him as 'a businessman who lives in the environment of international finance' and who therefore could not loyally serve the nation.[106]

Despite his engagements abroad, Volpi had remained active at home, notably with the founding in 1905 of the Società Adriatica di Elettricità (SADE, Adriatic Electric Company). SADE sponsored major hydro-electricity development in the Italian Alps and fed the resultant supplies through most of the Veneto and Romagna. During the First World War, SADE's capital rose by 84 per cent. Gaggia helpfully took a seat on the national committee supervising electricity supplies to the nation's industry, ensuring thereby that SADE served the nation and the nation served SADE.[107] For Volpi and his associates, world war may have been unlooked for, but it brought at least as much gainful opportunity as had peace.

But the grand step was taken in 1917. Now Volpi and his friends initiated the Società Porto Industriale di Venezia (Venice Industrial Port Company), aiming to bring to fruition pre-1914 schemes for a new harbour at Bottenighi. It was, Volpi would maintain, a choice between a 'pure' but dying Venice and a 'modern' one.[108] Volpi's group also established a Società Veneta per Imprese Fondiarie (Venetian Company for Land Development), which perspicaciously acquired much real estate in the area at a good price.[109] On 23 July 1917 the government in Rome, acting with what many observers judged as record bureaucratic speed by dealing with the matter in seventy-five days, signalled official approval for what was thereafter to be called Porto Marghera.[110]

The presence of Foscari in the Cabinet and the political contacts of Antonio Fradeletto among the Liberal elite in Rome assisted the team in Venice. It must also have been helpful that the scheme was blessed by the leading nationalist politician Luigi Federzoni,[111] whose public support indicated that Gray's charge that Volpi often acted like an undesirable alien was to be forgotten. Within Venice, Mayor Grimani, a doubter in earlier times, now also swung behind Volpi, ensuring that the necessary approval by the Comune was rapid and complete.[112] Even the socialists offered backing, pleased with the idea that employment opportunities would increase.[113] So, too, did Molmenti.[114] As a flattering biographer put it with a hint of ambivalence, Volpi, with the founding of Porto Marghera, 'once more showed himself to be not so much an industrialist as a financier and service provider'.[115] His partner Vittorio Cini was an even greater enthusiast, telling a meeting of the Rotary Club in 1935 that Marghera was a 'poetic, complete and disinterested creation'.[116] As we shall see, not all observers agreed.

In 1917, however, Foscari, who, the year before, had been sure that the Austrians were Italians' permanent racial enemies, just as socialists constituted unappeasable foes within,[117] was ready to spell out the manifold advantages of the planned development. Marghera, he wrote, would be the basis of 'a more ample dominion' for Venice, paving the way for a return of its empire. Growth on the other side of the lagoon must lessen the 'overcrowding of the presently too narrow inhabited area'. All real cities had suburbs, and now Venice could have them, too. There would be more room for new museums, swimming

17 Marghera in its infancy

baths and gymnasia. The health of ordinary Venetians would improve and their addiction to drink lessen. Even hoteliers would gain from the city's becoming 'thriving and hard at work'. If Marghera did not go ahead, Foscari concluded with what might seem a pessimistic thought about the current war's potential results, Trieste would prove too fierce a competitor.[118]

Hardly was the ink dry on the legal deeds approving the new port when the Italian armies were all but routed at Caporetto, while, in many eyes, socialist revolution of the sort now occurring in Russia threatened the home front. There may have been a precarious rebuff of the Central Power forces on the Piave, but, for some weeks, the military authorities feared that Venice must fall. It was now that Thaon di Revel advised that, in final battle, no time should be wasted on protecting art treasures, fearing more generally that the city could not be defended from direct attack.[119] After some hesitation, however, and when it had become apparent that the advance by the Germans and Austrians had stalled, Vittorio Emanuele Orlando, the prime minister and a liberal Sicilian lawyer, ordered that the city be saved, coining the slogan 'Per Venezia non si passa' (You can't get through Venice).[120]

The implications for Venetians were immense and terrible. What should the surviving population do? In many cases their first reaction was flight, resulting in chaotic scenes at the railway station as civilians and military personnel struggled to find a place on any available train. Informed of many derelictions of duty in those territories to the north-east that had fallen to the Central Powers, Orlando formally ordered on 7 November 1917 that Venetian public officials should stay at their desks. Class division and the widespread fear of social breakdown had their own implications. In mid November Orlando explained that he did not mind if the unemployed and 'dangerous elements' left; indeed he favoured their departure. All, however, must occur in good order, any sackings of shops or warehouses to be avoided as fatal to the national good name. A detachment of Carabinieri should stay in the city to 'safeguard order and property'. They could be seconded by 'good citizens', forming a paramilitary Civic Guard.[121]

Ordinary people, workers, minor officials, even nurses and medical staff, however, continued to leave (as early as 15 January, the moderate liberal paper *Il Gazzettino* did not refrain from commenting that the city's Jewish businessmen, lawyers and engineers had speedily recreated a community or pressure group in Rome, well behind the front).[122] The official tally was that 68,329 Venetians had left by October 1918, equal to 39 per cent of the population, encompassing 21,742 families.[123] Among the institutions that now ceased work was the Arsenale, whose employees had been unwontedly busy between 1915 and 1917, largely making fast motorised raiding vessels, or MAS (Mezzi d'Assalto), most of the profits going to a new company headed by Foscari. But in late 1917 production was transferred to La Spezia.[124]

In their displacement, Venetians, visited in a minor but often dislocating way by the experience of 'population transfer' that would murderously dog Europe's twentieth-century wars, drew rival lessons from the event. Some were national and patriotic, their spokesmen determined to resist and conquer for the nation. Other effects were local, encouraged by Venetians' edgy meetings with Italians from different places, who were themselves frequently unhappy or bemused at welcoming (government-sponsored) 'refugees'. Could the strangers be 'Austrians', some asked plaintively?[125] Venetians, sent as far south as Taormina, were equally reported to be dismayed by the 'low morality' of the locals in that pre-war gay tourist resort, whose history of a cohabitation of glamour, sexuality and poverty had ironical parallels with that of Venice.[126]

Eventually the war ended and did so with an Italian victory (despite D'Annunzio's labelling it 'mutilated' as early as October 1918, reflecting sourly, presumably without reference to his own alluring body odour, 'I smell the stench of peace').[127] George Ward Price, a journalist who would acquire greater fame from his sympathetic interviews with Europe's interwar dictators[128] but here writing in *The Times*, provided his readers with striking images of Venice as a post-war era gradually became imaginable. Early in 1918, he found a city without tourists or Venetians, inhabited by fewer than 60,000 people: 'A dreamy silence rests like an enchantment on the place, for the gravity of the hour has banished all the modern incongruities that peacetime exploitation has grafted here.... Last night I ... walked through miles of stilled and empty streets, across and along canals rippled only by the winter wind, with the cold moonlight silvering into the most exquisite detail the bridges, marble columns, arches, and delicate tracery of a deserted Fairyland.'[129]

After summer, however, with the Central Powers retreating on most fronts (except the Italian ones), he reported that 10,000 of the departed population had drifted back to the city; officials would tally 85,000 inhabitants in January 1919 and 156,839, almost the same number as in 1914, by the end of the year.[130] Meanwhile, when Ward Price visited again in September 1918, he found that, despite the rigours of wartime, 'the bathing season has started again on the Lido', where not so long before German and Austrian women had loafed around in the most daring bathing costumes. 'The sand is now dug and revetted into trenches, and a thick barbed wire entanglement runs right across the part of the beach where bathers bask in the sun after their swim.' In the cabins still lining the shore (their wood cannot have been requisitioned) were pinned 'notices ... that sentries have orders to fire on any bather going beyond the limits of the water fixed for the establishment', and 'as one leaves the bathing place, too, there is scrutiny by military police to be undergone, perhaps to defeat any attempt by the Austrians to land troops disguised as bathers'. Back across the lagoon, beauty was resurfacing: 'Few places in the war-zone can be more agreeable than Venice is now.... Last night there were hundreds of people standing between the Doge's Palace and the gleaming lagoon to look at the red flashes of anti-aircraft shells along the Piave front where Italian machines were bombing the enemy trenches.'[131]

Somewhere beneath Ward Price's sentimentality lay the key dilemma for the Venice that was to emerge from battle. Could normal service be resumed as though devastating war had never been? Could the city restore the sweet, soft, *belle époque* mix of cosmopolitan tourism and a gorgeously specific Venetian history that could hold the West (and more) in fee? Certainly one ordinary British soldier given leave there in February 1919 was impressed: Venice, he scribbled, was 'one of the most wonderfulest cities in Italy ... We put up at the Grand Canal Hotel, and we was alright.'[132] But were beauty and history really enough, or should Venice become a model of modern capitalism, 'Venezia grande', as Volpi and his associates wanted? Could there instead be some form of socialist revolution that would bring to power the workers of the world or the city? Or was the nation's total war to be protracted into a totalitarian peace as the nationalist propagandists had urged and as Mussolini would soon seek to put into practice across the country?

In July–August 1919 the pages of *Il Gazzettino* provided evidence that each of these possibilities existed in the post-war city. The cost of living was up. Strikes were frequent (even the waiters at the coffee shops of Piazza San Marco – though not Florian's – joined in) and could be accompanied by the spontaneous seizure of property and other kinds of social violence. The military guarded the paper's offices when 'bolscevichi nostrani' (our very own Bolsheviks) struck in a printing dispute. Perhaps the sudden arrival of frozen meat supplies could stave off threatened food riots. But work prospects for dockers at the port were meagre. There had been a meeting at the Gritti Palace hotel of the local 'fascio di combattimento', or soldiers' union, the body that in 1921 would be converted into the National Fascist Party, while refugees and nationalists were loudly prosecuting their campaign for annexation in Dalmatia. Thaon di Revel, the Duke of Aosta (handsome soldier-cousin of the king) and Diaz came on separate formal visits, the last being greeted by a 'grandiose demonstration of all Venice in praise of its army and Leader [*Duce*]'. Ca' Pesaro was staging a new art exhibition, while a show on the production of Venetian decorative arts had successfully opened in New York. The Excelsior sponsored a fencing competition and then a charity ball for the 'freed and redeemed lands'. The sea glistened and 'the Lido is heavily booked, all the hotels and private houses being occupied by outsiders [*forestieri*] come from every part of Italy to enjoy the beauty of our beach'.[133] In this Venice, lapped by many alternatives, the post-war path from past to future was not yet fully plain.

CHAPTER FIVE

Peace and the imposition of Fascism on Venice, 1919–1930

A few years ago, Giovanni Volpi, the son of Giuseppe Volpi's old age (born in Lausanne, Switzerland, in 1938, to the Algerian Nathalie El Kanoni, who became Volpi's second wife in 1942 in a union graciously blessed by Pope Pius XII), gave an interview to *Il Gazzettino*. His catchphrase headline was 'Venezia ingrata' (Ungrateful Venice), as he lamented that the city had not named a major *campo* or piazza after his father. Giuseppe Volpi, he maintained, had won the admiration of many leading Americans and was a personal friend of Winston Churchill. Despite such a high global reputation, an accompanying website explained further, a proper precious marble memorial to him was stymied after his death in 1947 as part of a widespread but totally unfair rejection of his legacy. It was only through the intervention of Patriarch Roncalli, the future Pope John XXIII, a man with 'unquestioned authority' in the city who then took pains to get the backing of Pius XII, that suitable burial was finally allowed on 9 February 1955 in Santa Maria Gloriosa dei Frari, 'the greatest Gothic church in the city' (see map 5).[1]

Volpi's sarcophagus, easily located today, is criss-crossed with historical ironies, since it sits between a massive seventeenth-century monument to Doge Giovanni Pesaro and an Austrian bomb (here called a 'bomba germanica') that penetrated the ceiling of the church during the raid of 26–7 February 1918 but did not explode. Pesaro's tomb depicts four black 'Moorish' slave caryatids with bare feet and tattered trousers, struggling to hold aloft the praying doge. Black skeletons on either side of the lower part of the shrine clutch scrolls, listing his qualities and achievements. By contrast, Volpi's own memorial is modest in size but transmits messages through what is recorded and what is not. Volpi held very many posts during his lengthy career, but those mentioned on his sarcophagus are his title, Count of Misurata in Libya (duly passed on to his son), and his most prestigious position within the city as Primo Procuratore

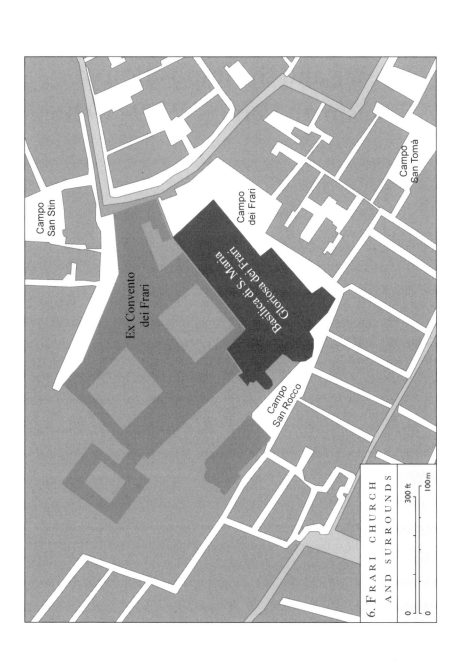

Campo
San Stin

Campo
San Tomà

Campo
dei Frari

Ex Convento
dei Frari

Basilica di S. Maria
Gloriosa dei Frari

Campo
San Rocco

6. FRARI CHURCH
AND SURROUNDS

300 ft

100 m

0

0

di San Marco. He thus is girded in death with imperial and local histories but not with a national one, and there is no reference to Fascism (or Marghera). Giovanni Volpi's mother, Nathalie El Kanoni, died only in December 1989, at which point she joined her husband in the tomb. Absent is Volpi's (patrician) first wife, Nerina Pisani (died November 1942), the mother of his two daughters, themselves important figures in Venice's history after 1945 but without salute at the Frari.

In pleading for greater recognition of his father, Giovanni Volpi did admit that Giuseppe Volpi had become a Fascist. But not, his son stressed, until he was forty-seven, and then he had anyway 'tranquillised the regime', which might otherwise have had a baleful impact on Venice. In spite of Mussolini, Volpi had advanced the city's happiness and prosperity on many fronts. It was totally unjust and unreasonable, his son urged, that his donning of a black shirt in the interwar period had thereafter blackened his historical fame.[2]

Yet, as is apparent at Volpi's tomb and at many other city sites, any visitor to contemporary Venice does not have to look far to find relics of the generation of Fascist dictatorship (and of an anti-Fascist opposition to it). Giuseppe Volpi

18 Volpi, by now Count of Misurata, in double-breasted suit and not black shirt – Venice's necessary magnate

is not as obscured in memory as his son has argued. A Fascist past lives in Venice alongside many others.

It can be conceded, nonetheless, that the sites of Fascist memory offer a complex rather than single insight into governance by a xenophobic, nationalising and aspiringly 'totalitarian' tyranny that would end its history as the 'ignoble second' of Nazi Germany. One location for such reflection is the 'Colonna Rostrata', a celebratory column topped with a Winged Victory holding aloft a laurel wreath, sedulously modelled on a pattern designed in classical Rome (see map 7). The Colonna stands in the Giardini, not far from the pavilions of the Biennale, which, in a process that began in 1907, belong to many countries and confirm the exhibition's global span and globalised nature. The column has a more circumscribed reach. A marble panel in German explains that it records the achievement of Archduke Ferdinand Maximilian, vice-admiral of the Habsburg fleet, who was victorious at the Battle of Lissa fought against the Italians in 1866, during that paradoxical war which resulted in the national annexation of Venice.

Why, then, is this foreign monument set in Venice and why is the column perched on a marble plinth equipped with a lunette displaying the triumphant Venetian lion? An iron plaque in Italian answers these questions: 'This rostral column, [originally] erected at Pola [Pula] by the Austrian navy to honour Archduke Maximilian, was carried to Venice by the Italian fleet, having avenged Lissa, as a testimony of victory. Today it is a symbolic gift from the sailors of Italy to the Queen of the Adriatic in remembrance of companions fallen for the redemption of our sea. 4 November 1918 – 4 November 1929 Anno VII [Fascist Year 7].'[3] A second, longer statement is transcribed from Thaon di Revel's speech of 22 March 1919, the day when the crestfallen ships of the Habsburg fleet sailed into Venice in solemn acknowledgement of their Empire's loss of the war. Such an admission had been greeted by applauding crowds in a festival that culminated at 9 p.m. with a massive fireworks display.[4]

In sum, the Colonna Rostrata stands for national victory in the First World War and for the Fascist regime's determination to translate the conflict's practical and spiritual history into the peacetime life of all Italians. On 4 November, 'Vittorio Veneto Day', 1929, at a festival that strove to appear as much national as Fascist, the regime's representatives and the city's worthies assembled in the Giardini to proclaim their unstinted patriotism.[5] Back towards the lagoon, there would soon be urban reconstruction, with the prolongation of the ample Riva degli Schiavoni from the end of the Via Garibaldi towards Sant'Elena. This pathway was formally opened in 1937 and named the Riva dell'Impero, following the proclamation of the Empire in May 1936 with Italy's bloody victory over Ethiopia. This Riva's propinquity added imperialism to the

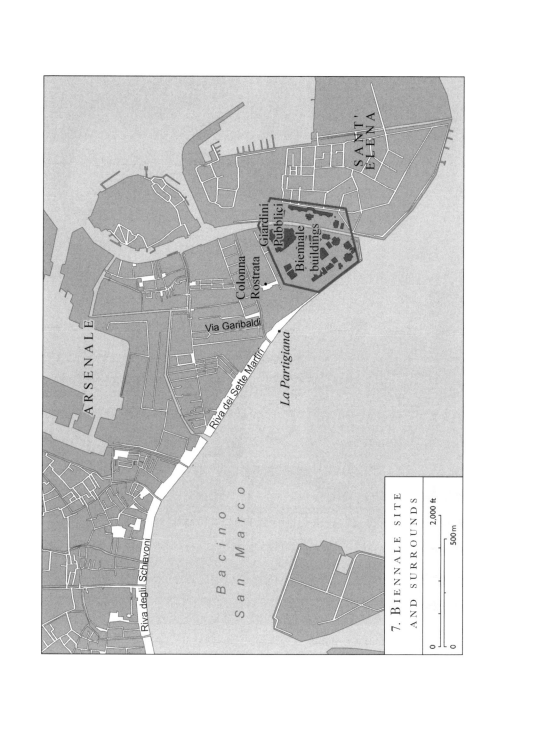

ARSENALE

Colonna
Rostrata

Via Garibaldi

Giardini
Pubblici

Biennale
buildings

SANT'
ELENA

Riva degli Schiavoni

Riva dei Sette Martiri

La Partigiana

Bacino
San Marco

7. BIENNALE SITE
AND SURROUNDS

0   2,000 ft

0   500 m

19 Colonna Rostrata, Giardini

nationalism expressed by the Colonna Rostrata. The amalgam did not last, however. After 1946, under the Republic, the Riva was renamed in honour of the 'sette martiri', who, as we shall see, were seven anti-Fascist 'martyrs', shot without due legal process by the Nazi-fascist authorities on 3 August 1944.

The Colonna Rostrata and its environs thus well reflect the expansionist ambitions of Mussolini's dictatorship and its unrepentant violence. But the Riva dei Sette Martiri and the higher profile of the Biennale pavilions than of the First World War memorial also suggest the greater credibility in that part of the city of an anti-Fascist comprehension of Venetians' experience of the regime.

More stylish and less contested in its preservation of echoes from Mussolini's regime is the Nicelli airport, located at the north-east of the Lido, near the church of San Nicolò (see map 4). Pioneer efforts at flying were common on the Lido, since, before 1915 and then during the war, Cagno, D'Annunzio and their comrades used land facing the channel between the lagoon and the Adriatic as a convenient runway. On 18 August 1926, in prime tourist season, the airstrip was passed from military to civilian ownership, with the first flight out ironically connecting Venice and Vienna. The aerodrome was now named after Giovanni Nicelli, an 'ace' in the First World War, born in the hills behind Piacenza rather than in Venice, and shot down by the Austrians in March 1918. Most of the airport's traffic was organised by the Società Anonima di Navigazione Aerea Transadriatica, among whose directors was Domenico Giuriati, of the leading Venetian Fascist family, a worthy who, in 1929, also joined the board of the Cassa di Risparmio, the key local bank.[6] The Transadriatica adopted the conspicuously Fascist name of Ala Littoria (The Lictorial Wing) in 1934. A year later, with times still good for Italy and its dictatorship, the Nicelli was equipped with a new airport lounge in the modish art deco style, rendered virile by the hanging of Futurist *aeropitture* (aeropaintings) there. By 1939 the airport counted an annual traffic of 4,000 planes and 23,000 passengers.[7]

For some decades after the war, the Nicelli airport mouldered, hindered by its associations with dictatorship. Come the new millennium, however, with its diminishing hostility towards the Fascist *ventennio* (twenty years) and Berlusconi's pronouncement that 'Mussolini never killed anyone',[8] the place was beautifully restored (between 2002 and 2008). It may lie off the city tourist beats, but the Aeroporto Nicelli is back in business. To be sure, it is used more for joy-flights by plane or helicopter than for regular aerial connection, and it scarcely competes with the main airport across the lagoon at Tessera, where a blandly modern terminal was inaugurated in 2002 (nine years later it welcomed eight and a half million passengers, making it Italy's fourth busiest airport).[9] But the Nicelli is not bland, and it is circled by the multiple histories of Fascism.

20 Aeroporto Nicelli, Lido

21 Interior of Aeroporto Nicelli with *aeropitture*

It is, after all, situated on the Lido, a locus more of leisure than of war, as well as a part of Venice where the twentieth century mattered and earlier eras did not. Certainly, by definition, the airport is 'modern', both generically and in its expression of the Fascist determination to modernise the city. As if in proof, in 1920, 1921 and 1927 the Schneider Airspeed trophy was disputed there by airmen from many countries; Italians won in 1920–1 and the British in 1927, when the Italian machines were painted red and the British blue, the scene reminding a guileless *Times* journalist of Canaletto.[10] In 1920 the speed achieved was 70 kilometres per hour;[11] by 1927 it was over 450.

The act of flying often seemed the quintessence of Fascist masculinity, a pilot being a devil-may-care individual propelled dauntlessly into the skies to challenge lesser mortals, himself and God. Mussolini personally led those Fascists who flew, emerging from a crash in March 1921 with only a twisted knee and a few scratches. Across Europe and beyond, other fascists or fascist sympathisers similarly took to the air, Goering, Mosley, Hinkler and Lindbergh among them. At the restored Nicelli, the *aeropitture* still evoke this radical, or radical-seeming, Fascism. As a style, 'aeropainting' began in 1929, launched in yet another Futurist manifesto, this one signed by Marinetti, his young, some-times domineering wife and the enduring Fascist Fortunato Depero (a promi-nent figure in the 1932 and 1934 Biennali, while *aeropitture* featured in the exhibitions of 1932 and 1938; on this last occasion, its adepts gleefully cele-brated Italian bombing prowess in Ethiopia and Spain).[12] *Aeropitture* proclaimed a 'revolution' through an artistic perspective that renounces any terrestrial base. Whether or not such an assertion should be given credence is a problem, since the Fascism of this artistic approach can scarcely be taken as read. During the interwar period, flying was a rich man's activity, scarcely affecting the lives of ordinary people. The Nicelli may reflect a 'hard', radical, modernising, Fascism, but it simultaneously hints that wealthy young men may not have been put out of kilter by the 'soft' version of 'totalitarianism' most often seen in Venice.

The first spread of Fascism into the city did nonetheless possess many harsh and violent features. Before the March on Rome, Venetians endured something of the social travails that accompanied the rise of the *fascisti* to power nation-ally, the socialists being, as in other places, the main victims. In the early months of peace, the socialists had taken the political initiative, Elia Musatti and Cesare Alessandri, each on the 'maximalist', extreme wing of their move-ment, and Eugenio Florian, a more cautious 'reformist', winning seats in the Chamber of Deputies in the elections of November 1919. For a time, strikes were frequent and widespread, be they of waiters, ferrymen, dockers, gondoliers, metalworkers, nurses, postmen, bank clerks or hairdressers. In a new-year editorial for 1920, *Il Gazzettino* expressed the bewilderment of the best people at such social dislocation at the hands of their inferiors, charging that, 'against any principle of justice or fairness', the post-war world was going 'blindly . . . to its doom', overwhelmed by 'anarchy, civil war and the destruction of any healthy civil association'.[13] Venice had become a city where, the paper lamented, so noble a figure as Foscari could be brazenly mugged at the station just after he had stepped down from his first-class compartment.[14] A few months later, *Il Gazzettino* added dramatically that socialist opposition to the war and the brazen summoning of soldiers to desert could never be forgiven or forgotten. This socialist 'collective crime' insulted the 'teaching of nature', the paper pronounced, since all men, animals and even vegetables loved the land that bore them.[15] The respectable classes were equally outraged when leftists formed a pro-Soviet Russia committee, seeking, according to *Il Gazzettino*, to force locals again to bow 'beneath a foreign yoke'.[16]

By contrast, the left was so jauntily sure of victory that a notice was published in the hostile columns of *La Gazzetta di Venezia* insultingly advertising a funeral ceremony in Piazza San Marco for what it implied to be the city, Italian and world bourgeoisie. Socialists boasted that the square was no longer a 'bourgeois stronghold' but had fallen to 'our unchallenged domination', reminding contemporaries that, whatever had been the unifying political role of the square under the Republic, it was now, had been and would long remain the prime urban site of class conflict and meaning.[17] As if in proof, one after-noon in the summer of 1920 a socialist 'invasion' of Piazza San Marco, at which demonstrators yelled 'Down with the bourgeoisie', forced the town band to stop its merry playing. Local Fascists then assumed the task of expelling these invaders, given that, as *Il Gazzettino* put it, 'the royal police shone by their absence'. Hurling chairs from Florian's and Quadri's to great effect, they drove their foes into the centre of the square, a push that was rendered more dramatic by two revolver shots and the throwing of a hand grenade. The explosion injured seventeen bystanders (and was blamed on the socialists). A squad of sailors then arrived and cleared the area. The following day, bourgeois Venetians were still thronging the site to see where class victory had been won.[18]

Battle was not over, however. Two months later, on 20 September, the anni-versary of the fall of papal Rome to Italian troops in 1870, an attempt by 'patriots' to demonstrate beside the Garibaldi monument in Castello failed to seduce local socialists through its implied anti-clericalism. Instead it resulted in another punch-up, at which workers proclaimed lasting socialist domina-tion of this part of the city.[19] That same day, according to a Fascist account, 'Reds' insulted uniformed officers in Piazza San Marco, while 'traitorously' evoking Caporetto, only to be slapped under citizen's arrest by outraged Fascists and handed over to the otherwise inactive police.[20] Nationalists and Fascists had swiftly reaffirmed full command over Piazza San Marco; as early as July 1920 the socialists' *Secolo Nuovo* lamented, 'The proletariat must not enter Piazza San Marco; it must stay sacred to the speculations of the hirelings of the bourgeoisie, of parasites of all sorts and of the exploiters of women.'[21] One part of the city, Venetians perforce accepted, was red; another black.

Throughout these tumults, the urban administration remained in anti-socialist hands. In 1919 Grimani finally vacated the mayor's office to be replaced by Davide Giordano, a surgeon at the local hospital (and Freemason) who had underlined his wartime credentials by divulging how doctors could identify self-inflicted lesions and so distinguish them from 'glorious wounds', while patriotically blaming the Germans for 'this horrible, insane and pitiless war'.[22] Giordano had arrived at the Ospedale Civile in 1894 and earned a repu-tation as a moderniser, while remaining a stern patriarch. Whenever he showed up at the hospital, a colleague later recalled, the person who first noticed his arrival rang an alarm three times to signify that any who worked there, 'be they porters, nurses, Sisters, junior doctors, and why not the sick', should at once spring to attention and remain alert until the great man had issued his orders. Despite being busy on many fronts, Giordano was said to have carried out 25,000 'major' operations throughout his career.[23] Nonetheless, the new mayor, a man of Jewish extraction and Waldensian faith (not born in Venice), aroused suspicion in the mind of Cardinal La Fontaine, who pregnantly remarked that Venice in the past had always been 'a city of Catholic tradition'.[24] Despite such priestly mutterings, Giordano's administration won backing from the Partito Popolare Italiano (PPI, Catholic Popular Party).[25]

The PPI constituted the first new mass party of the post-war era. Its national leader, the Sicilian priest Don Luigi Sturzo, visited Venice on 18 March 1919 and, in a meeting with La Fontaine, agreed that Catholics should launch a paper, to be entitled *L'Avanguardia*, implying that it would be at the vanguard of post-war modernity. In the November 1919 national elections, the PPI won 3,156 votes in the city (together with 3,200 for the liberals and 3,329 for the democrats) against a socialist tally of 9,883. (In the province, as became usual, the PPI did better, with 16,699 compared with 25,323 socialist voters.)[26] La Fontaine was not fully convinced by this new Catholic course, however, and he welcomed the efforts of Paganuzzi and other local conservatives from the old Opera dei Congressi to steer the party to the right; he always made plain his view that the PPI should not win too much freedom from hierarchical control.[27] When, in October 1921, with Fascism on the rise, the PPI held its national congress in Venice, La Fontaine sternly warned his priests against political activism, while joining Volpi in a campaign to stress the special history of local shipbuilders whose slogan was 'the Arsenale to Venetians', countermanding the socialists' cry of 'the Arsenale to the workers' of 1919.[28] A year later, after the installation of Mussolini as prime minister, the patriarch instructed Catholics to pay 'obedience and respect' to the new government 'for the good of the *patria*', while observing with clerical sagacity that 'Providence will do what is best for Italy'.[29] A happy patriot, he also accepted the title of 'Patriarch of the War'.[30] La Fontaine had already met Mussolini in June 1921, when the Duce temptingly implied that he was open to a resolution of the Roman Question that had dogged Church–state relations since the Risorgimento.[31] In the political warfare between Fascists and their socialist foes that, through 1920–2, seethed through the squares and *calli*, Venetian Catholics had quite a few reasons to be 'as neuter'.

Given their commotion during the war, it was predictable that nationalists would be highly visible in Venice after a troubled peace was restored, and would all but automatically take their place at the highest social level. The pre-war irredentist lawyer Giovanni Giuriati, who had heroically lost a hand in fighting at the front, led their cause, while also taking on the presidency of the elegant 'Yacht Club Veneziano'. Advised by D'Annunzio that the foreign-sounding name should be removed, he piloted through a change to the 'Compagnia della Vela di Venezia'.[32]

The children of the bourgeoisie were also alive with patriotism and a thirst to carry forward their elders' victory. In April 1919, local high school students followed their teachers in applauding patriotic speeches delivered at Palazzo Faccanon insisting that Venice 'return' to Dalmatia. A month earlier, D'Annunzio had bellowed from the loggia of the Doge's Palace his 'solemn reaffirmation of the Italic people's rights over all the lands of San Marco'.[33] Thirty-five Venetians joined the poet on 12–15 September 1919 in his armed 'expedition' of 'legionaries' from Venice to Ronchi near Trieste and on to Fiume, a town he seized in defiance of the government in Rome, then headed by the cautious economist Francesco Saverio Nitti. Venice remained an important reserve base for D'Annunzio's 'poetic dictatorship' in Fiume over the next fifteen months, with its mixture of radical and militant words, racist nationalism, cocaine and other comforts.[34] The city was rewarded in a fashion on 31 March 1920, when a legionary plane flew over Venice in imitation of D'Annunzio's wartime raid on Vienna and dropped manifestoes denouncing the 'Cagoia' (shit-bag) Nitti.[35]

Giuriati was a prime supporter of D'Annunzio and his expedition. Entering Fiume, he would later recall, he hoped 'to bid farewell forever to an Italy that was social-communist, parliamentary, Masonic and cowardly; the Italy of Caporetto'.[36] He quickly devoted himself to bringing welfare to the population, making sure that bakeries produced enough bread, while preaching the need for a 'Latin alliance' to fend off the global depredations of Germans, Anglo-Saxons and Slavs. No more than a 'faithful legionary', he assured his 'Comandante', D'Annunzio, in words that would prove easily adaptable to addressing a Fascist dictator, he would till the crack of doom march 'modestly but resolutely' behind him.[37]

Once at the poet's side, however, Giuriati discerned that, although a 'Great Man', D'Annunzio was a prey to superstition, blind to economics and finance, possessed of limited administrative skill, incapable of running a modern state, and a leader who did nothing to curb drug-use among his more 'amoral' supporters.[38] In January 1920 Giuriati moved to Paris to represent Fiume there and began a drift that would soon have him accept Mussolini rather than D'Annunzio as his Duce. In the May 1921 national elections, Giuriati lined up with the thirty-five Fascists under Mussolini who took seats in the Chamber of Deputies.

The de facto alliance within Venice of the Nationalist Association, the respectable classes and at least some Fascists could always be summoned at patriotic events, such as the granting of the Merit Cross for the city's war effort in June 1920, or, a month later, the erection of a monument to Battisti.[39] The term 'Fascist' was as yet fuzzy in meaning, with an announcement in January 1920 that local liberals had established a 'Fascio Giovanile' (Youth Fascio) for their movement, unconnected with the *fascio di combattimento* that owed allegiance to Mussolini.[40] On occasion, patriotic demonstration grew boisterous, as in September 1921, when a French military mission visiting Venice was hooted by a crowd composed of Fascists and Nationalists, prompting Camille Barrère, the long-term and notoriously exuberant French ambassador, to seize one young demonstrator and shake him, while the police stood passively by.[41]

Their boss, Agostino D'Adamo, the youthful and exceedingly chubby prefect in the city from April 1920 to October 1923,[42] did little to hide his own patriotic and anti-socialist preferences, happy to utilise D'Annunzio's term 'olocausto' to evoke the grandeur of the victorious war.[43] By September 1922 D'Adamo advised Rome that 'the state of mind of the [best] people is absolutely favourable to the Fascist movement'. Should he attempt any repression of their cause, he added, he would be 'firmly blocked by the popular response'. Within the city, he stated, there were now more than five thousand members, divided into eleven active squads, while the socialists faced 'full decline' and the Catholics had peaked. A few difficult elements had grabbed places in Fascist ranks, he acknowledged, but city businessmen and landowners in the province, individually and through their organisations, actively supported the movement. In this prefect's mind, at least, the Fascists were worthy of power in Venice.[44]

A *fascio di combattimento* had been founded in the city in spring 1919 at a meeting called in the offices of the conservative *La Gazzetta di Venezia*, the city's oldest newspaper. This *fascio* claimed to be the 'second-born' in the country after that founded in Milan by Mussolini on 23 March. In the months that followed, members inveighed against the wave of leftist strikes, while engaging in sporadic violence, such as the bombing of Musatti's house in prosperous Santa Maria del Giglio in November. Who might be the 'Leader' of the Fascist path to the future was by no means yet clear, however, the movement applauding D'Annunzio on 2 September 1920 as 'the spiritual Duce of Fascism'.[45]

In regard to this and other issues, Venetian Fascism was not identical with that surging across the rest of the country in 1920–1. Mainstream Fascism was being pushed to the right through the border conflicts between Italians and 'Slavs' in Trieste and the repression of an organised 'socialist' peasantry in the hinterlands of Florence or Bologna. In Venice, the movement was given an idiosyncratic cast by the leadership until the middle of 1922 of the nationalist lawyer Pietro Marsich, a man who underscored the movement's radical purpose socially, and who was willing for it to disembarrass itself of Mussolini.[46] Marsich long shared the local fascination with D'Annunzio, being appalled by the Treaty of Rapallo negotiated with Yugoslavia, the diplomatic prelude to D'Annunzio's expulsion from Fiume in what he and his fans melodramatically dubbed 'the Christmas of blood' of 1920. When the news reached Venice with (false) rumours that D'Annunzio had perished, his supporters crowded into Piazza San Marco 'mute and grave' and forced the Communal flag to fly at half-mast.[47]

Marsich's line in this matter lost him funding from Volpi, who favoured the deal with the Yugoslavs and who joined the Fascists only in July 1923, when they were safely in office, although his ticket was courteously backdated to 26 January 1922.[48] In the summer of 1921, Marsich, not a Fascist member of parliament, led purist opposition within the movement nationally opposing Mussolini's stratagem of signing a 'pact of pacification' with the socialists. Marsich pronounced that such a deal would surrender Fascism to 'the banking plutocracy and the liberal and social democrat state', proof, he remarked, of the cowardice of the Venetian bourgeoisie.[49] 'We are not disposed to sacrifice Fascism to Mussolini,' he added impertinently, nor, he implied, to Volpi, nor even to Giuriati.[50]

Such criticism drove Mussolini to resign as the Fascists' leader, although within weeks he was reinstated to that office as the movement converted itself into a full-fledged party, the PNF, pledged to greater discipline than in the past. With Marsich and his faction now giving ground, Mussolini contended virtuously that his Venetian rival stood for a 'Fascism of the lagoon' that had renounced the nation.[51] In June 1922 Marsich's paper, *Italia Nuova*, was forced into closure, making a final complaint that D'Annunzio was the lost leader, a charge that prompted Giuriati publicly to express his loyalty and that of proper Fascists to Mussolini.[52] Three months earlier, Marsich had left the party. He did not recover his position after the March on Rome and died young in 1928. His legacy in Fascist ranks, however, was never fully rooted out, especially among those who resented the (often competing) powers of Volpi and Giuriati and the identification of much of Venetian Fascism with the respectable classes.[53]

Before October 1922 matters were further complicated by the hubbub of a group who loudly designated themselves the Cavalieri della Morte (Knights of Death), under Gino Covre, a returned soldier from Friuli, who had been expelled from the national movement for 'moral unworthiness'.[54] It was Covre's squad who, in November 1921, had sacked the city branch of the Partito Comunista d'Italia (PCI, Italian Communist Party), which had broken from the socialists in January.[55] Six months later, the prefect D'Adamo moved to suppress the Cavalieri, announcing that they were bad Fascists who should not be confused with the good. Despite their talk of patriotism, he reported, they had acted like hooligans towards their political opponents and any who stood in their way, breaking into houses and gaols, filching property and insulting public authorities and the army.[56] D'Adamo failed to add that eight deaths had already resulted from thirty politically inspired brawls that had disfigured the *calli* during the first half of 1921. Despite the advance of the rightist groups, the left clung to its redoubts in the Via Garibaldi, Cannaregio and Campo Santa Margherita, ensuring the city was not fully subdued to the Fascist cause until after the March on Rome.[57]

The day of this Fascist half-coup in Rome passed peacefully in Venice under Giuriati's weather eye, although by evening packs of young men were tramping from one square to the next, singing raucous Fascist and patriotic songs, while at Mestre the undefended socialist Casa del Popolo (meeting place) was stormed by armed squadrists.[58] In the historic centre, theatres and cafés remained open as usual, the only incident occurring when a Frenchman was slapped after he failed to rise to his feet when the Quadri band played the 'Leggenda del Piave', a song exulting in Italian resistance after Caporetto. He was released when he explained diplomatically that he had not recognised the music but would of course have saluted it had he done so.[59] Iginio Maria Magrini, a Venetian airman and lawyer, operating as 'Consul of the San Marco Legion' on the mainland at Giuriati's behest, issued a public declaration of victory: 'The long struggle for liberation and the Risorgimento of our country is now over.'[60] On 30 October the city rang with more general applause for the new government (and for Giuriati's promotion within it to Minister of the Freed Territories; he soon assured the Comune that, in Rome, he would stand up for Venice's interests, which he was sure would not conflict with Italy's).[61] It did so notably at Piazza San Marco, where the municipal band did not forget to play the PNF anthem, 'Giovinezza' (Youth). Nationalists, liberals, sportsmen and members of the Pro Dalmazia association joined Fascists in celebration. The local naval commander expressed his pleasure at Fascist 'moderation in the Italian style' and looked forward to an Italy that could 'confront its destiny'.[62]

The new coalition government that Mussolini headed in Rome, in part a political deal with the monarchy, the army leadership, the Vatican and the rest of the national establishment, ensured the utter defeat of the socialists in Venice as well as a paradoxical suppression of the radical aspects of local Fascism. The young activist Girolamo Li Causi had already been advised by D'Adamo to pack up and leave, a departure further encouraged when he was beaten up by the Cavalieri della Morte near San Cassiano in September 1921.[63] Anita Mezzalira, the organiser of socialist women at the tobacco factory, also endured Fascist assaults. In February 1923 she was arrested and ordered brusquely to end her employment and her politicking; she remained under surveillance until Fascism fell.[64] From the last months of 1925 the use of the Roman salute became compulsory, although, on occasion, the tobacco workers may have deployed it mutinously. Ever the genial middleman, in October 1928 Volpi made an official tour of the workplace, where the Dopolavoro, or Fascist leisure organisation, now included a library, meeting hall, bar, theatre (seating 250 and decorated with shields of the Savoy dynasty) and changing room. Volpi spoke ingratiatingly of how his early ownership of the tobacco monopoly in Montenegro made him 'a tobacco worker, too', and alleged that the factory was the most beautiful in the country. He ended his speech in Venetian.[65]

The tares in its rule hidden at such moments, Venetian Fascism for the most part softened its deeper, more 'totalitarian' and populist purpose. Some initial compromises had been evident in June 1923, when Mussolini arrived in the city wearing a top hat and butterfly collar to be saluted in the usual Venetian manner by being borne ceremoniously down the Grand Canal. Naturally enough, he did not fail to make an endorsing visit to Marghera.[66] Rotund prefect D'Adamo kept the menus of the two gala dinners held in the city for the new prime minister, the first of which ran judiciously from caviar through chicken Forlì-style (Mussolini's father had run a hostelry there) to 'crema nazi-onale' and 'frutta d'Italia'. The other menu, more equivocally, was offered in Venetian in honour of 'So Eçelenza . . . presidente del Consegio dei Ministri'.[67] This feast took place at a restaurant next to the Fenice (owned by Foscari),[68] where Mussolini, lulled by his Venetian hosts into being little more than another tourist, was serenaded by a staging of Venetian composer Ermanno Wolf-Ferrari's pre-war comic opera with an Italianised title, *I quattro rusteghi* (based on Goldoni's play *I quatro rusteghi*).

22 Mussolini, the uniformed Giordano and a hefty prefect, June 1923

Where, after all, did Volpi and the comfortable classes stand in the new system, with its crowing about 'revolution'? Equally, what did Fascism mean for the tourist industry, which had fluttered back to life at the Biennale of 1920 (when Papadopoli and Jesurum headed a civic committee aiming to revive spectacles of all kinds and to do so, or so they said, across the class barrier) and 1922, the art exhibition visited by Victor Emmanuel III that May (when he returned in April 1924 for the next Biennale, *Il Gazzettino* reported waves of popular enthusiasm for 'the Head of the race and the country')?[69] In 1922 the king had more than one purpose, since he also presided over the opening of the new Victor Emmanuel III canal that had been dug to facilitate shipping to the Marghera site, which he toured with studied respect.

Volpi was, after all, more and more evidently the 'big man' in the city. His span of interests was ample, as reflected in his being the CEO or vice-president of twenty different companies, while serving on the board of a further forty-six.[70] His field of action was scarcely confined to Venice, moreover, since he had also served on the Italian delegation to Versailles in 1919. Soon he added his name to the Consiglio Supremo Economico, helping to negotiate the Treaty of Rapallo and dish D'Annunzio at Fiume. He was elevated to the Senate. In July 1921 he accepted office as governor of Tripolitania, a post that would win him that euphonious title of Count of Misurata. He nonetheless found time regularly to return to Venice, where, at least while D'Adamo remained prefect, he could rely on a Lucullan dinner in his honour.[71] So capable and ruthless was Volpi that, even though he had been appointed by Minister of Colonies Giovanni Amendola, an anti-Fascist destined to die in exile in 1926 after a vicious beating the year before, he was kept in office by Mussolini and actively pursued the 'reconquest' of Tripolitania. Under his aegis, in February 1924 Italian forces reoccupied Gadames, deep in the interior (a success well timed to coincide with a visit to Tripoli by the once Nationalist minister Federzoni), and Volpi personally sponsored the career of the then Colonel Rodolfo Graziani, destined by the end of the decade to impose a 'Roman', Fascist or genocidal peace on the whole colony of Libya.[72] The first 'concentration camps' and 'rastrellamenti' (forcible round-ups) in Tripolitania date to October 1923.[73]

In 1925 Volpi was replaced at Tripoli, only to be promoted by Mussolini, now a dictator aspiring to build a 'totalitarian state' rather than merely prime minister of a coalition, to become Minister of Finance. Volpi held this office for the next three years, a crucial period for the regime in its securing of American loans and its adoption of the deflationary 'quota novanta' policy of a strong lira. In this role, Volpi was punctilious in praising his leader (even if he may have blanched privately at the Duce's announcement that his intuition was infallible, obviating the need for any hard study of fiscal matters).[74] In his official writings, Volpi took care to endorse Fascism's pretentions to offer Italians a civic religion, asserting loftily that the regime bore 'the spirit of the war' into an armed peace, almost as though he himself had fought in it.[75] Operating in many fields with aplomb, Volpi assisted fifty-four Catholic banks in the Veneto to survive and prosper, a solicitude for the Church's interests that may have smoothed progress towards the Lateran Pacts.[76] His immense political skills were recognised on his ministerial retirement, when he received flattering farewells from his 'Presidente' (as he still in traditional manner addressed the Duce), from J. P. Morgan and even from E. M. Gray, who acknowledged politely that his past 'rancour' towards Volpi had turned to 'love', allowing him to offer a comradely if not ideological 'handshake'.[77]

While busy with national duties, Volpi did not overlook the local. In 1928 he took pains to instruct his lieutenant Achille Gaggia to ensure that his return to the city be hailed as a triumph by Gino Damerini, the adaptable editor of *La Gazzetta*,[78] destined to be eulogised on his death in 1967 by the city's best people but also persona grata to Fascist officialdom.[79] Moreover, in 1924 and 1926 Volpi twice restructured credit arrangements at Marghera, each time to his own advantage. According to a critical historian, he succeeded in doing business at the new port, 'be it industrial or commercial, entirely at the expense of the state.'[80] Volpi's portrayal of his purpose was rather different, with an emphasis that Marghera had been honed into a 'new city of work', destined to teach Venetians the meaning of modernity.[81]

In practice, however, there was a downside. Even if, by 1939, 18,000 were employed at Marghera in the pay of ninety-one different, though often linked, firms (15 per cent of Venice's active workforce), and 80 per cent of Italy's aluminium production was concentrated there together with other major segments of industries preparing for war, most workers were peasants from the hinterland rather than Venetians. Their deep ties to the land ensured that they constituted a quiet workforce, their docility enhanced by the high turnover in employment, despite the resultant hindering of their acquisition of modern skills. The claim of the early 1920s that housing around the factories would create an elegant modern 'garden city' of 30,000 inhabitants was anything but fulfilled, only 5,000 in fact living there, many in by no means ideal conditions.[82] Of these, just over 400 had been born in Venice.[83] There were thus many reasons why contact between Venice and the port was 'weak'; most Venetians were reported as regarding Marghera as a 'foreign' settlement.[84]

At home, Volpi may have been accustomed to presenting himself as the model of a Fascist rather than a capitalist businessman, happy to instruct English-language readers in 1937 that the dictatorship's corporate system was now fully functional.[85] But an extensive tour of the USA in 1926 during his

23 Marghera as Fascist garden city

period as minister allowed him to appear abroad as a proponent in Italy of something akin to liberal capitalism. The ideological detail, a historian might conclude, scarcely mattered so long as the profits rolled in.

Certainly Volpi's interest in and seeming admiration for the United States slotted readily into Venice's revived tourist purpose after the war and into its renewed competition with Paris as the key venue for global leisure. Throughout the roaring twenties the city was enlivened by many lavish high society parties, featuring such rackety celebrities as Elsa Maxwell, Diana Manners (later Cooper), John Barrymore, Irving Berlin, Coco Chanel, Cecil Beaton, Serge Diaghilev, George Gershwin, Cole Porter, Noel Coward, Winston and Clementine Churchill, Oswald Mosley and assorted royals, Italian and foreign, men and women whose experimentation with sex, drugs (newspapers often mentioned cocaine arrests until the regime's puritanism ended such reporting) and modern dance was hard to reconcile with spartan Fascism. In the summer of 1926, for example, Cole Porter, who had rented Ca' Rezzonico on the Grand Canal for that season and the next, paid for a 'negro orchestra' to tour the canals every night on a floating *galleggiante*, playing jazz to any who cared to listen.[86] Two years later, however, the American went too far, and was politely asked to leave after the police, at least according to Antonio Foscari, Piero's grandson, raided his palace to find 'a "river" of cocaine and Cole, in the company of a dozen or more young Venetians, dressed – when they were – in Linda's gowns [Linda was Porter's wife], while she was away in Paris.'[87]

For the most part, Volpi nonetheless viewed such behaviour benignly, and his elder daughter was noticed one summer at the Excelsior dancing the black bottom with the rest of the gilded set.[88] There, a much vaunted 'Saturnalia' in August 1924 involved more risqué dancing, but apparently went off well,[89] although one unkind English visitor thought the Adriatic reeked with the tang of 'hot saliva, cigar ends floating into one's mouth', made even worse by the habitual 'shoals of jelly fish'.[90] Cecil Beaton recalled everyone being seductively dressed in pyjamas, even if he added snidely that the 'vulgarity' of the Excelsior made him think himself in 'a Hippodrome revue – meretricious but rather fun'.[91] Well into Fascist rule, 'the insinuating rhythms of jazz' featured at a masked Lido festival, although its profits were worthily passed on to the Balilla.[92] The Biennali continued in regular succession, Volpi assisting the king and, perhaps less happily, Giuriati in the official opening ceremony of the 15th exhibition in April 1926, an event that earned a full description in the London *Times*.[93]

According to Noel Coward's biographer, holidays on the Lido featured 'indiscriminate sexual experimentation, heavy drinking was commonplace, and hashish, opium and cocaine were tried by most' of the high society set.[94] Certainly plenty of rich gays took their leisure there. Fascism officially disapproved of homosexuality, seen as bad for the reproduction of the race. In the course of the dictatorship, however, only two men in Venice were punished with 'confino' (forced residence) for 'unnatural sex', and then belatedly in 1937; 38 out of a national tally of 298 were found guilty of 'pederasty', but no celebrity was among them.[95]

In its tourist garb, it was clear, Venice remained a place where many different people danced to their own tunes, being readily permitted to ignore the harsher aspects of Fascist rule. Accommodation could take idiosyncratic forms, as appeared in the case of one ephemeral sightseer from the USA who hit the local headlines. On 13 October 1924 Chief 'Wite [sic] Elk Tewanna Rey' entered Venice on what *Il Gazzettino* explained was a world tour – the 'redskin prince', the paper avowed, was the son of a tribal chief but at one and the same time the cousin of Empress Zita of Austria and grandson of Maria Teresa di Borbone.[96] As he approached the portals of the Hotel Danieli, Chief White Elk was cheered by those Fascists who had congregated there. Perhaps they admired his garb – a 'white antelope skin, fringed along the seams', 'hemmed with ermine' and 'blazing with jewels', and a great black cloak that he slung over his shoulder, these impressive garments being completed with a pair of sandals and a large ebony stick topped by a 'hippopotamus [sic] horn', which he clutched in his hand.

His dress might appear outlandish but Chief White Elk soon made himself at home. He could understand some Italian and was charmed by the warmth of the Fascist welcome. Indeed, rather than reposing at his luxurious hotel, he bravely marched off with those Fascists who had greeted him. Together they crossed Piazza San Marco 'in a small band and to the sound of drums'. On reaching party headquarters in the city, Chief White Elk offered a generous donation to the Fascist cause and was rewarded with the gift of a Fascist banner, which he saluted in the Roman manner and then solemnly kissed. Talking 'quietly', 'in a mixture of English, French and Italian', he commenced an oration praising Mussolini and Fascism, and complaining about the manifold sins of journalists (*Il Gazzettino* supposed, self-righteously, that he must have had troubles with undisciplined rags in the USA). Whatever the case, his enumeration of these charges caused the Chief to wave his ebony stick threateningly and to 'show off the numerous gold teeth that glittered in his mouth'.

His dramatic entrance to Venice over, Chief White Elk retreated to the Danieli for a siesta, dropping his wallet on the way. It was returned by an honest citizen whom the chief rewarded with 1,000 lire. Later in the afternoon, despite running a high fever, he was again out and about in the city. His Fascist friends escorted him to a gondola and rowed the party up the Grand Canal. There was a brief alarum when the vessel bumped into a ferry and capsized. Onlookers feared that drownings must ensue, but, to the reported consternation and then presumed relief of the vessel's passengers, Chief White Elk and his local acquaintances scrambled up the ferry's side as though they were boarding it but without any piratical intent. This adventure over, someone found the Chief a red fez to wear and a new gondola to sit in, and he was escorted to the Rialto. After another distribution of money, this time 300 lire for the children of Venice, the happy pilgrim returned to his hotel at sunset, declaring in heartfelt cliché, 'Venice exceeds all dreams.' One further ceremony remained. In the evening the Chief took his seat in a box at the Teatro Malibran to watch an operetta, *Mille luci*, but not before acknowledging standing applause both from the audience and from the cast. The following morning he left for Trieste.[97]

This Venetian Fascist meeting with native America was to prove more fleeting than that with other forms of show-biz. Another, more worthy outsider to visit the city, however, was the Indian scholar Rabindranath Tagore, who, in 1925, spoke at the Ateneo Veneto 'on Venice'. He evoked Marco Polo and the city's long history in order to urge, in un-Fascist phrases, 'if we cannot cultivate a respect for all humanity, if we are obsessed with the spirit of our own separateness, which makes us contemptuous of that to which we are not accustomed, then we have no right to travel across our own boundaries.'[98] Chief White Elk one day, Tagore the next, jazz musicians most nights, gays and straights, 'beautiful people' – the tourist whirl, it was plain, had not ended with the *belle époque* and scarcely bowed to the more rigid rules of totalitarian dictatorship.

Nonetheless, by the mid 1920s Fascism was doing something to implement its avowed revolutionary purpose in Venice. The city's squares could now fill with uniforms and parades, if sometimes in ragged formation, *The Times* vividly describing one such event in Campo Santo Stefano in April 1927: 'Here are seen boy Fascists in black shirts and bright blue ties, of every age from four upwards, with bands and banners and (curiously enough in Venice) bicycles; hither come the processions of some 20 different trades, each with its flag, the gondoliers labelled as the "Company of Internal Navigation", the Glass-Makers, the Furniture-Makers and so on. They are in civilian costumes, save for an occasional black tie, but they are marshalled into companies by officials glorious in full uniform.' There were girl Fascists, too, the journalist noted patronisingly, and 'the Fascist song is continually played, sometimes in slightly divergent forms'.[99]

Yet, in many instances, the regime's thrust could be read more than one way. Davide Giordano was ousted from his mayor's office, first by a Commissario Straordinario, Bruno Fornaciari, from August 1924 to September 1926, and then by the nationalist historian Count Pietro Orsi, who was awarded the Fascist title of *podestà* in December 1926, lasting until June 1929. He was followed by a further interregnum, until Mario Alverà, another patrician and one with solid ties to Volpi and Cardinal Patriarch La Fontaine, took office from July 1930 to September 1938. *Podestà* was a Fascist office; its incumbent was appointed, not elected. Yet the tenures of Orsi and Alverà hinted that, for the best people, Fascism's rule in Venice was largely changing things so that they could remain the same. After all, as one local lady put it primly, Alverà was 'a gentleman of good breeding, in love with his city'.[100]

Perhaps Giorgio Suppiej, the PNF secretary or *federale*, the party chief in Venice and its province 1924–5 and 1928–35, could impose a more strenuous line. He had served as a lieutenant on the Alpine front and joined the movement in its early days. Yet he was another lawyer, born in Vicenza province on the mainland, and related by marriage to Gianpietro Talamini, the founder of *Il Gazzettino*.[101] He was also a loyalish client of Giuriati, although he blamed him for his being dropped in 1925, allegedly because he was overzealous in seeking that the PNF in the city remain independent of those who had flourished there before 1922.[102] He may have been equally dismayed when, at around the same time, Giuriati's adopted son, also called Giovanni, had with a whiff of nepotism been accorded the task of editing a well-illustrated propaganda magazine on local Fascism, *Le Tre Venezie*. No doubt Giovanni Giuriati junior and Suppiej belonged to a faction that did not automatically follow the lead of Volpi.[103] But their claims to revolutionary purism had limits.

In terms of factional dispute, it was Giovanni Giuriati, Minister of Public Works between 1925 and 1929, a man with rich funds at his disposal, who made the first move. On 3 March 1928 he summoned Vittorio Cini, Volpi's most loyal lieutenant, to his presence. Cini began their discussion with praise of Marghera and of Volpi. Giuriati responded in vexed tone, however. He was 'neither a socialist nor the son of a socialist' and he admitted the need for 'financial groups to prosper and gain'. But economic achievement was not all that life, especially Fascist life, was about. Capitalists had 'social duties, too'. Irritation, he stated, had spread across Venice at the behaviour of the 'Volpi group'. It was especially notable among old Fascists, who charged that Volpi was insensible to the wretched conditions of ordinary Venetians, a matter underlined recently by the lavish celebration of the marriage of Volpi's elder daughter, Marina, into the upper echelons of the aristocracy. It was equally deplorable that Damerini, Volpi's tame journalist, had declared that a new road bridge was more important to Venice than the urgent improvement of the hospital. It was just not good enough, Giuriati concluded, that 'we have maximum trade at the port when we have maximum poverty in the city'.[104]

In launching this attack on Volpi's Fascist devotion, Giuriati was scarcely being original. At around the same time, Luigi Federzoni, himself a convert to

Mussolini's regime from the ANI and never loved by the Duce, remarked maliciously on the Venetian's endless 'rounding up of support inside and outside the party'. 'Someone has defined him as the Nitti of Fascism. He is brilliant, witty, plausible, business-like, lacking convictions and serious ideals, just like Nitti.'[105] More furtive complaints, assiduously conserved by Mussolini's private office, alleged Volpi was making millions from shady stock market deals in Italy and elsewhere, using the profits to place 'devoted and faithful' followers in key commercial positions.[106]

Volpi knew that he had garnered as many enemies as friends, but, for the most part, geniality was his best policy. When criticism had a Venetian base, however, he needed to react, and the day after that on which Cini had been told of his shortcomings, Volpi met Giuriati. In his emollient way, Volpi, although underlining the tremendous value to the nation of Marghera and all being done there, obligingly agreed that he and his partners should become more active in 'Venetian social life'. At the same time he adroitly had Giuriati admit that improved communications between Marghera and the historic centre would be all to the good. By the end of their discussion, the two men had happily wandered into imagining a future in which a casino could be profitably opened in Venice, Volpi remarking that he had recently toured the French Riviera to find gambling profitably occurring in every town. There was no serious investigation whether such a venture would alleviate popular poverty in the city, and Giuriati accepted that all such local issues should first be passed to Suppiej and Fascist officialdom.[107] In the interim, Giuriati did not forget to reinforce his own position as a Fascist by sending a grovelling letter to Mussolini, informing him of Giovanni Giuriati junior's impending marriage. It would be too much to expect the Duce to attend, Giuriati noted politely, but could he send a photo so that 'the image of the Tutelary Deity can inspire and protect the exquisitely Fascist family that they intend to found'?[108]

Aware of such personal conflicts and instances of back-sliding that were threading Fascism in many parts of Italy, Mussolini summoned Suppiej and other *federali* to Rome in January 1930, commanding full reports on the standing of the regime in their parts of the country. First came statistics, Suppiej stating that forty-six branches were at work in his province (with thirty-eight 'fasci femminili', or women's groups), embracing more than 11,000 people.[109] He reported that 22,157 had enrolled in the Dopolavoro clubs and 3,256 in the paramilitary Milizia Volontaria per la Sicurezza Nazionale (Voluntary Militia for National Security). The various scouting organisations were also well attended, 11,650 boys parading in the Balilla (covering the ages eight to fourteen) and 4,412 in the Avanguardisti (fourteen to eighteen), while the girls could count 7,708 Piccole Italiane and 2,592 Giovani Italiane. The Fascist university group, GUF (Gruppo Universitario Fascista), had so far won a more modest 515 ticket-holders.[110] In regard to other issues, Church–state relations were good; a year earlier Mussolini and Pope Pius XI had signed the Lateran Pacts. In Venice, the situation was outstanding, Suppiej commented proudly, since the patriarch 'is really with us and helps us always'.[111] The local financial situation was reasonable, he added, although business flourished mostly at Marghera, where, however, peasants rather than Venetians constituted the main workforce. Given the collapse of Wall Street, the tourist industry was not as florid as in the past, employing 4,500 in summer and 2,000 in winter. The CIGA hotels on the Lido were making only modest returns and any benefit to the city was 'indirect and of little importance'.[112]

At this point, Mussolini interjected that Fascism must concentrate on the land and those who lived there. 'In a city, everyone just looks after himself and his interests etc. and produces nothing,' he remarked sententiously. In response, Suppiej echoed his master's voice, fearing that Venice possessed too many people who 'adored' it, an attitude that stimulated harmful 'apathy' towards such modernisation plans as the 'Littorio' road bridge, designed to connect Mestre with what would be named Piazzale Roma, which was about to be built. Alert to hints of possible opposition, Mussolini urged its rout, arguing loutishly that there were Byzantine arches all over the place and there was no need to take such aesthetic matters seriously. Artists, women and the English had besieged him with complaints about the alteration that the bridge would bring to the Venice cityscape. But, as befitted a Duce, he stated boldly, he enjoyed ignoring them.[113]

After this moment of self-satisfaction derived from the expression of plain, blunt, Fascist thoughts, the two turned back to the state of the party. There, Suppiej confessed, those of Liberal background still held every conceivable post. Giuriati, Volpi and Magrini, now a deputy in the Fascist parliament[114] but one who was thought to have been a Freemason,[115] he observed, wrangled constantly. Each wanted to be city boss. Giuriati stood for 'disinterested purity and Fascist faith' but was not the best of organisers, Suppiej conceded. Volpi, by contrast, had earned his party ticket at the Ministry of Finance and was undoubtedly 'a financial power of the first order', Suppiej reflected, choosing his words with evident malice (and presumed impotence).[116]

Yet whatever might have been the doubts that lurked in Fascist party minds about Volpi's ideological commitment, his was the authority that, into the thirties, would prove the greater in Venice, while Giuriati's slipped away, despite what now seemed a chance for total victory. Not long after his discussion with Suppiej, Mussolini, ignoring the *federale*'s advice about organisational inadequacy, appointed Giuriati secretary of the PNF. He was to govern the party

between October 1930 and December 1931 and endeavoured to make it sterner
in theory and practice, earning the ire of Patriarch La Fontaine, for example, by
campaigning rudely against surviving Catholic scouting organisations.[117] It
was a period of major shift in PNF history, since the Venetian attempted a
purge of corrupt and unbelieving elements, in what he asserted was a totalitarian manner, expelling 120,000 members.[118] He demanded that, in future,
membership be granted only after 'the most severe and conscientious' review
of an applicant's background.[119] In particular, he urged, there must be a meticulous inspection of the dating of party entry, a policy that would have revealed
Volpi's own belated accession to Fascist ranks. He also took in scuttlebutt about
his old rival from the Cavalieri della Morte, Gino Covre, filing the information
that Covre was renting a flat on the Lido with his lover, while his legitimate
wife 'found herself in Rome with two children at her charge, apparently living
as the concubine of a pensioned-off colonel'.[120]

Soon, however, Giuriati was dropped by a cynical Duce,[121] who chided him
that moral reform was impossible (and did not counter rumours from Giuriati's
successor, Achille Starace, that the man was a pederast).[122] Ironically, as far as
Venice was concerned, Giuriati's mission in Rome freed Volpi to entrench his
own urban authority and that of his wealthy and not always ideologically
driven friends. Not for nothing was Volpi rather than Giuriati installed by 1930
as the president of the local yacht club. In the following decade, his schooner,
euphoniously if predictably named the *Misurata*, became celebrated for its
cruises in the lagoon and beyond, an invitation to board it being eagerly sought
by all in high society.[123]

In any case, perhaps Giuriati should have had targets further down the
social order in Venice if he envisaged a city humming with revolutionary dynamism. In 1928, for example, a police investigation of the functioning of Fascist
unions in the city uncovered blatant corruption. The local leader, protected by
his 'intimate friendship' with senior Fascist unionist Edmondo Rossoni, was
said to 'frequent the most aristocratic or, better, plushest venues . . . often in the
company of party girls and spending a great deal on champagne. He wears
evening dress and the most elegant clothes', despite being so heavily in debt that
restaurant owners preferred him not to enter their portals. His behaviour, the
report ran sternly on, ensured that, 'in Venice, among the worker mass, there is
no sympathy for the [Fascist] union', a sad situation blighting Fascist appeal
among the tobacco, textile and heavy industrial workers. Any who had joined
the Fascist union had done so 'as a result of pressure and not conviction'.[124]

Meanwhile, the ability of the best people in Venice to adapt to the regime
while leaving their own interests and lifestyles intact was evident in urban
welfare practice and the role of women within it. In January 1924 Giuriati had

decorously blessed the standard of the local *fascio femminile*, remarking in paternalist vein that he was not an unthinking opponent of female suffrage yet knew women had separate social and party roles from men. Since 'they inspired the best human actions and the most worthy social phenomena', charity was and should be their first nature.[125] And despite the occasional anathema from the Church at even minimal change in the gender order – in May 1924 La Fontaine issued a pastoral letter urging the retention of 'severe dress' for women and berating the fashion industry as 'lying and silly'[126] – Venetian Fascism did foster (and so, by implication, politicise) female charitable work. Its leader was Maria Pezzè Pascolato.

She had been born in 1869 in a palace on the Grand Canal into a distinguished bourgeois and politically active family. Her father was a member of parliament and her brother was editor of the staunchly rightist *La Gazzetta di Venezia* until his early death in 1914. Pezzè Pascolato married a doctor and followed him to a practice in Tuscany, only to return, alone and childless, to her family in 1896, formally to look after her widowed father.[127] Thereafter she made a mark in the city in many fields, translating such authors as Carlyle[128] and Ruskin, publishing poetry and children's literature, and preaching that youthful learning came best when kids had fun.[129] From 1897 she acted as an inspector of schools, while struggling to improve local educational standards. She was also busily charitable, devoting herself notably to the cure of such endemic childhood diseases in the city as rickets and such adult woes as alcoholism.[130] No feminist, she agreed that high politics was men's business, while women must focus first and foremost on their domestic duties.

Despite such modesty, she became more open in her political stance after her brother's death, quickly opting for interventionism in the war after the July crisis, and, in 1916, editing a work entitled *Piccole storie e grandi ragioni della nostra guerra*, directed at explaining the military effort to the young.[131] She also joined a number of civilian committees backing the military. After 1918, Fradeletto, another who had arrayed himself behind the national cause,[132] elevated her first to the Ateneo Veneto and then to a teaching position as *assistente* at the local university, Università Ca' Foscari di Venezia, rare honours for a woman. In such roles, she gave advice on children's literature to the heir to the throne, Umberto, and his Belgian wife Maria José, and was allegedly invited into the Fascist movement by Mussolini himself.[133] In eventual repayment she would tell the Duce, with local pride, that he was 'another Manin', a dictator whose 'purity, self-abnegation and good judgement' stirred all Venetians.[134]

Donning her black blouse with aplomb, she pressed on with good works, finding room in Venice for a children's library and accepting leadership of the Fascist organisation for the better health of women and girls, ONMI

(Opera Nazionale Maternità e Infanzia), from its foundation in 1925. Writing in the staccato paragraphs and Caesarian third person favoured by her Duce, she urged female Fascists, for all their gender weaknesses, into action. The 'new woman', she vowed, would not 'use foreign perfume or Americanise herself, she did not care about politics or tally votes and had nothing to do with psychoanalysis'.[135] But she did care for the people. At times, Pezzè Pascolato pilloried Fascist patriarchalism, as she did under party secretary Augusto Turati (1926–30), though she got on well with his successor Giuriati.[136] Her death on 26 February 1933 prompted the suspension of Carnival, or what Fascism had left of it (as early as 1924 officials had deprecated the idea that people could traverse the city masked),[137] and induced widespread mourning among the elite, the *fascio femminile* and the popular classes.[138]

Pezzè Pascolato's case is telling, since it questions just how deeply the ideology had penetrated into the people's mind (in 1928 a washerwoman seemed to be having a bet each way when she christened her triplets Vittorio, Benito and Romano).[139] Class divisions remained gaping in Venice, and it is clear from Pezzè Pascolato's phrasing that there were few connections between the life experience of Venetians like her and the popular classes, who were still identifying primarily with their families and those who lived in their neighbourhood, as well as enduring a poverty that made each day precarious.[140] Fascist welfare may have brought minimal comfort to those poor who were deserving in Fascist eyes. But much more was needed even in a relatively well off city like Venice. As if in proof, in 1933 an observer reported that, in early summer, typhus was still endemic among the more wretched inhabitants, despite Fascist efforts to improve the housing stock. He estimated that 40 per cent of the population harvested their food supplies by picking molluscs off the rocks or from the mud at low tide, a choice that could be deadly given the fact that raw urban waste trickled directly into the lagoon.[141]

The yawning gap between rich and poor could scarcely be denied. In March 1930, only a few weeks after his session with Suppiej, Mussolini received a lengthy missive from Roberto Papini, a distinguished art historian, just then promoted to the editorial board of *Il Corriere della Sera*, the major Milan daily. Papini told his Duce that 'today the economic conditions of Venice are distressing indeed. Venice is inhabited for the most part by poor people, who, with the Arsenale stagnating, business impoverished and trade directed to the port at Marghera, suffer from complete misery.' It would be good if the road bridge were built – Mussolini had just telegraphed the prefect with instructions to ignore idle artistic chatter hostile to it, though conceding feelingly that it would take 'millions, many millions, to erect'[142] – but much more was needed. 'Venice can only be adapted to modern life', Papini urged, through a detailed plan that would widen and straighten its main alleyways, clean up building stock, and speed public transport through the historic city, across the estuary and on to the mainland. A 'courageous and totalitarian solution' was needed, with the 'creation of an emergency regime' for the city, headed by a 'serious, competent and impartial chief'.[143] After all, unemployment kept mounting, provoking a daring illegal demonstration by lace workers on Burano in February 1931 and, that autumn, a female occupation of the Murano Comune.[144] Even before then, it is estimated that there were 4,000 street people in Venice (vastly more than today) and 10,000 without formal work.[145] In 1931 the official tally of unemployed had risen to 13,172.[146] For those who were employed, ancient traditions could linger. According to a contemporary account, the hundred active fishermen who lived on the Giudecca automatically passed their calling from father to son; their families were known to all as descendants of people who had arrived from Chioggia or Pellestrina centuries before.[147]

In seeking a Leader for Venice, Papini plainly did not have Volpi in mind. Yet the canny entrepreneur had ever more arrows in his quiver, as the regime began to talk about Venice being the 'vetrina', or showcase, of Fascism. Indeed, on the very same day that Papini wrote to Mussolini, Volpi also sent the Duce a handwritten letter. Every time he came back to 'this, our incomparable city', he reported sadly, he found it ever more 'bloodless'. The 'fault', he knew, was 'that of men'. No doubt there were historical fatalities afflicting the place. But 'new life can return, new breathing space can be opened and a great part of the problem can be resolved with a better communications system'. So they must get on with the bridge and assume that suitable finance could be found for it.[148]

In the interim, there were always tourists, just the people who should peer into a showcase and applaud. So, as the tenth anniversary of the regime was being celebrated in 1932, Suppiej fell back on evocations of Venice's international allure. Fascism, he remarked properly, had not repeated the unsightly misdeeds of the Liberals, with their crass cutting through of pathways and burying of canals. Rather, it aimed to 'march boldly towards the future respecting the glories of the past'. Already that year, Venice, 'the most desirable tourist site in all the world',[149] had attracted 161,000 Italian visitors and 237,355 foreigners. In the years to come, those numbers, he implied, could only increase.

No doubt the Depression had afflicted some of the leisured classes, but high society rhythms were resuming quickly enough. Harry's Bar, a collaboration between American Harry Pickering and Giuseppe Cipriani, a waiter from Verona, opened in May 1931, just around the corner from Piazza San Marco. Its first guest book bears the signatures of Arturo Toscanini, Guglielmo Marconi, Somerset Maugham, Noel Coward, Charlie Chaplin, Barbara Hutton,

Peggy Guggenheim and Georges Braque.[150] At that time, Diana Cooper told her husband of light-heartedly watching the sights on the Grand Canal from the windows of Palazzo Volpi in elegant surrounds, noting, 'No one goes to bed here and the drinking is formidable.'[151]

But, during the new decade, the nature of tourism had to adapt to the regime's shift towards populism (the Duce was suggesting that modern theatre should look to audiences in the thousands).[152] New, bigger, better shows was the answer, in art, music, theatre, film and even sport. Circuses were easy enough to stage whereas a search for bread might challenge the authority or even the wealth of the best people, a sceptic might conclude. During the 1930s, at least while peace lasted, Venice was indeed to become the showcase of regime performance to a national and international audience. But it was simultaneously a city where Mussolini had to share the bill with Volpi and where any social revolution was again postponed.

CHAPTER SIX

Venice between Volpi and Mussolini, 1930–1940

On 14 June 1934 the social and political set in Venice were abuzz. The city was welcoming another tourist to view its art and its exhibitions – the 19th Biennale was open to visitors – in this case, one who was also a statesman, ideally to be persuaded by Venetian comforts and hospitality to negotiate in friendly vein with his Italian partner. Adolf Hitler, the Führer of Germany, was scheduled to meet the Duce, Benito Mussolini. It was Hitler's first official trip to a foreign country. From the instant Hitler landed at the Nicelli airport, however, garbed, as Mussolini would sardonically observe, 'like a plumber in a mackintosh', the meeting stuttered. Even the Biennale did not appease the sometime artist, who looked askance at its eclectic collection of paintings and sculpture, much of it too modernist and 'degenerate' for his Nazi and petit bourgeois taste.

Newsreel clips from the state-run Istituto Luce ruthlessly display the gap between the dictators. Greeted on arrival by assembled soldiers and sailors (they followed custom in bringing their hands to their brows in the military manner), Hitler saluted feverishly from one man to the next in fascist mode; Mussolini strode smiling on, hands at his sides, ending with a single salute that was half Roman and half a cheery, almost cheeky wave to those he was sure loved him. Later, when they had a moment to chat in the Pisani garden at Stra, a suited Hitler appeared even more uncomfortable than he had in his mackintosh, nervously fingering the brim of his soft hat, while a super-cool and confident Duce carelessly left his hands in his pockets. Throughout the visit, Mussolini was blatantly playing at home, effortlessly assuming the role of senior dictator, whether at the Biennale (a telling photo shows Volpi in full Fascist uniform meeting Hitler in civilian clothes at the Giardini),[1] reviewing marching boy scouts at Piazza San Marco, appraising Marghera or orating to an 'oceanic crowd' back outside St Mark's.[2] It did seem true, as Giovanni Giuriati junior put it in *Le Tre Venezie*, that the Duce's appearance in the city had been greeted with 'breathtaking enthusiasm'. The whole population, he maintained, had 'seen, rejoiced in and been satisfied by the multiple aspects of the grand figure of the Chief', a 'good, smiling, profoundly human Chief', who had set every heart racing when he proclaimed Venice to be 'a divine and heroic City, the heir of Rome'.[3]

As far as Hitler was concerned, these days were less blissful. Even the venues for the official meetings were inappropriate, be they the grandiose Villa Pisani on the mainland (where the mosquitoes were reported to be as big as quails and where Mussolini could imagine support from the ghost of an 'Italian' Napoleon who had bought the place in 1807) or the clubhouse of Venezia Golf (not a sport that gratified either dictator). According to Damerini's wife, Maria, a luncheon at the latter venue went badly, since only the most blue-blooded patricians had been invited; their wives 'spoke English well but had very little German' and could not divert the Führer. The splashier reception at Stra was still more vexing. 'The women looked suspiciously at the pallid Hitler, with his chilling eyes', such a contrast with Mussolini of shaven skull and Caesarian profile; Venetian females responded girlishly to 'his magnetic glances, half laughing, half thrilling, with inviting glances of their own'.[4] A German account states that, by the end, Hitler was wittering. He just wanted to get back to Berlin so he could talk to Goebbels, he expostulated pettishly, a remark prompting Mussolini to interject knowingly that he relished 'seeing all kinds of different people'.[5] In sum, the contrast between the German and Italian dictators seemed to prove that, in surrounds cherished by the best people of Venice (and its international tourist set), Mussolini was a gentleman and Hitler was not.

For those who seek sites in contemporary Venice bearing the record of this history, one obvious place for reflection is the city's golf club, still open for play at Alberoni, at the southern end of the Lido (see map 4). The course's origins go back to the 1920s and to Volpi's congenial line on American culture. In 1924, he, Cini and Achille Gaggia had presided over the founding of a Venetian branch of Rotary International.[6] In the summer of 1926, one American tourist who came to the Lido, naturally staying at the Excelsior, was Henry Ford. The American businessman brought his golf clubs with him, but found nowhere to play. He must have made his disgust evident, because he was taken urgently to meet Volpi, who courteously took time to accompany him on a search for an appropriate location for a Venetian golf course.

At Alberoni, a deserted area of dunes, marshland and pine trees, protected by an old fort dating from the days of Austrian rule, they discerned the ideal setting. Two years later, work began, supervised by a Glaswegian architect called Bobby Cruickshank. By September 1930 a nine-hole course, par thirty-five, was ready, and the Circolo Golf Venezia was inaugurated with a membership of twenty-five, mostly from patrician families. Among the first visitors were Queen Marie of Romania and an *équipe* of accompanying royals, who were entertained at the clubhouse in May 1931 by a number of local counts and countesses, a Mr Roger Sulton and a Major Charlton. In breathlessly describing the event, *Il Gazzettino* declared that the elegant lunch proffered to the visiting queen demonstrated that the Alberoni club was 'becoming more and more Venice's most fashionable sporting centre for leisure activities'.[7]

Volpi, never averse to assuming another prestigious office, had been appointed the club's first president (with Gaggia as his faithful deputy). He was succeeded by Count Giovanni Revedin (from a dogal family) in 1933–4, Count Cesare Cicogna (husband of Volpi's second daughter) in 1935–6, Count Andrea Marcello (another who could claim dogal background and the son of a senator) in 1937–40,[8] Ingegniere Giovanni Cicogna in 1941–6, and, with no hint of a break in continuity with the Fascist years, Count Giuliano Foscari (dogal again) in 1947–50.[9] It is true that the Fascist regime placed considerable emphasis on modern sport, with the implication that it was spartan training for war. Mussolini liked being photographed swimming, skiing, fencing, playing tennis, horse riding and kicking a ball with his sons. Golf was not his forte, however, even if it was the regular pleasure of his son-in-law and implied dauphin Galeazzo Ciano, a choice that deepened his wife's dislike of Ciano. The Circolo Golf Venezia, glamorous, cosmopolitan and patrician, may have had a modern side, but it was another sector of Venetian life that was hard to integrate into waffle about a Fascist social revolution.[10]

The golfers therefore had many reasons to forget Hitler's visit to their club. But the impact of Nazism on Venice, and of the Axis alliance between Hitler and Mussolini from 1937, is more readily visible in the *centro storico*, where, from 1938, the city's ancient, patriotic and well-integrated Jewish community found that its devotion to the *patria* could not save it from the enveloping anti-Semitic legislation, nor, eventually, from the Holocaust.

The place where passers-by are most obviously reminded that the fundamentalist Nazi-fascist determination to liquidate the Jews possesses a Venetian history is the ghetto, located towards the western end of Cannaregio (see map 1).[11] The origin of the word 'ghetto' is the Venetian 'ghèto', meaning 'slag', a foundry having been located on the island on which, from 1516, the Republic confined its Jews. On 25 April 1980 a monument to those deported from the city for extermination was opened in the square of the Ghèto Nuovo. Its internationally celebrated sculptor, Arbit Blatas, was born in Kaunas in Russian Lithuania in 1908, before making a career in Paris and New York and escaping the Holocaust. On 19 September 1993 the site was extended, President Oscar Luigi Scalfaro giving formal endorsement to the positioning of Blatas's

24 One of the Blatas panels

The Last Train, a set of seven bronze tablets depicting the fate of Venetian Jews
rounded up fifty years earlier under the Salò Republic and transported to extermination camps in the east. It is a deeply moving memorial, one into which
Blatas, who by the 1990s was assisted by architect Franca Semi (a Venetian who
had trained under Carlo Scarpa), was able to inscribe anger as well as suffering.
It is all the more remarkable (although typical of the underplaying of modern
history in many studies of Venice) that major recent English-language accounts
of the city's art and architecture ignore it.[12] The security business, however, has
not, and in recent years the site has been watched over by armed police in
another intrusion of global history even into Venice.

Of Venice's Jews, 246 perished in the Holocaust (only eight re-emerged
alive from the camps), while 1,050 survived, concealed in the city or its hinterland in 1945. The first victim was community president Giuseppe Jona, who,
on 17 September 1943, committed suicide rather than bow to Nazi-fascist
demands that he hand to the new authorities a list of his members. Seventy
years later, there are only five hundred Jewish inhabitants in Venice. As few as
thirty reside in the ghetto, despite the presence of kosher restaurants, a Jewish
museum and a number of synagogues,[13] allowing the claim that it remains a
major 'memory place' for Venetians of all sorts.[14]

25 Holocaust memorial guarded in 2012

In 1871 there had been 2,667 Jews in the city, although the figure dwindled thereafter as religious identity weakened. It had fallen to 2,474 by 1901, to 1,814 by 1931, and to 1,471 by 1938, when the Fascist dictatorship suddenly introduced severe anti-Semitic legislation, forcing separate development or worse onto the nation's Jews.[15] Venetians of Jewish culture had long been integrated into urban political, commercial and social life, their patriotism being clearly expressed in March 1923 in a marble memorial to the community's war dead at the Tempio Spagnolo. At its inauguration, Rabbi Adolfo Ottolenghi, destined to die in the Holocaust, orated patriotically while tracing a 'parallel between the wars of ancient Israel and the Jewish sacrifice for the Italian *patria*'.[16]

A Gruppo Sionistico Veneto had been established in 1903. Two years later, with an alleged membership of two hundred, the Zionists mourned the death in Vienna of the philosopher of modern Israel, Theodore Herzl, hailed as their 'Duce defunto'.[17] Here were potential divisions, exemplified in the countering appeal of the Italian Nationalist Association to some Jewish leaders. Such divided identity manifested itself starkly during the first half of the 1930s, when 40 per cent of children born to the community were reckoned to result from 'mixed' marriages. Giorgio Coen, a community leader, now warned

Zionists against being distracted from their prime loyalty to Italy, 'perhaps the only State that respects its Jewish fellow citizens'.[18] As telling about the mechanics of Fascist rule and the compromises with it made by Venetian Jews is a small file in Mussolini's secretariat, where, in May 1931, Giuriati, then the ostentatiously purist party chief, backed a claim for financial support from the wealthy Sullam brothers, whose agricultural dealings on the mainland had run into financial trouble. Mussolini approved the subsidy.[19]

Even if, practically speaking, the Fascist regime never ceased to be criss-crossed by patron–client networks, once Starace had replaced Giuriati as PNF secretary the dictatorship, as it 'went to the people', became more active in imposing totalitarian rule and therefore more troubled by difference among its citizens. So, in January 1935, the Ministry of the Interior nominated a young Fascist lawyer, Aldo Coen Porto, to be government commissioner over the Jewish community in Venice (three of his immediate relatives were destined to die in Auschwitz). Coen Porto's administration, and that of his successor from April 1937, the businessman and PNF member Aldo Finzi, for the moment proved satisfactory to the authorities, the prefect Giuseppe Catalano praising the 'profound patriotism' of the Jewish community and applauding their gift of four kilograms of silver to the nation, stripped voluntarily from the syna-gogues.[20] Eighteen months earlier, Volpi had naturally led the city's gold collec-tion during the Ethiopian war, joined publicly by Rabbi Ottolenghi.[21] In November 1936 the Jewish community formally consigned 50,000 lire to the local branch of the Fascist party as part of the celebration of the empire now established in East Africa.[22] The wealthy Max Ravà, who moved in Volpi's circle, was even more determined in his accommodation of Fascism, backing the Jewish Fascist newspaper *La Nostra Bandiera* (Our Flag), edited in Turin.[23] Converting to Catholicism, Ravà survived the Holocaust, as did all but three of 336 Venetian Jews who had taken this course before 1938.[24] Those who rejected that option had a worse fate in store.

War was coming. But for most Venetians, rich and poor in their different ways, the city remained insulated through the 1930s from the political crises that were battering this country or that. Both Fascist party members and the better-off citizens could bask in apparent success and comfort. At long last the furious dispute over the road bridge was settled, complaints from so self-important a foreign organ as the London *Times* that a vehicular crossing would destroy the 'unique beauty so jealously preserved throughout the centuries of the Queen of the Adriatic' being airily ignored.[25] The Ponte del Littorio (Lictorial Bridge, to become the Ponte della Libertà, or Freedom Bridge, after 1945) was opened with Fascist fanfare and a blessing from Patriarch La Fontaine on St Mark's Day 1933. It was supplemented by the cutting of the

Rio Novo, which accelerated water traffic between Piazzale Roma and Piazza San Marco. Both Mussolini and Volpi took credit for such progress, but Giuriati was numbered among those who opposed the forging of easier contact with the mainland. The bridge, he warned his Duce, in echoes of D'Annunzio, Foscari and the pre-war theme of Venetian-inspired imperialism in the Adriatic, would 'strike a decisive blow against the surviving sea-going traditions of Venice, while equally violating its glorious, singular beauty'.[26]

Trimming to the times, his sometime client Suppiej took the occasion to inform whingeing foreigners that 'the good sense of Venetians' and 'the wisdom of the Fascist government' could always be relied on to defend the city's past, present and future. What a joy it was that now two thousand cars could park at Piazzale Roma, he declared, and then detailed a long list of the extensive works and up-to-date technology that had been utilised to build the bridge and the 'autorimessa' (it must not be called by that un-Italian term 'garage'). With a hint of complaint against Volpi, Suppiej noted that, so far, Marghera had expanded more to the benefit of the mainland than of the city. The accessibility provided by the bridge would, he was sure, help to rectify the situation, as well as opening the way to a fresh wave of tourists.[27] Moreover, the name, Piazzale Roma, meant that Venice now offered a 'Roman' face to the world; as part of its enthusiasm for *romanità*, the regime had decreed that every town and village in the country have at least one space named for Rome. Half suggesting that he might be making the best of a bad job, the journalist Elio Zorzi told readers of the establishment journal *Nuova Antologia* that Piazzale Roma and the bridge beyond, sparkling from their nightly illumination, seemed to ordinary Venetians 'a fantastic spectacle, like a gigantic Luna Park'.[28]

A few months earlier, to mark the dictatorship's tenth anniversary, or Decennale, Suppiej had already used *Le Tre Venezie* to offer an official reckoning of the glories of Fascism in Venice city and its province. Naturally, he expatiated on the growth of Marghera, where he now claimed that sixty-eight different firms were in action. He also praised the Nicelli airport, which offered flights to and from seven sites elsewhere in Italy, as well as to Munich and Vienna. Within the city, commodious new housing was being erected at Sant'Elena.[29] He did not add that the area there, in something of an urban historic compromise, was known as the Quartiere Vittorio Emanuele III, to match the Quartiere Benito Mussolini that had grown up around Santa Marta during the 1920s and the Quartiere Giuseppe Volpi at Marghera.[30]

Nor did Suppiej acknowledge that the improvements were proceeding too slowly for most Venetians. The level of actual deprivation in the city was exposed in another of health officer Raffaele Vivante's detailed reports in 1935. In reality, Vivante claimed, because of the Depression, since the end of the

1920s all building activity had ceased, despite the desperate continuing need for it. The result was that 'the health and the decorum of citizens' lay in the balance. If only Venetians could live in 'more hygienic conditions', then 'the grave [moral] deficiencies that still characterise such a large number of our inhabitants' could finally be overcome.[31] His political point by implication made, Vivante proceeded to enumerate the uninhabitable dwellings (they had increased since his pre-war study), while demonstrating that there was more wretchedness in Castello, the Giudecca, Dorsoduro or Cannaregio than in zones frequented by the rich. Some modern conveniences were arriving, but in the *contrada* of Sant'Angelo Raffaele in Dorsoduro over 20 per cent of houses were not connected with electricity, and more than a quarter of dwellings in San Francesco in Castello lacked running water. In the city as a whole, only 11.3 per cent boasted the modern comfort of a bath or shower; in prosperous Santa Maria del Giglio the figure was 34.6 per cent and in San Francesco it was 2.1 per cent.[32] Much effort, Vivante advised, was still required to introduce contemporary standards of hygiene to Venetian homes. Much time, he was not rash enough to add, would have to pass before class difference could be surmounted, despite Fascism's claim that such was a basic aim of its 'revolution'.

What, then, can be discovered more generally of the Fascist impact on ordinary Venetians during the 1930s? How did totalitarianism, Italian-style, work there? Very partially is the answer. Contrary to propaganda about an all-embracing ideology and an all-powerful party, a recent study of everyday life in the city has demonstrated that poorer Venetians continued to rely on a 'currency of favours and connections and networks of family, friends and acquaintances' that Fascism scarcely infringed. As late as January 1935 an essay prize organised for nine and ten year olds produced entries that displayed 'a distinct apoliticism and ambivalence' rather than what organisers had hoped would be effusive Fascism. Similar ambiguity clung to the 'revival' in 1934 of the Festa delle Marie, held on 2 February for the Purification of the Virgin, a local festival that allegedly dated back to 973 and may well have had lingering purchase among the populace.[33] (It would be revived again in 1999, this time with openly commercial and tourist intent as part of Carnival.) Equally, despite some grandiose public funerals, the Venetian way of death remained traditional for all classes.[34]

Other evidence about attitudes in the city, whether to the Fascist party, Fascist ideology or the charismatic dictator, carries complex messages. One telling file is that on Giuriati's niece Fernanda and her husband Domenico. Their first approach to the Duce came late in 1931, when their request for a signed photo was seconded by Fernanda's influential uncle, who described Domenico appealingly as 'a Fascist from the very beginning and a wounded and decorated soldier'. Soon a photo arrived and Domenico sent a polite thank-you. Three years later the correspondence blossomed, since Fernanda was one of those *signore* who cheered Mussolini on his visit to the city with Hitler. She was so emotionally moved that she was impelled to write to tell the dictator that 'from Your [sic] magnetic glance and Your dear, wide smile we have had the most precious gift, the most sought-after recompense'. His long-sought presence in the city had 'renewed our enthusiasm and our will to obey You. If something displeased You in Venice, forget it, please, Duce, and remember only that we love You with a profound and pure passion, capable of any sacrifice'. When he looked down from the Excelsior balcony and seemed to fix on her 'Spanish shawl', joy and gratitude 'stopped her throat' and she could only 'tremble and babble'. 'May God bless You and Your immense work, oh Duce, for the good of Italy', she concluded ardently.

But could Fernanda's surrender to charisma bring advantage? Six months later she wrote to Edda Ciano, Mussolini's daughter, although her missive was plainly directed higher. The Duce was and would be her and her husband's 'Credo in terra' (Fount of all Wisdom), she explained, yet life was arduous for her family. Her husband was thirty-nine, knew three languages, was expert in the law of the air, but had not won a proper job. Worse, he was financially embarrassed. Could something be done? In March 1935, the file reveals, Mussolini said yes and Domenico Giuriati found regime-endorsed 'sistemazione'.[35]

While Fernanda Giuriati's efforts to tailor Fascism to her own needs were not unique, countering hints of more active dissent occasionally surfaced in the city. Even after glorious victory in Ethiopia, the workers at Marghera were convinced that France was more enlightened in its labour policies than Italy. They were passionately split over the Spanish Civil War, although most expected Franco to win.[36] During that conflict, one agent alleged that 'Fascists disguised as workers' (and therefore, it must be assumed, not workers themselves) were tramping suspect zones of the city by night, notably the Giudecca, 'watching and waiting to pick out the guilty' who might scrawl anti-Fascist slogans on a handy wall or switch on Spanish Republican radio. Resentment bubbled up, the policeman added, over the harshness of secret police measures during another visit by Mussolini in August 1936, but so did fear that, one day, 'the Duce might somehow no longer be there, with incalculable consequences for the destiny of the Patria'. Furthermore, even those who were glad that Fascism had intervened in Spain expressed unease over the possibility of another world war.[37] Local workers remained especially anxious, one secret police report from the end of March 1939, when Franco had just won, noting that worse-off locals wanted 'peace and employment' thereafter.[38] A speaker at the Ateneo who warned that the next conflict was likely to be an 'aerial-chemical' one is unlikely to have made his respectable audience feel particularly jolly, especially when he expanded on the need for aerial defence, albeit with more historical reference than contemporary detail.[39] For *podestà* Alverà a graver issue was the irritation evinced by Mussolini on one of his visits over the amount of noise coming from traffic in the canals. New regulations, he hastened to assure his petulant master, would put an end to such annoyances in the future.[40]

But doubts and worries did not yet darken too deeply Venice's experience of Fascism. In the highest echelons of the Church, La Fontaine, who was buried as a soldier of Christ and the nation in the Tempio Votivo on the Lido, with pious salute from all the city worthies, had been succeeded by Adeodato Giovanni Piazza. The new patriarch, born in the hills near Belluno in 1884, was even more accommodating in his dealings with the regime than his predecessor had been. Piazza had served as a war chaplain in the battles that, in 1915–18, had raged not far from his family home. After the war he published patriotic poetry, in which he did not forbear to borrow from Carducci and D'Annunzio.[41] In his holy office, Piazza stood forward as a stern opponent of 'communism', 'immoral cinema', modern female dress and lascivious dancing. Simultaneously, he urged respect for the Fascist authorities, joining their celebration of victory in Ethiopia and exulting in the national flag, 'the symbol of a civilisation flowering in a genuine faith in Christ'.[42] He fervently blessed Franco's 'crusade' in Spain. Typically, on the fourteenth anniversary of the March on Rome in October 1936, Piazza held an outdoor mass where he thanked God for those who had 'carried Italy to undreamed-of heights of grandeur' and who had resisted and continued to resist the 'Bolshevik hell', in which 'art, progress, humanity, social collaboration, good behaviour, tradition, religion and education' were all obliterated. Apposite quotations from Mussolini and the Gospels boosted his sermon.[43]

On occasion the Church's social values proved more conservative than those of the regime. In May 1938 Piazza unsuccessfully petitioned the Duce to open a Facoltà di Magistero (Teaching Faculty) at the local university, Ca' Foscari, on the grounds that it would protect female students from the moral dangers they would face if they had to leave the close supervision of their families to be schooled outside Venice.[44] He was, however, quick to express his gratitude to the dictator when, in May 1940, Volpi, as Primo Procuratore di San Marco, transmitted the glad tidings of Mussolini's 'personal' special grant of one million lire for the Basilica's restoration fund.[45] Nor was Piazza dismayed by Fascism's choice of enemies. In a pastoral letter of February 1938, following or even nudging forward the spirit of the times, Piazza publicly labelled Jews 'Christ killers', adding his anathema against the 'deicide people' who could always be found in the 'most shady sects from Freemasonry to Bolshevism, the bloodiest revolutions and the most ferocious wars'. Almost as dastardly were Protestants, 'dried branches' who needed to be lopped off the Church and diverted from their continuous attempts to overthrow the true faith, people who had the temerity to set up business in Venice as though it were a 'barbarian land'.[46]

At Epiphany that year, the patriarch was fulsome in his identification of the preoccupations of Church and state, noting how proud all must be 'to belong to a people who, with their reborn national consciousness, highlight the best gifts of the race: physical fitness and a deeply healthy morality, prolific fecundity and a genial autocratic sense, the Roman equivalent of thought and action and an admirable dedication on the fields of sacrifice'. It was, he concluded, proper that they ally themselves with the 'great people' of Nazi Germany.[47] Here was a prelate who was only too delighted to render unto a (sawdust) Caesar that which was Caesar's, even while he told himself that he was helping Venetians to stay in touch with God.

Meanwhile, any who ponder whether Catholicism was possessed of a totalitarian urge of its own in the 1930s should examine the ferocity of the campaign launched against swearing and blaspheming in the city, an issue that had first prompted legislation in 1261. Luigi Picchini acted as propagandist for what Piazza hailed as a 'really magnificent crusade' against the habit, one that should lead to the extirpation of cursing and other such forms of 'impurity' from 'our Italy'. A Fascist law of 1 July 1931 by which fines for such bad behaviour were increased to 3,000 lire should, Picchini urged, be applied to the letter, loyal Catholics denouncing sinners to the authorities and pressing for the imposition of monetary penalties or, better, imprisonment, given that 'cursing . . . is Satan's preferred weapon'. Blasphemy, he wrote, with what sounded like 'racial sense', contravened 'Italic traditions'.[48]

If the Church positioned itself on the austere side of Fascism, Volpi – seemingly happier to be snapped at an art exhibition or on his yacht than as the hard-working boss of Marghera – presided over a radiant city, contentedly pursuing its contest with Paris as a global capital of culture and leisure. Volpi took the credit for initiating not only the successive Biennali but, from 1930, an International Festival of Contemporary Classical Music and, two years later, a similar but more popular event devoted to film. The usual compromises with the ambiguities of Fascist authority were evident. The publicity for the music festival steered an expeditious course in calling itself 'Fascist and royal'; it was conducted with 'the moral and material assistance of Benito Mussolini' while saluting Crown Princess Maria José as patroness. The festival featured the work of most modernist composers, drawing to the city such open sympathisers with Fascism as Stravinsky but also rival musicians who believed their ideas lay on the left. The impressive list of those whose works reverberated at the 1930 festival included Bartók, Dallapiccola, Gershwin, Honegger, Hindemith, Kodály, Malipiero (a local), Prokofiev, Respighi, Rota, Villa Lobos and Zandonai,[49] backed by such distinguished predecessors as Busoni, Debussy and Scriabin. Lavish receptions were held for the more sociable guests in the opulent palaces of the Grand Canal, whether owned by Volpi (Palazzo Pisani near Rialto)[50] or the more strictly patrician Casa Morosini.[51]

The music festivals were widely trumpeted, but the Biennali had not lost their lustre or their artistic breadth. (In 1930 Patriarch La Fontaine banned his clergy from viewings, Pope Pius XI seconding his attack on 'art divergent from the spirit of Christian morality'.)[52] No doubt, the exhibition's bureaucratic format was now fascistised as part of that process whereby all Italian civil society paid obeisance to the regime and its ideology. From the late 1920s the organisation of the international art exhibition passed from the Comune to the Ente Autonomo Esposizione Biennale Internazionale di Venezia, a state-funded body whose directorate was appointed in Rome and reported there. Such centralisation was countered, however, by the fact that Volpi was, and remained, its president through to the last wartime festival of 1942. From the late 1920s his chief aide was Antonio Maraini, a sculptor and journalist with few immediate connections with Venice and who was nominated in Rome.[53] Despite being mocked by Marinetti as conversing with a 'grave solemnity' that the robust Futurist deemed 'effeminate',[54] Maraini moved in the circle of Margherita Sarfatti, who, through the 1920s, was a key figure in national cultural life. Even when her influence faded, Maraini steadily increased his profile in the corporatist Sindacato Nazionale degli Artisti (National Fascist Artists' Union).[55]

In office at the Biennale, however, Maraini advanced any radical Fascist takeover slowly, despite stipulating in 1932 that the 18th Biennale must display 'the twentieth-century-style vitality of Fascist Italy conquering the tiredness of the nineteenth century'.[56] Since one of its prizes went to a painting of the port of Marghera, and another awarded by the Rotary Club Italiano to a portrait of Giuriati, a desire to get on well with local notables was unmistakeable.[57] Then and thereafter, Maraini scarcely took the art exhibition to the people, although he did move the Biennale office from Ca' Farsetti, home of the Comune, to the grander and more historic Palazzo Ducale. Maraini was adroitly solicitous in keeping the dictator personally informed about events at the successive Biennali, always remembering to give him its glossier publications. Similarly, he did not forget to send a wedding present to Mussolini's laddish eldest son and film entrepreneur, Vittorio, in February 1937.

Maraini's Anglo-Polish writer wife, Yoï, proffered family support when she was moved by a summer visit to Britain in 1935 to bring the Duce abreast of sad developments in that country. There, she complained, Freemasonry had run amok and the British were disgracefully sustaining those who blocked Italian ambitions in Ethiopia. Anthony Eden was the worst in culpably misunderstanding 'the constructive civilisation of Fascism'. He was a fool who would not mind if Italy were reduced to 'anarchy'. To avoid that calamity, Yoï Maraini assured her Duce sturdily, she was 'ready to serve You and Your country from the beginning and for ever'.[58]

But for all his and his wife's assiduity in keeping a shine on family relations with their dictator, Maraini saw no reason to quarrel with Volpi and his well-off friends, underlining his disgust at the Nazi murder of Engelbert Dollfuss in 1934, for example (the Austrian strongman was killed immediately after Hitler's return from Venice and while his wife and children were staying in the Mussolini beach house at Riccione). Maraini must have felt he was currying favour with the Duce, Volpi and all right-thinking Italians when he showed personal initiative in laying a laurel wreath in memory of the Austrian chief outside that nation's pavilion at the 19th Biennale.[59] He and the Venetian elite had every reason to cheer when the international exhibition attracted more than 360,000 visitors that year, even if the numbers were not quite back to those of the pre-war period (a peak of 458,000 had been achieved in 1909). Maraini also collaborated with Volpi in a globalisation programme that saw Italian art sent to New York in 1932, to Paris in 1935 and as far as Sydney in 1936.

The desire to steer between the shoals of international politics was similarly manifest in the first of the new theatre festivals, inaugurated in 1934. The well-chosen highlight was the outdoor performance of Shakespeare's *Merchant of Venice* at Campo San Trovaso. The play was directed to critical acclaim by Max Reinhardt, the Austrian-Jewish director who had made his name in Weimar Berlin but had transferred to Vienna in 1933 (in 1938 he would move to Britain and then the United States; he died in New York in 1943). Reinhardt was known for fusing stage design, music, choreography and words in his productions in an avowedly modernist way. The open-air staging of the play could for the moment seem to express Fascist populist ambition to favour 'mass theatre' and thereby represent 'the myths of a living Italy',[60] although it is likely that few Venetian poor attended. By contrast, Umberto, Prince of Piedmont, was prominent in the 'select audience' one evening in July 1934.[61] In the years that followed, outdoor performances continued. In the tightening atmosphere of 1938, D'Annunzio's *La nave* was revived, staged on a platform anchored out in the lagoon in a manner to be repeated in the Pink Floyd concert fifty years later. As is always true of this play, precisely what an audience made of its themes is uncertain.

It was the film festival that really stole the headlines, however, from 1935 becoming an annual rather than biennial event, assisted by the fact that

Mussolini had declared cinema, with its amalgam of artifice and modernity, *the* Fascist art, while King Victor Emmanuel III and Giuseppe Bottai, the most avowedly intellectual of Mussolini's ministers, were convinced that too much laboured propaganda made cinema unwatchable.[62] Fans of film could be found everywhere, the first festival drawing to Venice the Prince of Wales and his high-living brother the Duke of Kent, each in pre-war-style ostentatious incognito.[63] Other vaunted visitors that year included ex-King Alfonso of Spain, Randolph Churchill, Oswald Mosley and Randolph Hearst with his actor-lover Marion Davies, takings exceeding 155,000 lire.[64]

Film stars were even harder to pin down in their social and political attitudes and behaviour than were musicians, a matter of concern as Fascism accelerated towards the overt anti-Semitism of the policies formulated after 1938 and the Nazi alliance. Goebbels was already a notable presence in 1936[65] and formally opened the 1939 show on 8 August (the Duke of Windsor was one high society visitor that year).[66] Ciano had inaugurated the 1935 festival, party chiefs doing for film what, at the Biennale, was still usually left in the decorous hands of members of the Italian royal family. At the initial show, Helen Hayes took the Coppa Volpi for best female actor, Katharine Hepburn winning it in 1934 (when forty-three films were shown, originating in sixteen countries), Bette Davis in 1937 and Norma Shearer in 1938. In this last year of political crisis, with the Munich conference imminent, Leslie Howard was judged the best male actor. The first two Mussolini Cups for best foreign films went in 1934 to a production crafted in Eire and in 1935 to one made in the United States, while the fourth went in 1937 to France, before German directors began to dominate, first with Leni Riefenstahl's *Olympia* in 1938.[67] Nonetheless, that year, at least according to a British administrator, Volpi went out of his way 'to be friendly on all occasions' while keeping pointedly distant from the Germans.[68] Moreover, *Snow White and the Seven Dwarfs* earned more popular applause than did Riefenstahl's epic. Walt Disney had already won an award for his cartoons in 1936. Two years earlier, it had doubtless been a sign of success when the French cinema journal *La Cinéopse* noted sniffily that the festival was 'better organised to serve the interests of Venetian hoteliers than those of the cinematic art'.[69]

These and other cultural events allowed Volpi to claim that his city was achieving 'an absolute world primacy' in the showcasing, if not in the production, of the high arts, with the implication that he was assisting their more general popularity in the modern Fascist manner, as well as making Venice a 'vetrina' for Fascism.[70] Flushed with success, he moved to reinforce his power in the city and further whittle away Giuriati's stature. He had bought *La Gazzetta* in 1926, leaving the biddable Damerini as editor. In 1934 the death of

Talamini, the owner of *Il Gazzettino*, whose paper was then in deep financial trouble and had been singled out by Mussolini as being in need of a change in political direction, gave Volpi the opportunity to control this too.[71] He completed his takeover in 1936, judiciously appointing first Giorgio Pini and then, in 1937, Giorgio Rocca, each with direct personal ties to Mussolini, to run the paper.[72] Although he and his juniors took pains sedulously to applaud the dictatorship's every act, Volpi controlled the coining of words in Venice at a more immediate level than did the dictatorship.

Volpi was equally pleased when Suppiej, once thought to be Giuriati's man in Venice, was dropped as *federale* in 1934, to be replaced by the obliging Michele Pascolato, a Venetian lawyer related to Maria Pezzè Pascolato. In 1937 Pascolato would reap benefits from his participation in the city elite, being promoted to the board of the Cassa di Risparmio.[73] Sure in his domestic base, from October 1934 to July 1943 Volpi assumed another national role as head of Confindustria, the big business league, now 'corporatised' but with a retained sense of its significance in bonding the nation's industrialists, men who seldom found that Fascism infringed their profits or weakened their control over their workers. There were thus many reasons to believe that the third regional conference of Rotary International which assembled in Venice between 15 and 19 September 1935 would confirm Volpi's mastery over the city and his ability to represent it as a mutually agreeable combination of practical and efficient Fascist dictatorship, global business and elegant culture, where wealthy locals presided over a polite and tranquil populace who had no reason nor wish to trouble their betters.

Prosperous guests arrived from more than thirty countries to be entertained with pleasant excursions across the lagoon and into the mountains and with dulcet concerts at the Fenice. The world president of Rotary, American Edward R. Johnson, was among the speakers, emphasising stoutly in capitalist vein that Rotarians stood for no politics except 'improvement'. The local vice-president, Alfredo Campione, was also apt in his phrasing, complimenting Volpi's 'grandiose achievements' in Venice, 'a really titanic work to which the Duce has given and continues to give his highest support and which could only be fully and happily carried through in the climate of Fascist Italy'. *Podestà* Alverà, yet another pleased to be a Rotarian, did not demur. Even the German delegate was gracious, inviting the transatlantic visitors to return to Europe the following summer so that they could attend the Berlin Olympics.[74] It was all very business-like and jocund.

Yet a cloud lay not far off on the horizon. On 3 October Italy launched a massive attack on the free African empire of Ethiopia, a member of the League of Nations. Aggressive war and Fascism had finally come together, not just in talk but in reality, even if the well-off young of the city were reported to be urgently enrolling at the local university in order to avoid conscription for an imponderable African campaign.[75] The die had been cast, however, and from October 1935 Fascist Italy was almost constantly engaged in war. How were Volpi and his circle of friends to deal with this new and potentially menacing world in which tourism and leisure began to seem out of place and in which business, too, was confronting new risks? What, after all, were Fascists of the late 1930s meant to make of Volpi's employment of tall, handsome, black, askari as servants in his *palazzo*,[76] a choice that was scarcely unknown in the best social circles of other European empires but was hard to reconcile with the Axis and Fascist drift towards racism?

In 1936, following Fascist aggression in Ethiopia and the resulting imposition of League of Nations sanctions, attendance at the Biennale fell to 195,000 (the numbers including Mussolini, who came on a 'surprise' visit in early August, flying his own seaplane, sporting a summery white uniform and accompanied by his schoolboy son, Romano, wearing shorts and looking owlish in his glasses).[77] The king had opened the event back in June.[78] Not even the expansion of outdoor theatre in the city could restore crowds to their previous levels and salve communal finances, which were falling into the red.[79] Just before this 20th exhibition opened, as a possible bad omen, Piazza San Marco had been flooded to 147 centimetres on 16 April, the worst *acqua alta* for many decades.

By 1940 the Biennale's visitors had halved again to 89,000 (down from an already modest 175,000 in 1938).[80] Although a residue of pro-Fascists, including, for example, Coco Chanel, still brought some social panache to the city beaches,[81] 'Mussolini's Italy', an ever closer partner in the Axis with Adolf Hitler's Germany, steadily lost appeal as a site for cosmopolitan partying. More and more people now decided that Mussolini and Hitler were 'twin dictators' and quite a few disliked the sight. As Margot Asquith underlined in an article in *Vogue*, 'We do not believe in mock-Mussolinis, silly shirts, self-advertising upstarts. We detest dictators.'[82] For those best people who had once flocked to the Lido, such invitations as that for beach-goers to participate in a contest launched by the local branch of the PNF in the summer of 1936 to build sandcastles on the theme 'the new Roman Empire' began to fall flat.[83] An elite absence from Venice was not fully compensated by the arrival of Nazi-sponsored groups, which in the autumn of 1936 included a squad of 'Hitlerian youth' followed by a delegation of industrialists.[84] Their extravagant welcome in the press was a sign of the times by contrast with two years earlier, when the secret police opened a file on a journalist of the *Kölnische Zeitung* who, it was claimed, had taken up residence in Venice as a Nazi organiser and spy.[85] Nor did other organised squads from such friendly states as Austria and Hungary or from other parts of Italy, brought in to view the sites on so-called 'treni popolari' (popular trains), with cut-price tickets, the precursors of those day-trippers who rouse the ire of contemporary Venetians, really compensate for the absent global clientele.

Whatever the changes that Fascism espoused or implemented, Volpi remained adaptable and sinuous, positive and with an eye to the main chance. He had long worked closely with friends in Venice's Jewish community, whether in business or in culture. When the dictatorship moved against its Jewish citizens, however, Volpi took the opportunity further to expand his portfolio of offices. In 1938, he became director of Assicurazioni Generali, the great national insurance company that had started out in Trieste. In this office, Volpi perforce sacked those Jews who, until then, had formed a majority on its board, although not with the thoroughness that party radicals wanted; after September 1943, his enemies in the Salò Republic would damn him as 'a total creature of the Jews'.[86] Other horizons could still beckon. According to Ciano, at a meeting in 1937 Volpi hinted that 'he would like to be Minister of Colonies, but he denies it, blushing like an embarrassed schoolboy'.[87]

Within Venice, the major debating point of 1936–8 was the placement of the casino (the first gambling site in the city had opened in 1638), in regard to which, as has been noted, Volpi had detected potential advantage during the previous decade. Patriarch Piazza was a predictable opponent, but Volpi spoke out in the Senate in Rome using the plausibly marketised argument that Venice faced international competition as a tourist venue and must equip itself with what (rich) foreigners desired and expected. The real issue was exactly where play should be located. The ideal site, Volpi was sure, would be near his CIGA hotels on the Lido.[88] In such a plan, however, Volpi was opposed by *podestà* Alverà, who wanted the casino to open in a palace on the Grand Canal and announced in June 1936 that such a choice had been made. He claimed with Fascist virtue that profits from urban gambling would sluice not into private hands but into party coffers. There the accrued funds could assuage 'social and humanitarian' needs. In this ambition, Alverà was joined by his deputy, Alessandro Brass, who lamented that, presently, ordinary children in Venice could not enjoy a single proper playground (or swimming pool),[89] while popular housing stock too often consisted of putrid 'hovels' rather than what might be expected under Fascism.[90] In January 1937, however, it was announced that the Duce, as so often in practice endorsing Volpi's line, had come to his decision: gambling was to be located on the Lido.[91] It was only in 1946 that a casino, under the direction of the Comune, would open at Ca' Vendramin Calergi on the Grand Canal, and then only for the winter season; in summer, play continued on the Lido.

Perhaps the dispute over the casino had become too strenuous. In Fascist terms it was time for a 'changing of the guard', and in September 1938, with the communal budget running into trouble for the first time in years,[92] Alverà was replaced by Giovanni Marcello, thus paying the penalty for his public disagreement with Volpi. The new *podestà* sprang from a patrician family and, it is unnecessary to add, was persona grata with Volpi.

Yet Fascism continued to sharpen its own image and mutinous mutterings grew louder among radical party members who had not renounced their view that Volpi's city exhibited his wealth and influence rather better than it did Fascist revolution (and, worse, failed to provide them with cushy and well-rewarded jobs).[93] To be sure, the urban streetscape was altered to proclaim the glory of expansionism and the value of war with the opening of the Riva dell'Impero (Empire Embankment) on 23 March 1937, a day sacred to Fascist memory, given the foundation of the movement in Milan on that day in 1919. But the date had no particular Venetian reference and the newly paved path beside the lagoon might be read as scarcely embracing the people. It debouched into the anonymous-looking housing on Sant'Elena, where, notoriously, placid clerks rather than militant Fascists found their homes.

A more thorough Fascist effort to implant a new culture in the population can still be viewed at the Liceo 'Raimondo Franchetti' at Mestre, planned from 1931 but actually built in 1939–40 as the first elite local high school outside the old city. Baron Franchetti, an intrepid explorer in Africa, had been born in Florence but his family were Venetian and no one mentioned their Jewish origins. Importantly, Franchetti had died 'heroically' in an air crash in Egypt in 1935 and it was easily implied that the perfidious British were somehow responsible. A major commemoration of him in the city that September focused more on his royal connections, however, and noted that he gave his four children African names (Simba was the eldest), while recalling his advice to Venice Rotary in 1930 regarding the great economic advantages to be gained from 'penetrating' Ethiopia.[94] Here, it might be thought, lay more than one complication. Yet, once the empire of Africa Orientale was won, everyone agreed that Franchetti 'possessed in the highest grade the virtues proclaimed by the ethics of the New Fascist Italy'.[95]

Work at the Great Hall of Ca' Foscari in the city under the charge of the young architect Carlo Scarpa had allowed the painting there of (still extant) Fascist frescoes by Mario Sironi (*Venice, Italy and Study*) and Mario Deluigi (*School*), the latter in cubist vein. Sironi's work (which has recently been restored and made the object of regular tourist viewings)[96] did not fail to include an image of a student athlete, embodying the Fascist slogan 'Libro e moschetto, fascista perfetto' (Book and rifle, perfect Fascist), and added a representation of the *patria* celebrating empire in Ethiopia. Such national themes were, however, conditioned by the local: a Winged Lion and the domes of San Marco. In practice, it was easier to epitomise the regime at Mestre than in the historic centre, where the urging of 'com'era e dov'era' was always likely to surface in opposition to major change. Without such limitations, the Liceo's assembly hall at Mestre could therefore be lavishly decorated with images pompously invoking 'the greatest geniuses of the race'. They omitted any religious figures, ranging from the emperor Augustus, Livy and Virgil through Dante, Leonardo and Galileo to Marconi, Verdi, D'Annunzio and Mussolini. (Eventually, after the war, they would be rechristened, less stridently, the 'greatest Italian geniuses'). The hall's scenario was completed with busts of Mussolini and Victor Emmanuel III and a map of the Italian empire. The portals of the Liceo were also given what is today called an entry statement in modernist Fascist bas-relief. On the left is an allegory of 'Venice, lady of the sea, art and trade', and on the right a representation of 'the physical and spiritual evolution of the young', worthily expressed by boys clutching books and rifles and girls grown to womanhood with babies. The school library was filled with regime-approved texts and took a subscription to *La difesa della razza*, the most virulently racist of party-sponsored periodicals. All was meant to underline the Liceo's didactic purpose to be 'monumental, disciplined and elite', a place where pupils learned to be 'new Fascist men and women'.[97]

Annibale Zerbetto, the first headmaster, zealously endorsed the foreign policies that, on 10 June 1940, pushed Italy into the Second World War, although there may have been hints of complications in a major speech of October 1941, when he charged his teachers not to forget 'the importance of the anti-communist struggle that Italy and its German ally are fighting'.[98] In any case, precisely how Zerbetto's words were comprehended by his staff and pupils must remain doubtful. As ever a gap may have lingered between what Fascism claimed to be doing and its reception by the people. A local spy reported in early November 1939, for example, in regard to the notorious campaign by Starace to persuade Italians to abandon the use of 'Lei' (a polite third-person form allegedly transferred corruptingly into Italian from Spanish) for the more militant 'Voi', that gondoliers at San Tomà were nonplussed when asked whether they addressed their clients as 'Voi'. 'Roba da siori, roba da dotori' (a matter for gentlemen and professional people), they replied scornfully, 'quà se parla come ne gà insegnà mare e basta' (here we speak as our mother always taught us and that's enough).[99] Their robust localism, a sceptical historian might note, may have become public at that time since the unpopular Starace had just lost office.

The secret police provide more detailed evidence of the response of Venetians to the coming of European war in August–September 1939, to

Mussolini's reluctant decision to opt for 'non-belligerency' over the next nine months, almost as if Fascist Italy was about to replay the history of Liberal Italy in 1914–15, and finally to the entry into combat on 10 June 1940, after Nazi armies swept aside French defences and soon stood at the gates of Paris. In July 1939 there was already a report that those involved in urban politics feared that Mussolini was no longer well appraised about 'the Italian internal situation and the life of the people', given that his immediate circle (presumably code for Ciano and Starace) had fenced him off from such matters.[100] A month later, the tone was even more pessimistic. People were just trying to keep themselves amused and stayed silent on international developments, although willing to express irritation about 'the cinematic poses' of some Fascist bosses. 'Today no class of Italian devotes itself to the problems of the nation,' the agent lamented self-righteously, and Venetians particularly discounted what the Fascist press and radio told them.[101]

The Danzig crisis and the signing of the Ribbentrop–Molotov pact (23 August), with its U-turn on anti-communism, did little to allay Venetian fears, although some locals unheroically thought that it happily guaranteed that the next war would be fought far from Venice, unlike the last one.[102] On 28 August an agent heard talk of prosperous people wanting to flee to sanctuary on the mainland. Memories of the First World War were alive enough for what the spy vaguely called 'anti-Fascists' to suggest that one day Germany would ask for the Trentino and Trieste 'back'. The precipitate flight of foreigners from Venice and its hotels was prompting more immediate concern, even if the agent did add ingratiatingly that people still had faith in their Duce and were waiting for him to speak. A pious handful expected mediation from Pope Pius XII but, more generally, Venetians had given up listening to their leaders. Rising prices for consumer goods were widely noticed and people were beginning to hoard food.[103]

The following days remained tense in the city, the secret police reported, with half-hopes in the Duce's word being clung to, together with an expectation that this crisis, like its predecessors, could have a diplomatic solution, perhaps one in which Italy's 'ambitions' were well satisfied, another Mussolini triumph. In any case, people reiterated, with an apparent ignorance of the implications for civilians of aerial warfare, mechanised modern battle could be left to the soldiery, would not demand mass mobilisation and might be ignored in Venice, destined to be a blessedly long way from the front.[104]

Unfortunately the archive contains no secret police reports about urban responses to the German invasion of Poland of 1 September and the consequent British and French entry into the conflict. Certainly, what war would eventually entail was not initially evident in Venice, that year's film festival proceeding as usual, bolstered by the glamorous presence of Cary Grant and Mary Pickford. The British selection of *The Mikado, The Four Feathers* and *Young Man's Fancy* underlined the fact that light entertainment was still the preferred choice of some in Venice.[105]

By the time the next season came round, however, Italy was at war. Ex-*podestà* and historian Pietro Orsi gave a patrician's imprimatur to the Duce's policies in *Le Tre Venezie*, linking the decision for war in 1940 with that of 1915, and praising Victor Emmanuel, the 'soldier king', as well as the dictator, that 'marvellous Statesman who has revived in the whole nation the ancient voice of the Race'. Italy's decisive war entry, Orsi maintained, would win the 'eternal gratitude of Italians', joyful to stride out again across the imperial pathways of Rome and Venice in a process certain to make Italy 'greater, more respected and more powerful'.[106]

Yet for the most part Venetians received the momentous news with a shrug. According to the local press, the city's rhythm scarcely missed a beat. The municipal band played in Piazza San Marco, its repertoire including lively, happy pieces by Rossini and Johann Strauss. During the day, the Lido was crowded, although bathers were expected to be more self-disciplined than in peacetime.[107] True, the number of foreigners had declined, and, as one commentator averred, girls now wandered back from the beach talking to each other about Leopardi and Schopenhauer, rather than gossiping as they would once have done.[108] Nonetheless, quite a few film stars were holidaying on the Lido and may be presumed not to have retired every night with a text by Schopenhauer as their only comfort. Perhaps the Festa del Redentore was more focused on its 'religious essence' than in the past.[109] Yet the annual international tennis tournament commenced play on the Lido as the sporting calendar said it should. Venezia Foot-Ball Club began what for its players and fans was a good war that would bring victory in the national cup in 1941 and the attaining of the unparalleled height of third in the championship in 1942, assisted in these triumphs by Valentino Mazzola, in some eyes his nation's greatest player, on loan from service in the navy. At Alberoni, patrician golfers were still missing or sinking putts, and in the evening they could beguile themselves at the Teatro Malibran, where *The Barber of Seville* was sung frolicsomely.

The occasional oration (Cardinal Piazza distributed an episcopal letter exhorting national victory) or ceremony (the Riva dei Giardini was renamed after the dead Italo Balbo, the nation's first celebrated casualty of the war) may have emphasised the gravity of the international situation.[110] But Venice was not immediately dislocated by this war, even though Thomas Cook and the Berlitz language school had their premises forcibly shut down. The official line denied that anything much had changed: 'The most absurd stories are circulating in the city and its province about a fixed date for the closure of hotels and beach and about other measures allegedly soon to be applied to the city of Venice,' *Il Gazzettino* reported. The police had identified the rumour-mongers and would take action against any who aimed to fret the magnificent national spirit. 'Venetians . . . must not permit a handful of Jews or Masons, or widows inconsolable about long-dead times, to find ears ready to listen to such poisonous lies.'[111]

The special proof of surviving normalcy was to be the usual round of festivals, whether of art or of film. King Victor Emmanuel showed up again for the 22nd Biennale,[112] at which Volpi orated, grandly and as though he meant it, about the nation's primacy in high culture and the contrast between the splendidly novel 'totalitarian and revolutionary concepts of Fascism' and 'the old world of demo-plutocratic hegemony'.[113] Maraini acted as a loyal second, praising Hitler's overturning of past aesthetic assumptions, and expressing his certainty that an Axis victory would produce 'a higher civilisation and a greater justice'.[114]

At the film festival, which opened on 1 September, Italy and Germany, it was confidently expected, would display their European leadership in film production, though Swiss, Swedish, Hungarian, Romanian and 'Bohemian' (if neither American nor Soviet) movies were also to be screened.[115] The whole event, it was announced, would demonstrate the superiority of the 'totalitarian powers'. Even in war, they, unlike their opponents, could devote time to the silver screen, because they understood cinema to be 'a school' of the nation or race, an art form that was 'propagandist' in the positive sense of the word.

Although Alessandro Pavolini, the Minister of Popular Culture, presided over the opening ceremony, Volpi, as ever on the lookout for rivals and versatile in his arguments, took special credit for the occasion. England and France, he remarked, had wanted the war, as Germany and Italy did not, and that made 1940 a crucial year in the history of the world. Bravely, he had never for a moment thought of cancelling the film show. Cinema was 'a necessity of our modern life'; the Duce had personally willed the Biennale's continuation, while the Duke of Genoa signalled royal approval.[116] The present, Volpi asserted, was a good time to reflect on 'the European economy of tomorrow' and on the likely reordering of the lineaments of the world following the certain triumph of the Axis. Then Italian industry would develop ever more swiftly under the happy impulse of autarky and in deep military collaboration with Germany, providing 'permanent expression of that dynamism that animates the Italian people and guides them towards the highest economic destiny'.[117]

At the Ateneo, Gino Damerini similarly stood up for the nation in war, advertising a public course on Venetian history that would illustrate the marriage between the city's long past and the nation (and its dictatorship). His purpose, he explained, was to show how the Venetian Republic, with its own imperial glory, acted as the crucial bridge between the First and Third Romes. Venetian conquests amounted to a 'mystical' process, as did the way that people and patricians had fused to serve their country. Such wondrous past unity could now be replicated when Italy and Germany stood 'shoulder to shoulder' in arms virtuously to restore international justice and complete Fascism's 'Mediterranean and imperial destinies'.[118] Only the gloomy comment of the local prefect that the Comune's budget was sinking into still deeper deficit and that the utmost financial rigour would be needed during the coming year suggested that touristic Venice might not flourish as luxuriantly in wartime as in peace.[119] Perhaps, after all, Nazi-fascist war would, paradoxically, given the militant ideology that underpinned Hitler's and Mussolini's imaging of a new world order, be softer on the city than Liberal war had proved to be from 1915 to 1918. Again not entirely differently from wartime Paris,[120] in the autumn of 1940 the city elite hoped that battle would not shake their world out of joint, and told themselves hopefully that they could still sell its history, culture and comforts to an appreciative and part-foreign clientele.

CHAPTER SEVEN

Venice, Nazi-fascist war and American peace, 1940–1948

In early November 2012 Italy was hit by floods, a common phenomenon in autumn. In Venice, *acqua alta* reached 1.49 metres in Piazza San Marco (the sixth worst on record).[1] As a result, the evocative but often overlooked monument *La Partigiana* (The [Female] Partisan), which rests at water level below the Riva dei Sette Martiri near the Giardini ferry stop (see map 7), was festooned with seaweed, decaying plastic bags and a large branch. In this condition, she may have broadcast an environmental message about the city's present and future. Her more formal duty, however, is to preach a historical lesson about the Venetian Second World War, or, rather, an anti-Fascist version of it, with contrary resonance from the inscription of US General Mark Clark's victory proclamation outside Ca' Farsetti, noted in chapter 4.

The bronze statue, the work of Augusto Murer, is of a bound, drowned woman, with dishevelled clothes, her face all but concealed by her arms, her eyes blank. She lies contorted on a concrete base, the *mise en scène* being the work of Carlo Scarpa. Born in the city in 1906, Scarpa was an independent, radical, globally celebrated and politically adaptable figure, committed to connecting Venetian and Japanese culture while also anxious to transpose Frank Lloyd Wright's ideas into Venice. Scarpa proved able, like many another, to make the conversion from success under Fascism to overt anti-Fascism.[2] By the early 1960s he was entrenched as the most celebrated architect in the city. In his design, *La Partigiana* is framed by a set of irregular prisms chiselled from the same Istrian marble that constitutes much of the city fabric. When the site was inaugurated on 25 April 1969 – conveniently both Venice's Feast of St Mark and the national Giorno della Liberazione (Liberation Day) – the female figure was intended to float up and down depending on the tide, the undulation reminding viewers to remain alert in the permanent but fluctuating struggle against Fascist tyranny.

26 *La Partigiana*

Unfortunately, the technology soon broke down and the statue went into a long period of 'restoration', with seemingly little effect other than the erection of an unsightly steel fence that kept the lagoon away. Eventually, however, the work was complete, and, on 6 June 2009, President Giorgio Napolitano, an ex-communist, taking time off from a visit to the latest Biennale, endorsed the statue's reappearance. Venice, it was now proclaimed on a small protecting wall, dedicated itself to *La Partigiana*. Read simplistically, the words suggested that Venetians had accepted one and only one historical comprehension of the Second World War.

The idea of representing Resistance in Venice had arisen before the insertion of *La Partigiana* into the cityscape beside the lapping water. In 1953 a campaign began for a permanent monument to wartime anti-Fascism. It was led by members of the Istituto per la Storia della Resistenza delle Tre Venezie under Egidio Meneghetti, a socialist-appointed rector of the University of Padua in the immediate aftermath of the war. A national commission that included such celebrated art historians and architects as Giulio Carlo Argan and Bruno Zevi, as well as veteran poet, journalist and cultural organiser in Venice Diego Valeri, chose an Umbrian, Leoncillo Leonardi (an ex-partisan), for the job.

27 The city dedicated to *La Partigiana*

Cocking a snook at the nostalgic, Leonardi furnished a strikingly neo-cubist design that, in September 1957, was erected in the Giardini, with an official oration from Ferruccio Parri, Italy's first post-war prime minister and a Resistance hero.[3] It showed a nameless young woman fighter striding alone to her glory (but doing so in fragile majolica). The monument proclaimed the 'grand and self-sacrificing contribution' of females to the Resistance, while also implying that all people of good will stood behind her in her brave and unabashed determination to fight Fascism to the death.[4] As if in proof, when, in July 1960, Christian Democrat Ferdinando Tambroni sought to form a government in Rome with neo-fascist support, the Riva dei Sette Martiri was the natural venue for a major demonstration in protest, backed by twenty-eight different parties, clubs and associations in the city.[5]

Its original red neckerchief toned down on official request to brown, the statue was positioned among the collection of patriotic busts in the Giardini. These include nationalist poet Giosuè Carducci and irredentist Guglielmo Oberdan, the latter executed in Trieste in 1882 after a failed assassination attempt on Emperor Franz Josef (his bomb killed two bystanders). Evidently, the past they represented jostled with the 'myth of the Resistance' embodied by Leonardi's statue. This leftist representation of history did not last long, however, since, on the night of 27–8 July 1961 it was dynamited into a thousand pieces by local members of a neo-fascist group called, with re-evocation of Mazzini, Giovane Italia (Young Italy).

In response, the Christian Democrat mayor, Giovanni Favaretto Fisca, who was experimenting locally with that 'opening to the left' (embracing the socialists) which had not yet become national policy, pledged swift replacement, so that 'memory of the Resistance could continue to be passed on to future generations'. His stance was applauded by city unions, partisan and women's organisations and the Jewish community.[6] *La Partigiana* was the result. Eventually, on 25 April 2005, for the sixtieth anniversary of Liberation, a copy of the original statue complete with red kerchief, which had been discovered in Leonardi's studio after his death, found sanctuary in the entrance hall of Ca' Pesaro, the city's gallery of modern art. Venice today therefore boasts two monuments to female partisans. Ironically it does so in an era in which neither the supporters of Silvio Berlusconi (no feminist he) nor purist neo-liberals give weight to what during the 1960s and 1970s was portrayed as the bright, democratic and modern cause of anti-Fascism. In a new millennium, *La Partigiana* may have been restored to transmit her message to passers-by, but whether they notice her and ingest her history lesson is another question.

How had Venice fought its second global war of the twentieth century under a regime that was the prime ally of Nazi Germany and went down to destruction with its partner in war crimes in 1945? As in the first conflict, thousands of young Venetian men fell in Italian armies on the various fronts. In a few cases, their memory is kept locally alive in lists of sacrifices to the *patria* on memorial stones set on church façades throughout the city. The First World War's history, however, is more easily recalled than that of the politically charged Second, when, in any case, the great majority of the city's soldiers perished far from Venice in a national sacrifice that constituted less than two-thirds of that of 1915–18.

The Second World War is notorious for having brought death to at least as many civilians as soldiers, on and behind its many blood-soaked fronts. Were Venetian residents similarly afflicted once Mussolini had cast his nation's lot in with Hitler? Venice had suffered mightily during the First World War, by 1918 being reduced to little more than a naval garrison, its ordinary population driven into exile, its economy in ruins, and its servicing of cosmopolitan leisure disdained by nationalism, xenophobia and encroaching Fascism. Venice's two wars may not perhaps be accurately summarised by Marx's formula 'first time tragedy, second time farce', but, paradoxically, given the horror that dominates most memories of the Second World War, Venetians, in the main, experienced a soft war. Despite the extremity of Nazi-fascist ideology and the slaughter that it perpetrated, Venice in the years from 1940 to 1945 was to a considerable degree safeguarded by its ancient devotion to art, architecture, leisure and tourism. As a repository of old history, 'sacred to civilisation', it stood safe most of the time from the aerial bombardment and other kinds of violent incursion that were then wrecking so many European cities. The Allies identified Venice and, remarkably, Torcello, together with Rome and Florence, as 'cities' the bombing of which was to be avoided without the highest authorisation.[7] As far as Venice's presence in the Axis was concerned, when nationalism and racism were merged and when Nazi-fascist chiefs opted for drastic, final solutions, the city was cushioned by its localism and by the reiterated idea that its evident pasts made it, as Diego Valeri claimed in a 'sentimental guide to Venice', published in mid battle in 1942, a 'city of life', not death. As he had already phrased it in January 1940, before Italy's war had begun, Venice carried in its bones 'universal love' that could waft unimpaired around the current disputes between universal fascism, universal communism and universal liberal democracy.[8]

Despite Italy's entry into the war, and despite the humiliating failure of Mussolini's attempt to run a blitzkrieg in Greece from 28 October 1940 until rescued by his German ally, whose forces swept through Yugoslav and Greek defences in April 1941, Venice, at least according to its press, concentrated on lighter matters. That spring like every other, readers of *Il Gazzettino* were informed, the sun shone and 'the most beautiful beach in the world' was 'preparing for its season in a smile of sweet-smelling roses on the water'. This time the grand hotels would not have to put up with 'false barons' and 'false talk' of a 'false cosmopolitanism'. Unmissed would be the English, 'those angular wandering skeletons, with their half-French hair-dos and make-up and their vulgar horsey laughs from mouths much worked over with the gold of London dentists'.[9] The French, too, were happily absent, a speaker at the Ateneo tracing the troubles of the world back to the 'brutal, stupid and iniquitous dismembering' of the Republic by Napoleon in 1797.[10]

Equally gratifying was the fact that Volpi, as his journalist employees politely explained, was perpetually attentive to his city's smallest needs; in a meeting with Fascist party officials at the prefecture he had developed a 'precise' hotel and entertainment programme for the summer, in which the film festival would play an even more important role than usual.[11] First on the leisure schedule were moonlit concerts in Piazza San Marco, with a harmonious repertoire of Donizetti, Verdi, Puccini, Beethoven and Wagner.[12] Later would follow an exhibition of eighteenth-century engravings, the usual round of *feste*, regattas and other sporting events, and the outdoor staging of plays by Goldoni and Schiller, performances at the mass 'Theatre of 4,000' continuing until mid September in the square faced by Santa Maria Formosa.[13]

The contemporary music and film festivals would open in their usual way; when the film season began, Volpi echoed Goebbels in urging that 'a continental European consciousness' be nurtured to frame the Nazi-fascist order, a schema that would in time disencumber itself from national particularisms. This refreshed Europe, Volpi added, seemingly renouncing his past admiration for the New World, was destined to triumph over the United States.[14] No wonder that it was at this time that a lavish volume was published recording the completion of the restoration of the Post Office in 1939 (blessed by Volpi) at the Fondaco dei Tedeschi, a building whose name recalled the ancient ties between Venice and the Germanic world.[15] A more academic speaker self-righteously informed his elite audience at the Ateneo Veneto that the sanctions campaign of 1935–6 had been led 'with sadistic diligence' by *The Economist*, 'the major organ of Jewish-British finance'; now vengeance was nigh through Fascism's 'Roman vision' and its scuppering of 'Greek individualism and Slavic-Eastern communism'.[16] In the city hotels, American guests might be fewer than in the past, but other foreigners turned up in regular procession, a cosseted visitor that year being the Croatian tyrant Ante Pavelić.[17] Only occasional mention of the unavailability or high cost of fruit, or reference to new and more energetic measures to ensure that price controls were applied and the black market frustrated, hinted that, across Europe, there was a war on.[18]

As the summer reached its peak, the press contended that the city was reliving its old glories. A special high fashion exhibition was announced (linguistic austerity and patriotism meant it was of 'alta moda' and not of 'haute couture'). Volpi and the Duke of Genoa joined agreeably in opening it, as they had done for so many peacetime shows. 'Venice for a few brief days will become a refined department store, an elegant emporium [offering goods] with the unmistakeable brand of *italianità* and good taste,' *Il Gazzettino* reported cheerfully. On this occasion, too, Italian textiles, fashion and artisanship would effortlessly lead the world. So, too, would Italian autarky. The coats and collars on display were made not from ermine or mink, but from wool, moleskin or Sicilian rabbit skin, as well as from the perhaps more easily obtained cat fur.[19] With the Fascist new order offering such delights, no wonder one local journalist could look back on the season as especially happy, free of French loafers and American Jews, pulsing instead with the vibrancy of Fascist labour.[20] Even on the terra firma, times were good; in early 1942 the workforce at Marghera, busily engaged in war production, peaked at 22,000,[21] tame journalists not forgetting to tell local citizens that work there brought high honour to Fascist Italy.[22] When, in autumn 1941, Mussolini received Volpi in Rome in order to review the successes of that summer and plan the 23rd Biennale for the following year, he gratifyingly saluted the authority and the achievement of the 'new doge': 'No Venetian can ignore what the name "Volpi" means for Venice.'[23]

While Venice remained at leisure, there were momentous developments at the front. On 22 June 1941 the Germans launched 'Operation Barbarossa', their surprise attack on the USSR, without informing the Italians beforehand. Soon, Fascist troops were supplementing an Axis tally of four million soldiers ravaging the Russias. Six months later, on 7 December, the Japanese entered battle through their own raid on Pearl Harbour and with rapid military triumph over the British and Dutch empires in Asia. Until the war's end, Italy would now be in combat with the two colossi of the USA, the former recipient of many Italian immigrants, and the USSR, the engine of global communism and master of the Italian Communist Party (PCI), whose cadres were to constitute the most numerous, obvious and committed segment of anti-Fascist resistance.

So what, Venice seemed to say. At least on the surface, tourism held sway in the city through the summer of 1942 as it 'always had'. The Biennale inevitably attracted fewer spectators than in peacetime, but it did open and, according to its advertisers, the clientele was more select and knowledgeable than it had been in the past. Diego Valeri was even permitted to evince a lingering independence of aesthetic judgement in praising the winning Croatian entry while expressing dismay at the 'scholastic and rigid' German contribution.[24] The sun glittered on the Lido, even if, as *Il Gazzettino* explained worthily, this season had 'a very special aspect': now 'people go to the beach for a deserved holiday, in order to recover, and out of an honourable need for leisure. But they go seriously, without excess, without clamour. These holidaymakers reflect the triumph of the family.'[25] In Piazza San Marco, music still echoed mellifluously, now on occasion provided by the Hermann Goering Regimental Band, which played Bach and Liszt.[26]

The customary tourist events had not been cancelled. The 'Theatre of 4,000' filled its stage, this time at Campo San Polo, under the auspices of Minculpop (the Ministry of Popular Culture) and with the populist promise that it presented 'the opportunity for all to attend performances that hitherto have been reserved for a narrow group of privileged beings'. Ordinary people, it was said, could there express the 'enthusiasm of their simple and open souls, beating at every expression of beauty'. At the Malibran and Fenice, *Cavalleria rusticana*, *Aida* and *Tosca*, 'the music of our great men, the real, magnificent music of our geniuses', could, it was stated, swell the hearts of every audience.[27]

Art, too, was still displayed. To supplement the Biennale, Venice played host to an exhibition of popular religious painting and sculpture. Volpi and the Duke of Genoa were once again twinned at its formal launch, underlining the inspiration given to contemporary religious creativity by the 'crusade' against the Soviet Union.[28] Conferences were still held, the Amici del Giappone (Friends of Japan) advertising a lecture series. Later in the year, a Croatian Exhibition got under way, luring visitors with a martial statue of the 'Poglavnik'. So, too, did a show of 'female activity', displaying the 'many tiny skills' of 'the perfect housewife'.[29] A 'historic' regatta rowed down the Grand Canal.[30]

There was even another film festival, the tenth since 1932, which, Volpi declared, would illuminate 'how Venice had learned to become a centre of formidable economic interest', as well as demonstrating that Italy, despite the heavy burden of its war effort, still gave time to 'art'.[31] Pavolini and Goebbels arrived to prove his point. To at least one journalist, all then was for the best in a 'Venice without the English'. He did not miss 'Mme Chanel and her exotic cosmopolitan friends', he noted, forgetting the French fashionista's erstwhile friendship with Fascism, but it was the absence of the English and their pet dogs that best cheered him. It had been the English, after all, who, 'with the excuse of leaving in Venice Byron, Browning, Ruskyn [sic] etc., took us for incurable idiots and acted like masters [padroni] in our house'.[32]

Yet some may have detected hints of dissent. In spring 1942 Count Mario Nani Mocenigo, director since 1922 of the naval museum and protector of the Arsenale, was brave enough to state publicly that 'racist doctrine' possessed no serious scientific basis, even while his historical sense told him how just it was for Venice to 'return' its rule to Dalmatia.[33] Picking up this latter theme, the city podestà took the opportunity provided by Axis gains in Yugoslavia to pester Mussolini with the request that Venetian lions, 'desecrated by the vile Slav plebs', be restored to Dalmatian towns.[34] Another speaker depicted a happy future in which the 'Jewish bacillus' was completely eliminated from 'the European organism' and Jews were no longer permitted 'to wander around our cities, under scarce surveillance', as they presently did.[35] More crudely still, Rabbi Ottolenghi had his face slapped when Fascists congregated in the ghetto, and, soon after, rocks and rubbish were hurled at the synagogue, which was stained with graffiti urging 'death to all Jews'.[36] Ordinary Venetians mostly seem to have been unconvinced by anti-Semitic campaigns in the Fascist press, although one secret agent reported in April 1942 that some Venetians disliked the way that federale Pascolato – and behind him, it might be assumed, Volpi – protected Jews.[37] Six months earlier, another spy had passed on the information that audiences 'in the stalls enthusiastically applauded' the anti-Semitic Nazi film Jew Süss when it played at the San Marco cinema.[38]

Despite such Nazi-fascist racist bravado, the war was inexorably closing in a little, even in Venice. (A German army was first trapped and then destroyed in Stalingrad between August 1942 and February 1943, while in October–November 1942 Allied victory at the second battle of El Alamein precipitated rapid Axis retreat in North Africa.) Attentive newspaper readers were now receiving instructions as to how ordinary people could build air raid shelters in a city whose nature made digging difficult.[39] By the summer of 1943 hoteliers had been ordered to pass to officials lists of their sheets and other bedding supplies and not on any account to dispose of such useful wares.[40] Although Toti Dal Monte sang in *La traviata* at the Malibran and fifty young men and women were arrested on the Lido for wearing overly skimpy bathing costumes, any change in domicile now had to be reported and justified.[41]

On the surface, however, life in Venice seemed much the same, even as the Fascist regime tottered to its fall in Rome on 25 July 1943. As one young visitor told his intellectual anti-Fascist parents in the middle of June 1943, 'in this place it really seems as though you are living in another world. This evening there was a band in [Piazza] San Marco. It played the Boccherini minuet in the moonlight as if nothing was happening. If you wander around the streets, or rather the *calli*, everyone is singing, accordions resound from the open windows and the shops are crammed with festive displays as though everything were still in abundance.'[42] As far as this observer and the Volpian press were concerned, Venice remained Venice, despite the lethal combat occurring somewhere beyond the lagoon. Ordinary urban life was surviving better than had been possible during the First World War.

An archive of police reports, while not challenging this view, manages to penetrate below the glitzy, half-cosmopolitan, half-tourist surface to depict a grouching, unhappy population, doubtless glad to be Venetians but convinced that they should not practise war in fundamentalist Fascist mode. Thus, as early as Christmas 1940, the local *questore* reported to the new national police chief, Camillo Senise, that Venetians were less than wholehearted in their commitment to battle. In curious phrasing about a party that was meant to have fused with the masses in totalitarian completeness, he described 'the Fascist element', plainly a small minority in his mind, as 'tired and disoriented' by the news that the attack on Greece had gone badly. The majority, scarcely at one with Fascism, felt depressed and anxious, blaming the army and its leaders for the failures at the front, as well as what the *questore* called 'the organs believed to be responsible' (a coded reference to Ciano and his high-living friends).[43]

Within the city, everyday life similarly suggested that class difference had scarcely vanished into a patriotic *union sacrée*. From its inception, rationing prompted concern over its inability to supply pasta and flour to the less well off; in April 1941, 40,000 in the city were officially deemed 'needy', a figure that was ironically much the same as it had been in 1866.[44] Many were murmuring sullenly against 'the richer businessmen, who are drawing excessive monetary advantage from the war'. The people were downcast, but hardly likely to revolt, the policeman concluded. They were sure that the world was unjust, and that the lives of their families remained a struggle that was destined to get worse not better, ancient ideas that were deeply inscribed in their psyches but were scarcely what was promised by 'revolutionary' Fascism.

Such a candid assessment of Venice's urban tone scarcely shifted as the war dragged on. In 1941 the prospect of spring did little to dispel widespread sense of alienation from the dictatorship's presumed war aims. Now openly registered was deep local suspicion of relying on an ally that was permanently 'Pan-German' in its approach to Europe and the Italian peninsula. Memory automatically cast the 'tedeschi' (Germans) as the city's ancient foes (reinforced by a vivid lingering recollection of the First World War). Hitler's latest speech, it was reported, had been heard in glum irritation as 'a paean of pride in the German race, advancing to European hegemony'. Italy's war effort, by contrast, was viewed as being slowed by 'incurable deficiencies'. A morose populace watched the 'Anglo-German duel, without sentimentality or illusion', sure that, whoever won, Italy would not get the 'brilliant pay-off that Fascism had guaranteed'. People were not appeased by the news that Ciano had been (belatedly) sent to the front, cynically doubting that he would be exposed to real danger there. The result was that anti-Fascist, anti-German and anti-war graffiti were appearing on city walls as the only way 'spontaneously' to express 'the public view'.[45]

A gap between populace and party-state yawned. Thus, the police maintained that a meeting between Mussolini and Franco had been judged worthless by urban opinion. Moreover, when local Fascists, an ever more isolated minority, moved to counter anti-war graffiti with wall posters of their own, few were persuaded by their arguments. 'Such propaganda has no useful effect, both because of its complete unoriginality in phrasing and because it is produced in identical form, thus making abundantly clear its preordained and bureaucratic origin'. Worse, the police insisted, was that party members showed an asinine preference for words over facts and their thorough and serious analysis, thereby confirming Venetians' discountenance with the Fascist style of war.[46]

In the months that followed, even the sweeping Nazi victories on many fronts failed to check popular discontent or curb the fervent hope that peace might come soon. The Germans continued to be feared rather than loved, and, even when they advanced to save Italian forces in the Balkans, Venetians briefly feared that their city might be exposed to an overwhelming countering attack from a Yugoslav army. Nothing could be done to amend the reality, entrenched in the popular mind, that Italy was not an actual Great Power. The prospect of conflict with the Americans did not please. Above all, the war was scrutinised for its local meaning, which confirmed that the rich were exploitative, Fascist corporatism was far from its promised efficiency, modernity and equality, corruption was endemic and national military might an illusion.[47]

The attack on the USSR briefly allowed greedy hankering for economic gain to surface among Venetians, hopeful that their families' poverty might be ameliorated by whatever means. It was known, however, that Britain stood undefeated in North Africa, and, not long into the campaign in Russia, the police were again reporting 'a mute disgust at the useless destruction of so much wealth'. 'By contrast with the time of the First World War', the telegram in question ran, 'every ideal fount of patriotism seems to have run dry.' Thanks to its ludicrous hyperbole, the party press was believed by none. The Germans were mistrusted. The rationing system functioned so badly that women of the popular classes regularly poured into the *calli* and *campi* in protest against it. Fascist efforts to incite local anti-Semitism better expressed the cheap ambitions of party fanatics than anything real in the population.[48] In August 1941 the Fascists had gone out of their way to put up a notice at Harry's Bar saying, 'No Jews here', but did so complaining that the powers that be in the city had done little to implement the racial laws and charging generally that the national habit of corruption was allowing Jews to buy fake Aryanisation.[49] Such diehard Fascists thought 'radical' German policies the ideal. Yet there were few signs that their ideology won sympathy outside 'squadrist' circles. Perhaps some 'humble workers' could be persuaded to blame 'Jews and Masons' for their woes.[50] But the racial message was conditioned by a class one, people muttering that poorer Jews were bowing before the newly severe measures, while the rich were not. Better-off Venetians and 'intellectuals' were also said to have given up wearing the Fascist party badge, as well as being hypocritically disconsolate over the fate of their Jewish friends.[51]

Even the 'heroic' death of Mussolini's second son, Bruno, saddened few, since people believed that it amounted to 'a common flying incident that had anyway happened away from the front'.[52] Worse was a visit to the film festival in September 1941 by Goebbels and his entourage.[53] Envious rumours spread that the Nazi bosses had rapaciously bought up clothes and shoes, while ostentatiously living the high life and contemptuously ignoring the rules about food rationing that ordinary Venetians had to follow.[54]

A pattern had been established that no victories at the front could amend. Stalingrad was soon causing concern.[55] The next film festival again demonstrated that Fascist law was unequal for all, Goebbels and his friends marking themselves out by their consumption of 'liqueurs, fruit and caviar'. Mind you, the police reported reprovingly, those Venetians who could do so tried to ignore the war, sauntering out to the beach and crowding other leisure sites, blatantly spending whatever money came their way.[56] But soon harsher realities set in, the American landings in Morocco from November 1942 raising the imminent prospect that 'a catastrophic future awaited the Italian *patria*, with the loss of its African dominions and perhaps the mutilation of some of its provinces and islands'. The city was now threaded with rumours of a pre-modern type that all was not well at the top of the ruling regime. Was Mussolini seriously ill? Had the king abdicated or some royal princes fled to England? Was the 'Farinacci faction', a coven of party radicals, secretly plotting an armed takeover?[57]

Not even a speech by the Duce could dispel the gloom, and the populace, the police contended, rejected the latest campaign for Italians to hate their enemies, even if complaint against the dictator was soon forgotten in the anxiety of each to look after his or her own interests.[58] Bombing was especially feared in Mestre and Marghera (the latter was badly hit in a raid as early as January 1941), but also in Venice. Would the bombers strike the Junghans factory on the Giudecca, which manufactured military fuses, or popular housing at Sant'Elena, where the battleship *Conte di Savoia* had taken anchor in the lagoon and was slow to sail away, people asked nervously? After all, they told each other, the city 'by its nature made it impossible to dig bomb shelters below ground and what has been constructed [above] is derisory in its nature'.[59]

Religion was another area of Venetian life in which the peacetime cohabitation with Fascism was turning sour. By early 1943, reports maintained, city clergy were engaging in a 'pacifist, evangelical and social' campaign, exploiting local 'religious sentiment' to their own benefit rather than that of the war effort. Now every class found sanctuary in church, where spiritual 'contemplation could bring comfort in regard to the difficult events of the moment'. Local Jews, the policeman added, as though such people were defined by religion rather than race, lived in tranquillity, convinced that 'the saddest days of racial struggle are past and also hoping, as a logical consequence, in a German defeat'.

Mutinous sentiment did not mean rebellion, however. Active anti-Fascism was rare, despite frequent bitter recollection of the positive military achievement of the Liberal government in the First World War by contrast with the failures of its Fascist successors. It was as though a generation of dictatorship had bled Venetians of the power to act. Both the soldiers who returned from the front to find rest and resuscitation in Venice and the residents who greeted them, each man and woman, entirely lacked 'national vigour', the police reported with some ambiguity. They were sure that any commitment to Italy on their part would only help the Germans, whose fanatical mixture of nationalism and racism envisaged a world in which Italians could be conceded only menial status.[60]

The police portrait of the Venetian response to the first three years of the Fascist war is thus largely consistent, despite the swaying to and fro of military success at different moments in the conflict. Here was a still touristic city that battle was treating relatively gently but whose populace were unengaged, disapproving, anything but fanaticised and fundamentalist subjects of a totalitarian regime. As troubles multiplied in their minds (and, for those with sons or husbands serving in the armed forces, in reality), Venetians sought solace in the traditional succour proffered by church and family. In their despair, they exchanged melodramatic gossip about what might be going on at the heart of the dictatorship, while being sure that the rich were unshaken by Fascist 'revolution', impervious to reform in their rapacity and cynicism.

Among the leading figures in the city, Antonio Maraini was one of the few casualties, even if his fate was more bathetic than tragic. His elder son Fosco, born in 1912, had been pursuing a cushy wartime career in Florence. One evening, an extended party ended with Fosco and gilded friends, tipsy or worse, dressing up to imitate Mussolini, Hitler, a Soviet OGPU agent, a Scots guard and an American soldier, presented in what the secret police condemned as 'ridiculous poses'. The matter leaked; Fosco Maraini was arrested and speedily sentenced to three years' *confino*. His father was sacked and left to protest to the Duce's office that the regime was thereby throwing away his 'twenty years of unquestioned Fascist faith and that passionate work' which he had selflessly devoted to 'the Patria, Fascism and Victory'.[61]

Only a few days later Mussolini fell, having been voted down by his Fascist colleagues in a meeting of the Fascist Grand Council, and on 25 July he was arrested at the king's order. The population celebrated the news of the dictator's fall in carnival mode in Venice as in other Italian cities, with behaviour that had accompanied the overthrow of tyrants in pre-modern times. The old leftist Armando Gavagnin was carried shoulder-high to speechify, first from a table outside Florian's and then standing on the Garibaldi monument in Castello. He persuaded the Duke of Genoa, still the local naval commander, to release anti-Fascist political prisoners. It was suggested that Gavagnin become editor of *Il Gazzettino*, although in the event the more decorous Diego Valeri took the job. Gavagnin may not have assisted his chances by ignoring a request from Volpi, who had taken refuge in Rome, for a meeting.[62] Other urban personnel, from the prefect down, were also replaced, amid emphasis that citizens were now again equal before the law.[63] A certain contradiction obtained, however, in relation to the ideological thrust of this post-Fascist city, where officialdom still praised Venetians for their 'totalitarian' acceptance of what was happening.[64]

Before a new national order could settle snugly over the city, on 8–9 September the king and his new prime minister, Field Marshal Pietro Badoglio, bungled their attempt to take Italy out of the war and fled ignominiously to sanctuary in Puglia with the invading Allies. Now Venice, like the rest of northern Italy, became subject to a revised version of the Mussolini dictatorship in the form of the Repubblica Sociale Italiana (RSI, Italian Social Republic), an ostensibly radical Fascist partner of the Nazis. On 11 September the Germans occupied Venice without a shot being fired, the Duke of Genoa following the royal example in a precipitous skedaddle south by hydroplane.

Those who had favoured or accepted Mussolini's fall in July were now in clear and imminent danger. Volpi and Cini were both arrested, although neither suffered the fate of Ciano and other former members of the Grand Council, who were executed in Verona in January 1944. Cini, who had been elevated to Count of Monselice in 1940, had resigned from the Fascist government on 24 June 1943 at either a responsible or an adroit moment. But in September 1943 his action looked disloyal to fanatical Fascists and he was arrested, enduring uncomfortable days in Dachau. In 1944, however, he was able to take sanctuary in Switzerland, from where he arranged to send financial help to the Resistance – fifty million lire in total, according to a friendly source – a gift that after the war helped to obscure his earlier dedication to Fascism. He was, it was then announced, 'a rare example of hard work, creative skill, political rectitude and patriotism'.[65]

Volpi's fate was simpler. Back in September 1943, *Il Gazzettino* had naturally acquired a new editor, Guido Baroni, a client of Rodolfo Graziani, himself once the client of Volpi in Tripoli but now the most Fascist of generals.[66] At this moment of Fascist restoration, Volpi's palace in Rome (though not the one in Venice) was sacked, and the richer and more historic contents sent to that rapacious art lover Goering. Despite his losses, the sometime 'doge' was not reduced to helplessness, however, his connections with Graziani and other supporters of Salò helping to bring about his release from prison in November 1943. He made it over the Swiss border in July 1944.[67] From there, he contributed what was said to be eighteen million to the Resistance and also passed ownership of *Il Gazzettino* to the Democrazia Cristiana (DC, Christian Democrat Party).[68]

For all such melodrama in the life of the 'last doge' and his associates, surviving police reports, despite being written by men who had committed themselves to the RSI, portray a Venice doing its best to avoid the harsher features of Nazi-fascist war. An account on the last day of 1943 underlined the 'diffidence and scepticism' of 'the great mass of the public' towards the new Partito Fascista Repubblicano (PFR, Republican Fascist Party) – in January 1944 it had enrolled 4,140 members in the city, 0.6 per cent of the population, as against the 88,684 who had been PNF ticket-holders in January 1943.[69]

'Workers' may have had their interest kindled by the greater 'social' equality pledged by the RSI, an agent noted, but they soon told themselves that, 'in the current state of affairs, only the conclusion of the war can decide the fate of the peoples and their regimes'. And, 'for the great part of the population, the war is lost'.

Furthermore, the German ally remained deeply unattractive, despite the fact that the 'occupation' had not so far resulted in 'incidents'. 'Nonetheless, the aversion nourished by the populace towards German troops, without any direct motive, is notable', enhanced by 'the many negative accounts of how Italians held in Germany were being treated', a report ran.[70] Nor were class divisions and those between city and terra firma healed, despite Volpi's flight. The socialist Arduino Cerutti later recalled that when he took refuge on an estate in the Po delta, where he joined the son of the rich Jewish Sullam family, 'the peasants, who knew very little about Fascism or anti-Fascism, looked at us with suspicion. [Sullam] was none other than the son of the *padrone*, and when with him and his friends you had to stay on your guard'.[71]

Nor was the situation dissimilar in the city. In the last year of the war food often ran short in Venice and Mestre. Yet 'the richer segments of society press the people down to their last drop of sweat', it was reported. Sacrifice was never equal; rather 'there are those who, in wartime, have multiplied their fortunes tenfold and do not fear the high cost of living, matching the increased expense with increased earnings'.[72]

Early in the new year, amid concern among police officials at the contempt with which they were treated by the more 'squadrist' of local Fascists (in some *calli*, squadrists had engaged in armed skirmishes with Carabinieri),[73] the message was bleaker. 'In the little world of the popular quarters, in tiny restaurants and outlying coffee shops, any notion of the *patria* and national honour is almost completely lost.' Perhaps, when Mussolini's image appeared on a newsreel, some handclaps could be heard, if only because his personal suffering was apparent on his face and elicited charitable sympathy. But no such feelings were generated by the rest of the RSI leadership, 'of whose names the great majority of the people are ignorant'. RSI propaganda was of dismal quality, and, in regard to the priorities of everyday life, its writ did not run; in daily food supplies, 'the black market imposes its prices unopposed'.[74] Despite RSI talk of social revolution, Venice in 1944 was an even less reliable Fascist redoubt than it had been in 1942.

Spurred by ancient assumptions about the imponderable life of the great, rumours readily circulated. In spring 1944 tidings spread that peace would break out on 24 April (the eve of St Mark). Other 'news' was even more sensational. Had Hitler been assaulted by Goering? Had the Führer gone mad and committed suicide? Germans in the city were meanwhile not making them-selves loved; everyone registered the fact that their disdain for Italians fell only a little short of what they reserved for Jews.[75]

So Venice's war drifted to its end through what a local historian, a little grandiloquently, has labelled the 'bloody summer' of 1944 and its aftermath, when survival became the key to family hopes and fears.[76] Now people had to put up as well as they could with the rationing of salt, the severe curtailing of hospitality over Christmas, the denunciation of Florian's for marketing contra-band coffee and a hyperbolic anti-Semitism.[77] Perhaps the leisured classes could draw some comfort from the fact that, in 1944, ninety-seven separate art exhibitions were slated for the city.[78]

'Race' was inevitably the determining factor in many people's suffering. In the elegant hall of the Ateneo Veneto, Giocondo Protti, an eminent and extrav-agantly Fascist local doctor who had earlier written how, of all political systems, only a modern dictatorship fostered genuine spiritual independence,[79] spoke on 'The Jewish Question as an Illness of Humankind' to alleged applause from an educated and respectable audience. The *Protocols of the Elders of Zion*, he urged, demonstrated why Jews should be treated like a cancer.[80] He had previ-ously advised the police that the real Church was as deeply anti-Semitic as it was anti-communist and denied the significance of occasional priestly doubts about the German alliance.[81] Within the city, two major raids on the night of 5–6 December 1943 and in August 1944 (ruthlessly involving a Jewish conva-lescent home housing the mentally and physically ill) carried Venetian Jews to their deaths.[82]

What Venetians made of such savagery is unclear, as ordinary people were driven to focus on family subsistence. Now, on occasion, the water supply to the city ran dry as a result of the bombing of Mestre and Marghera; 10 per cent of Mestre's housing stock was eliminated and a further 50 per cent damaged, while Marghera, attacked on 19 May, 6 June and 10 October 1944, lost 144 inhabitants to the bombers and witnessed the destruction of the Asilo Nerina Volpi (Nerina Volpi Kindergarten, restored after the war and still surviving, as a testament to the charity of Volpi's first wife).[83] To escape the bombing, pupils from the Liceo 'Raimondo Franchetti' were sent from Mestre to sanctuary in Venice, most lessons being suspended altogether from March 1945.[84] Life seemed almost medieval at times, as women queued by the city wells to collect water.[85] All restaurants were closed from January 1945, to be replaced by 'mense collettive di guerra' (state-run wartime canteens).[86] On the mainland, the ancient curse of malaria had returned in epidemic proportions by 1943–4. To eradicate the disease, the war victors sprayed the entire coastline from the Po to the Tagliamento with DDT every year between 1946 and 1951.[87]

Although conditions in Venice scarcely replicated the barbarisation of warfare on the eastern front, every day battle drew nearer. Protected by its reputation as the site of beloved histories and art, the city continued for the most part to be treated by the approaching Allied air power as 'open'. Nonetheless, a raid on 15 August 1944 hit a hospital ship off the Salute and its surrounds, taking forty-four lives. On 11 February 1945 the Scalzi bridge near the railway station was struck, resulting in two deaths. Six weeks later there was a serious assault on the Stazione Marittima, made graver by its explosion of a German mine store; the blast killed twelve and blew out the glass, some of it precious, from many of the city's churches.[88]

Death could also come from political action within the city, where anti-Fascist activism was stirring. On the night of 7–8 July 1944 a Fascist raid into Cannaregio in retribution for the shooting of a naval officer and two local Fascists ended in the butchering of five locals thought to be anti-Fascists. A couple of weeks later, on 26 July, Ca' Giustinian, the command post of the PFR's Guardia Nazionale Repubblicana (GNR, National Republican Guard), was bombed by the Resistance, inflicting thirteen fatalities, not all of them military. In retaliation the authorities executed thirteen imprisoned members of a partisan band from San Donà on the Piave, and exposed their bodies to public view. A week later, seven further political prisoners were shot in an execution that local people were dragooned into watching. The justification was that a German had drowned, probably because he stumbled into the lagoon when drunk. It is these victims who are still commemorated at the Riva dei Sette Martiri.[89]

Yet an alternative narrative might accept the assessment made by Giorgio Amendola of the Italian Communist Party, who, in September 1944, on a tour of inspection, upbraided the local party for being dominated by a 'shameless and ingenuous wait-and-see line'.[90] Certainly Eugenio Montesi, the PFR's initial *federale* in the city, although a self-consciously radical Fascist who did not recant after the war, tried to negotiate a deal with the anti-Fascists in the mutual hope of 'saving what was saveable'.[91] Montesi had to fight off less appeasing elements in the PFR, led by Idreno Utimperghe,[92] and, early in 1944, was replaced in his office, first by an outsider, Pier Luigi Pansera, and then by Pio Leoni, an old follower of Marsich.[93] Leoni, too, failed to unite the local Fascists, and was in turn ousted in October by Enrico Jtoyz, a unionist. At the top of government, the inability of the RSI to find a coherent political line in Venice, as elsewhere, was further evident in the fact that five prefects succeeded each other over the nineteenth months of the Republic's existence. While the Fascists of various persuasions squabbled, the more activist anti-Fascists fled to partisan bands in the hills on the mainland, given that the city was not an ideal place wherein to hide or engage in violent action.[94] For the most part and whatever the motive, therefore, Venice, rather than being a site of active resistance, at least until the end of 1944 remained a place of leisure for supporters of the RSI, of rest and recuperation for German officers and men lucky enough to be granted furlough, and of guarded passivity by the growing number of Venetians who were sure that Fascism was dying in the dishonour of military rout on the mainland.

The RSI never established a proper capital, and its ministries, whose activities were circumscribed by the all-powerful Germans, were scattered across northern Italy, Venice becoming the sanctuary of a large part of the Ministry of Foreign Affairs. More than 10,000 bureaucrats found a comfy base there – too comfy, in envious local eyes, to judge from the frequent anonymous denunciations of the newcomers as Freemasons or Mafiosi, or as being notorious for their ties with Venetian Jews. One irritated complainant drew police attention to a man deemed guilty of being 'a clerical of ineluctable cynicism'.[95] The city gave similarly uneasy welcome to the RSI's film and newsreel industries, with their raffish crew of actors, male and female, writers and the rest. In March 1944 an irked *federale* Leoni reported that 'restaurants, cafés, places to stroll are crowded from morning to curfew. Venice seems to have become a branch of the Via Veneto in the capital.'[96] Other Italians can be found resenting the city's exemption from the hardships of war and bombardment,[97] but Rome and Florence were more likely to be condemned in that regard, and Venice did allow less pampered refugees further to swell the population. By the end of 1943, it had reached a record high of 200,000.[98]

One Sard visitor and radical Fascist, Stanis Ruinas, who, immediately after the war, backed by Montesi and other ex-party radicals, tried to revive a Fascism of the left, painted a jaundiced portrait of the city during these last months of the Nazi-fascist new order. At the Hotel Luna on the Grand Canal near San Marco,[99] as he recalled after his arrival at the end of 1943, a regime salon was established, 'an elegant antechamber where you ate, you drank, you concocted business schemes, you intrigued'. By 9 p.m. every night it had transmuted into a high-class casino and bordello, thronged with 'bejewelled women with plunging neck lines'. Spies, writers, politicians and film people pullulated across the city, men who 'worked little, gained a lot and lived abundantly. A real paradise.'[100] Among the more decorous entertainments on offer was a season at the Fenice that, in 1943–4, opened with Mario del Monaco in *La Bohème*, with a supporting cast including Gianna Pederzini (Farinacci's quarrelsome lover) in *Mignon* and *Carmen* (although the addition of *La forza del destino*, *I vespri siciliani* and *Mefistofele* to the season's repertoire may have borne more subtle meaning). The following year Toti Dal Monte sang *Madama*

Butterfly, the show on 24 April 1945 being suspended at the request 'of the Committee of Liberation, which [called on] all citizens to join the national insurrection'.[101]

By the summer of 1944 a wartime curfew had finally been instituted, Ruinas remembered, to the dismay and confusion of 'the poor people who lived in the rat-holes of Castello, Malcanton and Santa Margherita'. The darkness enhanced rumours about the orgies veiled by it; the bourgeoisie dined richly at 11 p.m. and thereafter 'danced, gambled and made love' until the curfew ended at 6 a.m. Ruinas counted sixty bottles of foreign liqueur consumed on one occasion.[102] At Christmas 1944 even Ruinas had to confess that the Church was the only surviving bastion against the 'destructive madness' on all sides, committed as it was to 'saving what still remained of moral and artistic patrimony and material wealth in the Republic'. Nonetheless, at Easter 1945 he took his little daughter to the beach at the Lido, hoping against hope in a miracle weapon or in a separate peace with the Russians, who, he noted, had not bombed Italian cities in the vicious manner of the Anglo-Saxon countries.[103]

It was around this time that Venice saw the most dramatic resistance act of its war, the so-called 'Beffa del Teatro Goldoni' (Goldoni Theatre Jape), the name scoffing at D'Annunzio's heavily publicised raids – notably the 'Beffa di Buccari' of February 1918 – during the previous war. On the evening of 11 March 1945 the city worthies, still applauding or tolerating Nazi-fascist rule, gathered in the elegant theatre to watch Pirandello's *Vestire gli ignudi* (To Clothe the Naked), a play written in 1922. It had what might seem the ironical theme of a woman driven to pretend to be what she is not, reduced to suicide when the belief of others and self-belief finally dissolve. At 9.16 p.m. that evening, a band of ten partisans from the communists' Brigata Garibaldi (Garibaldi Brigade), including the post-war historian of Marghera Ivone ('Cesco') Chinello, seven other men and two women, armed and masked, burst onto the stage, proclaiming themselves representatives of the Committee of National Liberation. They announced the certain and imminent fall of Mussolini and Hitler, urging those watching to join them. They also distributed leaflets defending their cause and then, warning falsely that the theatre would be surrounded by snipers for the next half-hour, melted into the *calli* outside without casualty. It was indeed a verbal coup, and a witty one, as Radio London and other stations soon broadcast.[104]

As if seeking to deny the craven confusion evident during the Beffa, the following month some local *repubblichini* positioned machine guns at the PFR headquarters in Ca' Littoria and rambled about converting the city into another Alcázar, the fortress in Toledo successfully held by Francoists in the Spanish

Civil War. Their fanaticism evaporated, however, at the news of the Allied approach, and they fled.[105] The Germans talked of blowing up the city, but forwent such retribution following an appeal from Patriarch Piazza. The American and other Allied forces arrived on 30 April, although a Fascist X-Mas naval commando formation at Sant'Elena did not lower its flag until 7 May.[106] Perhaps among them were some who had watched a year before as a Venetian grandmother saved her sixteen-year-old grandson, the post-war cartoonist Hugo Pratt, from their band by wielding the point of her umbrella so forcibly that the commander allowed her to drag the boy back to the family house.[107]

Pratt's bathetic fate is an appropriate note on which to end an account of Venice's Second World War. With a number of exceptions, Venetians had a softer experience this time than between 1915 and 1918. Despite Fascist bombast (and Nazi terror), Venice had remained a place that was as much local as national. It similarly retained its special character as being devoted to cosmopolitan leisure, while being universally accepted as a treasure-trove of past history somehow exempt from present travails, whether by Nazi Germans seeking rest and resuscitation, or by Allied bombers venting their destruction on Marghera and Mestre but not on the 'historic city'. Venice's war was not the ferocious one that ravaged Leningrad, Warsaw, Belgrade and Berlin, nor the baleful one that brought many deaths to London and Naples. A little like Paris, a much greater city but one that also experienced a softish war, Venice was guarded from encompassing disaster by its possession of sacred urban histories of universal appeal and by being a holiday site. While perhaps a hundred million died in the rest of the world, in Venice the show went on. It was not therefore so much Volpi who gave his citizens relative tranquillity in the age of Nazi-fascism as the city's tourist vocation, which provided both the populace and the trimming and canny entrepreneur with the chance to avoid too fervent a fundamentalism. The surge of old histories and their deep roots in the tourist mind protected Venetians from the more devastating potential effects of Nazi-fascism, whether in power or in defeat. The question now was what this idiosyncratic experience of catastrophe circumvented would mean in the next world order to be imposed on the city, Italy, Europe and elsewhere in the decades after 1945.

Would it, for example, express the spirit of the Resistance and anti-Fascism in a determination ruthlessly to root out Nazi-fascists? Would victory mean punishing their 'fiancheggiatori' (fellow-travellers) and all profiteers of interwar Venice through social revolution, as many partisans avowed? Or would tourism, history and the city's holiday and leisure vocation condition the peace to an even greater extent than it had the war?

It did not take long for the city elite to suggest that they should retain their control. On 6 May Patriarch Piazza held a Te Deum in honour of the outbreak of peace. But, he made clear, it would be best if it were the peace of his conservative brand of Catholicism. As he phrased it, with a clerical sleight of hand that fused the erstwhile enemy, Nazi-fascism, with the Cold War foe to come, communism, 'Liberation from an absolute and despotic power, which became tyrannical when it served the foreigner, will doubtless long continue to be the merit and boast of the heroic volunteers for liberty'.[108]

For the moment, however, as far as the Allies were concerned, or at least those lucky enough to be presently stationed in Venice, social and ideological disputation seemed out of place. As *The Times* told its readers only a few days after Piazza's homily, the city was already in 'holiday mood'. 'Gondoliers are enjoying a rich harvest of trade and their favourite passenger is the one who will add a cigarette to the payment of the fare.' 'Happily', the city had 'suffered hardly any damage during the years of war', a striking contrast with the 'almost total destruction' of the industrial sites at Mestre and Marghera. Moreover, the paper added politely, much was due to the excellent contacts between the local chiefs of the CLN and the Allies. The Resistance had worked effectively, 'rounding up Fascists [and] preventing sabotage'. They had been scrupulous in not 'taking the law into their own hands against their oppressors', and one pleasant result was that 'supplies of food stocked in the city were surprisingly plentiful, especially sugar and flour'.[109]

Had Venice, then, simply shrugged off 'the horror, the horror' of the Second World War, to resume its jolly role as what so many foreigners thought was the 'paradise of cities'? Perhaps. At the most senior level, its urban politics transferred the putative unity of the Resistance into the mayor's office. In 1945–6, with the nominated post of *podestà* eliminated as a relic of Fascism, the interim *sindaco* chosen by the CLN was the Christian Democrat Giovanni Ponti, a Catholic whose world-view was not identical with that of Venice's cardinal patriarch nor with those of Volpi and Cini. Shortly after liberation, Ponti urged that 'the interest of the collectivity stands above that of the individual'.[110] Ponti, who had fought in the First World War and belonged to a family proud to be 'Garibaldinian' and Catholic, had been among the first in Venice to plan the reappearance of a Catholic party in early 1943 and made his anti-Fascist views plain after 25 July. With the advent of the RSI and German occupation, he was forced to flee, living for some months in disguise in Padua. In January 1945 he was arrested, and, together with his twelve-year-old son, first tortured and then sentenced to death, a punishment that was averted through the good offices of Carlo Alberto Biggini, the leading Catholic in Mussolini's last governments.[111]

Elections in April 1946 resulted in a sweeping leftist victory and entailed Ponti's replacement by Giovanni Battista ('Giobatta') Gianquinto. He had similarly been active in the Resistance, where he was one communist anxious for collaboration with democratic political groupings, adopting a vocabulary that sounded more populist or Mazzinian than Marxist or revolutionary.[112] Gianquinto maintained friendly relations with Ponti. As has been noted, each is properly commemorated outside the office of the Comune at Ca' Farsetti. In 1945–6, the two seemed to embody a victorious anti-Fascism, united in its ample and genuine popular base.

It remained easy for an attachment to the local to divert minds from the national and ideological. As Cerutti of the CLN recalled when he first re-entered the city after many years in anti-Fascist exile, 'An inexpressible emotion seized me. I felt my body tremble almost as if I had an invisible material bond with these houses and this water.' For a time he could not speak, as he traced his way back to where his wife, children and mother lived. Quickly he took over the Fascist branch offices in Castello and San Polo, automatically switching into Venetian when he needed to make an oration, since it seemed to him 'the most immediate tongue and that best fitting present circumstances'. The telephone system, he added, was still working.[113]

The relative moderation of Venetian fascism and the quietude of Venetians' war experience made it likely that the sometime followers of Mussolini would be saved from drastic purge. Volpi, Cini and Giuriati, as ex-ministers, were all arrested and arraigned but soon released, Volpi to die comfortably off in Rome on 16 November 1947. He left to his heirs his *palazzo* on the Grand Canal, a three-hundred-room palace in Rome and a four-thousand-acre property in Libya.[114] Cini lived on until September 1977, becoming in the post-war era a key player in urban cultural politics, in his turn Primo Procuratore di San Marco from 1955; in that most prestigious city office, he succeeded Ponti. Giuriati for a while seemed likely to face more political squalls, but he, too, was cleared of his record under Fascism and alleged corruption. He circumvented the condemnation he had received in absentia from the RSI in January 1944 to find a significant place in the post-war neo-Fascist Movimento Sociale Italiano (MSI, Italian Social Movement), which he retained until his death in May 1970. He was not shy of remarking that he still viewed both democrats and 'social-communists' as his 'enemy', people whom he believed had led the *patria* to 'catastrophe'.[115] He was also an unrepentant patriarch, doubting that women would want the vote if they found that politics interfered with their natural maternal role.[116]

Some humbler Fascists fell victim to peremptory justice. Captain Waifro Zani and Milite Ennio Cafiero of the National Republican Guard and Umberto Pepi of the Brigate Nere (BN, Black Brigades) were swiftly executed on 12 July at the firing range near San Nicolò on the Lido; their public trials had been conducted to loud public applause.[117] The city gaoler, Urbano Bazzeghin, was lynched without trial, and there were three further killings, the last in Cannaregio on 17 October.[118] In the main, however, Venetians did not engage in the murderous retribution that stained other parts of northern Italy during the first months of peace. For quite a few Venetians, the most shocking case of retribution in the city may have been the public attack on Cardinal Piazza as he led a Corpus Domini procession. The mother of one of the seven Resistance 'martyrs' had come to town, and she openly abused the patriarch for his record under the dictatorship. She was joined by others, who forced the priests accompanying Piazza to take sanctuary in the church offices beside San Marco.[119]

With due process, the Corte d'Assise Straordinaria (Emergency Assizes), before being shut down at the end of 1947, brought charges against 440 individuals (eight of them women) in Venice and its province. Of the 234 that were found guilty, 12 were given death sentences, 11 sentences for life and 51 sentences of between twenty and thirty years.[120] None faced trial for murdering the city's Jews.[121] Generally, as was true throughout Italy, the thirst for legal vengeance was soon slaked and most Fascists rapidly amnestied. Gianquinto intervened to lessen the sentences imposed on the *federali* Montesi and Leoni.[122] The story of the Liceo 'Raimondo Franchetti' at Mestre was typical. The headmaster, Zerbetto, was sacked on 9 May 1945 (although he resumed his career at Rovigo the following year). A temporary replacement from within the staff lasted only until 1948, when Armando Michieli was appointed head. He was a Venetian educator who had found no reason to quarrel with Fascism, having published in 1942 an anthology with the title *Fede e impero* (Faith and Empire). He had bypassed the danger of purge in 1945 and took office promising 'maximum discipline'.[123]

Meanwhile the pattern of urban cultural life was rapidly resumed, Ponti organising an exhibition of 'five centuries' of art in Venice (terminating judiciously in 1797) at the Correr by July 1945. The Ateneo Veneto soon reopened, its members readily forgetting the Nazi-fascist tirades they had listened to not long before to hail instead Venice's timeless cultural contribution to the nation, while not forgetting to thank the Allies for 'leaving intact the enchanting City of Art'.[124] They did find occasion respectfully to commemorate Giuseppe Jona, a doctor, president of the Ateneo (1925–9) and the city's first victim of the Holocaust. But they also mourned the death of Mario Alverà, saluted as a man who had loved Italy and Venice and 'was, on every occasion, courteous and affable, a true gentleman, ready to take counsel and favour good works'.[125]

The Fenice similarly resumed its repertoire, with the sage additions for a post-war world of Modest Mussorgsky's *Boris Godunov* and Dmitri

Shostakovich's *Lady Macbeth of Mtsensk* in 1946. Further adaptability was evident during the following season, when the city welcomed back the German conductor Herbert von Karajan to perform Richard Strauss's *Metamorphosen*.[126] A film festival of a kind had opened in August 1946 and another, in more ambitious vein, in 1947, although, in the decades that followed, the event lost ground to the one held at Cannes, from 1951 in spring, thereby pre-empting Venice. More celebrated was the revived, 24th Biennale of 1948; by its end, it had claimed an audience of more than 216,000, thereby surpassing its recent predecessors. In an atmosphere of post-war austerity only fifteen nations presented their works. The 'anti-Fascist' Picasso, however, banned under Mussolini and Volpi, was now accorded a retrospective show. The exhibition's organisers supplemented his work with contributions from Max Ernst, Paul Klee, Joan Miró, Piet Mondrian, Salvador Dalí, Wassily Kandinsky and the cream of the avant-garde. The contemporary music festival also recommenced – in October 1948 – although without ever replicating its pre-war reverberation.

Of most lasting significance was the return to the city of Peggy Guggenheim. Born to a wealthy family in New York in 1898, by the 1930s she was a renowned bohemian and art collector. Having retreated to her home city from Paris in 1941, five years later she reappeared in Venice. Much of her extensive collection was featured at the 24th Biennale, and in 1949 her presence in the city became permanent through her purchase of Palazzo Venier dei Leoni in Dorsoduro (encouraged by Elio Zorzi, another member of the city's cultural establishment who flourished both before and after 1945). After Guggenheim's death in 1979 the *palazzo* became and remains the site of the splendid Guggenheim Museum. Before her death she was made an honorary citizen of Venice, although her posthumous summation of the city was not free from sentimental cliché: 'There is no normal life in Venice. Here everything floats. . . . To go out in a gondola at night is to reconstruct in one's imagination the true Venice, the Venice of the past alive with romance, elopements, abductions, unaccountable deaths, gambling, lute playing, and singing.'[127]

Despite the post-war devotion to constructing welfare states as payment to the people for toppling Nazi-fascism, it did not take long for high society to resume in Venice, whether at the successive art and film festivals or at a party attended by the Aga Khan and his set at Palazzo Labia in 1951. There, the ballroom was frescoed with romantic scenes involving Antony and Cleopatra, painted in the eighteenth century by Tiepolo and others. Age had not withered Lady Diana Cooper, and she stole the show, it was said, by appearing as the Egyptian queen in a tableau imitating Tiepolo, richly dressed by Cecil Beaton and Oliver Messel. Her arrival in this garb was greeted by a cheering crowd of four thousand.[128] As Ponti had acknowledged in 1948 as he advanced towards an eventual posting as Minister of Tourism in Rome (1955–6), 'the tourist industry is what gives life to Venice'.[129]

While the beautiful people, in the immediate post-war period, numbered Venice among their preferred locations, their lives as ever connected little with those of ordinary Venetians, troubled by their housing conditions, unemployment and contestation between employers and labour over pay and conditions (even in 1943–4 there had already been major strikes at Marghera, requiring the deployment of troops for their suppression in March 1944).[130] Despite such wrangles and the damage inflicted on it by bombing, the industrial site was soon back in business, with a workforce that totalled 20,000. Major companies based there now included Edison, AGIP, Breda, Fiat, Montecatini, Shell and Esso.

It was not long before the business elite had triumphed in the city over union and other leftist political activism, which for a time had been dynamised by the 'spirit of the Resistance'. Perhaps remembering the cowardice of the Duke of Genoa on 8–9 September 1943, almost 60 per cent of Venetians voted for a Republic on 2 June 1946. In the elections for the Constituent Assembly held that same day, the communist-socialist, Partito d'Azione (P d'Az, Action Party), bloc won just short of 50 per cent of the vote, well ahead of the Christian Democrats' 38.3 per cent. That spring there were still 40,000 unemployed Venetians, and real wages stood at less than 50 per cent of pre-war levels. Strikes were common, a procession to Campo San Luca in July 1946 marked by cries of 'Fuori le donne' (Out with women workers). A year earlier, another ancient social division became manifest when 'women of the people' from around the Rialto marched through the *calli*, yelling 'Down with the peasants', the latter assumed to be greedily responsible for the high cost of basic food.[131] On another occasion the poor held together, as anti-Fascism suggested they should, a major demonstration at Mestre including women; their male comrades applauded loud female shouts of 'Death to speculators'. On 29 June 1947 a hostile crowd greeted Christian Democrat prime minister Alcide De Gasperi when he appeared in Piazza San Marco inciting the police to open fire; thirty were wounded and thirty-three arrested.[132]

Wages and employment were not the only issues. The poor in Venice continued to live in a wretchedness that was hardly imaginable among the refreshed party-goers in the *palazzi* on the Grand Canal. The indefatigable Raffaele Vivante had survived Nazi-fascist anti-Semitism to publish the last of his surveys of Venetian housing in 1948. Its findings were little different from those of earlier surveys, the number of what he considered to be 'uninhabitable' homes (1,769) being even greater than in 1935 (1,245). The achievement of Fascist welfare in this sector, he lamented, had been minimal, what work there had been being attributable to private initiative. The result was that many citizens lived in hovels, 'without a hearth, without toilets, without running water, scarcely lit, damp, with decaying floors and walls, overcrowded'. Castello and Cannaregio still counted two people in every room.[133] Emergency improvement must be the Comune's policy, Vivante once more advised.

Despite or perhaps because of such social conditions, by the April 1948 national elections the population of Venice and especially the Veneto had less sympathy for the Marxist parties. The communist-socialist bloc still won 39.6 per cent of the vote, but it fell well behind the Christian Democrats' 46.2 per cent (50.4 per cent in the Comune as a whole). The Christian Democrats carried Mestre and Marghera and the Giudecca, one of the poorer *sestieri* where some industry still functioned.[134] Cheering this swing to the right was Cardinal Patriarch Piazza, who, in typical phrasing, summoned loyal Catholics to mobilise as 'soldiers' in an anti-communist crusade to 'save God's Church and Christian civilisation for our people'.[135] In practice, it was Piazza's last throw in Venice, the Vatican transferring him to become secretary of the Congregazione Concistoriale in Rome in October 1948; he died there in October 1957. His replacement as patriarch from 1949 to 1952 was the moderate Carlo Agostini, whose installation as patriarch was, according to the prefect, 'spontaneously applauded and hymned . . . by the biggest and best part of the population'.[136] Agostini had been born in the Veneto in 1888 and pursued much of his career within the region. Predictably anti-communist but soon succumbing to poor health, after his initial flourish he made little impact on the city.[137]

The Church may have become a less strident urban force under Agostini than it had been under Piazza, but it was in practice the left that was being reduced to near impotence in both Venice and Marghera, a fact that a general strike and partial factory occupation on 14 and 15 July 1948 could not hide.[138] Some local communists undoubtedly wanted to maintain their rage, but rumours in May 1948, given credence by the prefect Gregorio Notarianni, that a Marxist paramilitary apparatus was readying to resume armed Resistance proved alarmist.[139] More acute was an account Notarianni gave in October, emphasising that 'public opinion' in relation to politics was still 'disoriented and depressed', whether in Venice, Italy or across the globe, unsure about employment prospects and fearful of the consequences of another harsh winter.[140] Wartime refugees were subsisting in regrettable 'hygienic and moral conditions' and must soon be cleared away, he noted.[141] Tourism, by contrast, had revived in a major way during the previous summer and brought in useful profits. But the prefect was uncertain whether they were sufficient to overcome the array of local problems and to sustain Venetians throughout the year.[142]

By the end of 1948 the new world order of the Cold War was settling over Venice and making it clear that talk in the Resistance about a social revolution to accompany the overthrow of Fascism had proven hollow. The dictatorship had been destroyed but its boasted totalitarianism could quickly be papered over as having been little more than an unfortunate interregnum – what the liberal philosopher-historian Benedetto Croce called a 'parenthesis'. Fortified by this cosy version of the past, those comfortable classes who had fellow-travelled with Mussolini throughout the interwar period could readily resume their lifestyles and belief systems without too much disruption to their wealth and culture. Venice today may, beside the Riva dei Sette Martiri, pay tribute to *La Partigiana*, with her promise of continuing anti-Fascist victory through permanent struggle. But neither the city's experience of a Second World War nor its peacetime condition by 1948 provide compelling evidence of a historical reality that might give body to this myth.

CHAPTER EIGHT

The many deaths of post-war Venice, 1948–1978

Thrice in the twentieth century patriarchs of Venice left for Rome to become popes: Giuseppe Sarto (patriarch 1894–1903, Pius X 1903–14, canonised 29 May 1954), Angelo Giuseppe Roncalli (patriarch 1953–8, John XXIII 1958–63, beatified 3 September 2000, to be canonised April 2014) and Albino Luciani (patriarch 1969–78, John Paul I 26 August to 28 September 1978). One memory site of the two post–1945 prelates is the Piazzetta dei Leoncini, on the northern side of San Marco, across from the sarcophagus of Manin (see map 3). Directly opposite the Risorgimento hero's tomb is a weathered medallion of Roncalli, an accompanying inscription noting that the Piazzetta (its little lions here upgraded to 'Leoni') was 'dedicated to Pope John XXIII by the unanimous vote of the communal council, 16 May 1966'. Away to the north-east stands the grand, nineteenth-century Palazzo Patriarcale, converted into the administrative centre of Venetian Catholicism after the transfer of cathedral status from San Pietro in Castello to San Marco in 1807. The left side of its façade bears another memorial inscription to Roncalli, here lauded for having engaged in the same urban 'mission' as Saints Pius X and Lorenzo Giustiniani (1381–1456, the city's first patriarch), while preparing for 'the ecumenical breadth and innovative ferment of his pontificate'; it concludes with a note of his beatification during the 'Holy Year of the Millennium' in 2000. On the other side of the portal, an observer can pay more modest homage to John Paul I, praise of his short pontificate recording that he 'opened the path to new hope' (by implication, paving the way to the populism of his successor John Paul II, the death of communism and 'the end of history').

If the Piazzetta dei Leoncini echoes with the somewhat discordant sounds of Catholic and patriotic memory in Venice, the Molino Stucky on the Giudecca offers pasts, and presents, both capitalist and worker, as was appropriate for an Italy and a Venice contested by the Christian Democrat Party (DC) and its

28 Roncalli remembered

Marxist rivals, notably the PCI, for two generations after 1945 (see map 1). Following the murder of Giovanni Stucky, founder of the mill, in 1910, the business was directed by his son Giancarlo, a bachelor with a taste for languages and a passion for motor boat racing and the arts. For a time he was a generous patron of Mariano Fortuny. Giancarlo Stucky cherished close ties with Volpi, Cini and the Venetian financial and business establishment, joining them in initiating the urban branch of Rotary. Completing what must have seemed his gratifying insertion into the interwar city elite, his sister married the brother of *podestà* Mario Alverà.[1]

The mill fell into financial travail after the Wall Street crash, however, Stucky failing in lengthy attempts to wring compensation from the state for alleged war damage. Giancarlo, like his father, was a Swiss citizen, and in 1917 the mill had a large Swiss flag spread across its roof to ward off Austrian attacks. Whether or not as a result, it was not bombed as heavily as were the Cotonificio Veneziano or the tobacco factory. Its business did suffer from raids on the Giudecca, however, and from the general dislocation of Venice's First World War, from which it recovered only haltingly. By 1932 the Banca Commerciale had cut off its credit, and in the years that followed Giancarlo Stucky relinquished family control over the mill, sold his art collection and passed what had been his ownership of the neo-classical Palazzo Grassi on the Grand Canal to Cini (who managed to divert an attempt by PNF secretary Starace to seize it for Fascist party use). By 1939 the business located at the Molino Stucky was just another part of Volpi's massive holdings in the Società Adriatica di Elettricità (SADE), while Giancarlo Stucky was a lonely old man, bedridden and awaiting death in a rented apartment.[2]

The transfer of the mill to Volpi's commercial empire failed to stem its decline. In 1955 the premises were abandoned and left to rot, cliché enjoining that a late nineteenth-century structure had no justification in a Venice that should treasure only buildings erected before 1797. The site was nonetheless acquired in 1994 by the Gruppo Acqua Pia Antica Marcia, a Roman concern dating back to Pius IX's rule before 1870, directed by the adventurous entrepreneur Francesco Caltagirone Bellavista. It sponsored a major restoration of the Molino, despite being hampered by a serious fire of 15 April 2003, in which much of the historic interior, including the mill chapel, was destroyed. In June 2007, the building reopened as the Hilton Molino Stucky, and so it remains, described by its website as a five-star hotel, equipped with a spa, a ballroom that can cater for a thousand guests, and major conference facilities. Twinned with the Redentore church at the other end of the Giudecca, the Stucky hotel, despite rumours of renewed financial troubles, dominates the *sestiere*'s streetscape.[3]

29 The Stucky Hilton today

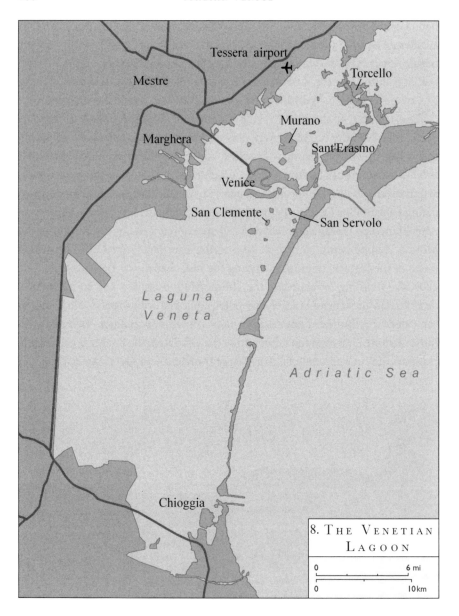

Mestre

Tessera airport

Torcello

Murano

Marghera

Sant'Erasmo

Venice

San Clemente

San Servolo

Laguna
Veneta

Adriatic Sea

Chioggia

8. The Venetian
Lagoon

0   6 mi

0   10 km

The hotel's blurb makes much of the 'Skyline Rooftop Bar', recommending its fine views over the city. For those aware of Venice's modern historics, at least as good is the expansive vista of the Marghera industrial site, a business zone crucial to the urban economy during the Fascist years and a major contributor to the war effort, as we have seen, and of still greater significance and controversy after 1945. Anyone who ponders the fate of the city's economy, its class conflicts during the post-war era and those environmental troubles that drastically surfaced in the great flood of 3–4 November 1966 might well pay the cost of a coffee or Campari at the Hilton bar so that they can scan Marghera – all 11,000 square metres of it (the site is larger than historic Venice).[4] After all, in a perhaps not too distant future, tourists may well be lured by the pasts of two Venices, one the old city, the other the industrial archaeological site of Marghera, where the triumphs and follies of twentieth-century industrialisation will be represented for all to see.

It is no surprise to find that the theme of death in Venice became all but automatic as the post-war decades succeeded each other. Although the number of those living there may have been at its highest when Venice was giving sanctuary to refugees in 1944–5, the official population of the historic centre peaked in 1951 at 174,808 (218,845 if inhabitants of the islands in the lagoon were included). A decade later, the tally in old Venice had sunk to 137,150, and it continued to fall. In 1971 there were 108,426 Venetians, in 1981 93,598, in 1991 76,644 and in 2001 65,695. Ten years later the urban population counted a meagre 59,635. About half as many were living on the islands and three times the number made their homes at Mestre or in the outlying villages that constitute the Comune di Venezia.[5] An alarmist but typical press report of 2006 suggested that by 2030 old Venice would be empty except for tourist throngs. Certainly, in strictly numerical terms, Venetians might better be viewed in our age of ever more mighty metropolises not as citizens of a city but as dwellers in a large village.[6] In the 1950s environmentalists launched what proved to be an ongoing debate as to whether the world was facing the physical death of Venice. By the new millennium there could be little argument that Venetians, at least if narrowly defined, were dying out without sign of arrest.

During the first years of peace, however, in which the city was embraced by the world system of the Cold War, Venetians mulled over more immediate concerns. The most obvious was the renunciation of the idea that anti-Fascist victory entailed a social revolution, or indeed any shaking of Venice's class structure and economic order. Prefects kept a careful watch on support for the Communist Party and the social conditions that sustained it, levels of unemployment being registered with particular nervousness, closely followed by poor, damp living conditions.[7] The arrival of tourists, still viewed as seasonal (commencing around Easter), was therefore greeted with relief as hotels filled and employment rose, while celebrities were said to be bringing a refreshing atmosphere to the city.[8] Long after the war, *Il Gazzettino* sedulously applauded a return visit by the ageing Cole Porter.[9]

In the official mind, from which residues of attitudes under the dictatorship had been scarcely purged, 'social-communists', such as those grouped from 1944 in the Confederazione Generale Italiana del Lavoro (CGIL, Italian General Confederation of Labour), were deemed alien to the nation, especially after the exit of Christian Democrat and Social Democrat unionists to found rival bodies in 1948. The PCI was thought to serve the 'interests of the Soviet state' and to subordinate its local policies to that end.[10] In reaction, prefects reported as though it were the norm their approval of intervention by the Carabinieri to 'preserve the freedom to work' and to counter strikes.[11] Prefectural scolding was similarly elicited when, in October 1949, the local branches of the national partisan organisation, the Associazione Nazionale Partigiani d'Italia (ANPI), another body based on a popular front alliance, called for a month-long celebration of the Resistance in Venice.[12]

Much of the atmosphere of the post-war city was encapsulated at the textile factory, the Cotonificio. In 1948 it had been taken over by the national concern SNIA Viscosa, which centred its main production elsewhere. Labour agitation by the largely female workforce, notably in 1946–7 and 1951–2, was greeted curtly by management. Business was backed by the local priest, who fixed an 'enormous cross, clearly visible from land and sea', on the factory chimney; its message, he preached, was the urgent need for 'the redemption of a working class and of a city that had fallen into the hands of the left'.[13]

Employment at the Cotonificio and the other surviving industrial sites dribbled away. Any serious activity at the Arsenale also ceased, after a flurry of public protest in 1957 that briefly united the Christian Democrat mayor Roberto Tognazzi (1955–8) and the socialist and communist unions. Even *Il Gazzettino* praised a (fifteen-minute) work stoppage on the morning of 1 March, the struggle being defined as for 'the rights of the *arsenalotti* and the historic rights of Venice itself'.[14] Patriarch Roncalli similarly hailed the 'noble initiative' and promised to pray for its success.[15] But not even he could arrest the Arsenale's decay as a work site, despite many rhetorical invocations of the place's glorious history.

In 1971, 6,999 artisans were employed in the city and its islands (their number more than halved over the next two decades).[16] But historic Venice was losing its labouring people. Class tussles were therefore fought out not so much in old Venice as across the lagoon at Marghera. There, the Breda heavy industrial and shipbuilding business was the most fiercely contested battleground between bosses and workers, anti-Fascists not forgetting that its buildings had been aggressively stamped with the regime's slogan 'Vincere' (Fight to Victory) during the Fascist war.[17]

Once Fascism had been vanquished, on 27 April 1945 armed workers had occupied the Breda factory yard, and in the months that followed they pushed hard to reduce the sixty-seven-hour week and improve pay and conditions. After the CGIL had established a 'permanent agitation committee' in the summer of 1949, matters came to a head. On 5 January 1950 a demonstration in the historic centre of Venice so galvanised its supporters that they took an hour and a half to file into Campo Santo Stefano. The workers protested that they and their 2,000 comrades had not been paid for two months,[18] a union chief announcing that the assembly represented 'a united, strong, worker Venice omitted in the tourist guides'.[19] In response, on 1 February the management sacked 400 blue-collar and 150 white-collar workers. The strike continued, Venice's mayor Gianquinto showing solidarity by joining unionists at Marghera on 14 March. The next day, on police instructions, soldiers fired on strikers, wounding three. Another demonstration followed, this time intruding into what was once again being established as the bourgeois site of Piazza San Marco, where the bloodied shirt of one of the injured was hung from the Ala Napoleonica.[20] Gianquinto was then arraigned for the crime, left over from the dictatorship, of 'inciting disrespect for and abuse of institutions, the law and constituted authority', as well as for infringing 'the freedom to work'.[21]

For all the passion of their protests, the workers were not destined to win. The prefect reported his disgust at Gianquinto's 'irresponsibility' in favouring the strike, claiming that 'every social class' in the city was 'absolutely hostile' to the demonstrations. The majority, he added, fully approved of police actions and had been waiting for the authorities to restore order. After all, the first tourists were now filling the hotels; given the Holy Year proclaimed by the pope in Rome, there should be more of them that summer.[22] Faced with such opposition, the ability of the labour movement to resist weakened. Breda reopened in May, employing a workforce half the size of six months earlier, mostly on short-term contracts.[23] Marghera was back in the hands of the employers, even if, throughout the Venice region, two million work hours were lost to strikes during the two years that followed the 1948 elections and another general strike was called on 21 December 1950.[24]

Thereafter, union agitation faltered. With productivity rising faster than the wage bill, Marghera could move into new and profitable manufactures, 31,000 men and women being employed there by 1970 in 218 separate concerns.[25] 'Improvements' at the port were widely supported, including a grand scheme to dig a new and much deeper Canale dei Petroli from Malamocco (14.5 metres as against the 4 metres of its original construction and 10 metres in 1900, with a resultant acceleration of the tidal process from two and a half hours to half an hour).[26] The increased commercial traffic to be fostered was to allow expansion of the site into a 'third zone', vaster than the total development at that time. Production had rocketed 150 per cent between 1949 and 1955,[27] a growth rate that made Venice part of what was being called the national 'economic miracle'.

Early in the 1950s, the Società Industrie Chimiche Edison (SICE, Edison Industrial Chemicals Company) began fabricating plastics, the wonder product of the moment, with know-how deriving from the vast American firm Monsanto, confident that neither Venice nor Italy was going to veer from the right side of the Cold War.[28] As in the interwar period, SICE's workers were more likely to be peasants hired from the Veneto than citizens of Venice itself. Factory conditions remained harsh, with strictly enforced rules about breaks in labour (a 'smoko' must not last an instant more than the smoking of one ciga-rette), rigid checks on theft after a shift and constant discouragement of union activity (in 1967 only 7 per cent of the workforce were members). Rather than prating about social solidarity, Edison preferred a wide gap between worker culture and that of the management and technicians. Worst was the pollution, 'airless workplaces, very high temperatures, dust, smoke, acid and poison gas spills', which, as one commentator has eloquently put it, 'chiselled their labour onto the bodies of the workforce'.[29]

Through the 1950s Marghera flourished sufficiently to offer employees a degree of well-being, albeit at a price. Elsewhere in the city and its comune, poverty and unemployment stayed at troublingly high levels, officials recording 20,000 without work in 1954, a figure not helped by the imminent closure of the Stucky concern on the Giudecca.[30] Three years later, two-thirds of the city's housing stock was pronounced in need of restorative work, only a quarter possessed a bath and 10 per cent central heating. As in the past, the worst living conditions were to be found in Castello, Cannaregio and the Giudecca and the best in the richer *sestieri*. More than 13 per cent of houses still placed their toilet facilities in the kitchen (Castello 21 per cent, San Marco 5 per cent).[31] Despite the economic miracle, there were many Venetians to whom prosperity had scarcely trickled down, and who scrimped through, as in the past, if often indirectly, from tourist monies and familial deals.

Contrary to initial expectations, the 1950 season had not been a bumper one and the prefect was inclined to blame poor organisation for the relatively low turnout at the 25th Biennale[32] and the 11th film festival (despite the presence of an 'elegant international public' at the latter).[33] While another tourist summer passed, police spent their time in such humdrum activities as expelling pickpockets and checking the physical health of prostitutes, both arriving on cue with the tourists.[34] As he congratulated himself in late October, however, 'for a long time now, the left-wing parties have no longer organised demonstrations in the Capital [Venice], their leaders doubtless preoccupied that, if they did, a failure would result'.[35]

Who, then, ruled the city, now that the tremors caused by the dictatorship and its fall had been stilled? The formal answer was the same in Venice as it was, after the 'Cold War' election of 1 April 1948, in Rome: the Christian Democrats. Local elections held in May 1951 saw Gianquinto and his leftist allies defeated. Angelo Spanio, a local doctor like Davide Giordano in 1919 (though a less splenetic one), became mayor, an office destined to remain in DC hands until 1975. A prefect may have remarked acerbically that the Catholic party lacked members of real calibre and was inferior to the communists in discipline and organisation.[36] But for a decade and more the city and its surrounding province became citadels of social Catholicism, Italy-style.

Tourists ebbed and flowed. In 1950 the annual tally of those who lodged in the historic centre surpassed one million, rising by a further 500,000 over the following decade.[37] This influx prompted the first discussions of what the arrival of the 'masses' entailed, even if for the present that term meant 'middling' Americans rather than working people on package deals.[38] One immediate effect may have been that ordinary Venetians were exposed to fashions from the wider world as never before, now consuming on an everyday basis spaghetti, pizza and the tomato, a southern diet that had previously been alien to them.[39] From 1961 until his death in 1972, the formerly pro-Fascist American poet Ezra Pound and his long-term lover Olga Rudge were prominent among the expatriates who found a home in the city and were lionised there. In return, at least according to journalist Judith Martin, Rudge paradoxically led the rescue of the work of Venetian baroque composer Antonio Vivaldi (1678–1741) in what had been his city. Martin adds tersely, 'the good news is that [today] there is a choice of small concerts in Venice every night. The bad news is that they all play Vivaldi.'[40]

Of celebrities with more fleeting contact with the city, Princess Margaret, the younger sister of England's queen perennially in search of a role for herself, was reported to 'love' Venice and did, from time to time, attend the parties staged there or on the terra firma by Volpi's daughter and granddaughter and other members of the elite.[41] Venice retained, and retains, high society attractions. Yet the post-war era gave the beautiful people a more global panorama than had been the case before 1939. Margaret, for one, was soon more often to be found at Mustique in the West Indies than at the Gritti Palace, which had looked after her on her first trip to Italy in 1949, when she was still naively musing on the difficulty of remembering every painting in every museum and every church.[42]

For those who thought of themselves as the arbiters of taste, Venice was not what it had once been, even if they had not yet fully abandoned the Lido for Sardinian or more exotic beaches, as they soon would. Like the princess, they might still accept invitations to parties at one or other of the *palazzi* along the Grand Canal. As Cecil Beaton recorded in his diary in August 1961, some were captivated by the annual ball held by Volpi's widow, 'Lili' (Nathalia). Among those in attendance were a Rothschild or two, and Elsa Maxwell, who, he wrote, 'looked like a terrified buffalo' as she was hauled from a gondola by 'husky servants' and ushered up a red carpet into the patrician residence acquired by Giuseppe Volpi. Distressingly, Beaton observed, 'the great assemblage was exactly the same group of Venetian society as it was last year and all the years before . . . there was no note of originality. No dress was outstanding. Only Lili Volpi's beehive hair-do was remarkable in the boldness of its proportions.' But even she looked wan at the tedium of it all, berating her servants, and ill-naturedly charging her stepdaughter Anna Maria for the break-up of her marriage on the one hand and for the shortcomings of the orchestra hired for the event on the other. No doubt, 'the cold buffet was a triumph of the chef's art with huge octopi made of lobster; a gondolier rowing a decorated bass; two bleeding mountains of cascading beef; crawfish filled with crevettes, and pinnacles of shrimps'. But as a female guest murmured to Beaton, who could not but agree, the whole party was 'a terrible bore'.[43]

A different aspect of tourist interest and an accompanying unapologetic sense of the foreign ownership of Venice occurred in 1966, when 'two English women, Mrs Helen Saunders and Miss Mabel Raymond-Hawkins', caused a stir by going on 'mission' to the city on more than one occasion. Their purpose was to improve the lot of Venetian cats, winning for their pains a positive editorial in *The Times* headed 'Good Deeds in Venice' and any amount of local sarcasm.[44] Five years later, no less a figure than John Sparrow, the Warden of All Souls, Oxford, felt impelled to protest in the grand manner about the state of the city's pavements and to demand '*the absolute exclusion from Venice of the dog*' (his italics), an animal he described as 'that indefatigable and unsavoury engine of pollution', a greater threat than *acque alte*. Such flooding, he japishly suggested, gave proof that 'nature herself resents this new blot upon the city and is sympathetically anxious to efface it'.[45]

High culture was still promoted at the various annual and biennial exhibitions of painting, sculpture (thirty-six different nations sponsored exhibits in 1958), cinema, theatre (*Twelfth Night* was performed outdoors in 1951)[46] and music (Toscanini's return to the Fenice in 1949 was broadcast direct to BBC's

Radio 3).[47] Shortly thereafter, the arts were given an additional thrust through the establishment of the Cini Foundation in a restored monastery on the island of San Giorgio, just across from Piazza San Marco. The name was all the more appropriate in that Vittorio Cini was mourning the death of his son Giorgio, killed in a flying accident near Cannes in 1949 and eulogised by Nino Barbantini, a local cultural manager who had fought in the First World War and remained a leading figure in the organisation of artistic activity in the city under Fascism. Young Giorgio, Barbantini wrote deferentially after being appointed the Foundation's first president in 1951, was 'exuberant in his youthful vitality . . . of exceptional intelligence, alacrity [and] smiling good-will'.[48] He was also said to have helped his father's release from Dachau in 1944 through his adroit distribution of diamonds and other jewellery given to him by his actor mother, Lyda Borelli, to corrupt members of the SS. He deserved commemoration.

Certainly, then and thereafter, the Cini Foundation fulfilled a major role in expressing Venetian culture of an established kind. The body's first organising committee was studded with the top people of the city, including, among others, the patriarch, the prefect, the head of the local Court of Appeals, the mayor and the president of the Biennale. Its initial rubric worthily promised that, at a 'Centro Professionale', it would teach 'abandoned boys of the people' such helpful skills as printing, tailoring and building, while sailors could be trained at a 'Centro Marinaro'.[49] Over the years, however, the Foundation's prime emphasis became more scholarly than practical, with a reverential focus on the pre–1797 past rather than a tough analysis of contemporary events. Cini may have been the first to make what was to become a hackneyed parallel when he expressed the hope that Venice would not end up as 'a bad copy of Disneyland'.[50] The London *Times* registered the Foundation's commencement of activities on 14 July 1954 with an open-air staging at San Giorgio of a sixteenth-century mystery play, *Life and Resurrection*. As the paper put it vaguely (unusual in Britain in having momentarily forgotten the war), Cini 'is said to be one of the richest men in Venice'.[51]

But the most public face of the city was Catholic, its special symbol from 1953 the portly figure of the new patriarch, Angelo Roncalli (in 1958 he weighed 205 pounds).[52] Although Roncalli had worked for long years as a Vatican diplomat, stationed in Ankara during the war and Paris after it, he was represented in his new office as a man of the people. Born in a village in Bergamo province in 1881, a territory ruled by the Republic from 1428 to 1797, he readily asserted a special bond with Venice. He gave it religious colour through an alleged heritage from San Lorenzo Giustiniani, allowing his eulogists to maintain that he was 'deeply in love with Venice and its religious and civic traditions'.[53] The fifth centenary of Giustiniani's death fell in January 1956, and, with the vastly rich historical store of the Church to draw on, naturally provided an opportunity for contemporary teaching.

Before his first year in the city was out, Roncalli had politely seconded the aims of the Cini Foundation and those behind it as fostering 'a well-being that was civic, social and international'.[54] He wrote privately to his friend in the Vatican Giovanni Battista Montini, his eventual successor as pope, that he was delighted to be made ex officio Honorary Abbot of San Giorgio, whose Foundation, he was sure, would 'bring honour to our time and spiritual wealth to the future of Venice and Italy'.[55] His approval of the various kinds of capitalism operating across the lagoon was even swifter than his endorsement of establishment culture. Installed as patriarch at San Marco on 15 March 1953, twelve days later he took mass in the Cappella AGIP at Marghera.[56]

When Roncalli became Pope John XXIII, soon to summon the Second Vatican Council, he acquired clout for opening the Church to modern times and being willing to talk to such foes of Catholicism as Protestants, Jews, Moslems and communists. In Venice, his course in this regard was by no means clear, being mostly characterised by prudent endorsement of the hard-line stance of Pope Pius XII (1939–58). In 1956, for example, Roncalli preached to the faithful that 'a Catholic absolutely cannot give his vote to those lists which represent clear and specific opposition to Christian doctrine and which fight with a bitterness that knows no let-up against the Catholic Church throughout the world; I mean, above all, the Communists and that part of the Socialists who are their accomplices'. Any notion of an opening to the left, he concluded, must be eschewed. It would amount to 'a most serious doctrinal error and . . . a flagrant violation of Catholic discipline'. Marxism was, he insisted, 'the negation of Christianity'.[57]

Stiffening Catholic politics in Venice was the ghost of Cardinal Patriarch Sarto, Pope Pius X, elevated to sainthood by Pius XII on 29 May 1954. In Venice, this sanctification reminded spokespersons of the Church of parochial history: Sarto had left the city for his conclave pronouncing, 'Either alive or dead, I shall come back to Venice.'[58] Roncalli entertained fond memories of Pius X's role in his own early career (after his ordination in August 1904 he had enjoyed five personal audiences with this pope).[59] Fifty years later, he was glad to report to Montini that the first church to take the name of 'Saint Pius X' had opened at Marghera 'at the very centre of worker activity', where it still stands at Via Nicolodi 2, not too far from a parish devoted to 'Jesus the Worker'.[60] In January 1957 Roncalli sounded as hard-line as his anti-modernist predecessor when he damned the 'plagues' that afflicted 'the crucifix': liberalism, Marxism, 'democratism', Freemasonry and laicism.[61]

The fullest adaptation of Saint Pius X's history by the local Church had to wait until 1959 to be implemented, however, by which time Roncalli sat in Rome as Pope John XXIII and the Venetian-born Giovanni Urbani had become cardinal patriarch (he was to die in office in September 1969). Between Sunday 12 April and Sunday 10 May 1959, Pius X was accorded a month-long celebration in Venice. In Rome, Roncalli proclaimed that Sarto, 'a great Son of our stock' (*stirpe*), was returning to the city 'more alive than ever'. Pius X had been exhumed in May 1944 as part of his course towards beatification and then canonisation, his body eventually being reburied under the altar of the Chapel of the Presentation in St Peter's. Now it was removed, and, on 9 April, John XXIII, accompanied by the Palatine Guard bearing flags and playing suitably holy music, made his way to the Vatican railway station to salute the dead pontiff's remains. In an ornamented glass casket, the body then journeyed north-east, under the protection of a number of priests and some government ministers and under-secretaries, among them the young Oscar Luigi Scalfaro, destined to become his nation's president from 1992 to 1999. The train stopped briefly at Florence at midnight to be venerated by the local archbishop, the cortege reaching Venice at 4.10 a.m., where it was greeted by what was described as a 'massive' crowd, wide awake despite the hour.

A pause followed. At 4 p.m., however, the catafalque was transferred from the station, where the new archbishop of Vittorio Veneto, Albino Luciani, had joined the celebrants. Now televising of the event began, despite the difficulties confronted by the technology of the time in setting up in Piazza San Marco. One piece of equipment was said to weigh fourteen tonnes, while a number of thirty-five-metre-high pylons were laboriously erected.[62] At 4.30 Pius X's body floated down the Grand Canal in a superbly dressed vessel rowed by eighteen oarsmen in eighteenth-century garb, amid the clangour of the city's bells.[63] As the aquatic procession passed, onlookers fell to their knees in worship. At the Rialto, according to an official account, 'the crowd flooded the area and was impossible to contain'. Flowers rained down on the dead saint and a flight of doves fluttered auspiciously backwards and forwards over the boat, 'before the amazed and deeply moved onlookers'. Some recalled, with a Catholic certainty that right must eventually prevail, that, when Sarto had been appointed to Venice, his installation had been perversely delayed by the machinations of a 'radical-Masonic junta', headed by Selvatico. Now, it was implied in sweet revenge, such wicked leftists must turn in their unhappy graves. When the cortege reached the Molo, the pope's body was saluted by further members of the government, notably the Christian Democrat Minister of State Participation, Mario Ferrari Aggradi, and by representatives of the armed forces. The procession then marched in stately solemnity across the square to the Basilica, to the setting of a brilliantly shining sun. Pius X was 'back' in 'his' Basilica.

In the weeks that followed, an estimated 120,000 took communion, while up to 30,000 pilgrims queued daily to pay respect to the saint as he lay in his glass casket; on one day 15,000 pilgrims arrived from Padua alone.[64] In total, *Il Gazzettino* reckoned, one million had venerated the papal remains.[65] Special masses were held for the female members of the social-political organisation Azione Cattolica (AC, Catholic Action), while in a more drastic version of Catholic patriotism the Association of Julian and Dalmatian Refugees attended a service on the Feast of St Mark, 25 April, implicitly contesting the leftist view that it marked the anniversary of anti-Fascist victory in 1945. Urbani then sermonised, judiciously stating that Pius X's reappearance in the city best demonstrated the eternal centrality of Catholicism in Venetian life.

On 10 May it was time for effusive farewells, Cardinal Giuseppe Siri, the conservative archbishop of Genoa, maintaining that the battle Pius X had waged against modernism needed renewing, and Cardinal Giacomo Lercaro of Bologna offering a less pungent message. Another procession down the Grand Canal then began, at the end of which Pius X was loaded back onto a train and carried to Rome, with stop-overs this time at Mestre, Rovigo, Ferrara, Bologna, Prato, Florence and Arezzo. John XXIII, borne aloft in the papal *sedia gestatoria* by presumably muscular Vatican servants, greeted the cortege on its return, before the dead pope again settled into the holy place reserved for his body at St Peter's.[66] Back in Venice, the events of 1959 were already recorded on a memorial stone just short of the garage at Piazzale Roma, complete with a flattering bust of a square-jawed pope. Even though the petrol outlet is slated for closure, the monument stands as a reactionary Catholic entry-statement to today's city.

Despite his personal asceticism, Pius XII had presided over a Roman Church, gorgeous in its ceremony. Pius X's posthumous return to Venice might make it seem that, with John XXIII as pope, little had changed in Catholicism's concept of helpful publicity. Certainly Roncalli's elevation had been welcomed at the Ateneo Veneto with an obsequious paralleling of the successive pontiffs. The speaker did aver, however, that the new pope, despite his long experience and wide culture, was 'a son of simple people', whose choice of name prefigured a move to widen the Church's vision in the modern world.[67] And Venetians knew that, when he had been cardinal patriarch of their city, Roncalli had on occasion appeared to be his own man and not merely the agent of Pius XII's reactionary line.

Early in his reign in the city, he had explained that he treasured both the great and the small histories of Venice. He amplified that implied populism by

30 A militant Pius X blesses Venice

revealing that he favoured reviving a scheme of his predecessors under Austrian rule Ján Ladislaus Pyrker (1820–7) and Jacopo Monico (1827–51) to move the richly decorated medieval iconostasis in the Basilica to allow better public view of the sanctuary during religious celebrations. Perhaps ill-advisedly, Roncalli claimed in spring 1955 that he had been persuaded on the issue by 'discontent expressed by the faithful not only in Venice but especially among the very numerous foreigners who throng here from every part of the world'.[68] In the months that followed, a noisy campaign spread in objection to his plan, with the usual insistence that Venice must be preserved 'com'era e dov'era'. An alliance hostile to change embraced local notables Diego Valeri and Elio Zorzi, as well as such national figures as the environmentalist Antonio Cederna. By July 1955 communist deputies had raised the matter of the patriarch's 'vandalism' in the Chamber of Deputies in Rome. Roncalli had been able to rely on Cini's public backing, but obduracy became impossible. In his Easter message of 1957 the patriarch still expressed the hope that 'modern technology' might resolve the matter,[69] insisting that Venice must be more than a museum. Yet he also conceded grudgingly that it would be better if there were no major alteration to the internal architecture of San Marco.[70]

At the beginning of his appointment as patriarch, Roncalli had stressed his commitment to an aphorism of St Augustine: 'We must hate error but love those who err'.[71] In 1957 he gave a practical cast to such a charitable precept by welcoming socialists who were assembling in Venice for a party conference, suggesting that they be offered 'traditional Venetian hospitality'. He added that he hoped such 'brothers from all the regions of Italy' might move towards 'the ideals of truth, goodness, justice and peace'; their congress could have a positive impact on 'the immediate direction' of the country.[72] To the disgust of hard-line rightists, these sentiments nourished, whether intentionally or not, the idea then sprouting in some sections of the DC that there could be 'an opening to the left' that might expand the base of the government, lessen the reliance on neo-fascist backing (approved by Pius XII) and have the tactical advantage of separating the Socialist Party from that of the communists.

More significant than his good-heartedness towards visiting socialists was Roncalli's tolerance of the young Christian Democrat radical Wladimiro Dorigo, born in 1927, a man destined to play a major role in urban history in the following decades. The son of a socialist railway worker, Dorigo had fought in the Catholic resistance as a teenager, and during the 1950s rose rapidly to become a national chief of Catholic Action's youth organisation. It was not long, however, before he distanced himself from the reactionary line of Pius XII's Church, being one of the first in the DC to favour a compromise with the socialists. He was soon in trouble in Venice, where he edited a left-leaning Catholic paper and had taken charge of town planning on the local council. In a typical piece published in the *Rivista di Venezia* late in 1957, Dorigo took no hostages in fulminating against 'the power-crazed, chaotic, absurd anarchy' that, in his view, had previously characterised the city's urban planning or non-planning. Remedial action, he preached, was urgent.[73] Through such stinging words, he placed himself in a position of grave antagonism towards the Church authorities and the city establishment. In February 1958 he resigned from his various offices in Venice, although continued to represent himself as a 'Christian Democrat independent' for a number of years. Back in 1956 Roncalli had tried to divert elite anathemas by telling the Curia charitably that 'Dr Dorigo is an intelligent young man of unblemished life and fervent religious observation, foreign to any egotistical calculations, and yet very firm, one would say obstinate, in his ideas, which he defends with unusual dialectical ability'.[74] In his soul, the cardinal patriarch was not a fully reliable advocate of reaction in the way that Cardinals Piazza and La Fontaine (and Sarto) and Pope Pius XII had been.

Planning was a central idea in every post-war European city, and a revised city plan (*piano regolatore*) for Venice was drafted in 1956 (largely based on one approved in 1937) and then revised in 1962. While such schemes were being formulated, Venetians engaged in lively debates about such matters as housing development on Sacca Fisola, a marshy island beyond the Stucky mill at the western end of the Giudecca.[75] More controversial was the proposal to hire the celebrated American architect Frank Lloyd Wright to design a building in his modernist style on the Grand Canal, next to the baroque Palazzo Balbi.[76] The plan was welcomed by Carlo Scarpa among others, but opposed within the city and by 'lovers of Venice' outside, the London *Times* keeping its readers up to date on the issue. Fans of 'Venezia com'era e dov'era' were delighted when, in April 1954, the Comune refused building permission, stating primly that the Lloyd Wright proposal 'violated the existing rules with regard to height and distance from other buildings'.[77] Despite this rejection and the failure of Le Corbusier to proceed with a hospital at Cannaregio a decade later (in the 1930s he had been close to equipping Venice with a modish aquarium),[78] modernist architecture did penetrate the city, Carlo Scarpa's design of an Olivetti showroom in the Procuratie Vecchie under the colonnades of Piazza San Marco (1958–9) and his reworking of the Fondazione Querini Stampalia near Santa Maria Formosa (1961–3) being early examples.[79] Less than an architectural triumph was the headquarters of the Ente Nazionale per l'Energia Elettrica (ENEL, National Electricity Agency), the successor company to SICE, on the Rio Novo, its decaying building winning headlines in 2009 when part of the ceiling collapsed.[80]

In the 1950s the greatest novelty in urban politics was the rise of environmentalist concerns about the city, especially as marshalled by an organisation that called itself Italia Nostra (IN, Our Italy) and published a monthly magazine under the same name. Its first president, in 1955, was the Liberal senator Umberto Zanotti Bianco, an anti-Fascist from the summit of Italian society, with an English mother and excellent international connections. IN won over many in the national elite. In 1961 the Venetian subcommittee included quite a few patricians, among them Anna Maria Cicogna Volpi and Teresa Foscari Foscolo, each destined to make her mark in the organisation locally and nationally. Among other scions of families that had flourished during the interwar period who joined IN were Alessandro Marcello and Giorgio Marsich.[81]

IN's initial preoccupation had been the preservation of the historic centre of Rome. But it almost immediately began preaching that Venice, too, must be left 'com'era e dov'era' in its central zone, while being critical of recent housing developments on Sant'Elena, for example. It sternly rejected 'insane' schemes to build a road along the north edge of the city or to unite Venice with the Lido,

Iesolo and the various islands by another bridge or by an underwater tunnel, as well as opposing suggestions to expand parking at Piazzale Roma, a place, in its view, 'badly begun and worse continued'.[82] At the same time, in what would become a familiar attempt to square the circle, IN demanded that ordinary Venetians be found remunerative employment within the city, ideally at a revived Arsenale, and rejected a future in which tourism was the sole local industry.[83]

In 1962 IN sponsored a major exhibition entitled *Venice: Ten Centuries of History Confronted by Modern Urbanism*, which it took to Paris, London and other cities, Anna Maria Volpi speaking in its praise in both capitals. (*The Times* informed its readers chattily that she had had an English governess in Fascist Venice, when her 'tree-climbing and other unfeminine pursuits were the despair of her mother'.)[84] By this point major issues included the pollution of the lagoon[85] and the fact that the city was sinking, *acque alte* now flooding parts of Venice more often than in the past,[86] and falling masonry from decaying buildings becoming an everyday occurrence.[87] IN's reprimands remained polite and mild; even its journal initially welcomed the plan to deepen the 'petrol' canal between Malamocco and Marghera.[88] Dorigo, who was not an environmentalist and would soon express popular resentment at IN's elitism, spoke at the Ateneo, insisting that old Venice must not be separated from Mestre and Marghera and urging that all Venetians refuse unswervingly any idea that their city be subordinated to a tourist 'monoculture'.[89]

A more immediate controversy was aroused by the project of modernist architects Pier Luigi Nervi and Angelo Scattolin, the latter a Venetian, to raise a new head office for the Cassa di Risparmio di Venezia along the north-eastern flank of Campo Manin, a building of reinforced concrete that IN hoped to delay through talk about the need for more detailed planning of the insertion of modernism into the old city.[90] But for the moment too rancorous a debate on this edifice seemed inappropriate, since 1966, after all, marked the centenary of Italian Venice and demanded its proper celebration.[91]

Nature, however, was not in a joyful mood. On 3 November an autumnal storm hit Venice, the Veneto and the rest of Italy. An *acqua alta* was predicted. Six years earlier, on 15 October 1960 a 1.45-metre flood had washed through the city, the highest since 1.47 metres on 16 April 1936, while in late October 1966 Piazza San Marco had been under water almost every day.[92] Now again, the lagoon rose both there and in the other low-lying parts of the city. At 10 p.m. of 3 November the tide was meant to turn. It did not. Instead the surge grew stronger, driven by a scirocco of seventy kilometres per hour and swelled by heavy rain.[93] Ironically, 4 November 1966, the forty-eighth anniversary of the victory at Vittorio Veneto that had ended Italy's First World War and was now national Armed Forces Day, became the darkest in Venetian history. It was the moment when, as one commentator would graphically put it, Venice 'suffered a heart attack'.[94]

With more and more *calli* and *campi* inundated, city dwellers lost telephone contact and electricity supply; a few candles guttered. No bread was baked. Most shops were awash, their goods floating higgledy-piggledy in the waters. It would ultimately be claimed that 7,000 retail venues were destroyed and 15,000 dwellings inundated.[95] Boxes of fish, fruit and vegetables swirled around the Grand Canal, hindering navigation for some days. There was even a major fire in Cannaregio, quickly enough extinguished but causing major damage.

At 6 p.m. the tide once again failed to turn and the waters began to rise further, reaching 1.94 metres, well above any previously recorded level (the second worst to date is 1.66 metres on 22 December 1979). The *murazzi*, ancient city bulwarks, collapsed in ten places as the Adriatic raged against them. The island of Sant'Erasmo, traditionally the area where Venice's daily food supplies were grown, was swept by waves more than four metres high; 'the water dragged away furniture and houses, destroying fields of artichokes and cabbages, and drowning cattle, chickens and rabbits'.[96] Burano, its water pipe broken, seemed adrift in open sea. At Mazzorbo, waves flooded the new cemetery, breaking memorial stones as though they were made of cardboard. On the Lido, both the Casino and the Excelsior were swamped and 'permanent' beach cabins vanished, while Malamocco was submerged for only the second time in what *Il Gazzettino* declared its 'thousand-year history'.[97] Pellestrina, further south, was all but washed away. When the gale, which had blown ceaselessly, finally turned at 9 p.m., the flood receded with violent rapidity, leaving dead pigeons and rats in every square as a token of mortality, while viscous black mud lay a metre deep in every *calle*.[98] It was estimated that 200,000 tonnes of rubbish needed collecting (it was still rotting a week later).[99] *Il Gazzettino* described the whole event as 'apocalyptic'. The paper's editor nonetheless remembered to attack his political enemies, the communists, for reproaching the government with inaction, even while he summoned a general 'solidarity' among the afflicted populace.[100]

The main archives of the Republic were engulfed by waters to a level of 40 centimetres, damaging 3,648 boxes and 3,177 registers, the repositories of the city's history thus themselves assaulted by the flood.[101] The three ground-floor rooms of the Marciana library were covered in more than a metre of water and hundreds of books were inundated, although the rarest volumes were preserved safe on an upper floor. Seventy of the four hundred city gondolas were wrecked, notably those moored along the Riva degli Schiavoni. The water that lapped into the Cini Foundation buildings took days to subside and soaked

15,000 historic magazines and 4,000 photographic glass plates.[102] Worse, tank-
fuls of heating oil had seeped into every canal throughout the city, and when
the water drained away each building was found to be heavily stained. The
pungent smell of oil took days to disperse.[103] Even more drastic was the salt,
which, it became clear in the weeks that followed, had worked its way into
many *palazzi* and churches, resulting in the sullying of precious medieval,
Renaissance and baroque artworks. Venice, it would eventually be realised, had
come close to suffering the fate of Atlantis, supposedly swallowed by the sea.
After 4 November 1966 the possibility that another, greater flood would one
day come lay behind almost all debate about the city. In the meantime, the most
pressing question was what could be done to repair the estimated 40,000 million
lire loss to the historic centre alone. Local spokesmen, sure as ever that Venice
was the repository of a special and sacred universal history, thought that the bill
should fall to the 'civilised world', *Il Gazzettino* urging that even the *murazzi*
were a key component of the globe's 'most famous human patrimony'.[104]

The grim weather had also hit Florence, where much of the Tuscan city had
been flooded by the river Arno, for a time diverting attention from Venice. The
British ambassador, for example, was sure on 6 November that 'the damage is
worst in Tuscany', while three days later *The Times* reported that, in Venice, by
contrast with Florence, 'historic art treasures' had suffered little, even if the
paper admitted that Venetians might take some time to recover from the

31 Venice awash with water rather than beauty and history

'psychological shock' of the *acqua alta*.[105] A few weeks later, amid stories in the Italian press and internationally of tardy and 'chaotic' responses from the Italian government, a British official sniffed that 'the misfortunes of the Venetian shopkeepers' had proven 'somewhat exaggerated'.[106]

Italia Nostra took a broader line, an editorial invoking a predictable metaphor in comparing the effects of the floods on Florence and Venice to the 'barbarian invasions' that had brought down the Roman Empire. More recent twentieth-century wars, it added, had caused nothing like such 'irremediable damage'. The organisation's new president, novelist Giorgio Bassani, described the situation as 'dramatic', the *acqua alta* compounding the crisis already evident in the city's depopulation and threatening its 'rapid disqualification' from any hope of remaining 'alive'. Venetians, he was sure, hated the idea of being no more than a 'museum-city'. To save them from that fate, and from the 'eternal mental sclerosis' of bureaucrats and the 'eternal infantilism' of pseudo avant-garde intellectuals, men and women of goodwill, he asserted, like those who rallied in IN, must become ever more active in the city's defence. Another writer added that the *murazzi* must be restored and extended, and detailed further planning completed, if Venice was to be saved from the sea.[107]

Rotary was similarly anxious to lend its good offices to flood relief. By January 1967, it had already paid for Dutch experts to visit the city and share their knowledge of how to resist the sea.[108] Many other foreigners, then and later, tried to offer their own counsel in what was coming to be seen as a global crusade to save Venice.

Some Venetians retained older priorities. Not long after the flood, Vittorio Cini spoke eloquently at the Ateneo on the 'fiftieth anniversary of Porto Marghera', underlining that, 'when you say Marghera, you say Volpi'. Cini went on to praise the inauguration of a memorial stone to 'a huge enterprise owed to the bright ideas of a genial builder', Volpi. The heavy industrial and ship-building complex, Cini preached, displayed 'the grandeur of Man'; Volpi, like Thomas More, was 'a man for all seasons'. Profitable business still constituted the best defence of 'the undamaged artworks of the ancient islands that everyone loves so much'. Its third zone, expanding the area to 6,000 hectares from the current 2,000, should be got to work as soon as possible. Why not, he suggested brightly, rename the area 'Porto Marghera–Volpi'?[109]

In practice, however, clouds were building over Marghera. Cini's crass optimism began to seem out of place among not only the Venetian elite, who tended to group in IN and be troubled by environmentalist concerns, but also those best people throughout the globe who thought of themselves as the special friends of the city.[110] Sir Ashley Clarke, who had been ambassador in Rome from 1953 to 1962, and Lord Harewood, a cousin of the queen, led the first British relief efforts.[111] Their succour was originally directed at Florence as well as Venice. But it quickly became evident that it was the latter that had suffered the more profound damage and, worse, remained exposed to further threat. Soon Clarke became the vice-president of the 'Venice in Peril' fund, serving under historian John Julius Norwich.[112] In January 1971 the two wrote to *The Times* to press their mission: 'The plain fact is that if steps are not urgently taken, then within the lifetime of many children alive today, Venice as we know it will have ceased to exist.' Italian government initiatives were proving regrettably slow and inadequate, they remarked tetchily. In any case, they concluded, 'Venice belongs to us all. It is part of our own history. Few cities of similar size have contributed more to our civilization.'[113]

The British were not the only foreign group to involve themselves. IN was soon rejoicing in a charitable list that included Argentina, Australia, Austria, Belgium, Brazil, Canada, Colombia, Cyprus, Czechoslovakia, Denmark, Egypt, Eire, Finland, France, Germany, Greece, Israel, Japan, Luxembourg, Mexico, New Zealand, the Netherlands, Norway, Poland, Romania, San Marino, South Africa, Spain, Sweden, Switzerland, Syria, Thailand, the USA, the USSR, Venezuela and Yugoslavia.[114] The Great Flood had indeed made plain that Venice and (some of) its historics lived in hearts and minds across the wide world.

Of most immediate impact was a UNESCO report, issued in July 1969 at the initiative of two French members of the secretariat in Paris, and based on the determination 'We must save Venice'. They produced a five-point plan urging the restoration of damaged artworks, the protection of the city from the sea, the avoidance of a future that would depend on tourism alone, the fostering of centres of international learning within the city and the defence of Venice from man-made pollutants.[115] It was the last of these provisions that was the most immediately controversial, since the most obvious polluter of the historic centre was Marghera. By the summer of 1967, the city branch of IN had already passed a motion against proceeding with the Canale dei Petroli and the third zone. As Ennio Gallo argued in the organisation's journal, no proper study had been made of the long-term effects of the planned works, which would leave Venice surrounded by 'smoking chimneys'. The whole industrial development, he lamented, expressing a viewpoint that was becoming ever more common, served outside interests and gave nothing to Venetians.[116] In the next issue, another observer added that pollution from wind and rain had eaten into the celebrated Quadriga, the four horses standing above the Basilica di San Marco; their restoration would exercise even the most skilled expert.[117] As Teresa Foscari Foscolo concluded, she and her colleagues in IN did not nurture even the most minimal desire to interfere with private property but . . . something had to be done to save the city.[118] President Bassani underlined the lesson. The tanker trade into Marghera and its 'infamous' new canal must be directed elsewhere.[119] Even Pope Paul VI was happy to have been noted blessing the 'salvation of Venice'.[120]

Also prominent in the campaign to 'save Venice' was a cross-party body that called itself the Fronte per la Difesa di Venezia (FDV, Venice Defence Front), founded in 1968. It aimed to 'alert public opinion' to the degradation that man had visited on the lagoon and the city, condemning Marghera as, 'from Venice's point of view, a deal that was a total loss'. On 18 January an FDV-organised flotilla of seventy-five boats made its way down the Grand Canal, bearing such slogans as 'No more poisoned fish', 'No more *acque alte*', 'No more draining of the *barene*' (swampy areas on the lagoon's edge), 'No more industrial barbarities', 'Marghera is poisoning us'. Such environmentalism was mixed with what would soon turn into autonomism, further placards demanding 'Venice for the Venetians' and 'Lower taxes'.[121] The FDV also opposed a 'tourist monoculture' as Venice's future and, in what would become an endless but barren refrain, sought mass employment within the city.

The most sensational intervention in the now florid debate came from the radical conservative journalist Indro Montanelli. A series of articles in *Il Corriere della Sera*, Italy's most highly regarded daily, in October 1968 was followed by a documentary screened on RAI, Italian state TV, the following year. Montanelli, who also praised the protests being launched by the FDV,[122] demanded that something be done and done now. Marghera, he declared, was 'an industrial site that has profaned a temple of nature, the Venetian lagoon'. The whole idea to accord Venice a modern, industrial economy had been a mistake; instead the city should concentrate on becoming 'a residential centre of the most refined international elite, a capital of high cultural research and, by definition, the mecca of quality tourism, as it in fact already is'. No longer could Venice be 'abandoned, fatally wounded by pollution and negligence'.[123]

In his crusade, Montanelli was swiftly joined by such significant figures as Republican (and anti-Fascist) businessman and politician Bruno Visentini, Minister of Finance in 1974–6 and 1983–4. Visentini accepted the chairmanship of the Italian committee to save Venice, its members including such bankers, businessmen and society stars as Raffaele Mattioli, Gianni Agnelli, Leopoldo Pirelli, Ida Borletti and Giulia Maria Mozzoni Crespi.[124] In his capacity as CEO of Olivetti, Visentini bought Palazzo Grimani near Santa Maria Formosa as a model of meticulous restoration that might be imitated by his wealthy friends, adapting it into a conference centre. Born at Treviso in 1914, Visentini took to defining himself as a 'Venetian of the terra firma',[125] in 1977 becoming president of the Cini Foundation and there sponsoring the multi-volume *Storia di Venezia* that was finally published in 2002.[126] During his inaugural speech, Visentini characteristically cited communist thinker and 'martyr to Fascism' Antonio Gramsci with approval, while avowing in words that would soon be eschewed by neo-liberalism that intellectual labour should be entirely separated from thoughts about profit and any other form of capitalist interference.[127]

In 1972 Visentini had appeared as a witness for Montanelli in two sensational defamation trials between the journalist and, respectively, Christian Democrat mayor (1970–5) Giorgio Longo and Wladimiro Dorigo. Each case was resolved without conviction, although Montanelli stole the headlines on 25 January 1972 when he spoke uninterrupted for six hours about Venice's travails. Dorigo had tried to object to what he deemed Montanelli's unscientific exaggerations and, more significantly, the failure of the journalist and his rich friends, among whom he listed Anna Maria Volpi,[128] to focus on what Dorigo regarded as the most crucial urban issue: keeping employment for ordinary Venetians in some arena other than tourism.[129] 'Without Marghera and without the resulting and quite horrible conurbation of Mestre', he maintained, 'the economic and civil death of Venice' was certain.[130] Meanwhile that year, the Comune gave nostalgia in the city a boost by setting up an Ente per la Conservazione della Gondola e la Tutela del Gondoliere (Agency for the Preservation of the Gondola and the Welfare of the Gondoliere), thereby funding the restoration of the *traghetto* routes across the Grand Canal, which are still today the cheapest way for visitors to experience a (brief) trip in a gondola.[131]

In standing against the tide of opinion championed by Montanelli, the by now independent leftist Dorigo was occasionally joined by a wealthier Venetian. Eugenio Miozzi, engineer of the Ponte del Littorio in the 1930s, who as early as the 1950s had published a lavish history of the city's urban fabric, confident that it could adapt to modern change,[132] spoke twice at the Ateneo to argue that the city's sinking was caused by the extraction of water and gas on the mainland of the Veneto rather than by Marghera. He also unfashionably favoured a new bridge to join Venice to Cavallino to the north-east and other improvements in communications that, he claimed, would assist those employed at Mestre or Marghera.[133] After all, he added, Venetian workers were 'sober, savers, morally honest, very attached to their families', an ideal workforce; their devotion to labour meant the city could not die.[134]

But his was an increasingly isolated voice, and, in January 1972, IN formally pronounced that 'a further expansion of the industrial zone at Marghera at the expense of the lagoon is incompatible with hydro-geological, ecological and visual safeguarding of an environment that, together with the city of Venice, forms a unique and indissoluble bond of extraordinary importance for Italy and the world'. Its members piously reiterated their determination to avoid the place becoming a 'gigantic boutique' and 'a stone Disneyland'. The city must live, not die, IN urged, but without prescribing the means to arrest the population decline.[135]

While the national government lurched towards passing a 'special law' for the city in 1973, granting still richer funds towards Venice's 'salvation' (a policy that was almost immediately damned as ineffectual and/or corrupt),[136] Marghera was facing problems on a different front. Since 1968 Italy had been experiencing its 'anni di piombo' (bullet years) of left- and right-wing terrorism, as well as of union activism and widespread employer concessions. Given the working conditions at Marghera, it is scarcely surprising that it was an early site of 'contestazione' (protest). Toni Negri, the radical Marxist sociologist who had been born in Padua and worked at the university there, had followers in Venice, and his Potere Operaio (Worker Power) group commenced activity in 1967, although it would not be formally founded for another two years. Even before that, Negri had opened a free 'Marxist school' at Campo San Barnaba, where the young converts included later mayor of Venice Massimo Cacciari, a rising figure in the city's cultural debate.[137] Potere Operaio was soon distributing what it called 'the Porto Marghera workers' paper', urging autonomist action free from the rigid discipline of CGIL. The 'hot summer' of 1968 was studded with strikes, lockouts and demonstrations. Disturbances continued the following year, workers interrupting a meeting of the Comune on 7 November to preach their case. A month later, they won what seemed a 'historic victory' over their bosses at Montedison, the biggest firm operating at Marghera and the owners of SADE. The then state-controlled company conceded pay rises, a reduction of the working week towards a target of forty hours, an improved working environment, an acceptance of labour representatives on management committees, space in the workplace for union meetings and other reforms.[138] In 1973 the Brigate Rosse (BR, Red Brigades) made Marghera one of their first bases outside Milan, establishing a tiny cell in Petrolchimico.[139]

There had been further advances in pay and conditions in 1972, when the next contract negotiations fell due. Montedison was, however, simultaneously sinking deeper into the red. Moreover, by the end of the 1970s its state financing in an age that was turning neo-liberal was beginning to seem perverse. The conglomerate was reprivatised in 1981, a change applauded by the socialist Gianni De Michelis, once a student radical and by now the major political influence in Venice, where the socialist mayors Mario Rigo (1975–85) and Nereo Laroni (1985–7) headed the communal council.[140] Triggers to 'reform' came with a crisis created by a factory explosion on 22 March 1979, which killed three workers and was condemned in the leftist press as 'chemical terrorism'. Armed leftist reprisal in its turn made matters worse, the Red Brigades exploding a bomb five days later on the balcony of the factory director's home. In January 1980 they turned to murder, shooting Sergio Gori, the second in command of Petrolchimico, in central Mestre, and then in 1981 kidnapping Giuseppe Taliercio, the boss of the same concern, whom they held prisoner for forty-seven days before murdering him on the night of 5–6 June.[141] Such violence did nothing to stop the move to market-based 'reform'. Sackings and the cancellation of union rights followed. Yet neo-liberal nostrums did not save the petro-chemical business either. By the 1990s the total workforce at Marghera had fallen to 13,000 amid talk of the extinction of the working class, and plans began for the creation of an archaeological park in place of productive industry. Nor did the decline stop there.[142] In 2009 Montedison and its linked companies, laden with debt, ceased all work in the area, a closure reported in the press as another 'death in Venice'.[143]

Radicalism had conditioned other aspects of Venetian lives while the spirit of 1968 lasted. Cells of neo-fascist terrorists flourished for a while at the Liceo 'Raimondo Franchetti', where pupils included Martino Siciliano and Delfo Zorzi of Ordine Nuovo (New Order), a neo-fascist body that favoured violent action.[144] Although no one has ever been convicted for the crime, they may have been involved in the bombing of the Banca dell'Agricoltura on Piazza Fontana in Milan on 12 December 1969 with a device that had been assembled in a safe house on the Lido. The deliberately random attack killed sixteen bystanders and injured eighty-three.[145] Zorzi, who was found guilty in 2001 but was absolved on appeal three years later (going through a similar process in relation to allegations that he had managed another fatal rightist bombing in Brescia in 1974), is today a successful businessman living in Tokyo. He retains economic interests in the Veneto region.

During the 1970s, the left won out over the right at the Franchetti, an occupation of the school by the pupils in February 1969 being a high point of 'revolutionary' activism. Thereafter, the atmosphere remained volatile, even if students were not sure whether they fully identified with striking workers from Marghera, whose demonstrations often marched past the Liceo. Closer to their immediate concerns was the arrival of the 'sexual revolution', made manifest in March 1979 with the approval by the school governing committee of a feminist-sponsored questionnaire on sexual practice, provoking *Il Gazzettino* to the reproving headline 'They do sex at the Franchetti'.[146]

Within the old city, high cultural activities were themselves not exempt from newly vocal argument, the 34th Biennale of 1968 opening in an atmosphere of contestation that, in spring 1967, had seen students occupy the

Istituto Universitario di Architettura di Venezia (IUAV, Venetian University Institute for Architecture, founded 1940) for sixty-four days and do the same at Ca' Foscari from December 1967 to February 1968.[147] Demonstrations against the festival's 'elitism' began on 18 June and spread into Piazza San Marco. Waving placards stating 'We don't want the Biennale of the bosses', students tried to raise the Red Flag in front of the Basilica before being driven away by three hundred riot police. Luigi Nono, the avant-garde composer who arguably possessed the highest reputation among contemporary Venetians in terms of global culture and was a staunch anti-Fascist, told readers of the PCI's weekly, *Rinascita*, that the reaction to the Biennale was displaying local workers' and students' 'total opposition to the capitalist system'.[148] In response to official 'brutality', various artists endorsed the slogan 'The Biennale is Fascist', memories surfacing of Volpi's sponsoring of this and other cultural events. A formal opening did take place on 21 June but by then eighteen of the twenty-two Italian artists had withdrawn their works in protest at 'police brutality' with the backing of colleagues from France, Scandinavia and elsewhere,[149] amid sardonic talk of an 'International Police Exhibition' in which Pop Art had been replaced by 'Poliz Art'.[150] Now, it was also announced that the film festival, too, would be challenged as 'an instrument of the bourgeoisie'.[151]

Thereafter there were changes in Biennale organisation that liquidated any leftovers from the Fascist era. The 'elitist' awarding of prizes was suspended between 1969 and 1980 at the film festival and between 1969 and 1986 at the art exhibition, while in 1973 the Italian parliament approved a more democratic organising body for the various festivals, admitting union and other staff representatives, whose board elected its president, the (aristocratic) socialist and environmentalist Carlo Ripa di Meana. The new system lasted until the partial privatisation of the whole operation in 1998. There was no art exhibition in 1974 but a film festival mourned the overthrow of Allende's Marxist regime in Chile by 'fascist' military and American power. When the art exhibition resumed in the 37th Biennale in 1976, the works on show had a politically correct focus on the Spanish Civil War (Franco had died in November 1975, allowing Spain its transition towards democracy) and rhetoric about the centrality in modern life of Resistance values.[152]

While the Biennali seemed to have swung permanently left, Patriarch Luciani, who had been appointed to replace Urbani in December 1969, remained a stalwart of tradition. Throughout the 1970s, he made enough of a name for himself as a preacher to be elected to succeed Paul VI as pope in August 1978, his elevation being greeted as that of another humble 'man of the people' like John XXIII. Catholic publicists christened him 'the smiling pope'. John Paul I's reign lasted only thirty-three days, however, rumours circulating that his death had been hastened by his sense of total inadequacy as pontiff.[153] Certainly any reading of the monthly letters he published in the local Catholic press during his years as patriarch is scarcely impressive. He chose 'historic figures' as his imagined correspondents in order to pen gentle homilies that a critic might find hackneyed at best. Thus he told Charles Dickens that the Scrooge of *A Christmas Carol* was deplorably devoted 'to money and business'. Workers, despite residual woes, were better off than in Victorian times, he added cosily; trust in God could alone ease their continuing fears and insecurity. Holidays were now too frequent and too long, and, in reality, left men bored, irritated and forgetful of their religious duties.

An epistle to Empress Maria Teresa of Austria prompted the prelate to deplore the decay of morals that resulted when girls, even 'from good families', went out alone with boys in their cars or wore skimpy swimming costumes. Women, he preached primly, should rather 'dress with decorum and adorn themselves with modesty'. How dreadful it was, he observed in words of the 1930s, that contemporary women swore and cursed! Pinocchio was another recipient of his letters and a boy about whom he liked to moralise in his sermons. Mephistopheles, he warned, stalked every film festival and regularly found fresh Fausts to corrupt among the viewers of immoral films. Abortion brutally exposed how the advance of 'so-called feminism' had provoked the collapse of 'femininity and humanity'. Chatter about Marxist revolution seduced youth into violence, although, he added quickly, if capitalism was to obey the rules of the Church it 'must be profoundly modified'.[154]

Despite such evident naivety, Luciani must have convinced the Conclave that he deserved his reputation as an educator who reached out to embrace the people.[155] In retrospect, however, his innocent preaching lacked insight and dynamism. In his failings and frailty, this last Venetian pope might be thought to stand for the city as it was at the end of the 1970s. Patriarch Luciani had escaped the ineffectual attempts of his parishioners to avert the termination of their city's story only to find his swift and bathetic demise in Rome. Death, at the end of the decade, eddied all around: John Paul I's death, the death of Marghera, the death of the working class, the death of Venice as a dwelling place and what seemed to be its rapidly approaching physical death from rising sea levels, sinking land, chemical pollution in the air and water and the ever swelling 'barbarian invasion' of mass tourism. Venice, everyone was agreed, was still equipped and even cluttered with many pasts. But did it have a future?

CHAPTER NINE

Death postponed
through globalised rebirth
(and mass tourism)?

The islands of San Clemente and San Servolo are readily visible from Sant'Elena or the Giudecca, lying in the lagoon between old Venice and the Lido (see map 8). In recent years, San Clemente has been offering rich visitors up-market holidays. Its website used to tempt potential customers with an invitation to enjoy 'history, art, nature, relax: all based on a unique environment, specially designed for the Guest who can rejoice in the services and attention that only a five-star Luxury Hotel – a member of "The Leading Hotels of the World" group – knows how to offer.'[1] In 2013, however, it was suddenly closed, although it was soon announced that it would shortly reopen under new ownership. All in all, the acquisition of an elite hotel in contemporary Venice might sometimes seem as unpredictable a financial venture as purchasing a football team. (Venice's team, renamed the Foot-Ball Club Unione Venezia in February 2011, was bought by a consortium headed by the Russian entrepreneur Yuri Korablin.) New owners at San Clemente are sure to lay claim to history and beauty as fundamental to the island's appeal. As so often in Venice, however, it is a question of which history. The place certainly contains a church, whose origins date back to 1131 (although it was reconsecrated in 1750 and further altered in 1800, an old Augustinian convent there finally being shut down ten years later).[2] But the island brims with a darker history, about which heritage entrepreneurs may prefer reticence.

In 1855 the governing Austrian authorities decided that San Clemente was well fitted to become the Manicomio Centrale delle Provincie Venete (Central Lunatic Asylum of the Venetian provinces) for female patients. In practice, conversion was not complete until 1873 and it was the Italian government that inaugurated the asylum on 1 July that year. The stated charitable aim was to rehabilitate and resocialise the inmates, 620 of them initially, two-thirds deemed 'incurable'.[3] Administrators promised to proceed with the most advanced scientific methods, although simpler remedies could also bring results.[4] Among the curable were quite a few poor peasant women, whose diet, based on polenta and little else, had resulted in pellagra and its associated 'madness'; after some weeks of decent food, such patients' behaviour became 'normal' and they could be sent back to their ordinary lives.

In 1884 San Clemente was housing a thousand patients, among whom two hundred recalcitrants were chained to their beds.[5] Despite such cruelty, the place avoided scandal in the following century, perhaps because it was kinder to upper-class patients. More equivocally, it was where the bigamous Mussolini's 'other' wife Ida Dalser died of a brain haemorrhage in 1937 (she had been transferred to Venice from an asylum on the outskirts of her native Trento twelve years earlier, having been diagnosed as psychologically disturbed, a clinical decision encouraged by the Duce's brother and business agent Arnaldo).[6] But medical fashion was changing, and during the 1970s demands to close the asylum grew as part of the widespread determination to end institutionalisation. Eugenio Miozzi, among others, was doubtful, buoyed by his usual theme, however unhistorical, that there must be no infringement of the principle of 'com'era e dov'era'. In his opinion, San Clemente must stay as it was and bring its financial and employment benefits to Venice.[7] Yet in seeking to retain the asylum Miozzi was opposing the spirit of the times. Soon the island had to find another purpose. Once again in Venice, history changed.

San Servolo was for many years the twin of San Clemente, itself home in the middle ages to a community of Benedictine monks and other religious. Its hospital services went back to the 1720s, undergoing major modernisation in 1819. Thereupon it acted as the city's asylum, from the 1870s taking men only, after the opening of San Clemente. It closed in 1978 as part of the global fashion for de-institutionalisation of which the Venetian-born psychiatrist Franco Basaglia had been a prominent advocate.[8] The asylum was replaced by an Istituto per le Ricerche e gli Studi sull'Emarginazione Sociale e Culturale (IRSESC, Institute for the Study of Social and Cultural Exclusion), furnished with an archive of 13,000 photographic plates of the mentally ill and an extensive written record of the psychiatric history of confined men and women.[9] It also offers a rich museum collection of the medicines and equipment utilised in such places. IRSESC's main purpose was declared to be the academic study of 'the "beaten", "marginalised", "excluded" and "diverse" minorities viewed on their own terms in their daily lives', now to be charitably rescued from derision and forgetfulness.[10] From 1995 such worthy but poorly remunerated research was broadened. Most of the richly restored buildings became the home of Venice International University (VIU), a private body blessed by the two local state tertiary institutions, Ca' Foscari and IUAV. VIU's first head was the banker Carlo Azeglio Ciampi (1995–9), who then moved on to become president of Italy.

32 San Servolo as asylum

In 2012, the University of Padua, the most prestigious university in the region, joined VIU's team. By then the initiative had also won sponsorship from ENEL, the partially privatised national electric utility company. Instruction is in English, while the main university buildings promise good deeds through looking out onto 'Piazza Baden-Powell', although the founder of the Boy Scouts had no connection with San Servolo. Hoping to be a globalised institution in a globalised world, VIU has assiduously courted international contacts in the USA, Germany, Israel, Spain, Japan and China, with a particular emphasis on the last as the coming global power. Expensive redevelopment of buildings on the island now provides elegant space for exhibitions and conferences – twenty-six were held in 2012 – and a meagre library of 4,000 books. The VIU website and other publications speak of academic focus on such apt themes as 'intercultural dialogue, sustainable tourism and value adding to cultural patrimony'. One recent highlight was a workshop in collaboration with Harvard that examined 'Industrial pollution, regulation and growth: governance, challenges and innovation', and that attracted twenty-five 'world leaders'.[11]

So is Venice today a city in which internationalised luxury leisure and richly privatised global academic research have buried past madness? Can the developments on San Clemente and San Servolo rebut cheap talk about death in and of Venice? Perhaps. But a better site for contemplation of the effects of contemporary neo-liberal hegemony, and of Venice's place within it, is Piazza San Marco itself, a square where the class wars of the first half of the twentieth century have indeed lost traction. There, for some years now, the great buildings have been regularly festooned with hoardings advertising expensive watches and other fashion accessories, perfumes, stylish clothes, motor cars and food products of questionable environmental and health benefit, the capitalist present thereby blotting out direct viewing of the glories of the Republic, let alone exploration of the social conflicts of Liberal and Fascist Venice.[12] The justification for such an intrusion is the familiar one of the bottom line.[13] As any student of the city must concede, historic sites require expensive upkeep and restoration, and Venice more than others. In turn, Venice's fame, its history and beauty, mean that the Comune has something to sell and business something to buy. As a spokesperson of Coca Cola explained with specious virtue to the *New York Times* in 2010, when the façade of the Palazzo Ducale was hidden by its image: our company has 'chosen to advertise [there] . . . not just to help promote our brand, but because it would also help preserve some of the city's culture. When we advertise, we are always conscious of local artistic and cultural heritage.'[14]

33 Time on sale in Piazza San Marco

A seductive image can be reinforced by up-scale entertainment. In September 2006 Bulgari executives held a dinner for their 160 top clients in the Palazzo Ducale, with Cacciari, back in office and proving ever more adaptable to the hegemony of the market, the guest of honour.[15] Paolo Bulgari then spoke for business, hailing Venice as 'a city that is alive and international. It is rich in history and culture. It is a matter of great pride for me to be able to make one of its most precious symbols stand out again in renewed beauty.'[16]

Scholars did not demur. As if on cue, the American early modernist Thomas Madden composed a neo-liberal history of the city, arguing that, from the very beginning, Venetians had been 'businessmen through and through'. Throughout the Republic's story, he pronounced, 'entrepreneurs' had received backing from 'their pro-business government'; together, 'freedom and free enterprise . . . built a wonder'. Venice was 'a birthplace of modern capitalism'.[17] It was also a city 'com'era e dov'era'. According to Madden, 'by 1700 Venice looked much as it does today'. It had even made ready for tourists. Republican Venice 'was not only a vibrant city, it was a museum. And many people came to marvel at its exhibits.'[18] By contrast, in Madden's account, the travails of Italian Venice after 1866, and any contemporary history, deserve slight analysis, although he did enthuse that, from 1945, 'American perspectives on Venice would play a prominent role in shaping the city and its image. . . . To name even a few influential Americans in Venice is to leave out thousands.'[19]

In sum, through such scholarship, and as is made evident every day in Piazza San Marco, neo-liberalism is presently as dominant in the local setting of Venice as it is throughout the globe, perhaps more so, if, as Madden, Coca Cola and Bulgari executives contend, the city and the market go together like love and marriage. What might be more debatable is whether the promised advantages of marketisation have trickled down into the lives of the people of Venice, or whether, rather, a hint of madness and the nearness of death still hangs over the city, and not merely at the ex-asylums of San Clemente and San Servolo. How, it must be asked generally, have Venice and its complex pasts and memories dealt with what Francis Fukuyama labelled 'the end of history', the acceptance in our present era that a sole economic model and a sole political system have been and are viable? Is neo-liberalism enhancing or fretting beauty and history as it imposes its changes on Venice? Can a city that has long cried out for protection, where 'middle-class welfare' has habitually been extended to patricians and the super-rich, really yoke itself to the pure market?

If, back in 1978, the lonely death of Pope John Paul I in Rome resonated with the many pressing matters that threatened Venice's downfall, another contemporary event better foreshadowed the dawning of the era of market profit. Even while, in the national capital, the Christian Democrat Aldo Moro was from 16 March being cruelly interrogated and then, on 9 May, murdered by the Red Brigades, Venice was confronting a local controversy, one that jarred bathetically with national preoccupations. On 6 April, as politicians in Rome wrestled over whether or not to ransom gaoled members of the Red Brigades in a deal to save Moro, and Moro himself, facing death, suggested in letters passed to his friends that his family mattered more to him than did the nation, *Il Gazzettino* had a more banal issue to debate.

That day, Vincenzo Torriani, who for forty years from 1949 presided over the organisation of the national (and nationalising) cycle race, the Giro d'Italia, revealed his plans for the 1978 contest. Ever since 1963, he recalled, he had wanted to 'bring the Giro to Venice, right into the heart of the city, into Piazza San Marco'. Many obstacles had stood in the way of this dream, but now the Comune, under the socialist Mario Rigo, had declared itself willing to over-come them. At last, it seemed, Torriani could transport his cyclists to a stage finishing line beneath the Quadriga. As he mused, 'touring Venice *calle* by *calle* and *fondamenta* by *fondamenta* ... I observed the placards proclaiming "Venice is alive", "Venice must live", "Defend the Venetian lagoon". And then I said to myself that one way to make this marvellous city live is to bring the Giro right here.' The race would be not just a 'spectacle' but – he added in words that were soon to dominate political discourse – a 'good business deal'. Perhaps Torriani would have to put up with locals being divided on the matter, his deferential interviewer remarked. 'What a success it would be if the people were divided only in that sense,' Torriani retorted sardonically. 'Normally in Italy we are much more divided than that!'[20]

Opposition there certainly was, the patrician Count Lodovico Valmarana denouncing the 'absurd scheme', the 'cycling farce', the 'ugly spectacle', to the press. He wondered why those in charge of historic monuments and the normally active paladins of Italia Nostra had not led a protest. Valmarana mocked enticing suggestions that the city could benefit financially from the race; rather, the cost of temporary or adapted bridges, smoother pavements and security must outweigh any profits. In any case, he predicted piously, Venetians, who flocked to authentically historical and local events like the Vogalonga regatta, would scarcely be won over by such a worthless and foreign sporting activity as the Giro.[21]

Despite such charges, on 16 May, while the nation was still wrangling over the meaning of Moro's murder, the Comune gave the plan its final approval. An itinerary had been agreed. The cyclists would swing from the Tronchetto to the Zattere and race down its edge to the Salute and the Punta della Dogana. From there a bridge of boats would carry the competitors across the Grand Canal and into Piazza San Marco, with a finishing line right outside the Basilica.[22]

34 Cyclists on the Zattere

Five days later, the race took place, if not at full pedal. Morning rain had aroused 'authentic fears' that the surfaces might prove perilous and that the national champion Francesco Moser, from the Trentino, might skid into a canal. Who knew if a man from the mountains could swim? By the afternoon, however, the sun came out and the contest went ahead, despite grumbling from the cyclists that the track was 'impracticable'.[23]

In the long term, the experiment of bringing the Giro to Venice and attaching Venice's heritage of beauty, history and leisure to the national cycling race was only a partial success. The placing of a finishing tape outside San Marco has not so far been replicated, although stages of the Giro did end (1997) and start (2007) in the wider spaces of the Lido. After all, as *Il Gazzettino* complained in 1978, seating arrangements had scarcely allowed crowds to watch and applaud; rather, Venetian cycling fans had sagely stayed at home and viewed the contest on TV.[24]

Yet the market's restless search for a grand spectacle that could be rendered grander and more remunerative by a beauteous and historic Venetian setting continued unabated. A decade after the Giro, arrangements began for the cele-brated English rock band Pink Floyd to perform on a platform anchored out in the lagoon, close to the Piazzetta, the Riva and Piazza San Marco. Each of these spaces, advocates of the concert insisted, could happily be filled with fans. More imaginative still, in 1984–5 Gianni De Michelis had begun advocating that Venice celebrate the bicentenary of the fall of the Republic in 1797 by hosting an 'Expo' or World's Fair.[25] By this time, aided by what one critic labelled his natural bumptiousness,[26] De Michelis was making himself the city's most prominent national politician. He was very close to Bettino Craxi, the socialist who served as prime minister from 1983 to 1987 before falling into exile and death amid the corruption scandals of 'Tangentopoli' in the 1990s.

In March 1985 Craxi made a formal visit to Venice, endorsing the achievements of the mayor, Rigo, the man who was to be his successor, Nereo Laroni, and Craxi's friend De Michelis, and promising government subsidy for new plans to develop something more marketable on San Servolo than a foundation for the underprivileged.[27] In response, Laroni was soon urging that the World's Fair go ahead, contending pointedly that the time for nostalgia had passed. A modish focus on the advance in robotics, he added, could underline the city's future commitment to 'splendour and progress'. A display of the most novel technology could mark the passing of that 'industrial society' which had, after all, he admitted, caused 'some degradation in Venice'.[28] The Expo, Laroni and De Michelis maintained, could revive Venice's traditional place at the crossroads between East and West.[29]

By 1988 the Consorzio Venezia Expo was being directed by Cesare De Michelis, an academic and publisher, another socialist and Gianni's brother. He had won public support for the grand scheme from such giants of the business world as Benetton, Fiat (one sister of the Agnelli family lived in Venice, while another had a second home there),[30] Coca Cola, Mondadori, Olivetti and Fininvest.[31] Among linked projects was a vast development at Tessera, around the airport, where modernist architect Renzo Piano, celebrated over the decades for the Pompidou Centre in Paris, the Parco della Musica in Rome and the Shard in London, was reported to have agreed to redesign the place as the 'magnet' of the entire region. Some advanced the idea that it could be called Marco Polo City, thereby harnessing many histories, including a Chinese one.[32] Before Piano could proceed, however, other issues intervened, even though in 2006 the architect was still claiming soulfully that 'Venice is the place that I love most in absolute. . . . Here you can feel that, for centuries, different cultures have confronted each other and intermingled. At a time when everyone talks about globalisation, [the city] is a grand example of global culture', although one that, he advised, must be more than a 'luxurious shopping centre'.[33]

Gianni De Michelis rose to be his nation's Foreign Minister between 1989 and 1992, relishing the fall of the Berlin Wall; a decade later, having not altogether successfully fended off his involvement in Tangentopoli, he was still denouncing

Italian communism for being part of 'the supranational Soviet system', glad that Craxi had sundered workerist ties between the Socialist Party and the PCI. It was the communists, De Michelis avowed, rather than the demonstrable corruption of the Christian Democrat, socialist and other parties, who bore the blame for Italy's being 'an imperfect democracy'.[34] Back in the 1980s De Michelis had stood forward as the special Italian and Venetian symbol of the new era when quite a few were ready to proclaim that 'greed is good' and individuals must always dance to their own tunes. His thickly curling black locks and chubby body might not have appealed to everyone, but he was the only statesman to find value in publishing a personal guide to 250 discotheques scattered across the country; twenty-one were located in the Veneto, four at Jesolo Lido but none in the old city. He did, however, plug 'Ranch 5' at Mestre, which had floor-space for a thousand dancers, while also being equipped with two Olympic-size swimming pools and a restaurant of an 'uncommon quality' in that town.[35]

While great events loomed, in May 1985 the city rejoiced in a visit from Prince Charles and Princess Diana. Rigo found Charles 'extraordinarily cultivated', impressed by the prince's studious viewing of Tintoretto's portrayal of the Battle of Lepanto, an event he politely acknowledged to have been a pinnacle of world history. Diana was noticed taking a photo of Ca' d'Oro, but Venetians found her strangely silent, glum and unforthcoming, despite a toothsome lunch at the Locanda Cipriani on Torcello, then as now a better place to eat than most in Venice. Among the genteel guests were Count Valmarana, his wife and Anna Maria Volpi.[36]

A more beatific visitor was John Paul II, who came on mission across the Veneto in June, to be greeted by Rigo with the assertion that Venetian history was still treasured there.[37] Predictably, the pope found oratorical sustenance in the Church's regional past, exalting Pius X and John Paul I as his grand predecessors, while being more reticent about John XXIII (and Vatican II). At the Fenice, where he listened to Mahler's Second Symphony under the baton of Israeli conductor Eliahu Inbal, John Paul extolled Venice as 'a city that constantly gave birth to real humanity', all the more since 'art' expressed an 'experience of universality' that neither science nor technology could match.[38] At the same time, the pope did not forget to visit Mestre and Marghera, where at the church of Gesù Lavoratore he emphasised that he was neither a boss nor a unionist (ferry staff remained on strike throughout the visit, throwing city communication into 'chaos' according to *Il Gazzettino*) but 'just a worker'. Perhaps either in the knowledge of Marghera's fading position or out of resentment at the failure of employers to give their employees time off to salute him (any who did lost a day's pay), John Paul II eschewed neo-liberalism, asserting rather that 'the economy must serve man', an implied retraction from that variety of modern capitalism which maintained that there was no such thing as society.[39]

But neither British royals nor a Polish pope possessed the drawing power of Pink Floyd, whose concert was timed to coincide with the Festa del Redentore, an ever busier moment in the tourist season, during which the Zattere was connected to the Palladian church of the Redentore on the Giudecca by a bridge of boats.[40] More ironical in 1989 was the conjunction with the bicentenary of the French Revolution, which modish contemporary historians were doing their best to write off in Paris. Busy preparations began, and by 6 July it was formally announced that the British group would perform from two enormous pontoons anchored 182 metres out into the lagoon from the Riva degli Schiavoni. Together the platforms would extend over half a hectare; anyone listening from the platforms themselves would pay 200,000 lire for their seat and a cold buffet. City engineers, it was said, had discovered how to protect ancient buildings from noise vibrations, and Lloyds were insuring the event. Pink Floyd and their support staff were to stay at the Excelsior. Eighty million would watch on TV and tens of thousands in the city itself, whether from the waterfront or on giant screens to be erected in Campo San Polo, Campo Santo Stefano (two), the Lido, the Giudecca, the Riva (another two) and Piazza Erminio Ferretto (named after a partisan shot in the hinterland in 1944) in Mestre.[41] Venice, the press announced cheerfully, was being swept by waves of 'Pink fever'.[42]

Nine charter flights were delivering fans, headed by American film stars, among them Woody Allen, Mia Farrow and their children.[43] Organisers promised that the concert would amount to the biggest 'promotion' ever in the city, and would not cost it one lira. 'All' Venetians would be able to behold the swelling scene free. Reprimands from a number of intellectuals, including local philosopher and emerging politician Massimo Cacciari, who had reviled the event as 'a complete horror', were rebutted from London by Pink Floyd's manager Steve O'Rourke, who insisted that the group were 'not barbarians'. Rather they were 'the epitome of youth culture and modern culture more generally'. They were playing in Venice as 'an act of love . . . for one of the most beautiful cities of art in the world'.[44]

But the council, by now under Antonio Casellati, a Republican (a party whose leading local figure, Bruno Visentini, stood somewhere in the background), had not yet given the full go-ahead for the concert. Such official hesitation encouraged argument. While the Comune dallied, with socialists mostly in favour (although Rigo, now a senator in Rome, joined the opposition) and Christian Democrats leading the critics, pessimists prophesied that 300,000 young people would invade every nook and cranny of the city with deplorable effect.[45] Had not the original Redentore festival, they added brightly, celebrated the end of an outbreak of the Plague? Would this year's event, through its coin-cidence with the concert, inject a new plague into Venetian lives? Cacciari, a Marxist who had left the Communist Party and was conditioning his early beliefs through a reading of Nietzsche in preparation for becoming the leading local politician of the following decades (he was mayor of his city in 1993–2000 and 2005–10), stated dramatically that only God could save Venice.[46]

By contrast, Giorgio Lago, the editor of *Il Gazzettino*, pronounced that Pink Floyd provided music for the present times just as Vivaldi had once done. The band must be allowed to play. But, as dissent grew, the concert management gave ground on a number of fronts, such as a tolerable decibel level.[47] As a result, during the performance itself the band not only looked like demented manikins to their distant audience but could scarcely be heard. For fans of the music, it was much better to watch and listen on TV, although, as Venetians were soon lamenting, the coverage focused on Pink Floyd and scarcely displayed Venice at all.[48]

So the city confronted its fate on the evening of 15 July. Special trains had been put on to carry the anticipated crowds, but ferry workers shut down internal communications in the city in one of their long series of strikes.[49] A final hitch was avoided when, at 8.25 p.m., deputy mayor Cesare De Piccoli (PCI) gave formal permission for the event (Mayor Casellati had by then judi-ciously gone missing). The result was what the local papers would describe in the days that followed as a 'sack' of the city by 200,000 or more fans. Shortly after noon, the railway station was already swamped with people and reeked of marijuana. A five-mile queue blocked entry by car, each vehicle able to stagger forward no more than a metre or so every five minutes. Within the city, satura-tion had been reached; by 3 p.m. it took forty-five minutes in a crammed Piazza San Marco to edge two hundred metres in any direction. Quickly the crowds began to clamber onto any and all edifices that looked out over the lagoon, the police desperately summoning reinforcements, who were, however, unable to get through the crush from Mestre. Even the most minimal equipment neces-sary for a large crowd had not been provided. In the absence of toilet facilities, boys urinated against the doors of San Marco (church officials had wisely closed the Basilica at 10.30 a.m.). Unable to retreat when the concert was over, many exhausted fans slept out. On the morning of 16 July, locals had to zig-zag around piles of excrement and through squares and *calli* deep in rubbish.[50] Water in the canals stayed putrid for days.[51]

On that following morning, Gianni De Michelis sassily pronounced that 'it had been a terrific festival, with an extraordinary concert and a wonderful spectacle of crowds and fireworks'. But even he conceded that there had been teething problems in management. The coming World's Fair, he suggested

35 The Piazzetta after Pink Floyd

blithely, would have the advantage of being able to plan with 'the greatest professionalism'.[52] Few shared his sanguine outlook, however; even the cautious Cardinal Patriarch Marco Cé (in office 1978–2002) homilised against the show and its effects. Italia Nostra was predictably outraged. International criticism was even more pointed, *Le Monde*, the *New York Times* and the *Frankfurter Allgemeine Zeitung* berating the city fathers.[53] Some domestic critics drew parallels with the earlier extravagance of the Giro d'Italia in 1978, and calls grew for the mayor to resign. Within weeks the ruling junta did fall, although Casellati was not replaced until the following year, when his successor was the Christian Democrat Ugo Bergamo. Franco Rocchetta, the head of the localist 'Łiga Veneta', demanded that the prefect also depart, comparing the havoc of the concert not so much with the cycle race as with the 1966 flood.[54]

The major lesson, as proclaimed by a headline in *Il Gazzettino*, became 'Never again like this'. The resolve extended to Expo, architect Cristiano

Gasparotto, a supporter of the Green movement, arguing, 'It would be criminal to think of holding the Fair in Venice.'[55] The pre-planning for the event was soon abandoned, to the palpable disappointment of De Michelis and of business interests in Venice and the Veneto. Repulsed on one front, they sought advance on another. In November 1991 De Michelis issued a ten-point modernising scheme for the city's future. It advocated more rapid communications and the creation of a modern container port, while admitting that the best prospect for Marghera might be the opening of a 'scientific and technology park' and a new, vocational university rather than fresh industry. The Arsenale, De Michelis counselled, should be transformed into a site for scientific and cultural display. Tourism, he added vaguely, must be better administered. Finally, De Michelis sharply attacked those who had opposed Expo, suggesting instead that the World Art Forum should be held in the city in 2001.[56]

Shortly after De Michelis launched this latest plan for a great event the insurance firm Assicurazioni Generali announced that it was closing its Venice office on the Bacino Orseolo and in part of the Procuratie Vecchie in San Marco, further proof of the flight of what had once been the leaders of the urban economy to the mainland.[57] In its own bitter reflection on the twenty-fifth anniversary of 1966, *Il Gazzettino* noted that 2,200 pupils were currently enrolled in elementary schools, whereas in 1966 there had been 7,145. In the last year, 1,160 had perished in the city, scarcely replaced by 471 births; the 1966 figures had been 1,624 and 1,497.[58] With or without Pink Floyd and with or without the prospect of the World's Fair, Venice was dying.

What could be done to arrest this demise? The answer of the times was clear to the sometime proponents of the World's Fair, who rallied in a group rechristened 'Venezia 2000'. To spur a 'new vitality' in the city, one of their members, the centre-right sociologist Giuseppe De Rita, argued in words with a global ring, a 'business culture' must be implanted.[59] Venice no doubt possessed a special and glorious past, but this history should not be allowed to block sensible development. The obsession with preservation, 'com'era e dov'era', De Rita feared, favoured a focus on mass tourism rather than other, richer economic prospects. Rather than the weight of the past demanding a 'unique, immobile and unquestionable model for the city', history should be plumbed for the lesson of Venice's adaptability and skill at reinventing itself. 'Without the bridges, the train, the factories, the improved pathways, without Mestre, it is likely that the problem of Venice would have been resolved a century ago with its abandonment, and today the city would be a Pompei languishing in the marshes,' De Rita contended. It was a good moment to ponder what Volpi had done for Venice in the first half of the century; in the years to come, every programme should be propelled by modern development.[60]

De Rita was scarcely a voice crying in the wilderness. In 1995 the Biennale celebrated its centenary with fanfare. Two semi-official British observers took the opportunity to pay homage to the 'extraordinary setting, where east meets west, ancient meets modern, land meets sea', extolling the way the festival had developed a tradition of 'pluralism and inclusiveness', not 'exclusivity and single-mindedness'.[61] Perhaps cheered by such praise and by a French expert's concession that all ideologies had demonstrably failed and that even the avant-garde had reached the end of history,[62] others favourable to the Venezia 2000 bloc, who thought of themselves as 'the new bourgeoisie of the north-east', joined De Rita in support of 'privatising Venice'. Such an enriching neo-liberal victory, they were sure, should be achieved through the formulation of further grand schemes for the city. Only thus could the sterile hold of the 'alliance of rentiers, hoteliers, shop owners, bureaucrats and university professors' be broken.[63] Giovanni Cantagalli, writing for the Benetton group, warned lest promising advances be stymied by 'bureaucratic tangles', as, he believed, Expo had sadly been.[64] His own company, he added, was buying property in Venice not so much with the aim of 'pure restoration' as through 'a simple calculation of investment, from which they expected a return, a benefit' in their bottom line.[65] Even Cacciari, whose background did not lie in business circles, was persuaded to present the Comune's case on increased privatisation. Although he scarcely rejected the continuing presence of public funding and regulation in the city and could still argue that there was no such thing as a free market, the mayor did concede that Venice should accept finance from wherever it could.[66]

But before the latest flurry of ideas about making yet another 'great Venice' could get very far, another disaster struck. On the evening of 29 January 1996 the beguilingly lovely Fenice opera house burned to the ground. Tackling the blaze was made more difficult by the fact that Cacciari had recently approved the closing of the surrounding canals for badly needed dredging.[67] Without aquatic access, fire crews struggled to reach the theatre, and at midnight the flames were still leaping high into the sky, not yet doused by the helicopters that flew backwards and forwards from the lagoon 120 times, laden with water (they kept going until 4 a.m.). Their journeys were the more urgent because, for a time, it was feared that a firestorm could devastate the whole city. No Venetian, it was said, slept that night.[68]

The opera house had been closed for refurbishment in preparation for a Woody Allen concert, promoted as a highlight of the imminent Carnival. After a legal dispute it was eventually agreed that the fire had been caused by arson, the culprits being two electricians whose company faced fines over tardy contracted work. While the guilty were being identified, the loss of the Fenice

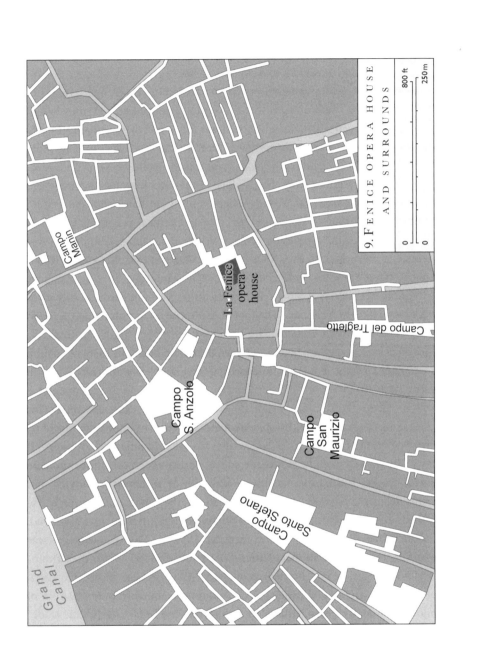

9. FENICE OPERA HOUSE
AND SURROUNDS

Grand Canal

Campo Manin

La Fenice opera house

Campo del Traghetto

Campo S. Anzolo

Campo San Maurizio

Campo Santo Stefano

0   800 ft
0   250m

all but automatically fuelled talk of the kind that had greeted the fall of the Campanile in 1902. 'Com'era e dov'era' became the predictable cry, endorsed by Cacciari among many others, the mayor promising rashly that the Fenice would reopen exactly as it had been within two years. In fact, it took until 2003 for its reconstruction as a concert hall to be complete, the first opera to be staged there being *La traviata* in November 2004.

Routinely voiced by Venetians as they surveyed the blackened remains of their opera house was the claim that the Fenice belonged to everyone. Was it not a bastion of timeless culture? Should not the world therefore join the city (and the nation) in paying for a new edifice? Rome was asked to contribute 30,000 million lire.[69] Generous offers from across the globe were quickly added, although a suggestion of marketing a video of the 1989 Pink Floyd concert did not win universal approval. Woody Allen, who might have been thought an ominous figure in the city, promised to come to Carnival as contracted and to donate receipts to the rebuilding project. Venice, he explained smoothly, was the ideal city in which to live, since he could walk out from his hotel without being irritated by motor traffic; he also loved the winter fog.[70]

True, an occasional carping critic worried that a rebuilt Fenice could never look exactly like the 'original'. (The first opera house on the site, constructed in 1790–2 and called 'La Fenice' (The Phoenix) because it had risen from the ashes of an earlier venture, had in fact been destroyed by fire in 1836, reopening a year later.) Might it instead resemble 'Disneyland'? For his part, Vittorio Sgarbi, an unrepentant self-publicist and swashbuckling cultural commentator close to Silvio Berlusconi, whom he would serve as Under-Secretary for Cultural Heritage in 2001, brashly demanded that no famous architects be employed on the reconstruction since their skills could only lead to 'fakery'. If they really wanted work in Venice, he added, perhaps such celebrities could be allowed to sketch the toilet facilities.[71] But with or without such advice, and despite delays occasioned by legal complications, the Fenice did eventually rise again, its delicate beauty restored and its technological infrastructure improved.

Meanwhile, Berlusconi (prime minister 1994–5, 2001–6, 2008–11) was beginning to bestride national politics. But in northern Italy it was the autonomist movements, which in 1989 coagulated into the Lega Nord (Northern League), that aroused almost as much comment, notably over the role of Umberto Bossi, who consolidated his position as the Lega's charismatic leader in 1991. Bossi summoned into being an imaginary country called 'Padania', formulating for it a usable past that was even more obviously falsified than most national histories. In 1996 he added a flag.[72] Equipped with such invented traditions, that September Bossi organised a 'long march' down the river Po (after which Padania was named), carrying phials of 'sacred water' from its source to Venice. His geography was as wonky as his comprehension of history, since the Po had always flowed into the Adriatic well to the south of Venice. But the city's store of time and beauty was irresistible, even to the ostentatiously straight-talking Bossi.

At least according to *Il Gazzettino*, when Bossi and his precious droplets reached Venice, the ceremony did not really fizz, Mayor Cacciari having advised his fellow citizens to stay at home. The event was not rescued by Bossi's proclaiming that the Padanian people had existed since time immemorial, and that, armed with such historical strength and virtue, they had been able to resist the 'colonial oppression, economic exploitation and moral violence' that the Italian nation had inflicted on them. After all, he added, with additional pretensions to linguistic scholarship, the name 'Italia' was in origin Calabrian, 'the worst race of all', people who, 'by culture and tradition, were native Fascists'.[73] A return visit by the Lega chief ten years later, on which occasion, it had been promised, he would be joined by 50,000 *leghisti*, similarly disappointed, with 'soaking rain and [not so many] resigned militants' mingling with the tourists, each as likely as the other to become lost in the city's labyrinth.[74]

In pushing for himself and the Lega Nord, Bossi was reducing to insignificance Venice's own autonomists and separatists, despite their loud protestations that they were girded with a real history, that of the Republic and its empire. Their key figure had been the federalist writer and activist Franco Rocchetta, who had been converted to the Venetian cause when a schoolboy. He had then won fame through being investigated by the authorities for graffiti lamenting in the Venetian dialect (or language) that Italy had joined the First World War. In 1978 Rocchetta founded the Società Filologica Veneta (Philological Society of the Veneto) and rapidly linked himself with other devotees of ways of speaking that were not endorsed by a current nation. By 1980 he and his followers were publishing a journal in the Venetian language entitled *Veneto libaro*. Rocchetta and his wife Marilena Marin had become the leaders of the Łiga Veneta, although it was quickly beset by debate, schism and purge.[75] Nonetheless, the Łiga garnered a degree of regional, national and European electoral success, and in 1989, although maintaining that 'the Łiga is the mother of all the leagues', Rocchetta accepted association with the Lega Nord, boasting typically that he had no more affinity with a Neapolitan than with a Frenchman or Armenian.[76] He became president of the Lega in 1991, a position he held until 1994. In that year, Rocchetta was awarded the important position of Under-Secretary for Foreign Affairs in the first Berlusconi government, perhaps because it was thought that the history of the Venetian Empire in Dalmatia gave him special understanding of the nationalist crises enveloping what was becoming the ex-Yugoslavia.

Rocchetta's view that the Lega should be a federalist body squared badly, however, with Bossi's centralisation and ambition, and in September 1994 he and his wife were expelled from the movement. In helpless disgust, Rocchetta compared Bossi's behaviour to that of Hitler in his bunker.[77] The expulsion marked what to all intents and purposes was the end of Rocchetta's political career, a situation confirmed by the ever more fissiparous nature of the many small local or autonomist movements. In the decades that followed, the Partito Nasional Veneto, for example, campaigned for a wholly independent Venetia, with a flag in which the Lion of St Mark was paired with a lime tree leaf beneath the claim that this combination had been 'sacred to Venetians for at least 3,000 years'. Perhaps more disconcerting was the banner of the Unione Popolare Veneta, which combined the Lion with the head of Che Guevara.[78] In the 2013 elections, the tiny Venetianist vote was split between movements calling themselves the Łiga Venezia Repubblica, Veneto Stato and Indipendenza Veneta. Between them, they drew 2.1 per cent of the vote in the region.[79] No wonder their chief historian has concluded that, since the foundation of the Łiga, 'the flag of St Mark has passed from one hand to the next, in an uninterrupted sequence of dissolutions, schisms, reprisals and always unsuccessful attempts to blend into a single voice the summons to the values, history, culture and tradition of the Serenissima'.[80] Electoral failure did not put an end to the bravado, however. In March 2013 a Lega MEP tried to persuade the European Parliament to accept a motion approving a referendum on the independence of the Veneto, and when rebuffed talked instead about establishing a 'liberation committee' to sustain the cause.[81] A year later, an unofficial online poll recorded 89% of those responding as favouring independence for the Veneto, parallels being drawn with the Crimean decision to go home to the Russian Reich, although, in the Italian case, the aim was to leave the nation, not join it.[82]

In 1997, the bicentenary of Napoleon's termination of the Venetian Republic and a year replete with more public history than most, one faction of the autonomist movement, calling itself the Veneto Serenissimo Governo (VSG), opted for bravado of a different kind, hitting the headlines and not merely in Venice. Initially, the anniversary of 12 May seemed to be approaching in a placid and predictable manner, the highlight to be a parade of eighty gorgeously dressed boats down the Grand Canal. The chief organiser, Antonio Salvadori of the Comitato per la Difesa di Venezia (Venice Defence Committee), had assured the populace that 'ours will be a demonstration of Venetians for Venice, without party brands and without claims for independence. That Sunday we shall invite all to come along who want a city that can return to being alive and liveable.'[83] The usual hint of crisis and complaint in his words was reinforced the following day when a surprise *acqua alta* broke the record for May, disconcerting a city in which the *passerelle* (duckboards) were not ready.

Good news there was, on the other hand, for business, since Arrigo Cipriani, the owner of Harry's Bar, announced that he had bought premises on Wall Street from Donald Trump so that New Yorkers, too, could enjoy his 'Venetian' cocktails and snacks.[84] Mayor Cacciari was even more often in the news. He may have been pleased to find the city's leading contemporary historian, Mario Isnenghi, saluting him as 'this singular figure of an intellectual nourished by the great decadent culture of Mittel-Europa, in a close personal and working relationship with artistic avant-gardes and with the world of music and painting, while also being equipped with a notably acute sense of the "artificial" and constructed character of the meaning of Venice'.[85] Certainly, the bicentenary was reinforcing the mayor's general fame, as was evidenced in his public debate with Carlo Maria Martini, the Jesuit cardinal of Milan, on the meaning of 'solidarity', in which each man appeared troubled by the recent gains of the rich, 'free' individual and rejected too narrow an identification with neo-liberal hegemony.[86]

But at midnight on 8 May, three days before the anniversary of Napoleon's suppression of the Republic, a number of locals sought to connect themselves and their city with history in a fashion that lay outside the established global discourse. Kitted out with machine guns and a camper van, and further armed with a road-digger camouflaged to resemble a small tank and furnished with a flame-thrower, twelve disciples of the VSG seized the last *traghetto*, or car ferry, to ply the route from Tronchetto to the Lido that night, immobilising the crew and cutting the ship's radio. They politely paid for their tickets but stopped other passengers or vehicles from boarding, and, at 12.20 on the morning of the 9th, headed for the Piazzetta, where they unloaded themselves and their 'tankette', as it would become known. They trundled it towards the Campanile, which they scaled and 'seized', perhaps imagining a long siege given that they had brought with them knapsacks 'filled with well-ironed underwear, food, wine and also a bottle of grappa, naturally enough from the Veneto'.[87] On the mainland, spokesmen with nerdish skills hacked into RAI 1 programmes to announce the coup, proclaiming that the 'Veneta Serenissima Armata has liberated Piazza San Marco. Today the Serene Republic of Venice is reborn. It resumes life because we have not abandoned our unshakeable faith that it is alive.' We know, they added, that it was, is and always will be 'an ornament of Europe and a bulwark of Christianity'.

By 1 a.m. paramilitary police had begun to arrive in the square, and the hours that followed saw a meeting of the city's emergency committee for security and public order. Mayor Cacciari, who was proud of his vivid social life,

36 The 'tankette' in Piazza San Marco

could not be located until he rang his chief assistant at 7.50 a.m., reaching San Marco some minutes later, somewhat belatedly. Before dawn, while Cacciari was being pursued and the police hesitated, the tankette had been driven twice around the square, belching fire. Once the police got moving, however, it did not take long for the 'terrorists' (or pranksters) to be hauled down from the Campanile and arrested. The VSG offered no resistance, except to declare grandly, 'We are political prisoners', producing identity cards stamped by 'the Republic of the Veneto'. Bemused locals (those, that is, who did not sleep through the entire proceedings) were said to have assumed that the group involved were 'Albanians', and to have continued their lives as normal.[88]

The seizure of the Campanile had no lasting significance. The perpetrators were treated with sensible mildness by the legal system, despite much huffing and puffing from the political world, whose denizens were nothing if not unoriginal in their views. Gustavo Selva of the ex-fascist Alleanza Nazionale (National Alliance) thought pompously that the attack further signalled the way government weakness fostered 'terrorism'.[89] The left-leaning historian Giannantonio Paladini, who had been interpreting the meaning of 1797 in the city in the pages of the local paper, feared rather that it smacked of 'Fascism'. In *La Repubblica*, senior anti-Fascist Giorgio Bocca warned that the Red Brigades had started in the same fashion as the VSG; the independence movement, he prophesied fearfully, might unleash a guerrilla campaign. In more patrician mode, Teresa Foscari Foscolo was sure that the assault on the Campanile had sprung from a deplorable general 'contempt for [pretty] history'. Preferring conspiracy theory, Bossi announced that the action was a provocation organised by the Ministry of the Interior in Rome. It was, he declared, a case of 'state terrorism', designed to discountenance autonomists.[90] In response, the VSG dismissed the Lega Nord as a 'neo-colonial instrument in regard to the nation of Venice'.[91] Their 'final communiqué' labelled Bossi a 'traitor', but did not forget simultaneously to reprehend 'the occupying regime of the wretched little Italy of the south'; in more learned tones and remembering the bicentenary, they at the same time condemned the politicians of the Congress of Vienna of 1815 for allowing Venice to die.[92]

Between the Pink Floyd concert with its related Expo debate and the comical seizure of the Campanile, Venice had experienced a decade studded with melodramatic events, ones that would not be replicated in the years to come. Yet, somewhere beneath such feverishness, the grand themes of Venetian life continued across the decades. A major one was the fate of Marghera, where the shutting down of one business was succeeded by that of another, culminating in August 2006, when Dow Chemicals announced their withdrawal from the site and sacked 180 workers. This multinational had gained unwanted headlines in November 2002 after a leakage of lethal gas, an industrial accident, critics charged, that 'could have killed part of the population of Marghera, Mestre, Venice and the surrounding area', even though in practice only four workers were lightly injured. 'The flames, the sirens, the loudspeakers, the state of alert for citizens, the escape of Dioxin into the air, the image on TV of the mayor, [Paolo] Costa, visiting the place wearing a gas mask', all confirmed the long-standing view that Marghera had always been a disaster and was best erased from Venice's future.[93] After all, the processes of globalisation were making the chemical and electrical businesses that had flourished there out of place in a Europe in which such heavy industry was everywhere moving offshore.

Greenpeace had already focused its environmental expertise on industrial Venice, exposing in detail the shameless dumping of waste into the lagoon. A spokesman stated that one plate of 'spaghetti alle vongole veraci' (actually based on the 'vongole filippine' that had replaced the historic stock some years earlier) contained levels of Dioxin that exceeded the recommended maximum daily intake, sometimes supplemented by traces of cadmium, chromium, mercury, DDT and various other poisons.[94] Although today Marghera remains a functioning industrial port and a number of industries continue production there, those who approve the place are likely to applaud its new 'scientific and technological park' rather than its lingering traditional businesses.[95] The potential for industrial archaeology may well be the best recipe. Indeed, an official report of 2013 concluded that 'for too many years there had been a search to save what could not be saved' and that old forms of business had no future in Marghera. The overall workforce had fallen to a little over a thousand, about a third of whom were still employed by 'industry'.[96] Meanwhile, it is telling that researchers have begun to record the memories of those who lived through the experience of post–1945 Marghera, even if it might not be a surprise to learn that old residents think of themselves as the 'poor relations of Venice and [even] Mestre'. In any case, they are now outnumbered in the streets where they live by extra-European immigrants.[97]

The greatest environmental issue confronting the city has remained the fear, triggered by the flood of 1966 and enhanced by the subsequent massive scientific demonstration of inexorable global warming, that, as nature runs its course, Venice will sink beneath the waves. In the minds of practical men, the solution to such a potential catastrophe must lie in machines and engineering works. As usual in Venice, despite the fashion for neo-liberal chat, it was automatically accepted that remedial action should be funded through the successive special laws passed by the national government for the city's benefit. Such subsidy could be matched by international largesse, whether arriving directly from sometimes bickering and usually high society private charitable organisations[98] or channelled through the numerous research projects devoted throughout the scholarly world to the 'Venetian problem'. The exhortation that 'time is running out for this loveliest of cities' has been one that even the most parsimonious of finance committees have found hard to resist.[99]

The grandest scheme to prevent the drowning of Venice was one to rework the *murazzi* in line with modern knowledge, creating structures that could block the Adriatic in an emergency while allowing the benign cleansing ebb and flow of the tides to work as it always had in normal circumstances. Thoughts on the topic have a long history, but it was on 31 October 1988 that the first colossal Modulo Sperimentale Elettromeccanico was lowered into the sea off Treporti as a trial.[100] The following year, the costly project was formally launched by De Michelis, who had won national backing from Giulio Andreotti, the durable Christian Democrat who would serve his last term as prime minister between 1989 and 1992. De Michelis predictably took the opportunity to suggest that the success of such engineering works could be a major theme at a Venetian World's Fair.[101]

The MOSE project was designed to baulk a raging sea at the three lagoon outlets (the Lido, Malamocco and Chioggia; see map 8) by means of a system of mobile gates, anchored to the sea bottom but able to rise to three metres above normal sea level, 50 per cent higher than the flood of 1966. Appearing tardily from the international competition advertised in 1975, the plan for the MOSE was first sketched in detail in 1981. Despite being initially dismissed by the city's Chamber of Commerce as 'crazy', the scheme convinced the people who counted, and by the end of the decade had developed a momentum of its own. In 1994 the national Ministry of Public Works signalled its approval, while international experts were, as ever, happy to provide their own support.[102]

The initial trial, however, had mixed results,[103] and at the end of the 1990s a committee investigating the environmental impact of the engineering involved reported negatively, prompting further delays. Italia Nostra had not conceded approval, and Antonio Cederna, one of the best-respected environmentalists in the country, attacked the insertion of the MOSE as 'hypertechnologisation'.[104] A Venetian observer agreed, lamenting that, in campaigning for the MOSE, the Consorzio Venezia Nuova (Consortium for a New Venice) had become an 'institutionalised monster', gobbling up huge funds to pay for its mechanical fantasies and ignoring the subtle natural reality of the lagoon.[105] A 'Comitato NoMOSE' drew considerable sympathy in the city, especially from the Green movement, and in 2006 the Minister of the Environment in the centre-left government headed by economist Romano Prodi suspended work.[106]

The project had, however, gained public promotion from Silvio Berlusconi, and when he returned as prime minister in May 2008 preparation for the insertion of the MOSE resumed. The work was now said to be 63 per cent complete and an end-date was set for 2014. Most recently, completion has slipped forward to 2016 or 2017, even though on Saturday 12 October 2013 the authorities celebrated the rising of the first four structures. Controversy and criticism have nonetheless continued.[107] Moreover, there are fresh worries that the gates could be overwhelmed by severe pressure from wind and sea and thus unleash a tsunami against Venice. Doubts prompted by the devastating effect of tidal waves in Asia are reinforced by older concerns that, in certain adverse climatic circumstances, flooding will be worse from the rivers that flow into the lagoon than from the sea; then, it is feared, the MOSE might operate to stop the waters flowing out.

A lay historian is not the person to adjudicate the science of the dispute. What cannot be denied, however, is the cost to the state and the profit to a number of businesses involved. By 2013 an initial estimated budget of 1,500 million euros had ballooned to 5,600 million, and that figure did not include upkeep. According to one critic's estimate, over the previous three decades Venice has received more than 10,000 million euros in subsidy, a little less than half of it having been consumed by the still unfinished MOSE.[108] If the sums are right, then this small city must have won a gold medal in enjoying benefaction outside the sober functioning of market profit and loss in a neo-liberal age. 'History' pays, it might be concluded.

While the MOSE project was being debated, plenty of other changes to Venice were mooted, proponents almost always seeking 'real' employment in the old city as opposed to that occasioned by mass tourism. Such searching, however, never reversed the decline in actual residents. Just as they had done when Volpi or Giuriati or Foscari had dreamed of a 'restored' great Venice, the minds of architects and engineers, financiers and entrepreneurs, once again teemed with grand plans, each certain to summon a usable history when an ideal way forward was plotted. As a new glossy magazine aiming to market the city's charms to a global public put it in 2000, modern Venetians 'are following the paths of history and acting as explorers of their own history'.[109]

Predictable in its proposed marriage of heritage, profit and sport was a suggestion from business groups led by Benetton, whose first headquarters were in nearby Treviso but whose attention was ever more drawn to the luminous heritage of Venice. They launched a campaign to hold the Olympics in the city and surrounding districts, 2020 seeming the ideal date.[110] The bid was announced in October 2009 by Cacciari, who had yielded to the neo-liberal process of the personalisation of communal politics and the accompanying dismissal of parties and class as irrelevant in modern times. On resuming the mayorship in 2005 he had already told a journalist from *La Repubblica* that, if he had to select a Maecenas for Venice, his choice would fall on Lorenzo Benetton.[111] The athletic dream that Cacciari and Benetton shared, however, lost official support when the economist Mario Monti replaced Berlusconi as prime minister in November 2011. Propelled into office by the parlous state of the national finances, Monti was quick to extract Italy from the expense of any such competition (a rival case had been mounted for the return of the Olympics to Rome).[112]

But a Venetian Olympiad was not the only proposal of these years. Benetton, for example, had devoted funds and energy to a controversial conversion of the Fondaco dei Tedeschi, until 2008 the main city post office, into what critics condemned as a crass shopping centre to be furnished with (debatably) elegant balconies over the Grand Canal.[113] Even more controversial was the fourth bridge across that waterway, known in the city after its architect, the Spaniard Santiago Calatrava. Cacciari launched the idea of a new crossing between Piazzale Roma and the railway station in 1996, but the construction provoked so much disputation that it was opened secretively at night twelve years later. Argument continued, on account of the expanding cost of the bridge's upkeep, notably of the people-mover that was meant to help the disabled over it but that functioned either badly or not at all.[114] None noticed what might be thought its greatest irony: the similarity of its elegant curve to that of the giant metal tube on the horizon at Marghera that has framed one view across the lagoon for the last half-century.

The Fondaco restoration and the Calatrava bridge were not the only costly modernisation proposals to divide Venetians. In 2010 the Fondazione Gianni Pellicani, named after a local communist who, like Cacciari, had gone with the neo-liberal flow, proposed the construction of four thousand floating houses. They could constitute 'a series of micro-cities with parks, squares, schools, super-markets', anchored to the lagoon floor.[115] Yet more flamboyant was the suggestion of the Dutch architect Julian De Smedt that, by 2060, the old city might, at a distance of a few hundred metres, be framed by a necklace of tall modern high-rises, each built on its own artificial island. Such a development, his company's publicity maintained, would make Venice 'the most fascinating city in the world', while the skyscrapers could protect the historic centre from *acque alte* and ensure, in some undisclosed manner, the place's repopulation with Venetians.[116]

Compared with this proposition, the suggestion of a group calling itself Nova Marghera, who exhibited at the 2004 architecture Biennale, to redevelop the entire waterfront of the lagoon might seem remarkably modest. Five years earlier, a conference of regional engineers had been sure that Venice could raise itself into a 'European metropolis', in its 'greatness' matching such places as New York, Tokyo, Seoul and Singapore, as well as London and Paris.[117] In 2011 their optimism appeared undimmed as they looked to changes across the lagoon that could convert it into Venice's 'eighth *sestiere*, composed of space for housing, leisure and work'.[118] While that prospect matured, in 2013 a group of busi-nessmen called for backing for 'Venezia Nord Est 2019: Capitale Europea della Cultura', wherein Venice and its province could together gain the prize as Europe's cultural centre; 'Venice has the history and the strength to win,' they urged.[119]

Half-plans to build a subway system under the lagoon that might extend from Iesolo and the Lido to Padua and beyond, thereby resolving the city's communication 'problem', had already been envisaged before 1914 and continued to drift in and out of urban debate. After the flood of 1966, for example, it was promised that the trip on a 'sub-lagunare' from Mestre to Piazza San Marco could be cut to 10.2 minutes.[120] Another recurrent issue was whether the old city and the settlements in the lagoon should be administratively sepa-rated from Mestre (and Marghera). One advocate of this change was Giorgio Suppiej, a prominent city lawyer from the family of the former *federale*.[121] The Lido, too, felt the thrust of the bottom line. There, the real estate concern EstCapital snapped up the old Ospedale al Mare, as well as the Excelsior, the Hotel des Bains (soon recast as sumptuous apartments) and the Forte di Malamocco, only to become bogged down in its developments by a complex law suit with the Comune by 2013.[122]

Equally persistent but slower in progress was the debate over the future of the Arsenale, the major issues being whether the navy should cede what it still owned there and what could best be done with the considerable space involved.[123] From 1999 parts of the site were regularly utilised for Biennale exhibitions, and nowadays, when the exhibitions are closed, concerts, lectures and other cultural events occur there often enough, the Comune having taken charge of most of the edifice from the nation state in 2013.[124] Heartfelt pleas that workers should find employment of some not too outlandish form in the old buildings have gone unheeded, however.[125] For all the regular evocation of their 'glorious' history, *arsenalotti* no longer exist, and the Arsenale is yet another part of Venice that may be 'dov'era' but is certainly not 'com'era'. A bright suggestion that it could be an excellent base for 'Montgolfier' or balloon trips over the lagoon in the style of 1848 has not yet been implemented,[126] but major archaeological work has received public and private finance, its first findings said to be 'stunning'.[127]

Another recurrent theme in Venice has been the expansion of the city's universities, tertiary education frequently being seen as an appropriate business for a place that aches with history and beauty. As a prominent local historian put it in least complicated form, 'Venice is a natural university campus.'[128] The rise of the VIU on San Servolo in this regard has already been noted, while Ca' Foscari and IUAV have continued to expand their student intake and to extend their co-operation with universities elsewhere in Italy and abroad. In the last decade, the sometime Cotonificio, near the Zattere, has been re-equipped and modernised as a teaching and housing venue for students in what most agree has been a harmonious and handsome manner, and there is a prospect that the empty tobacco factory will be used for the local law courts.

More controversially, a story surfaced late in 2013 that Carlo Carraro, the rector of Ca' Foscari (and an environmental economist), had lined up behind a scheme to transform San Biagio, the artificial island off the Giudecca where Venetian rubbish has been dumped in recent decades. The suggestion of Alberto Zamperla, CEO of a company that has worked at Disneyland Paris and Coney Island, New York, was to erect 'a centre of fun, history and learning'. As the entrepreneur put it, 'It will be about the history of Venice – one of my passions – but done my way.' Somewhat belying the promise of Carraro that the project would 'have a solid grounding from a cultural and scientific point of view' was the idea that a fun park might offer 'a big wheel, wagons shot at high speed across an artificial lake' and reproductions of the Turkish and Venetian ships that fought out the Battle of Lepanto. A 'virtual museum' would allow 3D 're-creation' of the 'Venetian past' (defined, of course, as that of the Republic rather than the modern city).[129] To adapt a Disney slogan, Zamperla seemed to envisage a place that could be a popular and populist vehicle of 'tall tales and untrue from the legendary past'.

According to American early modernist Joanne Ferraro, whose general history of the city was written before the debate on such vagaries began, most advances in tertiary education there should be applauded. 'Even as it has changed over the centuries', she observed, Venice, 'with the help of intellectuals, artists, and philanthropists, has preserved the culture from its greatest days, and everyone comes to see what has remained. If only for a few hours, it gives people the opportunity to share in Venice's historical legacy', she added with characteristic certainty that history after 1797 was of trifling significance and that the place enchanted only where it maintained the formula 'com'era e dov'era'. After all, she pronounced, Venice is 'an important international center of scholarship'. 'Besides the endless visits from foreigners [a euphemism for mass tourists and excluding poor immigrants], Venice is filled with scholars, writers, artists, and expatriates from around the world who have adopted it as home, or a home away from home.'[130] Yet despite Ferraro's admiration for the 'living presence' of Republican history and culture, the Venetian universities have not moved to the top of any of the global tertiary league tables, and it remains hard to imagine Venice equalling the breadth and depth of scholarship to be found in Paris, Oxford and Cambridge or the American Ivy League. It is thus all very well for a dewy-eyed recent observer to maintain that 'almost everybody' who resides in Venice 'is united by the desire to give this city another chance to live', while excoriating 'the daily violation of one of the earth's most glorious treasures by unregulated tourism'. But, in populist manner, she blithely assumes that someone else will pay for such protection.[131]

The city may attract thousands of undergraduate and graduate students, but of the estimated 12,000 commuters who enter Venice daily for reasons of work the great majority are employed in one 'industry' only, that of mass tourism. Ignoring *acque alte* and poisoned *vongole* (as well as the often direly exploitative and 'un-Venetian' nature of many food outlets in the city), tourists have continued to pour into Venice. In the cold, wet and fog of February, visitors flock to Carnival, a 'traditional' festival that was revived on private initiative in 1979 after years of neglect, bolstered by claims that it could help the city recover from the flood.[132] Its huge drawing power soon won the endorsement of the Comune as filling what had been a low point in the tourist year, although dismay at the numbers involved soon surfaced. The tourists also come in the heat and humidity of August, refusing to be put off by smelly canals (the algae problem is not fully resolved) and the difficulty of crossing every city bridge. Indeed, at any time of the year it is impossible to cross a canal without being blocked by a tourist taking a photo of another tourist from the bridge's summit, oblivious that the space has a more immediate practical use.[133]

The numbers are staggering. According to one local pamphleteer, in 2012 the official annual tally was 21.6 million. That total meant an average of more than 59,000 visitors daily, matching the number of surviving residents. In fact, he claimed, more than 30.38 million had entered the city in 2011, peaking in August at over 140,000 every day. At least 80 per cent were reckoned to be day-trippers, although the beds available in the city had risen to 37,000, up 75 per cent on a decade earlier, and 500 per cent greater than in 1957.[134] Whereas in that year 30 per cent of visitors had been Italians, thirty years later co-nationals composed only 17 per cent of the tourist trade.[135] Since then, the variety of incomers has continued to expand, as the global tourist market has spread among the new middle classes of Asia and South America. On one summer day in 2011, the tourists who had arrived by car, train or bus (in 2006, 72,000 coaches disgorged their passengers at Piazzale Roma)[136] were supplemented by 35,000 who disembarked from the massive cruise ships.[137] With the Comune's approval, what their critics lambasted as 'huge floating tins . . . inspired by Las Vegas style casinos' had taken to anchoring at the Stazione Marittima. Standing in some cases more than sixty metres high, in the cityscape they towered over ordinary houses that were a quarter as tall.[138] The wash they created when they sailed in or out of the lagoon added markedly to the damage already being done to buildings by the passage of other motorised vessels.[139] In November 2013 it was announced that a national ban would be placed on the 'largest vessels' using the Giudecca canal. They would still, however, be able to anchor at the Stazione Marittima.[140]

The epicentre of the tourist trade in the city is of course Piazza San Marco, the goal of visitors who have streamed down Strada Nova and similar routes, pathways equipped with innumerable shops marketing an array of goods, fashion, glass, masks and other trinkets more likely to have been made in China than in Venice. In other words, the great square, which earlier in the twentieth century had been vigorously contested by Venetians of different class and ideology, has fallen all but completely into the hands of the tourist masses. Nowadays, Venetians are said to try to avoid crossing the Piazza unless forced. In 2007 Cacciari won new headlines with a scheme to unleash a squad of volunteers of all ages – housewives, pensioners and students – to attempt to persuade tourists not to picnic in the Piazza or otherwise interfere with urban decorum. He continued, however, to block the suggestion that only paying ticket-holders be allowed to enter Venice, and a scheme to have a ferry line accessible only to locals also soon collapsed.

In 2006 Cacciari had made another splash when he urged a final solution to the pigeon problem, joking that the administration should erect placards with a skull and crossbones warning against any toleration of 'flying rats'.[141] Previous

37 Contemporary ferry stop notice, urging tourists to travel clothed and to accept that the Lido is the beach resort

proposals to use killer birds to frighten the pigeons away or to introduce anti-conception-laden food to stop them breeding had failed. Even though it was announced in 2008 that the sale of pigeon food and the feeding of the birds had been banned, today there are still pigeons, fluttering, defecating and nibbling, in Piazza San Marco. There are also plenty of tourists, feeding and photographing the pigeons and themselves. It might not require very much psychological insight to suggest that in many Venetian souls there lurks the thought that the tourists are more rat-like than the pigeons.

Among those serving or stimulating present needs are immigrants from the world beyond Europe, people known throughout Italy as 'vu cumprà' (do you want to buy?) and common wherever tourists gather. In 2005 observers noticed that, by contrast with the old city, there were no 'vu cumprà' in Mestre; ironically, it was as much of a 'non-place' to them as it was to supercilious intellectuals.[142] Non-European immigrants began to reach Venice from the early 1990s. Today they have carved out a continuing place there and should be acknowledged as part of the city's contemporary history, however much they are ignored in most debates about Venice's past and future.[143] By 2006 *Il*

Gazzettino was reporting that 6.5 per cent of school children enrolled in the province were foreign-born,[144] while Senegalese had allegedly split the city into sales zones and threatened retribution against any who might want to interfere with their scheme.[145] More recently, an *alimentari* (grocer's shop) in Castello stole the headlines by advertising its sale in its window in Chinese.[146]

One group who have provoked hostile public attention are Rom and Sinti, whose long presence in the region grew rapidly in the 1990s as a result of the Balkan wars and the greater indulgence in racial prejudice by post-communist regimes after the fall of the Berlin Wall. Matters were complicated in Venice by the populist racism of many in the Lega Nord and other autonomist movements. In September 2008 one such spokesman at the 'Festa of the Padanian Peoples' demanded 'double zero tolerance' as the proper line to be taken on any 'gypsy' presence.[147]

Ironically, the region had, in the past, led the way in Italy in acknowledging that 'nomadic culture' was part of the multicultural assembly of life in the Veneto. The settlement of newcomers, however, first at Marghera and then in greater numbers at San Giuliano outside Mestre, provoked attack,[148] and in February 2003 the encampment at San Giuliano burned down. Despite Cacciari's attempts to defuse them, troubles have smouldered, both within the 'community' and among old Venetians, unalleviated by the Comune's 'dispersing' of the immigrants around the smaller towns of the province.[149] The bemused comment of a social worker sent in the 1990s to report on the situation at Marghera – 'I came back to the office with the strong impression that I had seen a place out of the Fifth World just a few steps away from home' – remains a sad commentary on the continuing difficulty experienced by Venetians in absorbing too much 'difference' from the wider world.[150]

It is the mass tourists rather than those who serve or prey on them, however, who remain the hottest issue in contemporary Venice, there being an almost universal assumption that day-trippers and their ilk are annoying, ignorant and exploitative. They are the ugly aliens who push Venice into a sad fate as a Disneyland, amusement park or shopping centre, each the epitome of a 'soullessness' that wounds ever more gravely the city's holy 'beauty', each lacking a proper sense of history, each encumbering Venice and assaulting its greatness. As recent culturalist analysts have claimed, Piazza San Marco has become so 'touristed' that Venetians can no longer locate 'meaning' in it.[151] By definition, it is assumed, mass tourists do not understand and will never understand Venice. They typically get the blame for the legendarily poor quality of Venetian restaurants. No doubt it is possible to eat well if a hungry visitor is willing to search discerningly (and the locals do manage to find their own preferred sites), but it must be admitted that low-grade food is frequently purveyed in the city at very high prices, in a rip-off system that surely brings profits to some local interests. Yet the meals served near any historic centre are unlikely to give satisfaction to the gourmet or the seeker of the authentic, and in this regard, as in so many others, Venice's real problem is that it is little more than a 'historic centre'.

The same explanation is the best one for the other commonly condemned impacts of tourism: the groaning ferry boats, the swarming canals, the blocked *calli* and *campi*, the focus of most shops on the trinkets aimed at the short-term tourist, with the resultant lack of a large supermarket (necessitating a trip to Mestre or Marghera for residents). Those few tens of thousands who continue to live in the old city have to endure many annoyances, and are driven to put up with them by their wealth, their poverty or their special love for the peculiarities of Venetian life. Their endurance is often accompanied by complaint, and just as old history is revered and the more recent past ignored, so everyday life is frequently declared to be not what it was. According to one scholarly American visitor, writing an uncritical booklet in a local series that is almost always critical in approach to recent developments, mass tourism over the last thirty-five years has fatally disturbed the tenor of life in the Venetian *campo*; there, she claims, 'the community's basic needs' were until recently met, given that 'almost all transactions [were] between people who [trusted] each other'.[152]

Such naive sentimentality may be music to Venetian ears. But a more sceptical observer might wonder whether trust is ever an automatic part of life. More generally, it must be asked, how fair is it for the visiting throngs to be treated with the same contempt that used to be visited on peasants, or with the same 'condescension' that E. P. Thompson noticed falling upon the 'deluded followers of Joanna Southcott'? Perhaps a better approach to mass tourism would be to admit that, however briefly (and some day-trippers must return once, twice and more), the visitors bear histories of their own, some forged on their visits, that deserve recording. Perhaps, even when they clutter up the city squares and yield to the temptation of buying T-shirts woven in Fiji, glass manufactured in China rather than on Murano and plastic gondolas that glow in the dark, they too are, in quite a few senses, 'Venetians', and therefore deserve to have their heritage added to those many other histories that wash so richly through the place. Perhaps, today, their numbers and their delight contribute most to making twenty-first-century Venice a living city, or at least a living 'historic centre' of that world we like to call civilised.

Conclusion

Recent observers of Venice's 'tourist maze' have argued that those who tramp inexhaustibly through the *calli* are responsible for the city's being reduced to a place that is 'all in the mind', no more than 'a backdrop and a stage for one's gaze, emotions, and passions'. Venice, they contend, is the prime 'postmodern city, selling no product other than itself'. It is 'a city not just visited but *inhabited* by tourists'. Yet, they add, 'Venice's history actually offers little with which modern-day visitors can identify personally. Unlike Florence, Rome, or Athens, the city fits rather poorly into the general narrative of Western Civilization.'[1] With the supercilious pessimism that seems all but obligatory among such commentators, Giorgio Agamben, a philosopher with his own postmodern drift who worked for a time at IUAV, has phrased it differently but with similar implication. As far as he is concerned, contemporary Venice is no longer even a corpse, as it was when there was chatter about holding the Expo there. Now it is merely a spectre 'composed of signs', a ghostly being that 'constantly carries a date in its wanderings and is therefore an intimately historical being'.[2] But this history is dead, like the city; it records a lost past and not a living one.

This book has been written to reject the contentions of such melodious mourners, or at least to urge that they be heard sceptically. Its theme is that, in reality, if not always in discourse and imagination, Venice is awash with copious histories, plenty of them modern. One great matter has become clear in the course of these pages. However repeated may be the claims that the city is or ought to be 'com'era e dov'era', simply as it always was, in fact it has been as subject to change as any other place. Time has not stood still in Venice. Tides that began in the long history of the Republic have been pushed and patterned by the force of events and new structures since. Despite constant efforts to erase the recent past, with its overtly 'political' dangers and debates, in favour of cosily consensual Republican antiquity, Venice has actually experienced the full impact of contemporary history. Its local and parochial systems have adjusted to the arrival of the Italian state, as well as to regular passage into the city of political, social and economic influences from across the globe.

In the years after 1866, Venetians learned to live under the rule of nineteenth-century liberalism, with its worthy emphasis on the nation, 'improvement' and rationality (and anti-clericalism), even if quite a few still clung to a surviving piety, a staunch preference for Church over state, an unabated patriarchism, and other ideas and practices with an early modern cast. During these decades, a version of the industrial revolution enveloped the city, providing factory employment and heightening class strife, be it at Santa Marta, the Giudecca and Marghera or the never fully revived Arsenale. At the same time, the inauguration of the Biennale in 1895 and the fashioning of the Lido into one of Europe's most glittering beach resorts enhanced Venice's magnetism for tourists and intellectuals alike, whether the latter were optimists about modernity or driven by the view that nations were engaged in a Darwinian struggle for supremacy and survival.

The charm of the *belle époque* in its turn transmuted into the slaughter and terror of those world wars that blighted the first half of the twentieth century in Europe. Then, in part citizens of an Italy that was driven by the needs and delusions of the 'least of the Great Powers' and in part participants in an urban story that was special to their city, Venetians learned the meaning of modern battle and bowed to the modern nation state's ambition to run 'total' war. For most residents, the First World War demonstrated that the city's commitment to cosmopolitan tourism, leisure and an elegant high culture must yield to the particularist ambitions of the nation, local leaders talking glibly of a 'great Venice' sponsoring a 'renewed' Venetian empire that could be a natural supplement to that of the 'Third' Italy and its capital, Rome. Before long, such aggressive dreams were harnessed by Fascist and 'totalitarian' dictatorship. Mussolini was made prime minister in October 1922 and dictator in January 1925 to the relief and applause of the best people in Venice. Ironically, however, the Second World War, driven by the genocidal ideological obsessions of Nazi-fascism, largely passed Venetians by, the city resuming, even in the bitter days of 1943–4, its tourist vocation.

Under the aegis of Giuseppe Volpi, who shrugged off challenges from the radical Fascism of Pietro Marsich and from Giuseppe Giuriati's purist (if paradoxically self-interested) enthusiasm for the regime and its tyranny, Venice had undergone its own version of totalitarianism through the years of Mussolini's rule. Fascist brutality and corruption were always present – not for nothing was Volpi made Count of Misurata as a reward for launching Italy's murderous 'reconquest' of Libya – but so was high society gentility. Attracted by the expanded set of festivals and serviced by the elegant Nicelli airport and the golf course at Alberoni, a cosmopolitan elite continued to swell Venetian crowds until the late 1930s, their rackety behaviour exemplified by Cole Porter's 'negro orchestra' drifting down the Grand Canal while playing jazz (not a musical form of which the Nazis approved). Poorer Venetians were left to cope with the dictatorship and its secret police as best they might, on occasion seeking to manipulate the regime's inconsistencies and divisions to their own familial ends. Such ordinary citizens remained beset by bad housing and recurrent unemployment. Moreover, they increasingly faced the prospect of renewed war, made nightmarish to most by the memory of what had happened to the city between 1915 and 1918.

In 1945 General Mark Clark declared ringingly that Venetians had liberated themselves, a statement that, as has been noted, still hangs outside Ca' Farsetti as proof of the deep-rootedness of anti-Fascism in the city. Yet the reality was diverse during the war, when, rather than actively backing the Resistance, most Venetians did their best to keep their heads down, some not seeming to mind when their Jewish co-citizens were rounded up by the Nazi-fascists who ruled the city after September 1943. Then, the Holocaust left its appalling and shameful mark on Venice. Similarly, after the war, liberation scarcely meant the unchallenged triumph of the left, whether in the old city or in the factories at Marghera, where initial union gains from the Italian version of a people's war were soon rolled back after 1948. Much about Venice was summarised in the ironical conjunction of Liberation Day and the Feast of St Mark on 25 April, when the continuing power of Catholic history could offset any contention that Venetians had learned to treasure an anti-Fascist view of the world above all else. Under Christian Democratic rule, talk about the overcoming of class difference was as unreal as it had been in the Fascist 'revolution'.

Within the city, the Resistance was officially commemorated with the statues of *La Partigiana*. The choice of a female subject was some indication that the sociological effects of post-war prosperity – the 'Italian miracle', as it was known – were trickling into the city. Venetians were certainly learning to consume more than in the past, and differently. Furthermore, at least to some extent, the habitual patriarchy that had for centuries been entrenched across the classes yielded to modern ideas about women's liberation. Yet, even today, the heights of power in the city, whether business or governmental, lie in male hands. Venetians have never elected a woman mayor, and leading urban officials, newspaper editors and cultural commentators have been predominantly male. There are exceptions, but women who have been prominent especially in environmental debates, such as Anna Maria Volpi and Teresa Foscari Foscolo, spring from the patriciate, a group always likely to infringe social norms.

In this regard, Venice was little different from other parts of Italy, but in other arenas Venetians lived their own story. In an era when most cities were expanding and then expanding again, Venice from the early 1950s began to shed its residents, so that today, with a population of under 60,000, it may be better viewed as a small town or large village rather than as a metropolis. The great flood of 1966 marked a watershed in both the literal and the metaphorical sense. Thereafter, as global warming became irreversible, the possibility that Venice, a new Atlantis, would soon be dead could never be denied. How, became the insistent question, might that destiny be averted?

Soon the world entered the era of neo-liberalism, an ideology whose major principles of winding back the welfare state and allowing the market to rule were ill suited to a city that was, by definition, dependent on subsidy for its continued existence. Another datum of the 'end of history', that the individual must be free and personality celebrated, was easier to live with, Venice having hailed a 'great' mayor in Massimo Cacciari in recent decades, as well as various great capitalists, Lorenzo Benetton being the most active current example. At the same time, those who throng the city's alleyways and squares are increasingly looked after by immigrants from places far away, rendered mobile through the effects of globalisation on their home societies, but now, even when resident at Mestre, Marghera or the other towns on the mainland, become Venetians of some definition. While the urban poor have been thus ambiguously renewed, those with the opportunity to craft ideas have come up with a long series of grand (and costly) schemes, the Pink Floyd concert, the MOSE project and the plans for a World's Fair, the Olympics or becoming Europe's cultural capital notable among them. All have begun with claims that they would bring money into the city and thereby somehow 'restore greatness'; all have soon demanded subvention.

In these as in other instances, what is plain is that, since 1866, Venetians have experienced their own mixture of change and continuity, a set of pasts that are scarcely out of kilter with the time and tide of the rest of Italy, Europe and the contemporary world. For anyone who cares to listen, the city echoes with these histories as much as with those of the Republic and its *imperium*. But the central narrative about Venice is determined to deny contemporary history and to privilege instead those centuries when the city was the capital of an empire (however bloodily imposed and defended)[3] on which the sun took quite a while to set. The music of Vivaldi resounds, while that of Luigi Nono is seldom heard. The paintings of Tintoretto or Palma il Giovane must be viewed by all, while more modern representations (with the exception of the splendid cosmopolitan collection of Peggy Guggenheim exhibited in Palazzo Venier dei Leoni, an unrepentantly modernist building beside the Grand Canal) may be ignored. The Renaissance statue of Bartolomeo Colleoni is a wonder of the world, but who notices the monuments to Manin, Victor Emmanuel II or *La Partigiana*? The Contarini del Bovolo staircase is a must on any visitor's itinerary, but should anyone bother to locate the Scarpa staircase on the ground floor of the Querini Stampalia palace? When tourists float down the Grand Canal, every photographer is obsessed by the medieval and Renaissance palaces, even if few can identify where the multiple 'restorations' and alterations from the original have been made, or discern which buildings were erected not in the middle ages but in the nineteenth or twentieth centuries. Beside the Rialto bridge, who notices the splendidly kitsch architecture of the fish market? Who cares about the story of the *vaporetti* or of the alterations to the pathways of the city, when everyone longs to spend an hour with a lover in a gondola, musing on eternity and oblivious of present troubles? No doubt the curious assembly of early styles in the Basilica di San Marco deserves to be the cynosure of all eyes, but could not visitors also squinny at the period syncretism of the Excelsior hotel?

Throughout the old city, in sum, a history war has been fought and won whereby an 'old' past (however reinvented), a pretty past and a safe past have silenced a more bracing review of Venetian lives and identities over the last two centuries. The victorious history has much to be said for it. It portrays a shiningly beautiful Venice that glitters in the sunshine and smells of the sea in a way unknown in other cities, with enough complexity refracted into the fluctuating images that dance amid the lapping waters. Married thus indissolubly to beauty, this history allures and sells. It makes the buyers happy, delighted to be Venetians of the mind and soul for a day or a week or for ever in memory. It opens cheque books to pay for restoration and preservation in a generous and endless process that a rigorous market might suggest was better avoided. Yet it is also a history that has rejected the rigour of a discipline that seeks to record the crimes, follies and tragedies, the pomposities and greed, the bathos, the parochialism of humankind, together with the joys and successes. This Venice is not Disneyland, as has so frequently been alleged, but rather a prime contemporary venue of history with such history, or the great majority of it, left out.

Perhaps heritage value is all that can be expected of a 'historic centre', and Venice is the grandest, the most complete heritage site in the world, less the historic centre of the Veneto than of Western civilisation, with a periphery that extends beyond Mestre to every place of origin of its innumerable visitors. As such it is not surprising or humiliating to find it 'occupied' by mass tourism. Which historic centre is not? The difference between Venice and the rest is that most major urban tourist sites have peripheries that are not so far away and so combine the 'historic' with the 'real'. Certainly, it is impossible to deny that, in the twenty-first century, mass tourists 'make' Venice in their mind, or their mind's eye, seeing through their preparatory viewing of film and image as much as through gaze, taste and smell on the day. They constitute, compose and endlessly reinvent and reinvigorate Venice at least as much as do the surviving residents. They indeed inhabit the city, but by no means to its certain destruction; their versions of the past are as meaningful and serious as are the 'wromantic' and self-interested evocations of the pre-1797 Republic by the self-conscious elite of 'Venice lovers'.

But there is a limitation. When, in my previous book, I recounted the whispering histories that jostle their way through contemporary Rome, it was easy to find pasts that were multiple and contemporary, embracing rich and poor, men and women, fans of this ideology or that. In Rome, history wars were endemic, and are still being fought with passion and commitment, and with a resultant positive effect on democratic debate. In Venice, by contrast, contemporary histories have been and still are suppressed almost to nothingness. Their absence entails the failure to acknowledge the poor as well as the rich, the newcomers as well as ancient patrician families, the kaleidoscope of tourists as well as the dwindling residents. Few notice the contests that, over the last century and a half, have been vivaciously disputed between cosmopolitans, Italian nationalists, Venetian particularists and defenders of a Church that is simultaneously global and urban, between Fascists and anti-Fascists, between the classes, between unions and business, between men and women. If Venice is dead or is approaching death, a key reason is that it is too often imagined and marketed as though dressed by a single good history, when, in reality, like every other place in the world, it is washed by multiple pasts enjoying their historians or summoning them to write another telling story. The first lesson of contemporary Venice, its contents and discontents, is that history and beauty are joined there, but they are not, or should not be made, identical.

Notes

Introduction

1. Quoted in Toby Cole (ed.), *Venice: A Portable Reader* (New York: Frontier, 1979), xii.
2. Gore Vidal, *Vidal in Venice* (London: Weidenfeld and Nicolson, 1985), 11.
3. Quoted in Tony Tanner, *Venice Desired* (Oxford: Blackwell, 1992), 368.
4. Paul Morand, *Venices* (London: Pushkin, 2002), 11, 35.
5. Fernand Braudel and Folco Quilici, *Venezia: immagine di una città* (Bologna: Il Mulino, 1984), 50, 143.
6. Régis Debray, *Against Venice* (London: Pushkin, 2002), 9, 17, 22–47, 75.
7. Mark McKenna, *An Eye for Eternity: The Life of Manning Clark* (Melbourne University Press, 2011), 472.
8. F. Marion Crawford, *Gleanings from Venetian History* (London: Macmillan, 1907), 1–2.
9. Reginald Hill, *Another Death in Venice* (London: The Crime Club, 1976), 104.
10. Iain Pears, *Stone's Fall* (London: Vintage, 2010), 448.
11. Robert Coover, *Pinocchio in Venice* (London: Heinemann, 1991), 20.
12. Peter Ackroyd, *Venice: Pure City* (London: Chatto and Windus, 2009).
13. Ruskin's only memorial plaque in the city can be found on the Zattere at the Pensione Calcina, where, a shadow of his former self, he undertook his last stay in 1887. Aldo Andreolo and Elisabetta Borsetti, *Venice Remembers: The Faces, Lives and Works of the Venetians and non-Venetians Whom the City Has Wished to Commemorate in Marble* (Venice: Le Altane, 1999), 115.
14. John Ruskin, *The Stones of Venice*, vol. 1: *The Foundations* (London: Smith, Elder and Co., 1851), 17; vol. 2: *The Sea-Stories* (London: Smith, Elder and Co., 1853), 107–8.
15. Ruskin, *The Stones of Venice*, vol. 2, 301.
16. Quoted in Jeanne Clegg, *Ruskin and Venice* (London: Junction, 1981), 66.
17. Ruskin, *The Stones of Venice*, vol. 2, 52.
18. John Ruskin, *The Stones of Venice*, vol. 3: *The Fall* (London: Smith, Elder and Co., 1853), 208.
19. Quoted in Clegg, *Ruskin and Venice*, 83.
20. See, for example, Pompeo Molmenti, *I nemici di Venezia: polemiche raccolte ed annotate da Elio Zorzi* (Bologna: Zanichelli, 1924). A plaque sanctifies the house where Molmenti began his history writing. Andreolo and Borsetti, *Venice Remembers*, 89.
21. Pompeo Molmenti, *Venice* (London: The Medici Society, 1926), 49.
22. Monica Donaglio, *Un esponente dell'élite liberale: Pompeo Molmenti politico e storico di Venezia* (Venice: Istituto Veneto di Scienze, Lettere ed Arti, 2004), 227.
23. Molmenti, *Venice*, 51.
24. For yet another example, see Anna Somers Cocks, 'The Coming Death of Venice', *New York Review of Books*, 20 June 2013.

25. John Julius Norwich, foreword to Hetty Meyric Hughes (ed.), *Venice: A Collection of the Poetry of Place* (London: Eland, 2006), 11. Norwich mistakenly gives the year in which Venice joined Italy as 1867 (12).

26. Thomas Mann, *Death in Venice* (Penguin: Harmondsworth, 1955).

27. Comune di Venezia, *Venezia* (Venice: Ufficio per il Turismo, 1938), as cited by Kate Ferris, *Everyday Life in Fascist Venice, 1929–1940* (Houndmills: Palgrave Macmillan, 2012), 196.

28. For an example, see the balance in information heavily weighted towards medieval and early modern times in Richard J. Goy, *Venice: An Architectural Guide* (New Haven and London: Yale University Press, 2010).

29. Margaret Plant, *Venice: Fragile City, 1797–1997* (New Haven and London: Yale University Press, 2002).

30. Over the last fifty years, the deprecation of Venice's 'disneylandizzazione' has become all but mandatory in some circles. See, for example, Vidal, *Vidal in Venice*, 87; Enrico Tantucci, *A che ora chiude Venezia? Breve guida alla disneylandizzazione della città* (Venice: Corte del Fontego, 2011), 5, 25.

31. For the view that tourist trips, even to religious sites, are less than worthy, see Ruth Harris, *Lourdes: Body and Spirit in the Secular Age* (London: Penguin, 1999), 313.

32. Alvise Zorzi, *Venezia scomparsa*, vol. 1: *Storia di una secolare degradazione* (Milan: Electa, 1977), viii.

33. Norwich, foreword to Hughes (ed.), *Venice*, 13.

34. James Morris, *Venice* (London: Faber and Faber, 1960), 33.

35. The main Italian introductions to modern times in Venice are the multi-authored Emilio Franzina (ed.), *Venezia* (Bari: Laterza, 1986), and the mammoth and also multi-authored Mario Isnenghi and Stuart Woolf (eds), *Storia di Venezia: l'Ottocento e il Novecento* (Rome: Istituto dell'Enciclopedia Italiana, 2002). The essays there assembled contain a wealth of crucial detail but lack the overarching interpretation that might be provided by a single author.

36. See, for example, Giovannino Guareschi, *Mondo piccolo: Don Camillo* (Milan: Rizzoli, 1948), translated as *The Little World of Don Camillo* (London: Gollancz, 1951).

37. Gianfranco Bettin, *Dove volano i leoni: fine secolo a Venezia* (Milan: Garzanti, 1991), 91.

38. Ibid., 93.

39. Andreolo and Borsetti, *Venice Remembers*. It is telling that one of the publication successes of recent years, Andrea di Robilant, *Venetian Navigators: The Voyages of the Zen Brothers to the Far North* (London: Faber and Faber, 2010), begins with a plaque (and a map) and tells a labyrinthine story about a labyrinth of travel and story-telling.

40. http://www.hotelsanfantin.com/ (accessed 8 August 2012).

41. Giovanni Sbordone, *Nella Repubblica di Santa Margherita: storie di un campo veneziano nel primo Novecento* (Venice: Istituto veneziano per la storia della Resistenza e della società contemporanea, 2003), 31, 51.

42. For background to the idea, see Roberto M. Dainotto, 'The Gubbio Papers: Historic Centres in the Age of the Economic Miracle', *Journal of Modern Italian Studies*, 8 (2003).

Chapter One: Awaiting an Italian destiny

1. For background, see R. J. B. Bosworth, *Mussolini's Italy: Life under the Dictatorship, 1915–1945* (London: Penguin, 2005), 326–7.

2. For background, see John Foot, *Italy's Divided Memory* (Houndmills: Palgrave Macmillan, 2009).

3. See especially George Macaulay Trevelyan, *Manin and the Venetian Revolution of 1848* (London: Longmans, Green and Co., 1923).

4. Jonathan Keates, *The Siege of Venice* (London: Chatto and Windus, 2005).

5. Ibid., 36.

6. Emilio Franzina, 'L'unificazione', in Emilio Franzina (ed.), *Venezia* (Bari: Laterza, 1986), 41.

7. In 1871 there were 2,667. See Simon Levis Sullam, *Una comunità immaginata: gli ebrei a Venezia (1900–1938)* (Milan: Unicopli, 2001), 49. The Republic had toughened its anti-Semitic legislation in 1777. See Cecil Roth, *Gli ebrei in Venezia* (Rome: P. Cremonese, 1933), 397.

8. Simon Levis Sullam and Fabio Brusò, *Il Ghetto. Piazza Barche* (Padua: Il Poligrafo, 2008), 14–5.

9. Giovanni Sbordone, Giorgio Crovato and Carlo Montanaro, *Via Garibaldi. La Regata Storica. I Cinema 'Peocéti'* (Padua: Il Poligrafo, 2005), 11–13.

10. The original of this church was said to date from the seventh century. For its history, see Alvise Zorzi, *Venezia scomparsa*, vol. 2: *Repertorio degli edifici veneziani distrutti, alterati o manomessi* (Milan: Electa, 1977), 332–4.

11. The Byzantines had in their turn stolen them from somewhere, since they were made in Greece in the fourth century BCE. In the 1980s, in view of the damage caused by pollution, the horses were moved inside the Basilica and replicas put in their place outside.

12. *Daily Telegraph* (London), 10 January 2003. One trigger was the rediscovery of a Venice-made statue of the emperor that stood in Piazza San Marco between 1811 and 1814.

13. See, for example, François Furet, *Revolutionary France, 1770–1880* (Oxford University Press, 1995).

14. See Michael Broers, *The Napoleonic Empire in Italy, 1796–1814: Cultural Imperialism in a European Context?* (Houndmills: Palgrave Macmillan, 2005).

15. Bruno Bertoli, 'La Chiesa veneziana dalla caduta della Repubblica alle soglie del Novecento', in Silvio Tramontin (ed.), *Patriarcato di Venezia* (Padua: Gregoriana Libreria, 1991), 195.

16. Alvise Zorzi, *Venezia scomparsa*, vol. 1: *Storia di una secolare degradazione* (Milan: Electa, 1977), 22.

17. Richard J. Goy, *Venice: An Architectural Guide* (New Haven and London: Yale University Press, 2010), 208.

18. Luigi Casarini, *Sulla origine, ingrandimento e decadenza del commercio di Venezia e sui mezzi che nella presente di lei situazione praticare potrebbonsi per impedirne la minacciata rovina: memoria* (Venice: Picotti, 1823).

19. Zorzi, *Venezia scomparsa*, vol. 1, 190.

20. Keates, *The Siege of Venice*, 36–7.

21. Paul Ginsborg, *Daniele Manin and the Venetian Revolution of 1848–9* (Cambridge University Press, 1979), 6.

22. Pellico is remembered on city walls with two memorial plaques. One appears outside the Hotel Luna Baglioni, a building that will play a further part in this book. The other is located on the cemetery island of San Michele (see map 1), where the Austrians had imprisoned him en route to Spielberg. It was affixed to the island's wall in 1916, when war against the Austrians raged. Aldo Andreolo and Elisabetta Borsetti, *Venice Remembers: The Faces, Lives and Works of the Venetians and non-Venetians Whom the City Has Wished to Commemorate in Marble* (Venice: Le Altane, 1999), 229–30.

23. It is available in English translation as Silvio Pellico, *My Prisons* (London: Oxford University Press, 1963).

24. Andreolo and Borsetti, *Venice Remembers*, 29–30.

25. Quoted in David Laven, *Venice and Venetia under the Habsburgs, 1815–1835* (Oxford University Press, 2002), 211.

26. David Gilmour, *The Pursuit of Italy: A History of a Land, Its Regions and Their Peoples* (London: Allen Lane, 2011), 112.

27. Laven, *Venice and Venetia under the Habsburgs*, 20, 25.

28. Ibid., 25.

29. Henry Matthews, *Diary of an Invalid: Journal of a Tour in Pursuit of Health, 1817–1819* (Stroud: Nonsuch, 2005), 209, 212.

30. Laven, *Venice and Venetia under the Habsburgs*, 130–1.

31. Ibid., 113.

32. Alexander Bradley, *Ruskin and Italy* (Ann Arbor: University of Michigan Research Press, 1987), 8.

33. Sarah Quill (ed.), *Ruskin's Venice: The Stones Rediscovered* (Aldershot: Ashgate, 2000). Ruskin gave no thanks for the chance now to avoid his earlier complaint that his inn at Mestre equipped itself with 'a dirty table cloth' and soured its more genteel visitors with 'a close smell of garlic and crabs'. John Ruskin, *The Stones of Venice*, vol. 1: *The Foundations* (London: Smith, Elder and Co., 1851), 346.

34. See, for example, Piero Bevilacqua, *Venezia e le sue acque: una metafora planetaria*, rev. edn (Rome: Donzelli, 1998), 133.

35. Ernesto Corti, *Lido di Venezia* (Venice: C. Ferrari, 1919), 21–2.

36. Jeanne Clegg, *Ruskin and Venice* (London: Junction, 1981), 57. As far as Ruskin was concerned the increased number of hotels resembled 'Margate boarding houses'.

37. Ginsborg, *Daniele Manin*, 31.

38. Mario Dalla Costa, *La basilica di San Marco e i restauri dell'Ottocento: le idee di E. Viollet-le-Duc, J. Ruskin e le 'Osservazioni' di A. P. Zorzi* (Venice: La Stamperia di Venezia, 1983), 11–12.

39. Elia Barbiani (ed.), *Edilizia popolare a Venezia: storie, politiche, realizzazioni per le Case Popolari della Provincia di Venezia* (Milan: Electa, 1983), 12.

40. Alvise Zorzi, *Venezia austriaca, 1798–1866* (Bari: Laterza, 1985), 49.

41. Ibid., 46.

42. Zorzi, *Venezia scomparsa*, vol. 1, iii.

43. Filippo Maria Paladini, *Arsenale e Museo Storico Navale di Venezia: mare, lavoro e uso pubblico della storia* (Padua: Il Poligrafo, 2008), 23–4.

44. See, notably, Alberto M. Banti, *La nazione del Risorgimento: parentela, santità e onore alle origini dell'Italia unita* (Turin: Einaudi, 2000).

45. Ibid., 74.

46. Ginsborg, *Daniele Manin*, 66.

47. Paladini, *Arsenale e Museo Storico Navale di Venezia*, 24. See also Keates, *The Siege of Venice*, 61–4. The standard English-language study of the congresses is Kent Roberts Greenfield, *Economics and Liberalism in the Risorgimento*, rev. edn (Baltimore: Johns Hopkins University Press, 1965).

48. As we shall see, each acquired a statue in a prominent city *campo* that was renamed in his honour. Two further plaques celebrate Manin, one affixed to a house where he lived near the bridge of San Paternian in the *sestiere* of San Marco, and the other recording his birthplace at Ramo Astori in Santa Croce. Tommaseo is memorialised in the house in Calle del Remedio in Castello where he was living when arrested in 1848. Many other plaques celebrate other 'heroes' of the Risorgimento, especially those of 1848–9. Nine plaques elevate seventeen to hero status in the Calle Larga de l'Ascension, among them the Jewish economist Isacco Pesaro Maurogonato (see further below). Andreolo and Borsetti, *Venice Remembers*, 9, 23–6.

49. Keates, *The Siege of Venice*.

50. Ginsborg, *Daniele Manin*, 315–16.

51. Ibid., 114, 176.

52. Laven, *Venice and Venetia under the Habsburgs*, 224–30.

53. Zorzi, *Venezia austriaca*, 105.

54. Other exiles included Domenico Giuriati and his father, whose family was destined to possess a long political history in Venice. See Domenico Giuriati (ed.), *Duecento lettere inedite di Giuseppe Mazzini con proemio e note* (Turin: L. Roux, 1887). See also his *Memorie d'emigrazione* (Milan: Treves, 1897). When Garibaldi died in 1882, Giuriati gave the eulogy for him at the Ateneo Veneto. See *L'Ateneo Veneto*, June 1882, 345–62.

55. For some graphic visual evidence of the siege, see Margaret Plant, *Venice: Fragile City, 1797–1997* (New Haven and London: Yale University Press, 2002), 138–45.

56. Vincenzo Marchesi, *Settant'anni di storia politica di Venezia (1798–1866)* (Turin: L. Roux, [1894]), 209.

57. Ibid., 185–7.

58. Mary Lutyens (ed.), *Effie in Venice: Unpublished Letters of Mrs John Ruskin Written from Venice between 1849–1852* (London: John Murray, 1965).

59. Ibid., 69–70.

60. Zorzi, *Venezia austriaca*, 111–12.
61. Dalla Costa, *La basilica di San Marco e i restauri dell'Ottocento*, 10.
62. The Comune opened her rooms to the tourist gaze in 2012. See *La Repubblica*, 6 July 2012.
63. Zorzi, *Venezia austriaca*, 362.
64. Ibid., 109–10.
65. Ibid., 135.
66. Franzina, 'L'unificazione', 27.
67. For a lavish pictorial history, see Anna Laura Bellina and Michele Girardi, *La Fenice, 1792-1996: Theatre, Music and History* (Venice: Marsilio, 2003).
68. Zorzi, *Venezia austriaca*, 145.
69. William D. Howells, *Venetian Life* (Leipzig: Bernard Tauchnitz, 1883), 10, 15, 161, 304.
70. Ibid., 58.
71. Ibid., 49–51, 298.
72. Ibid., 79.
73. Ibid., 154.
74. Ibid., 321.
75. Ibid., 303, 322–3.
76. Ibid., 342, 378.
77. Ibid., 124.
78. Ibid., 336.
79. Ibid., 143, 149–50.
80. Ibid., 184.
81. Ibid., 16–25.
82. Marco Gioannini and Giulio Massobrio, *Custoza 1866: la via italiana alla sconfitta* (Milan: Rizzoli, 2003), 11.
83. Geoffrey Wawro, *The Austro-Prussian War: Austria's War with Prussia and Italy in 1866* (Cambridge University Press, 1996), 116.
84. Comitato Regionale Veneto per la storia del Risorgimento italiano (ed.), *L'ultima dominazione austriaca e la liberazione del Veneto nel 1866: memorie di Filippo Nani Mocenigo, Ugo Botti, Carlo Combi, Antonino Di Prampero, Manlio Torquato Dazzi e Giuseppe Solitro* (Chioggia: Giulio Vianelli, 1916), 256–9, 266–7, 329. This volume was published during the First World War to celebrate fifty years of liberation from Austrian tyranny.
85. *The Times*, 29 October 1866.
86. Andreolo and Borsetti, *Venice Remembers*, 9.
87. Mario Isnenghi (ed.), *Il diario di Letizia (1866)* (Verona: Novacharta, 2004), 2.
88. Ibid., 12–14, 32.
89. Ibid., 50–2.
90. Ibid., 78–80.
91. Ibid., 108–10.
92. Ibid., 112–20.
93. Ibid., 128, 140.
94. Ibid., 164–70.
95. Franzina, 'L'unificazione', 22.
96. Isnenghi (ed.), *Il diario di Letizia (1866)*, 190.
97. Ibid., 192–6.
98. Ibid., 204–6.
99. Carlo Leoni, *Cronaca segreta de' miei tempi*, ed. Giuseppe Toffanin (Cittadella (PD): Rebellato, 1976), 620, 628.

Chapter Two: The lights and shadows of Liberal improvement in Venice, 1866–1900

1. *L'Ateneo Veneto*, 1878, 88.
2. Camillo Boito, 'I monumenti a Vittorio Emanuele', *L'Ateneo Veneto*, March–April 1882, 137–60.

3. Ferrari was also responsible for a monument to Garibaldi in Rovigo, and for more controversial ones to Giuseppe Mazzini and Giordano Bruno in Rome.

4. For a positive review, see Raffaello Fabris, 'La Mostra Nazionale di Belle Arti in Venezia', *L'Ateneo Veneto*, 1887, 125–45.

5. For background, see R. J. B. Bosworth, *Whispering City: Rome and Its Histories* (New Haven and London: Yale University Press, 2011), 133–40.

6. Cf. Margaret Plant, *Venice: Fragile City, 1797–1997* (New Haven and London: Yale University Press, 2002), 160; Plant is not, however, tempted by irony.

7. The aristocratic, conservative and Catholic then mayor, Count Dante di Serego Allighieri, used 'illness' to avoid attending the inauguration on 24 July. Giovanni Sbordone, Giorgio Crovato and Carlo Montanaro, *Via Garibaldi. La Regata Storica. I Cinema 'Peocéti'* (Padua: Il Poligrafo, 2005), 20–1.

8. The sculptor was Luigi Borro, born in the Veneto, who arrived in the city still an illiterate and was, for a time, a success both there and in Rome. He died back in poverty in Venice in 1886. See http://www.treccani.it/enciclopedia/luigi-borro_%28Dizionario-Biografico%29/ (accessed 26 August 2012).

9. Debora Antonini, *Risorgimento a Venezia: impronte monumentali* (Venice: Corte del Fontego, 2012), 13–16.

10. See Daniele Francesconi, *La questione delle ceneri di Daniele Manin nella Basilica di S. Marco: osservazioni* (Venice: Tipografia del *Tempo*, 1868).

11. For a graphic description, see Plant, *Venice: Fragile City*, 159–60, which utilises the image of the event recorded by the painter Giambattista dalla Libera.

12. Sergio Barizza, *Il Comune di Venezia, 1806–1946: l'istituzione, il territorio, guida-inventario dell'Archivio municipale* (Venice: Comune di Venezia, 1987), 14.

13. For a list to 1946, see Mario Missori, *Governi, alte cariche dello stato e prefetti del Regno d'Italia* (Rome: Ministero dell'Interno, 1973), 509–10.

14. See Antonio Monti, *Il Conte Luigi Torelli: il Risorgimento italiano studiato attraverso una nobile vita* (Milan: R. Istituto Lombardo di Scienze e Lettere, 1931), 217, 273.

15. Alvise Zorzi, *Venezia scomparsa*, vol. 1: *Storia di una secolare degradazione* (Milan: Electa, 1977), 194–5.

16. Luigi Torelli, *Le condizioni della provincia e della città di Venezia nel 1867* (Venice: Tipografia della *Gazzetta*, 1867), 26–7.

17. Ibid., 12–13. After elevation to the Senate, Torelli became a partisan of the gum tree's grab for world power by favouring the planting of the eucalyptus in and around Rome as a counter to malaria. He was 'the earliest apostle of a national anti-malarial program'. See Frank M. Snowden, *The Conquest of Malaria: Italy, 1900–1960* (New Haven and London: Yale University Press, 2006), 9; cf. Luigi Torelli, *L'eucalyptus a Roma: memorie* (Rome: Tipografia dell'*Opinione*, 1879).

18. Torelli, *Le condizioni della provincia e della città di Venezia nel 1867*, 7.

19. Monti, *Il Conte Luigi Torelli*, 446.

20. Ibid., 455–6.

21. Bosworth, *Whispering City*, 97–8, 103–5.

22. Sbordone, Crovato and Montanaro, *Via Garibaldi. La Regata Storica. I Cinema 'Peocéti'*, 32.

23. Silvio Tramontin, 'Dall'alba del nuovo secolo al concilio Vaticano II: i patriarchi', in Silvio Tramontin (ed.), *Patriarcato di Venezia* (Padua: Gregoriana Libreria, 1991), 222.

24. Antonio Niero, *I patriarchi di Venezia da Lorenzo Giustiniani ai nostri giorni* (Venice: Studium Cattolico Veneziano, 1961), 192.

25. Bruno Bertoli, 'La Chiesa veneziana dalla caduta della Repubblica alle soglie del Novecento', in Tramontin (ed.), *Patriarcato di Venezia*, 204–8.

26. Ibid., 209.

27. The figure is confirmed in Giannantonio Paladini, 'Momenti ed aspetti della lotta politica e sociale a Venezia (1870–1874)', *Risorgimento Veneto*, 1 (1972), 45.

28. *The Times*, 16, 17 November 1874. In the 1870s, 4.6 per cent had the right to vote and about a third of them exercised it. See Barizza, *Il Comune di Venezia*, 13.

29. Carlo Calza, 'La vita e la salute in Venezia e la legge di popolazione', L'Ateneo Veneto, 1876.

30. Renzo Derosas, 'Appesi a un filo: i bambini veneziani davanti alla morte (1850–1900)', in Nadia Maria Filippini and Tiziana Plebani (eds), La scoperta dell'infanzia: cura, educazione e rappresentazione: Venezia, 1750–1930 (Venice: Marsilio, 1999), 60.

31. See, for example, the superb collection Daniele Resini and Myriam Zerbi (eds), Venezia tra Ottocento e Novecento nelle fotografie di Tomaso Filippi (Rome: Palombi, 2013), and its attached CD of 8,500 images.

32. Emilio Franzina, 'L'unificazione', in Emilio Franzina (ed.), Venezia (Bari: Laterza, 1986), 53.

33. Francesco Gavagnin, Sulle abitazioni dei poveri: lettere al compilatore (Venice: Tipografia della Gazzetta, 1866), 4–7, 12.

34. Francesco Meneghini, Delle abitazioni dei poveri: considerazioni pratiche (Venice: Antonio Clementi, 1866), 3, 5, 14–15.

35. Giovanni Distefano (ed.), Atlante storico di Venezia (Venice Lido: Supernova, 2008), 689.

36. Cesare Musatti, Dello insegnamento dell'igiene specialmente per le classi operaie: lezione popolare tenuta al Veneto Ateneo nel dicembre 1874 (Venice: Grimaldo, 1875), 6–20.

37. See C. Boldini, 'Risanamento di Venezia', in L'Ateneo Veneto, 1886, 124–44, and, at greater length, G. A. Romano and A. S. De Kiriaki, 'La fognatura della città', L'Ateneo Veneto, 1892, 311–55, 127–49; 17, 1893, 27–58, 297–360, 45–109; 18, 1894, 73–111; and A. S. De Kiriaki, 'Della fognatura della città', L'Ateneo Veneto, 1895, 236–54. In these accounts, Venice was typically measured for 'backwardness' against other European cities and found wanting, with modern toilets defined as an epitome of civilisation.

38. Elizabeth Horodowich, A Brief History of Venice: A New History of the City and Its People (London: Constable and Robinson, 2009), 221.

39. Maurizio Reberschak, 'L'economia', in Franzina (ed.), Venezia, 237.

40. Piero Bevilacqua, Venezia e le sue acque: una metafora planetaria, rev. edn (Rome: Donzelli, 1998), 137–8, 140, 143.

41. Giovanni Distefano and Giannantonio Paladini, Storia di Venezia, 1797–1997, 3 vols (Venice Lido: Supernova, 1997), vol. 3, 21.

42. Giampaolo Salbe, Storia dei trasporti pubblici di Venezia–Mestre–Lido (Cortona: Calosci, 1985), 18–24.

43. Sbordone, Crovato and Montanaro, Via Garibaldi. La Regata Storica. I Cinema 'Peocéti', 54.

44. Franzina, 'L'unificazione', 83, 89.

45. Alberto Errera, Storia e statistica delle industrie venete (Venice: Giuseppe Antonelli, 1870), 173.

46. G. Collotta, Intorno alle questioni ferroviarie nei riguardi della provincia, della città e del porto di Venezia (Venice: G. Antonello, 1873), 86.

47. Giorgio Bellavitis, L'Arsenale di Venezia: storia di una grande struttura urbana (Venice: Marsilio, 1983), 210.

48. Errera, Storia e statistica delle industrie venete, 447–8.

49. Luciano Pes, 'L'economia delle classi popolari a Venezia (1866–1881)', in Daniele Resini (ed.), Cent'anni a Venezia: la Camera del Lavoro, 1892–1992 (Venice: Il Cardo, 1992), 235–6.

50. Errera, Storia e statistica delle industrie venete, 711.

51. Angelo Papadopoli, Della necessità di un nuovo indirizzo nella pubblica beneficenza in Venezia (Venice: Marco Visentini, 1871), 7–8, 10–11, 13–14.

52. Ibid., 15–16, 19.

53. Ibid., 26.

54. Errera, Storia e statistica delle industrie venete, 706–7.

55. Papadopoli, Della necessità di un nuovo indirizzo nella pubblica beneficenza in Venezia, 37.

56. Ibid., 32–5.

57. Maria Teresa Sega, 'Lavoratrici', in Mario Isnenghi and Stuart Woolf (eds), Storia di Venezia: l'Ottocento e il Novecento (Rome: Istituto dell'Enciclopedia Italiana, 2002), 826.

58. A statistician reckoned in 1870 that lace makers were restricted to three hundred mainly female workers spread across Chioggia, Venice and Burano, supplemented by three hundred at Pellestrina. Errera, *Storia e statistica delle industrie venete*, 519–20.
59. Michelangelo Jesurum, *Cenni storici e statistici sull'industria dei merletti* (Venice: Marco Visentini, 1873), 8–9, 11.
60. Ibid., 37–9.
61. See, for example, Ugo Facco de Lagarda, *Morte all'impiraperle* (Venice: Evi, 1967), 341–7, which evokes the last of her trade, an old woman who had never been to the mainland and, indeed, had not ventured as far as Piazza San Marco since 1902.
62. Sega, 'Lavoratrici', 831.
63. Ibid., 842.
64. Pes, 'L'economia delle classi popolari a Venezia (1866–1881)', 238.
65. Giovanni Sbordone, *La Camera del Lavoro* (Padua: Il Poligrafo, 2005), 13–14.
66. Emilio Franzina and Ernesto Brunetta, 'La politica', in Franzina (ed.), *Venezia*, 127–9.
67. Maria Teresa Sega and Nadia Maria Filippini, *Manifattura Tabacchi. Cotonificio Veneziano* (Padua: Il Poligrafo, 2008), 20.
68. Ibid., 22–3. For period debate on the matter at the Ateneo, see D. C. Finocchietti, 'I bambini poveri', *L'Ateneo Veneto*, 1882, 1–19; 'Ancora dei bambini poveri', 265–83; 'Un'ultima parola sui bambini poveri', *L'Ateneo Veneto*, July 1884, 528–44.
69. Sega and Filippini, *Manifattura Tabacchi. Cotonificio Veneziano*, 29–31.
70. Ibid., 97–9.
71. Ibid., 101, 105–6.
72. For background and details on a number of other concerns there, see Sicinio Bonfanti, *La Giudecca nella storia, nell'arte, nelle vite* (Venice: Libreria Emiliana, 1930).
73. Jürgen Julier, *Il Molino Stucky a Venezia* (Venice: Centro Tedesco di Studi Veneziani, 1978), 8–14.
74. G. A. Zanon, 'A proposito del nuovo ponte in laguna', *L'Ateneo Veneto*, 1896, 141–7.
75. G. A. Zanon, 'Ancora sulla organizzazione di Venezia con la terraferma', *L'Ateneo Veneto*, 1898, 205–16.
76. Luigi Luzzatti, *Memorie*, 3 vols (Milan: Istituto centrale delle Banche Popolari italiane, 1966), vol. 1, 127.
77. Luigi Villari, 'Luigi Luzzatti', in Hector Bolitho (ed.), *Twelve Jews* (London: Rich and Cowan, 1934), 130.
78. Amedeo Nasalli Rocca, *Memorie di un prefetto* (Rome: Mediterranea, 1946), 247–8.
79. See, for example, Camillo Boito, 'I restauri di San Marco', *Nuova Antologia*, fasc. 29, 15 December 1879, 701–21.
80. Camillo Boito, 'Venezia che scompare: Sant'Elena e Santa Marta', *Nuova Antologia*, fasc. 20, 15 October 1883, 630, 643–5.
81. *The Times*, 22 September 1885.
82. See, for example, Helen, Countess-Dowager of Radnor, *From a Great-Grandmother's Armchair* (London: Marshall, n.d.), 185, 188–90. Among those to be sustained there before the war was 'Baron Corvo', the wayward Catholic English novelist. See Alphonse J. A. Symons, *The Search for Corvo* (Harmondsworth: Penguin, 1934), 170.
83. It is still open. See www.stgeorgesvenice.com (accessed 2 September 2012).
84. Horatio F. Brown, *Venetian Studies* (London: Kegan Paul, Trench and Co., 1887), 397.
85. Horatio F. Brown, *Life on the Lagoons* (London: Rivington, Percival and Co., 1894), 206–7.
86. Despite such local variation, a five-day bakers' strike in the city in 1897 provoked complaints that Venetians were now forced to eat 'foreign bread'. Sbordone, *La Camera del Lavoro*, 82.
87. Brown, *Life on the Lagoons*, 207, 219–25.
88. Horatio F. Brown, *In and around Venice* (London: Rivingtons, 1905), 3, 33.
89. Ibid., 35. Augustus Hare, the greatest English tourist writer about Italy, was equally sure that 'gravity' had been 'washed out of the Venetian character'. Augustus J. C. Hare, *Cities of Northern Italy*, vol. 2: *Venice, Ferrara, Piacenza, Parma, Modena and Bologna* (London: G. Allen, n.d.), 48.

90. *The Times*, 8 November 1879.
91. *The Times*, 17 November 1879.
92. *The Times*, 24 November 1879.
93. *The Times*, 18 November 1879.
94. *The Times*, 28 November 1879.
95. Reberschak, 'L'economia', 249.
96. Pompeo Molmenti, 'Delendae Venetiae', *Nuova Antologia*, fasc. 3, 1 February 1887, 413–14, 417, 420. In 1977 Alvise Zorzi endorsed Molmenti's attack. See Zorzi, *Venezia scomparsa*, vol. 1, 209.
97. Pompeo Molmenti, *I nemici di Venezia: polemiche raccolte ed annotate da Elio Zorzi* (Bologna: Zanichelli, 1924), 242. See also his *Venezia calunniata: discorso* (Venice: Fratelli Visentini, 1894).
98. For a useful modern biography, see Monica Donaglio, *Un esponente dell'élite liberale: Pompeo Molmenti politico e storico di Venezia* (Venice: Istituto Veneto di Scienze, Lettere ed Arti, 2004).
99. Donaglio, *Un esponente dell'élite liberale*, 5, 82.
100. See, for example, Giacomo Boni's nightmare quoted as one of the epigraphs to this book, and more generally in Giacomo Boni, *Il cosidetto sventramento: appunti di un veneziano* (Rome: Stabilmento Tipografico Italiano, 1887).
101. Giorgio Bellavitis and Giandomenico Romanelli, *Venezia* (Bari: Laterza, 1985), 211.
102. Franzina and Brunetta, 'La politica', 125.
103. As was lovingly recorded in *L'Illustrazione Italiana*, 5, 12, 19 May 1895.
104. Mario Isnenghi, 'La cultura', in Franzina (ed.), *Venezia*, 436.
105. For this national patriotic body, see R. J. B. Bosworth, *Italy: The Least of the Great Powers: Italian Foreign Policy before the First World War* (Cambridge University Press, 1979), 49–54.
106. Biennale di Venezia, *Le Esposizioni internazionali d'arte, 1895-1995: artisti, mostre, partecipazioni nazionali, premi* (Venice: Electa, 1996), 17.
107. Daniele Ceschin, *La 'Voce' di Venezia: Antonio Fradeletto e l'organizzazione della cultura tra Otto e Novecento* (Padua: Il Poligrafo, 2001), 20, 81–2, 86.
108. Lawrence Alloway, *The Venice Biennale, 1895-1968: From Salon to Goldfish Bowl* (London: Faber and Faber, 1969), 34.
109. Christian F. Feest (ed.), *Indians and Europe: An Interdisciplinary Collection of Essays* (Aachen: Rader, 1987), 387. Nietzsche, too, was in Venice that year.
110. Distefano (ed.), *Atlante storico di Venezia*, 725.
111. See, for example, Paulo Fambri, 'L'avvenire di Venezia', *Nuova Antologia*, fasc. 9, 1 May 1878, 151.
112. Gino Damerini, *D'Annunzio a Venezia* (Venice: Marsilio, 1992), 13.
113. John Woodhouse, *Gabriele D'Annunzio: Defiant Archangel* (Oxford: Clarendon, 1998), 74, 151.
114. Maurice Barrès, *Amori e dolori sacri: la mort de Venise* (Paris: Félix Juven, 1903).
115. Thomas Mann, *Death in Venice* (Penguin: Harmondsworth, 1955).
116. Damerini, *D'Annunzio a Venezia*, 28–9.
117. Woodhouse, *Gabriele D'Annunzio*, 125, 139. For Duse, see Helen Sheehy, *Eleonora Duse: A Biography* (New York: A. A. Knopf, 2003).
118. Gabriele D'Annunzio, *The Flame* (London: Quartet, 1991), 6, 9.
119. Ibid., 28, 46–7.
120. Ibid., 56.
121. Ibid., 153.
122. Giuseppe Sarto (Pope Pius X), *Le pastorali del periodo veneziano (1899-1903)*, ed. Antonio Niero (Asolo: Quaderni della Fondazione Giuseppe Sarto, 3, [1991]), 95–6.
123. Ferruccio Carli, *Pio X e il suo tempo* (Florence: Adriano Salani, 1941), 62–4.
124. Sarto (Pope Pius X), *Le pastorali del periodo veneziano (1899-1903)*, 8–9, 17, 28.
125. Giuseppe Sarto (Pope Pius X), *Le pastorali del periodo veneziano (1894-1898)*, ed. Antonio Niero (Asolo: Quaderni della Fondazione Giuseppe Sarto, 2, [1991]), 71, 94.

126. See http://www.sanpiox.it/public/ (accessed 7 September 2012).

127. See I. F. Clarke, *Voices Prophesying War, 1763–1984* (Oxford University Press, 1965).

128. Giorgio Moscarda, *Venezia nel 1930* (Venice: Tip. Società M. S. Fra Compositori, 1898), 36.

129. Ibid., 75–6.

Chapter Three: Venice in the *belle époque*

1. Comune di Venezia, *Il campanile di San Marco riedificato: studi, ricerche, relazioni* (Venice: C. Ferrari, 1912), 238.

2. Daniele Riccoboni, 'Il XIV luglio: per la caduta del campanile di S. Marco', *L'Ateneo Veneto*, July–August 1902, 69–71. Cf. another poem, this time about returning glories, in Antonio Trevissoi, 'Al campanile risorgente', *L'Ateneo Veneto*, January–June 1908, 151–2.

3. Anita Mondolfo, 'Bibliografia del Campanile dal crollo alla compiuta ricostruzione (14 luglio 1902–31 dicembre 1911)', in Comune di Venezia, *Il campanile di San Marco riedificato*, 251.

4. Benito Mussolini, *Opera omnia*, ed. Edoardo and Duilio Susmel, 44 vols (Florence: La Fenice, 1951–80), vol. 1, 9–10.

5. Lucy Hughes-Hallett, *The Pike: Gabriele D'Annunzio, Poet, Seducer and Preacher of War* (London: Fourth Estate, 2013), 237.

6. Gregorio Gattinoni, *Il campanile di San Marco: monografia storica* (Venice: G. Fabbris, 1910), 21, 121.

7. Ibid., 372.

8. Gino Damerini, *Amor di Venezia* (Bologna: Zanichelli, 1920), 21–5.

9. Giuseppe Sarto (Pope Pius X), *Le pastorali del periodo veneziano (1899–1903)*, ed. Antonio Niero (Asolo: Quaderni della Fondazione Giuseppe Sarto, 3, [1991]), 111.

10. Ibid., 111–12.

11. *The Times*, 15 July 1902.

12. *The Times*, 15–21 July, 26 July, 8 August, 20 September 1902. German elite opinion was equally doubtful whether the Italian government was sufficiently steeled completely to rebuild the tower. See Daniele Donghi, 'La ricostruzione del Campanile di S. Marco e della Loggetta del Sansovino', *L'Ateneo Veneto*, July–August 1912, 22.

13. Antonio Fradeletto, 'Prefazione', in Comune di Venezia, *Il campanile di San Marco riedificato*, v.

14. Ibid., vi, xix.

15. Pompeo Molmenti, 'La vita del campanile', in Comune di Venezia, *Il campanile di San Marco riedificato*, 25.

16. For details, see Giacomo Boni, 'Sostruzioni e macerie', Luigi Beltrami, 'Indagini e studi per la ricostruzione dal marzo al giugno 1903', and Gaetano Moretti, 'La ricostruzione dall'agosto 1903 all'aprile 1912', all chapters in Comune di Venezia, *Il campanile di San Marco riedificato*. Cf. Donghi, 'La ricostruzione del Campanile di S. Marco e della Loggetta del Sansovino'.

17. *The Times*, 25 April 1912.

18. Lonsdale Ragg and Laura M. Ragg, *Things Seen in Venice* (London: Seeley, Service and Co., 1912), 92.

19. 'Volframo', 'Teatri ed arti', *Nuova Antologia*, fasc. 735, 1 August 1902, 544, 551–5.

20. Davide Calandra, letter to the editor, *Nuova Antologia*, fasc. 741, 1 November 1902, 157–8.

21. James Rennell Rodd, *Social and Diplomatic Memories*, 3 vols (London: Edward Arnold, 1922–5), vol. 3, 155.

22. *The Times*, 27 April 1912.

23. *The Times*, 25 April 1912.

24. Scot D. Ryersson and Michael Orlando Yaccarino, *Infinite Variety: The Life and Legend of the Marchesa Casati* (London: Pimlico, 2000), 4.

25. See Guillermo de Osma, *Fortuny: The Life and Work of Mariano Fortuny* (London: Aurum, 1994). His career in the city was said to have been launched by the (first) wife of Giuseppe Volpi. See Ludovico Toeplitz, *Ciak a chi tocca* (Milan: Milano Nuova, 1964), 62.

26. Ryersson and Yaccarino, *Infinite Variety*, 56–7.

27. Ibid., 27.

28. Margaret Doody, *Tropic of Venice* (Philadelphia: University of Pennsylvania Press, 2007), 49–50.

29. See especially Luigi Picchini, *Tentati suicidi e suicidi con particolare riguardo alla città di Venezia*, (Venice: Sorteni, 1933).

30. Diana Cooper, *The Rainbow Comes and Goes: Autobiography* (London: Century, 1984), 93–4, 103–4.

31. Emilio Ninni, 'I colombi di S. Marco', *L'Ateneo Veneto*, July–August 1902, 72–8; September–October 1902, 245–55. Surely Franz Ferdinand cannot have known of Oscar Wilde's evocation of pigeons over the Campanile as gorgeously 'opal-and-iris-throated birds'. Oscar Wilde, *The Picture of Dorian Gray*, ed. R. Mighall (London: Penguin, 2000).

32. Gerald Campbell, *Of True Experience* (London: Hutchinson, n.d.), 35.

33. See, for example, accounts in *Il Gazzettino*, 26, 27 March 1911.

34. *The Times*, 14 October 1898.

35. *Il Gazzettino*, 25, 26 March 1914. Wilhelm had also passed through Venice in 1908, 1909, 1911 and 1912.

36. Ragg and Ragg, *Things Seen in Venice*, 147.

37. Frederic Eden, *A Garden in Venice* (London: G. Newnes, 1903), 67, 72, 75. His account was first published in *Country Life*.

38. Sicinio Bonfanti, *La Giudecca nella storia, nell'arte, nelle vite* (Venice: Libreria Emiliana, 1930), 128–9.

39. For the social whirl involved, see Helen, Countess-Dowager of Radnor, *From a Great-Grandmother's Armchair* (London: Marshall, n.d.), 190–4, 234, 237–8, 249, 255.

40. Its current website reiterates this view. See http://www.hotelexcelsiorvenezia.com/en/storia/hotel-excelsior.html (accessed 10 September 2012).

41. Achille Talenti, *Come si crea una nuova città: il Lido di Venezia: la storia, la cronaca, la statistica* (Padua: Angelo Draghi, 1921), 19, 45.

42. For social and economic background, see Ludovico Toeplitz, *Il banchiere: al tempo in cui nacque, crebbe, e fiorì la Banca Commerciale Italiana* (Milan: Milano Nuova, 1963), 71. The bank also underpinned Stucky.

43. Talenti, *Come si crea una nuova città*, 52–4.

44. Michele Casarin and Giancarlo Scarpari, *Piazzale Roma. Il Lido di Venezia* (Padua: Il Poligrafo, 2005), 51.

45. *Il Gazzettino*, 21 January 1914.

46. See it lavishly related in Aldo Luzzatto (ed.), *La comunità ebraica di Venezia e il suo antico cimitero*, vol. 1 (Milan: Il Polifilo, 2000).

47. Ernesto Corti, *Lido di Venezia* (Venice: C. Ferrari, 1919), 25.

48. M. R. Levi (ed.), *I bagni marini sulla spiaggia del Lido per i poveri scrofolosi di Venezia nell'estate 1868: relazione del Comitato Promotore e proposta dell'erezione di un ospizio marino veneto* (Venice: G. Antonelli, 1868), 3–5. In the new century, it would be respectablised into first a TB hospital for adults and then the grander sounding Ospedale al Mare (Hospital by the Sea). Maria Grazia Ciani and Maria Ida Biggi, *La spiaggia. Il Teatro La Fenice* (Padua: Il Poligrafo, 2006), 25.

49. Corti, *Lido di Venezia*, 22.

50. Ibid., 28.

51. Giuseppe Pasqualigo, 'Del Lido di Venezia e della sua malaria', *L'Ateneo Veneto*, July 1884, 108–36.

52. Corti, *Lido di Venezia*, 31–4.

53. Pompeo Molmenti, 'Il Lido di Venezia', *Nuova Antologia*, fasc. 912, 16 December 1909, 562.

54. *Il Gazzettino*, 19, 20 May 1911. The idea of a tunnel across to the city and on to the mainland was again backed in Alvise Manfroni, 'Attraverso la laguna – il tunnel

subacqueo Venezia-Lido', *Nuova Antologia*, fasc. 974, 16 July 1912, 292–300. Manfroni thought it would make Venice as attractive as Detroit.

55. Talenti, *Come si crea una nuova città*, 89–90.

56. Ibid., 113, 117.

57. *Il Gazzettino*, 20 February 1911.

58. *Il Gazzettino*, 5, 6 March 1911.

59. Sigmund Freud, *The Interpretation of Dreams*, ed. J. Strachey (Harmondsworth: Penguin, 1976), 599–601.

60. *Il Gazzettino*, 17 March 1911.

61. Klimt was a star at the 1910 exhibition. See Mario Pilo, 'La nona esposizione internazionale d'arte a Venezia', *L'Ateneo Veneto*, September–October 1910, 241–316.

62. For a review of the 1912 exhibition, see Michele De Benedetti, 'La X Esposizione Internazionale d'Arte a Venezia', *Nuova Antologia*, fasc. 970, 16 May 1912, 311–25.

63. *Il Gazzettino*, 26 May 1911.

64. *Il Gazzettino*, 1 June 1911.

65. *Il Gazzettino*, 12 July 1911.

66. Talenti, *Come si crea una nuova città*, 117.

67. Katia Mann, *Unwritten Memories*, ed. Elisabeth Plessen and Michael Mann (London: Deutsch, 1973), 60–4.

68. Frank M. Snowden, *Naples in the Time of Cholera, 1884–1911* (Cambridge University Press, 1995), 322–3. Snowden adds, however, that Italian officials disguised the real figures on outbreaks in Venice, Naples and other ports, also from the Americans.

69. *Il Gazzettino*, 20 June 1911.

70. Mann, *Unwritten Memories*, 63.

71. Amedeo Nasalli Rocca, *Memorie di un prefetto* (Rome: Mediterranea, 1946), 287.

72. Ibid., 266–8. When Luzzatti died in 1928, the ex-Nationalist Fascist Luigi Federzoni farewelled him as 'a Jew and a Venetian, each a scary thing'. Luigi Federzoni, *1927: Diario di un ministro del fascismo*, ed. A. Macchi (Florence: Passigli, 1993), 147.

73. Archivio Centrale dello Stato, Rome (hereafter ACS), Ministero dell'Interno, Direzione Generale della Sanità Pubblica, Atti amministrativi, 1882–1915, busta 181, 8 June 1911.

74. Nasalli Rocca, *Memorie di un prefetto*, 282–6.

75. ACS, Ministero dell'Interno, Direzione Generale della Sanità Pubblica, Atti amministrativi 1882–1915, busta 178, 1 June 1911, Ministry of the Interior to prefect. A file in this packet shows that there were 12,799 deaths from the disease in Italy as a whole between 1 January and 30 October, although the number in Venice constituted a small fraction of that total.

76. Nasalli Rocca, *Memorie di un prefetto*, 286.

77. *Rivista mensile della città di Venezia*, April 1923.

78. *Il Gazzettino*, 23 November 1911.

79. At the turn of the century, Vivante had investigated the presence of malaria in Venice and its surrounds, reporting positively on its relative absence. See Raffaele Vivante, *La malaria in Venezia* (Turin: Fratelli Pozzo, 1902).

80. Raffaele Vivante, *Il problema delle abitazioni in Venezia* (Venice: C. Ferrari, 1910), 33, 51, 54–6, 59, 63–5.

81. Ibid., 59–60, 63.

82. Ibid., 85–8. See also his follow-up study of TB in the city. Raffaele Vivante, *La lotta contro la tubercolosi in Venezia* (Milan: Stucchi, Ceretti, 1915).

83. *Il Gazzettino*, 2 January 1911.

84. Giovanni Sbordone, *La Camera del Lavoro* (Padua: Il Poligrafo, 2005), 21.

85. Giovanni Sbordone, *Nella Repubblica di Santa Margherita: storie di un campo veneziano nel primo Novecento* (Venice: Istituto veneziano per la storia della Resistenza e della società contemporanea, 2003), 101.

86. Jürgen Julier, *Il Molino Stucky a Venezia* (Venice: Centro Tedesco di Studi Veneziani, 1978), 16; Lavinia Cavalletti, *La dinastia Stucky, 1841–1941: storia del Molino di Venezia e della famiglia da Manin a Mussolini* (Venice: Studio LTL, 2011), 126–7. The worker was deranged.

87. *Il Gazzettino*, 1, 2 May 1911.

88. *The Times*, 19 September 1904.

89. Emilio Franzina and Ernesto Brunetta, 'La politica', in Emilio Franzina (ed.), *Venezia* (Bari: Laterza, 1986), 148.

90. *Il Gazzettino*, 30 September 1911.

91. *Il Gazzettino*, 16 November 1911.

92. Girolamo Li Causi, *Il lungo cammino: autobiografia 1906-1944* (Rome: Riuniti, 1974), 36-9.

93. *Il Gazzettino*, 13 May 1911.

94. Sbordone, *Nella Repubblica di Santa Margherita*, 21-2, 39-41.

95. Ibid., 122-3, 135, 142.

96. Maria Teresa Sega, 'Lavoratrici', in Mario Isnenghi and Stuart Woolf (eds), *Storia di Venezia: l'Ottocento e il Novecento* (Rome: Istituto dell'Enciclopedia Italiana, 2002), 845.

97. Clotilde Tiboni, 'La scuola femminile', *L'Ateneo Veneto*, January–February 1902, 72. Cf. a man's response urging that the modern woman must under no circumstances forget her family duties. Enrico Maggioni, 'La donna nuova in tempi nuovi', *L'Ateneo Veneto*, January–February 1906, 363–88.

98. Maria Teresa Sega and Nadia Maria Filippini, *Manifattura Tabacchi. Cotonificio Veneziano* (Padua: Il Poligrafo, 2008), 39.

99. Ibid., 48.

100. For an English-language biography, see Philip V. Cannistraro and Brian R. Sullivan, *Il Duce's Other Woman* (New York: W. Morrow, 1993).

101. Sega and Filippini, *Manifattura Tabacchi. Cotonificio Veneziano*, 35.

102. Silvio Tramontin, 'Dall'alba del nuovo secolo al concilio Vaticano II: i patriarchi', in Silvio Tramontin (ed.), *Patriarcato di Venezia* (Padua: Gregoriana Libreria, 1991), 223.

103. Mario Balladelli, *Anita Mezzalira (1886-1962): una vita per la democrazia e per il socialismo* (Venice: Comune di Venezia, n.d.), 7-9, 19-22.

104. Luisa Bellina and Michele Gottardi, *Osterie. Il Venezia* (Padua: Il Poligrafo, 2006), 101-3.

105. *Il Gazzettino*, 16 March 1911.

106. See the unnumbered pages of Gabriele Rossi-Osmida, *1872-1972: cento anni di sport a Venezia* (Venice: n.p., 1971); *Il Gazzettino*, 28 May 1920.

107. Giovanni Sbordone, Giorgio Crovato and Carlo Montanaro, *Via Garibaldi. La Regata Storica. I Cinema 'Peocéti'* (Padua: Il Poligrafo, 2005), 58.

108. Mario Isnenghi, Filippo Maria Paladini and Giovanni Sbordone, *Il Liceo Convitto Marco Foscarini. Canottieri e remiere. La Camera del Lavoro* (Padua: Il Poligrafo, 2005), 56-60.

109. Sbordone, Crovato and Montanaro, *Via Garibaldi. La Regata Storica. I Cinema 'Peocéti'*, 54, 58, 61-4.

110. Criminologist Cesare Lombroso, a man with a genuine period international reputation, admitted that he was puzzled by the relationship between the evident decadence of the city and the appearance of present-day Venetians compared with the past. See Cesare Lombroso, 'Perché fu grande Venezia?', *Nuova Antologia*, fasc. 647, 1 December 1898, 395-418.

111. See Peter Collier, *Proust and Venice* (Cambridge University Press, 1989).

112. John Pemble, *Venice Rediscovered* (Oxford University Press, 1996), 142.

113. Campbell, *Of True Experience*, 34.

114. Thomas Okey, *A Basketful of Memories: An Autobiographical Sketch* (London: J. M. Dent, 1930), 123.

115. Giordano Bruno Guerri, *Filippo Tommaso Marinetti: invenzioni, avventure e passioni di un rivoluzionario* (Milan: Mondadori, 2009), 107-8.

116. Ibid., 108-9.

117. John Woodhouse, *Gabriele D'Annunzio: Defiant Archangel* (Oxford: Clarendon, 1998), 232-5.

118. *The Times*, 15 January 1908.
119. Iain Fenlon, *Piazza San Marco* (London: Profile, 2010), 100.
120. Even in the Fascist years, her favourite tipple was noted as an unpatriotic Johnny Walker. Maria Damerini, *Gli ultimi anni del Leone: Venezia, 1929-1940* (Padua: Il Poligrafo, 1988), 121.
121. For a eulogistic biography, see Armando Odenigo, *Piero Foscari: una vita esemplare* (Rocca San Casciano: Cappelli, 1959).
122. Luciano Pomoni, *Il Dovere Nazionale: i nazionalisti veneziani alla conquista della piazza (1908-1915)* (Padua: Il Poligrafo, 1998), 43.
123. Ibid., 81-2. In the 1920s, Rocco would be the chief artificer of the Fascist Corporate State.
124. Piero Foscari, *Per l'Italia più grande: scritti e discorsi*, ed. T. Sillani (Rome: Edizioni della *Rassegna Italiana*, 1928), 68, 96.
125. Piero Foscari, *Il porto di Venezia nel problema adriatico* (Venice: F. Garzia, 1904), 7, 25.
126. Nasalli Rocca, *Memorie di un prefetto*, 235.
127. Giovanni Giuriati, *La vigilia (gennaio 1913-maggio 1915)* (Milan: Mondadori, 1930), 38.
128. For such matters and Giuriati's Fascist comprehension of the law's functioning, see Giovanni Giuriati, *La parabola di Mussolini nei ricordi di un gerarca*, ed. Emilio Gentile (Bari: Laterza, 1981), 39, 100, 105-6.
129. Giuriati, *La vigilia*, 40-1, 47-8.
130. Pomoni, *Il Dovere Nazionale*, 51-4.
131. Giuriati, *La vigilia*, 21, 86.
132. Ibid., 97-8.
133. Ibid., 119-20.
134. Nasalli Rocca, *Memorie di un prefetto*, 228-9. Nasalli Rocca noted that Giolitti backed him on this issue of not rashly opening the city to modern gambling.
135. For a detailed review of the matter, see Luciano Petit, 'Porto di Venezia', *L'Ateneo Veneto*, January–February 1905, 33–50, which underlined that the development at Bottenighi might allow old Venice, with its 'special characteristics of an absolutely artistic kind', to survive (43).
136. *La Gazzetta di Venezia*, 14 June 1904.
137. In 1926, however, Volpi complained that the Antivari company had never turned a profit but had assisted Italy's 'penetration and infiltration in Yugoslavia'. ACS, Carte Volpi, Volpi pro memoria, 4 September 1926.
138. See Richard A. Webster, *Industrial Imperialism in Italy, 1908-1915* (Berkeley: University of California Press, 1975).
139. Sbordone, *Nella Repubblica di Santa Margherita*, 111.

Chapter Four: Venice and its First World War

1. Disconcertingly, if you google 'Madonna's house' you are directed to a website about the American residence of the pop singer of that name.
2. Giovanni Scarabello, *Il martirio di Venezia durante la grande guerra e l'opera di difesa della Marina italiana*, 2 vols (Venice: Tipografia del *Gazzettino Illustrato*, 1933), vol. 1, 66–7.
3. *Il Gazzettino*, 12 July 1917.
4. Alvise Zorzi, *Venezia scomparsa*, vol. 1: *Storia di una secolare degradazione* (Milan: Electa, 1977), 237.
5. Andrea Moschetti, *I danni ai monumenti e alle opere d'arte delle Venezie nella guerra mondiale MCMXV-MCMXVIII*, rev. edn (Venice: C. Ferrari, 1932), 50.
6. He was well known enough to paint portraits of Giuseppe Volpi, his wife and family. Tito had been born near Naples, the son of a sailor and a Venetian. The family soon returned to Venice and Tito made most of his career there, his son and grandson continuing his traditions after he retired but in sculpture more than painting.

7. Silvio Tramontin, 'Il Cardinale Pietro La Fontaine, patriarca di Venezia, e il suo tempo', *Archivio Veneto*, 129 (1987), 46.

8. For a patriotic account, see Carlo Pignatti Morano, *La vita di Nazario Sauro ed il martirio dell'eroe* (Milan: Treves, 1922).

9. For the memory of Sauro in Trieste, where the border is indeed apparent, see John Foot, 'Memories of an Exodus: Istria, Fiume, Dalmatia, Trieste, Italy, 1943–2010', in Daniela Baratieri, Mark Edele and Giuseppe Finaldi (eds), *Totalitarian Dictatorship: New Histories* (New York: Routledge, 2013).

10. In August 1920 a plaque to Sauro had been erected for a time outside Quadri's in Piazza San Marco; it was inaugurated by Giuriati. *Il Gazzettino*, 8 August 1920.

11. Lega Navale Italiana, *The Adriatic Avenged: Apotheosis of Nazario Sauro* (Rome: Lega Navale, 1917), 12–13.

12. Ibid., 4. Mussolini did not get round to ordering his countrymen to hate the enemy until 1942, and then earned criticism from the Church and other commentators for his brutality in so doing.

13. http://www.military-today.com/navy/sauro_class.htm (accessed 21 September 2012).

14. Rosario Romeo, *L'Italia unita e la prima guerra mondiale* (Bari: Laterza, 1978), 147.

15. David Lloyd George, *War Memoirs*, 2 vols (London: Odhams, 1939), vol. 1, 32.

16. *Il Gazzettino*, 3 July 1914.

17. *Il Gazzettino*, 13, 16 July 1914.

18. *Il Gazzettino*, 18, 19 July 1914.

19. *Il Gazzettino*, 22, 26, 27, 31 July 1914.

20. *Il Gazzettino*, 2 August 1914.

21. Michele De Benedetti, 'La XI esposizione internazionale d'arte a Venezia', *Nuova Antologia*, fasc. 1026, 16 September 1914, 128–9, 132.

22. Marco Pilo, 'L'undecima Esposizione Internazionale d'Arte a Venezia', *L'Ateneo Veneto*, September–December 1914, 93–4.

23. *Il Gazzettino*, 9, 16 August 1914.

24. *Il Gazzettino*, 13 August 1914.

25. Quoted in Bruna Bianchi, 'Venezia in guerra' (unpublished thesis, University of Venice Ca' Foscari, 2002), 5.

26. Grimani may not have understood the role of illegal, often female, moneylenders, through the so-called 'casse peote', in lubricating the social life of Venice. For background, see Alessandro Casellato, 'I sestieri popolari', in Mario Isnenghi and Stuart Woolf (eds), *Storia di Venezia: l'Ottocento e il Novecento* (Rome: Istituto dell'Enciclopedia Italiana, 2002), 1594.

27. *Il Gazzettino*, 17, 18, 19 August. One graphic story that day was of a Hungarian homosexual tourist who had gone insane, torn apart by the dilemma of a call-up to the colours and leaving his lover.

28. *Il Gazzettino*, 23 August 1914.

29. *Il Gazzettino*, 15, 16 September 1914.

30. *Il Gazzettino*, 3 September 1914.

31. Bianchi, 'Venezia in guerra', 8.

32. *Il Gazzettino*, 9 October 1914.

33. Bianchi, 'Venezia in guerra', 11.

34. Lisa Bregantin, Livio Fantina and Marco Mondini, *Venezia, Treviso e Padova nella Grande Guerra* (Treviso: ISTRESCO, 2008), 15.

35. Maria Teresa Sega and Nadia Maria Filippini, *Manifattura Tabacchi. Cotonificio Veneziano* (Padua: Il Poligrafo, 2008), 119–20.

36. Moschetti, *I danni ai monumenti e alle opere d'arte*, 5–6; Daniele Ceschin and Anna Scannapieco, *L'Archivio dei Frari. La Casa di Goldoni* (Padua: Il Poligrafo, 2005), 27. The decision was taken after a meeting at the Albergo della Luna, a place that would become more notorious during the Second World War.

37. Piero Foscari, *Per l'Italia più grande: scritti e discorsi*, ed. T. Sillani (Rome: Edizioni della Rassegna Italiana, 1928), 113.

38. Giovanni Giuriati, *La vigilia (gennaio 1913-maggio 1915)* (Milan: Mondadori, 1930), 128, 151, 175.
39. Luciano Pomoni, *Il Dovere Nazionale: i nazionalisti veneziani alla conquista della piazza (1908-1915)* (Padua: Il Poligrafo, 1998), 381-2.
40. Ibid., 407, 440-3.
41. Giuriati, *La vigilia*, 190-3, 205.
42. Maurizio De Marco, *Il Gazzettino: storia di un quotidiano* (Venice: Marsilio, 1976), 36-8.
43. Monica Donaglio, *Un esponente dell'élite liberale: Pompeo Molmenti politico e storico di Venezia* (Venice: Istituto Veneto di Scienze, Lettere ed Arti, 2004), 243-8.
44. Pomoni, *Il Dovere Nazionale*, 477.
45. Ibid., 481.
46. Scarabello, *Il martirio di Venezia durante la grande guerra*, vol. 1, 57-8.
47. Ibid., vol. 1, 191.
48. Bregantin, Fantina and Mondini, *Venezia, Treviso e Padova nella Grande Guerra*, 17.
49. For background, see R. J. B. Bosworth, 'Tourist Planning in Fascist Italy and the Limits of a Totalitarian Culture', *Contemporary European History*, 6 (1997), 1-25.
50. Ezio Maria Gray, *La bella guerra* (Florence: Bemporad, 1912).
51. Ezio Maria Gray, *L'invasione tedesca in Italia (professori, commercianti, spie)* (Florence: Bemporad, [1915]), 62-6. There was an eventual version in English: Ezio Maria Gray, *The Bloodless War* (London: Hutchinson, 1917). Gray was one of the few people who took seriously the ramblings of English crime writer William Le Queux, who was at least as paranoid as Gray (258-9).
52. Ezio Maria Gray, *Il Belgio sotto la spada tedesca* (Florence: A. Beltrami, [1915]), 8.
53. Ezio Maria Gray, *Germania in Italia* (Milan: Ravà, 1915), 29.
54. Gray, *The Bloodless War*, 57, 167.
55. Gray, *L'invasione tedesca in Italia*, 129, 169.
56. Ezio Maria Gray, *Venezia in armi* (Milan: Treves, 1917), 20-1, 24.
57. Gray, *L'invasione tedesca in Italia*, 85, 101-5.
58. Ibid., 85.
59. Ibid., 185-6.
60. Gray, *Venezia in armi*, 3-4, 24.
61. Gray, *L'invasione tedesca in Italia*, 247-8.
62. Gray was scarcely original in holding this view. Other nationalists, such as Armando Cippico in 1915, had already proclaimed that 'whoever possesses Venice has to possess Valona and Dalmatia and Istria and Trieste'. See Luciano Monzali, *The Italians of Dalmatia: From Italian Unification to World War I* (University of Toronto Press, 2009), 323.
63. Gray, *Venezia in armi*, 126, 156, 159-64.
64. Ibid., 52, 58, 61.
65. Ibid., 69.
66. Ibid., 73-4. In this they could rely on outside support, Edmund Gosse (15 August 1916), Richard Bagot (14 October 1916) and Horatio Brown (25 January 1917) leading campaigns in *The Times* against the 'cynical barbarity' of Austrian bombing of Venetian treasures, while the historian G. M. Trevelyan commanded a British Red Cross section working through the war years on the Italian front. For his account, with its many period stereotypes of Italians, see George Macaulay Trevelyan, *Scenes from Italy's War* (London: T. C. and E. C. Jack, 1919). Trevelyan thought, for example, that the response to Caporetto was proof of 'the nobility and character of the race' and thus a replay of what had happened in classical times after the loss to Hannibal at Cannae (163-4).
67. Gray, *Venezia in armi*, 88, 97.
68. Gabriele D'Annunzio, *Notturno* (Milan: Treves, 1921).
69. Gino Damerini, *D'Annunzio a Venezia* (Venice: Marsilio, 1992), 143.
70. D'Annunzio, *Notturno*, 28.
71. Ibid., 275.

72. For an English description, see John Woodhouse, *Gabriele D'Annunzio: Defiant Archangel* (Oxford: Clarendon, 1998), 297–310.
73. Antonio Beltramelli, 'Venezia senza porpora (pagine di diario: 1916–1917)', *Nuova Antologia*, fasc. 1492, 16 May 1934, 168–9.
74. Henri de Régnier, 'Sur l'altana ou la vie vénitienne', *Revue des deux mondes*, 97, 1 November 1927, 93.
75. James Strachey Barnes, *Half a Life* (London: Eyre and Spottiswoode, 1937), 264–6.
76. Antonella Ercolani (ed.), *Carteggio D'Annunzio–Gravina (1915–1924)* (Rome: Bonacci, 1993), 158–9. Gravina became a major Fascist official in the League of Nations.
77. For the best English account of Italy's First World War, see Mark Thompson, *The White War: Life and Death on the Italian Front, 1915–1918* (London: Faber and Faber, 2010).
78. A list of the fallen, quite a number of whom are still unidentified, can be found at http://tempiovotivo.altervista.org/index.php?nav=Elenco%20caduti.5 (accessed 25 September 2012). In 1925 the Comune published a lavish volume listing locals who had been decorated for heroism in war. See Comune di Venezia, *MCMXV–MCMXVIII: Veneziani morti per la patria decorati al valore* (Venice: Umberto Bartoli, 1925).
79. Lisa Bregantin, *Per non morire mai: la percezione della morte in guerra e il culto dei caduti nel primo conflitto mondiale* (Padua: Il Poligrafo, 2010), 259. See also her touching case study of peasant losses from a village on the terra firma. Lisa Bregantin, *Caduti nell'oblio: i soldati di Pontelongo scomparsi nella Grande Guerra* (Venice: Istituto veneziano per la storia della Resistenza e della società contemporanea, 2003).
80. Bianchi, 'Venezia in guerra', 7, 19–23, 27.
81. Francesco Piva, *Contadini in fabbrica: Marghera, 1920–1945* (Rome: Lavoro, 1991), 33.
82. Sega and Filippini, *Manifattura Tabacchi. Cotonificio Veneziano*, 118–23.
83. Girolamo Li Causi, *Il lungo cammino: autobiografia 1906–1944* (Rome: Riuniti, 1974), 57.
84. Silvio Tramontin, 'Dall'alba del nuovo secolo al concilio Vaticano II: i patriarchi', in Silvio Tramontin (ed.), *Patriarcato di Venezia* (Padua: Gregoriana Libreria, 1991), 229.
85. Giovanni Sbordone, Giorgio Crovato and Carlo Montanaro, *Via Garibaldi. La Regata Storica. I Cinema 'Peocéti'* (Padua: Il Poligrafo, 2005), 32.
86. Sicinio Bonfanti, *La Giudecca nella storia, nell'arte, nelle vite* (Venice: Libreria Emiliana, 1930), 191–2.
87. See Public Record Office, London, Foreign Office (hereafter FO), 977/1 and 369/409, on whether the current occupant, Princess Aspasia of Greece, had paid for the property.
88. *Il Gazzettino*, 13, 15, 26 July 1917.
89. Umberto Bognolo, *Venezia eroica* (Rocca San Casciano: Cappelli, 1918), 62.
90. *The Times*, 2 November 1915.
91. H. G. Wells, *War and the Future: Italy, France and Britain at War* (London: Cassell, 1917), 68.
92. Laura M. Ragg, *Crises in Venetian History* (London: Methuen, 1928), 278.
93. Bognolo, *Venezia eroica*, 48–9.
94. Giordano Bruno Guerri, *Filippo Tommaso Marinetti: invenzioni, avventure e passioni di un rivoluzionario* (Milan: Mondadori, 2009), 171.
95. Scarabello, *Il martirio di Venezia durante la grande guerra*, vol. 1, 59–94, has full details.
96. Armando Gavagnin, *Vent'anni di resistenza al fascismo: ricordi e testimonianze* (Turin: Einaudi, 1957), 30–1, 42.
97. Beltramelli, 'Venezia senza porpora', 163.
98. Bognolo, *Venezia eroica*, 51
99. A proper biography of Volpi is badly needed. For some introduction, see the superficial Sergio Romano, *Giuseppe Volpi: industria e finanza tra Giolitti e Mussolini* (Milan: Bompiani, 1979), the eulogistic Associazione degli industriali nel 40° anniversario di Porto Marghera e del Rotary Club di Venezia nel 35° anniversario della sua fondazione (ed.), *Giuseppe Volpi: ricordi e testimonianze* (Venice: C. Ferrari, 1959), and the period Oreste Mosca, *Volpi di Misurata* (Rome: Pinciana, 1928).
100. Mosca, *Volpi di Misurata*, 11. A brother had also died in Italy's imperial adventuring in Africa.

101. Romano, *Giuseppe Volpi*, 20.

102. Cesco Chinello, *Porto Marghera, 1902-1926: alle origini del 'problema di Venezia'* (Venice: Marsilio, 1979), 79-80.

103. Enrico Coen Cagli, *Il porto di Venezia* (Venice: La Poligrafica Italiana, 1925), 8.

104. This love was endorsed by his son Ludovico, who noted that Volpi was a family friend. See his autobiographical accounts, Ludovico Toeplitz, *Il banchiere: al tempo in cui nacque, crebbe, e fiorì la Banca Commerciale Italiana*, (Milan: Milano Nuova, 1963), and Ludovico Toeplitz, *Ciak a chi tocca* (Milan: Milano Nuova, 1964).

105. See Nicolò Papadopoli, *Le monete anonime di Venezia dal 1472 al 1605* (Milan: L. F. Cogliati, 1871).

106. Romano, *Giuseppe Volpi*, 48.

107. Maurizio Reberschak, 'Gli uomini capitali: il "gruppo veneziano" (Volpi, Cini e gli altri)', in Isnenghi and Woolf (eds), *Storia di Venezia: l'Ottocento e il Novecento*, 1262.

108. Giuseppe Volpi di Misurata, *Venezia antica e moderna* (Rome: Atena, 1939), 29.

109. Other Venetian notables had moved that way as early as 1908. See Santo Peli, 'Le concentrazioni industriali nell'economia di guerra: il caso di Porto Marghera', *Studi storici*, 16 (1975), 196-7.

110. Reberschak, 'Gli uomini capitali: il "gruppo veneziano" (Volpi, Cini e gli altri)', 1263.

111. Chinello, *Porto Marghera, 1902-1926*, 159.

112. Ibid., 115.

113. Peli, 'Le concentrazioni industriali nell'economia di guerra: il caso di Porto Marghera', 190-1.

114. Zorzi, *Venezia scomparsa*, vol. 1, 244.

115. Romano, *Giuseppe Volpi*, 93.

116. Rotary International, *Terza Conferenza regionale Europa–Africa–Asia Minore, Venezia, settembre 1935* (Venice: Zanetti, 1936), 14.

117. Piero Foscari, *Nel cinquantenario della liberazione del Veneto* (Rome: L'Italiana, 1916), 3-5, 13.

118. Piero Foscari, *Per il più largo dominio di Venezia: la città e il porto* (Milan: Treves, 1917), 29, 70, 80-1, 93, 112-13.

119. Scarabello, *Il martirio di Venezia durante la grande guerra*, vol. 1, 189.

120. Ibid., vol. 2, 285.

121. Ibid., vol. 1, 189-90.

122. Daniele Ceschin, *Gli esuli di Caporetto: i profughi in Italia durante la grande guerra* (Bari: Laterza, 2006), 38.

123. Ibid., 242. In 1918 the government got round to paying them a subsidy on a sliding scale dependent on the number of children in the family, but starting at 3.60 lire for a family with two (101).

124. Filippo Maria Paladini, *Arsenale e Museo Storico Navale di Venezia: mare, lavoro e uso pubblico della storia* (Padua: Il Poligrafo, 2008), 71-2.

125. Matteo Ermacora, 'Assistance and Surveillance: War Refugees in Italy, 1914-1918', *Contemporary European History*, 16 (2007), 457.

126. Ceschin, *Gli esuli di Caporetto*, 154.

127. Damerini, *D'Annunzio a Venezia*, 240.

128. George Ward Price, *I Know These Dictators* (London: Harrap, 1937).

129. *The Times*, 8, 14 January 1918.

130. Luciano Pes, 'Il fascismo adriatico', in Isnenghi and Woolf (eds), *Storia di Venezia: l'Ottocento e il Novecento*, 1315.

131. *The Times*, 3 September 1918. A final Austrian bombing raid hit the city at 5 a.m. on the morning of 23 October 1918, but was ineffective. Scarabello, *Il martirio di Venezia durante la grande guerra*, vol. 1, 140.

132. Bill Lamin, *Letters from the Trenches: A Soldier of the Great War* (London: Michael O'Mara, 2009), 183.

133. *Il Gazzettino*, 5, 9, 14, 15, 18, 19, 21, 29 July, 1, 4, 8, 10, 15 August, 3, 5, 9, 10, 11 September 1919.

Chapter Five: Peace and the imposition of Fascism on Venice, 1919–1930

1. For the reburial, see Marco Roncalli, *Giovanni XXIII: la mia Venezia* (Venice: Canal e Stamperia, 2000), 56.
2. See *Il Gazzettino*, 18 October 2006, and http://www.vajont.info/volpiBIOlight.html (accessed 27 September 2012).
3. Giovanni Scarabello, *Il martirio di Venezia durante la grande guerra e l'opera di difesa della Marina italiana*, 2 vols (Venice: Tipografia del *Gazzettino Illustrato*, 1933), vol. 2, 497.
4. Ibid., 467–76.
5. *Il Gazzettino*, 5 November 1929.
6. Giannantonio Paladini, *Uscire dall'isola: Venezia, risparmio privato e pubblica utilità, 1822–2002* (Bari: Laterza, 2003), 106.
7. Michele Casarin and Giancarlo Scarpari, *Piazzale Roma. Il Lido di Venezia* (Padua: Il Poligrafo, 2005), 54–5.
8. For background, see R. J. B. Bosworth, *Mussolini*, rev. edn (London: Bloomsbury, 2010), 2.
9. See http://www.veniceairport.it/core/index.jsp?_requestid=168983 (accessed 1 October 2012).
10. *The Times*, 24, 27 September 1927.
11. For the event and the victory of Lieutenant Bologna, see *Il Gazzettino*, 22 September 1920.
12. Lawrence Alloway, *The Venice Biennale, 1895–1968: From Salon to Goldfish Bowl* (London: Faber and Faber, 1969), 108.
13. *Il Gazzettino*, 1 January 1920.
14. *Il Gazzettino*, 26 September 1920.
15. *Il Gazzettino*, 4 March 1920.
16. *Il Gazzettino*, 1 September 1920.
17. Giulia Albanese, *Alle origini del fascismo: la violenza politica a Venezia, 1919–1922* (Padua: Il Poligrafo, 2001), 21 n. 20.
18. *Il Gazzettino*, 23, 24 July 1920.
19. Albanese, *Alle origini del fascismo*, 31–2.
20. Raffaele A. Vicentini, *Il movimento fascista veneto attraverso il diario di uno squadrista* (Venice: Zanetti, [1934]), 14.
21. Ibid., 57.
22. Davide Giordano, *Conferenze di chirurgia in tempo di guerra fatte agli Ufficiali Medici nello Spedale Militare Principale di Venezia, Febbraio–Marzo 1917* (Turin: Editrice Torinese, 1917), 10, 15.
23. Enrico Polichetti, 'Elogio di Davide Giordano', *L'Ateneo Veneto*, 1954, 61, 73.
24. La Fontaine was also troubled by the mayor's approval of such heretical figures from the past as Paolo Sarpi, Galileo Galilei and Giordano Bruno. Silvio Tramontin, *Cattolici, popolari e fascisti nel Veneto* (Rome: Cinque Lune, 1975), 26. Giordano was born in the Waldensian redoubt of Torre Pellice in Piedmont.
25. Emilio Franzina and Ernesto Brunetta, 'Figure e momenti del Novecento politico', in Emilio Franzina (ed.), *Venezia* (Bari: Laterza, 1986), 163.
26. Tramontin, *Cattolici, popolari e fascisti nel Veneto*, 11–12.
27. Alberto Guasco, *Cattolici e fascisti: la Santa Sede e la politica italiana all'alba del regime (1919–1925)* (Bologna: Il Mulino, 2013), 104–5.
28. Francesco Piva, *Lotte contadine e origini del fascismo, Padova–Venezia: 1919–1922* (Venice: Marsilio, 1977), 84.
29. Tramontin, *Cattolici, popolari e fascisti nel Veneto*, 40–1, 49–50; Silvio Tramontin, 'Il fascismo nel "Diario" del card. La Fontaine', *Storia contemporanea*, 1 (1970), 370.
30. Ugo Camozza, *Il Card. Pietro La Fontaine: patriarca di Venezia*, rev. edn (Venice: Studium Cattolico Veneziano, 1960), 64.
31. Silvio Tramontin, 'Il Cardinale Pietro La Fontaine, patriarca di Venezia, e il suo tempo', *Archivio Veneto*, 129 (1987), 65–6.

32. Filippo Mariani, Francesco Stocco and Giorgio Crovato, *La reinvenzione di Venezia: tradizioni cittadine negli anni ruggenti* (Padua: Il Poligrafo, 2007), 43–4.

33. Vicentini, *Il movimento fascista veneto*, 3.

34. Luciano Pes, 'Il fascismo adriatico', in Mario Isnenghi and Stuart Woolf (eds), *Storia di Venezia: l'Ottocento e il Novecento* (Rome: Istituto dell'Enciclopedia Italiana, 1321–4).

35. Vicentini, *Il movimento fascista veneto*, 20.

36. Giovanni Giuriati, *Con D'Annunzio e Millo in difesa dell'Adriatico* (Florence: Sansoni, 1954), 18.

37. Archivio Storico della Camera dei Deputati, Rome, Archivio Giovanni Giurati (hereafter AGG), busta 2, fasc. 13, undated note, Giuriati to D'Annunzio.

38. Giuriati, *Con D'Annunzio e Millo*, 27–9, 41–2, 55–6.

39. Vicentini, *Il movimento fascista veneto*, 50, 54.

40. *Il Gazzettino*, 12 January 1920.

41. *The Times*, 26, 27 September 1921.

42. His private papers include two thick folders containing the menus of the official dinners he attended while in Venice. See ACS, Fondo Agostino D'Adamo, busta 3.

43. ACS, Fondo Agostino D'Adamo, busta 3, speech 23 May 1920.

44. ACS, Fondo Agostino D'Adamo, busta 3, report 3 September 1922.

45. Pes, 'Il fascismo adriatico', 1329.

46. For a review of Marsich's career, see Giulia Albanese, *Pietro Marsich* (Sommacampagna (VR): Cierre, 2003). Cf. the chief Fascist account, which glosses over party divisions; with Marsich safely dead, Vicentini hailed him as 'a magnificent, almost mystical figure in the Fascism of the Veneto' (Vicentini, *Il movimento fascista veneto*, x).

47. *Il Gazzettino*, 28 December 1920.

48. Sergio Romano, *Giuseppe Volpi: industria e finanza tra Giolitti e Mussolini* (Milan: Bompiani, 1979), 197.

49. Pes, 'Il fascismo adriatico', 1338.

50. For background, see R. J. B. Bosworth, *Mussolini's Italy: Life under the Dictatorship* (London: Penguin, 2005), 161–2.

51. Albanese, *Pietro Marsich*, 67.

52. *Il Gazzettino*, 10 June 1922. The paper talked about Venetian Fascism's 'grave crisis'.

53. Piva, *Lotte contadine e origini del fascismo*, 267.

54. Covre was destined to have a troubled financial and political history after 1922, but, in the way of sometime Fascists, never altogether lost contact with the upper ranges of the regime. See ACS, Segreteria particolare del Duce, Carteggio ordinario (hereafter SPDCO), 180148.

55. Piva, *Lotte contadine e origini del fascismo*, 1339.

56. ACS, Fondo Agostino D'Adamo, busta 3, report 8 June 1922.

57. Albanese, *Alle origini del fascismo*, 84.

58. Kate Ferris, *Everyday Life in Fascist Venice, 1929–1940* (Houndmills: Palgrave Macmillan, 2012), 35.

59. *Il Gazzettino*, 29 October 1922.

60. AGG, busta 2, fasc. 15, 30 October 1922, Magrini statement.

61. *Il Gazzettino*, 7 December 1922.

62. *Il Gazzettino*, 31 October 1922.

63. Albanese, *Alle origini del fascismo*, 167–8

64. Mario Balladelli, *Anita Mezzalira (1886–1962): una vita per la democrazia e per il socialismo* (Venice: Comune di Venezia, n.d.), 33, 39.

65. Maria Teresa Sega and Nadia Maria Filippini, *Manifattura Tabacchi. Cotonificio Veneziano* (Padua: Il Poligrafo, 2008), 59–60.

66. *Rivista mensile della città di Venezia*, June 1923.

67. ACS, Fondo Agostino D'Adamo, busta 3, menus of 2, 3 June 1923.

68. Elio Zorzi, *Osterie veneziane* (Venice: Filippi, 1967), 200–1. Two years later, it fed Mussolini's brother (and *portaborsa*) Arnaldo, very much to his satisfaction.

69. *Il Gazzettino*, 13 May 1920; 16, 17 May 1922; 26 April 1924.

70. Romano, *Giuseppe Volpi*, 123; Maurizio Reberschak, 'Gli uomini capitali: il "gruppo veneziano" (Volpi, Cini e gli altri)', in Isnenghi and Woolf (eds), *Storia di Venezia: l'Ottocento e il Novecento*, 1267.

71. See, for example, ACS, Fondo Agostino D'Adamo, busta 3, menu of 25 July 1921.

72. See the authorised account in Raffaele Rapex, *L'affermazione della sovranità italiana in Tripolitania: governatorato del Conte Giuseppe Volpi (1921–1925)* (Tientsin: Chilhi Press, 1937), 222, 275, 340, 354.

73. Ibid., 331, 350.

74. See, for example, ACS, Carte Volpi, 8 June 1927, Volpi to Mussolini.

75. Giuseppe Volpi di Misurata, *Finanza fascista: Anno VII* (Rome: Libreria del Littorio, 1929), 95.

76. Ernesto Brunetta, 'Dalla grande guerra alla Repubblica', in Silvio Lanaro (ed.), *Il Veneto* (Turin: Giulio Einaudi, 1984), 969.

77. ACS, Carte Volpi, 7 July 1928, Mussolini to Volpi; 7 July 1928, Volpi to Mussolini; 10 July 1928, Gray to Volpi; 12 July 1928, J. P. Morgan to Volpi. Volpi had assisted Gray to his well-remunerated position as head of the state tourist office, CIT.

78. ACS, Carte Volpi, 7 July 1928, Volpi to Gaggia.

79. Cf. Emilio Mariano, *Gino Damerini: cittadino dell'altra Venezia* (Venice: Fondazione Giorgio Cini, [1968]), and SPDCO, 509495, 17 February 1929, Coffari to Ministry of the Interior.

80. Cesco Chinello, *Porto Marghera, 1902–1926: alle origini del 'problema di Venezia'* (Venice: Marsilio, 1979), 196, 199.

81. Enrico Coen Cagli, *Il porto di Venezia* (Venice: La Poligrafica Italiana, 1925), 24.

82. Laura Cerasi, *Perdonare Marghera: la città del lavoro nella memoria post-industriale* (Milan: Franco Angeli, 2007), 41–7.

83. Francesco Piva, 'Il reclutamento della forza-lavoro: paesaggi sociali e politica imprenditoriale', in Francesco Piva and Giuseppe Tattara (eds), *I primi operai di Marghera: mercato, reclutamento, occupazione, 1917–1940* (Venice: Marsilio, 1983), 447.

84. Piva, *Lotte contadine e origini del fascismo*, 31–2; Piva, 'Il reclutamento della forza-lavoro: paesaggi sociali e politica imprenditoriale', 428.

85. Giuseppe Volpi di Misurata, *Economic Progress of Fascist Italy* (Rome: Usila, 1937), 9.

86. William McBrien, *Cole Porter: The Definitive Biography* (London: HarperCollins, 1999), 106.

87. Antonio Foscari, *Tumult and Order: Malcontenta, 1924–1939* (Zurich: Lars Müller, 2012), 92.

88. McBrien, *Cole Porter*, 91–2.

89. *Il Gazzettino*, 22 August 1924.

90. Robin Saikia, *The Venice Lido: A Blue Guide Travel Monograph* (London: Somerset, 2011), 12.

91. Cecil Beaton, *The Wandering Years: Diaries, 1922–1929* (London: Weidenfeld and Nicolson, 1961), 120.

92. *Il Gazzettino*, 19 February 1928.

93. *The Times*, 27 April 1926.

94. Philip Hoare, *Noël Coward: A Biography* (London: Sinclair-Stevenson, 1995), 163.

95. Lorenzo Benadusi, *Il nemico dell'uomo nuovo: l'omosessualità nell'esperimento totalitario fascista* (Milan: Feltrinelli, 2005), 141–4.

96. For an introduction to the history of Native Americans in Europe, see Christian F. Feest (ed.), *Indians and Europe: An Interdisciplinary Collection of Essays* (Aachen: Rader, 1987).

97. *Il Gazzettino*, 14 October 1924.

98. Rabindranath Tagore, 'On Venice', *L'Ateneo Veneto*, January–June 1925, 82–96.

99. *The Times*, 1 April 1927.

100. Maria Damerini, *Gli ultimi anni del Leone: Venezia, 1929–1940* (Padua: Il Poligrafo, 1988), 56.

101. Maurizio De Marco, *Il Gazzettino: storia di un quotidiano* (Venice: Marsilio, 1976), 64.
102. ACS, Segreteria particolare del Duce, Carteggio riservato, busta 49, 19 July 1925, Suppiej speech.
103. See, for example, Giovanni Giuriati, ' "Secondo tempo": lettera a Giorgio Suppiej', *Le Tre Venezie*, April 1929, 4–6.
104. AGG, busta 2, fasc. 11, 3 March 1929, memorandum.
105. Luigi Federzoni, *1927: Diario di un ministro del fascismo*, ed. A. Macchi (Florence: Passigli, 1993), 120.
106. ACS, Segreteria particolare del Duce, Carteggio riservato, busta 38, 19 February 1929, report.
107. AGG, busta 2, fasc. 11, 4 March 1929, memorandum.
108. AGG, busta 2, fasc. 11, 8 July 1929, Giuriati to Mussolini.
109. Suppiej rather carelessly used the same figures two years later, although he did then greatly amplify the number of those who belonged to the linked scouting and after-work institutions. See Giorgio Suppiej, 'Dieci anni di Fascismo nella provincia di Venezia', *Le Tre Venezie*, October 1932, 627.
110. Alessandro Bau, Antonio Marco Furio and Carlo Monaco, 'Il Veneto nei rapporti di Mussolini ai segretari federali (1930)', *Venetica*, 25 (2011), 158.
111. Ibid., 163.
112. Ibid., 159–60.
113. Ibid., 161–3.
114. See Emilio Franzina and Ernesto Brunetta, 'La politica', in Franzina (ed.), *Venezia*, 176.
115. *Il Gazzettino*, 18 September 1924. Giordano was also a Mason.
116. Bau, Furio and Monaco, 'Il Veneto nei rapporti di Mussolini', 163–4.
117. Silvio Tramontin (ed.), *Patriarcato di Venezia* (Padua: Gregoriana Libreria, 1991), 288. See also AGG, busta 6, fasc. 37, 29 June 1919, memorandum of Giuriati–La Fontaine talk.
118. Paul Corner, *The Fascist Party and Popular Opinion in Mussolini's Italy* (Oxford University Press, 2012), 104.
119. ACS, Segreteria particolare del Duce, Carteggio riservato, busta 47, 29 October 1930, Giuriati to *federali*.
120. AGG, busta 6, fasc. 35, 25 February 1931, prefect in Venice to Giuriati.
121. For a recent analysis (which, however, ignores the Venetian background), see Philip Morgan, ' "The Trash Who Are Obstacles in Our Way": The Italian Fascist Party at the Point of Totalitarian Lift-Off, 1930–31', *English Historical Review*, 127 (2012), 305–43.
122. Benadusi, *Il nemico dell'uomo nuovo*, 252–4.
123. Mariani, Stocco and Crovato, *La reinvenzione di Venezia*, 44–6.
124. ACS, Ministero dell'Interno, Direzione Generale di Pubblica Sicurezza, Divisione Polizia Politica, 1927–44 (hereafter DPP), busta 59, fasc. 5, 2 May 1928, report.
125. *Il Gazzettino*, 8 January 1924.
126. *Il Gazzettino*, 23 May 1924.
127. Nadia Maria Filippini, *Maria Pezzè Pascolato* (Sommacampagna (VR): Cierre, 2004), 15–21.
128. See, for example, Thomas Carlyle, *Gli eroi*, trans. Maria Pezzè Pascolato (Florence: G. Barbera, 1897).
129. Filippini, *Maria Pezzè Pascolato*, 43.
130. Alcohol was a problem for poor children, too. In 1924, 40 per cent of those in elementary school were reckoned to drink. Alessandro Casellato, 'I sestieri popolari', in Isnenghi and Woolf (eds), *Storia di Venezia: l'Ottocento e il Novecento*, 1594.
131. Filippini, *Maria Pezzè Pascolato*, 37.
132. See Antonio Fradeletto, *I martiri nostri* (Milan: Treves, 1918); *La missione di Venezia di fronte all'Austria* (Venice: C. Ferrari, 1926).
133. Filippini, *Maria Pezzè Pascolato*, 44, 110–11.
134. SPDCO, 14291, 29 October 1932, Pezzè Pascolato to Mussolini.
135. Maria Pezzè Pascolato, 'Fasci femminili', *Gerarchia*, 12 (1932), 113–14.

136. Ibid., 128–31.
137. *Il Gazzettino*, 10 February 1924.
138. Margherita Deleuse, 'Maria Pezzè Pascolato: commemorazione tenuta il 26 marzo 1933 nella Sala Maggiore dell'Ateneo Veneto dalla Fascista Margherita Deleuse, Vice Fiduciario prov. del Fascio femminile di Venezia' (printed pamphlet held in the Biblioteca Marciana, Venice); Lina Passarella Sartorelli (ed.), *Maria Pezzè Pascolato: notizie raccolte da un gruppo di amici* (Florence: Le Monnier, 1935).
139. *Il Gazzettino*, 11 March 1928.
140. For a neat case study of gender, honour and murder among the people, see Lucio Sponza, 'L'onore e la legge: un dramma d'onore a Venezia (1924)', *Quaderni di stori-Amestre*, 9 (2009).
141. Alessandro Ori, *La febbre tifoide a Venezia* (Venice: Libreria Emiliana, 1933), 4–7, 13–16, 21–3.
142. SPDCO, 501101/3, 1 March 1930, Mussolini to prefect.
143. SPDCO, 501101/4, 17 March 1930, Papini to Mussolini.
144. Nadia Maria Filippini, 'Storia delle donne: culture, mestieri, profili', in Isenghi and Woolf (eds), *Storia di Venezia: l'Ottocento e il Novecento*, 1632–3.
145. Laura Cerasi and Michele Casarin, *Marghera. Sant'Elena* (Padua: Il Poligrafo, 2007), 76.
146. Casellato, 'I sestieri popolari', 1586.
147. Sicinio Bonfanti, *La Giudecca nella storia, nell'arte, nelle vite* (Venice: Libreria Emiliana, 1930), 314.
148. SPDCO, 510101/3, 17 March 1930, Volpi to Mussolini.
149. Suppiej, 'Dieci anni di Fascismo nella provincia di Venezia', 637–8.
150. For Cipriani's account of its foundation, see http://www.harrysbarvenezia.com (accessed 17 February 2013).
151. Diana Cooper, *The Light of Common Day: Autobiography* (London: Century, 1984), 105.
152. Mario Corsi, *Il teatro all'aperto in Italia* (Milan: Rizzoli, 1939), 35.

Chapter Six: Venice between Volpi and Mussolini, 1930–1940

1. Alvise Zorzi, *Venezia ritrovata, 1895–1939* (Milan: Mondadori, 2001), 99.
2. http://www.thevenicelido.com/p/fuhrer-on-fairway.html (accessed 7 November 2012).
3. Giovanni Giuriati, 'Il Duce a Venezia, Venezia al Duce', *Le Tre Venezie*, July 1934, 363–5. The text was followed by three pages of photographs, which also featured Volpi but lacked any serious focus on Hitler. See also 'Mussolini a Venezia', *Rivista di Venezia*, June 1934, amplified by many photographs.
4. Maria Damerini, *Gli ultimi anni del Leone: Venezia, 1929–1940* (Padua: Il Poligrafo, 1988), 148–9.
5. Fey von Hassell, *A Mother's War*, ed. David Forbes-Watt (London: John Murray, 1990), 11.
6. Associazione degli industriali nel 40° anniversario di Porto Marghera e del Rotary Club di Venezia nel 35° anniversario della sua fondazione (ed.), *Giuseppe Volpi: ricordi e testimonianze* (Venice: C. Ferrari, 1959), 105.
7. *Il Gazzettino*, 16 May 1931.
8. SPDCO, 197599, 24 April 1937, Girolamo Marcello to Mussolini, respectfully introducing Andrea and his brother Alessandro to the Duce.
9. Circolo Golf Venezia, *Sessantacinquesimo anniversario del Circolo* (Alberoni: Circolo Golf Venezia, 1995), 1–2.
10. Fascism would eventually try to Italianise the national language, but in the 1950s the club's rule book included the words 'Albatros' (sic), 'bogie', 'fore', 'honneur', 'toppei' (topped) and 'waggle'. Golf Club di Venezia, *Regolamento ed etichetta del gioco* (Venice: n.p., n.d.).
11. For a lavish description, see Roberta Curiel and Bernard Dov Cooperman, *The Venetian Ghetto* (New York: Rizzoli, 1990).

12. For example, Richard J. Goy, *Venice: An Architectural Guide* (New Haven and London: Yale University Press, 2010), 123–6. Margaret Plant, in her otherwise exhaustive account of artworks in the city – *Venice: Fragile City, 1797–1997* (New Haven and London: Yale University Press, 2002) – also omits reference to it.

13. See http://www.jvenice.org/ (accessed 14 November 2012).

14. Simon Levis Sullam and Fabio Brusò, *Il Ghetto. Piazza Barche* (Padua: Il Poligrafo, 2008), 13–4.

15. Simon Levis Sullam, *Una comunità immaginata: gli ebrei a Venezia (1900–1938)* (Milan: Unicopli, 2001), 49–50.

16. Levis Sullam and Brusò, *Il Ghetto. Piazza Barche*, 17.

17. Levis Sullam, *Una comunità immaginata*, 39.

18. Ibid., 86.

19. SPDCO, 107757, 1 May 1931, Giuriati to Acerbo; 26 January 1932, departmental note.

20. Levis Sullam, *Una comunità immaginata*, 97.

21. Cesco Chinello and Giulio Bobbo, *La Breda. Da Ca' Littoria a Ca' Matteotti* (Padua: Il Poligrafo, 2006), 44.

22. SPDCO, 172097/7, 27 November 1936, Marinelli to Sebastiani.

23. Levis Sullam, *Una comunità immaginata*, 210–11, 223–4.

24. Paolo Sereni, 'Gli anni della persecuzione razziale a Venezia: appunti per una storia', in Umberto Fortis (ed.), *Venezia ebraica: atti delle prime giornate di studio sull'ebraismo veneziano (Venezia 1976–1980)* (Rome: Carucci, 1979), 133.

25. *The Times*, 31 May 1932.

26. Giovanni Giuriati, '"Secondo tempo": lettera a Giorgio Suppiej', *Le Tre Venezie*, April 1929; AGG, busta 7, fasc. 55, 26 May 1930, Giuriati to Mussolini.

27. Giorgio Suppiej, '25 aprile 1933', *Le Tre Venezie*, May 1933, 251–2.

28. Elio Zorzi, 'Il ponte del Littorio sulla Laguna', *Nuova Antologia*, fasc. 1469, 1 June 1933, 415.

29. Giorgio Suppiej, 'Dieci anni di Fascismo nella provincia di Venezia', *Le Tre Venezie*, October 1932, 631, 635–7.

30. Elia Barbiani (ed.), *Edilizia popolare a Venezia: storie, politiche, realizzazioni per le Case Popolari della Provincia di Venezia* (Milan: Electa, 1983), 21–2.

31. Raffaele Vivante, *Nuovo contributo allo studio del problema delle abitazioni in Venezia* (Venice: F. Garzia, 1935), 7.

32. Ibid., 18–21.

33. Kate Ferris, *Everyday Life in Fascist Venice, 1929–40* (Houndmills: Palgrave Macmillan, 2012), 31, 67–8, 119–20. See also Carlo Viviani, 'La Festa delle Marie nella storia e nell'arte', *Rivista di Venezia*, January 1934.

34. Ferris, *Everyday Life in Fascist Venice*, 155–87.

35. SPDCO, 154322, 12 October 1931, Giuriati to Chiavolini; 3 November 1931, Domenico Giuriati to Mussolini; 21 June 1934, Fernanda Giuriati to Mussolini; 18 January 1935, Fernanda Giuriati to Edda Ciano; 8 March 1935, Sebastiani note.

36. DPP, busta 8, fasc. 4, 29 September 1936, report.

37. DPP, busta 8, fasc. 4, 29 June 1937, report.

38. DPP, busta 220, 29 March 1939, report from Venice.

39. Alfonso Abbruzzetti, 'L'edilizia veneziana e la protezione antiaerea', *L'Ateneo Veneto*, August 1934, 71–3.

40. SPDCO, 501101/8, 2 June 1937, Alverà to Sebastiani.

41. Antonio Niero, *I patriarchi di Venezia da Lorenzo Giustiniani ai nostri giorni* (Venice: Studium Cattolico Veneziano, 1961), 212–13.

42. Bruno Bertoli, 'Indirizzi pastorali del Patriarca Piazza', in Bruno Bertoli (ed.), *La Chiesa di Venezia dalla Seconda Guerra Mondiale al Concilio* (Venice: Studium Cattolico Veneziano, 1994), 40.

43. *Il Gazzettino*, 29 October 1936.

44. SPDCO, 133113, 9 May 1938, Piazza to Mussolini

45. SPDCO, 133113, 21 May 1940, Piazza to Mussolini.

46. Bertoli, 'Indirizzi pastorali del Patriarca Piazza', 32–5.

47. Silvio Tramontin, 'La Chiesa Veneziana dal 1938 al 1948', in Giannantonio Paladini and Maurizio Reberschak (eds), *La resistenza nel Veneziano: la società veneziana tra fascismo, resistenza, repubblica*, 2 vols (Venice: Istituto Veneto per la storia della Resistenza, 1985), vol. 1, 457–8.

48. Luigi Picchini, *Venezia contro la bestemmia e il turpiloquio* (Venice: Libreria Emiliana, 1937), i, vi, 6, 235–52.

49. Shortly afterwards, Zandonai would tell Mussolini of his deep regard for him as 'the ardent animator of all the arts' in Italy. SPDCO, 550869, 27 February 1933, note.

50. According to a flattering biographer, Volpi's relationship with Nerina Pisani was based on a 'homely love', while Nathalie El Kanoni, twenty years his junior, was the 'love of his life'. The two got together in 1932. See Fabrizio Sarazani, *L'ultimo doge: vita di Giuseppe Volpi di Misurata* (Milan: Edizioni del Borghese, 1972), 276–7.

51. Damerini, *Gli ultimi anni del Leone*, 60.

52. Lawrence Alloway, *The Venice Biennale, 1895–1968: From Salon to Goldfish Bowl* (London: Faber and Faber, 1969), 105.

53. For further biographical detail, see http://www.treccani.it/enciclopedia/antonio-maraini_%28Dizionario_Biografico%29/ (accessed 16 November 2012).

54. Lorenzo Benadusi, *Il nemico dell'uomo nuovo: l'omosessualità nell'esperimento totalitario fascista* (Milan: Feltrinelli, 2005), 9.

55. See his eventual account in Antonio Maraini, 'Introduzione', in Sindacato Nazionale Fascista Belle Arti (ed.), *L'ordinamento sindacale fascista delle belle arti* (Rome: CFAP, 1939). See also Antonio Maraini, 'Preparazione della Biennale', *L'Ateneo Veneto*, September 1932, 250–1.

56. Antonio Maraini, 'XVIII Biennale', *Le Tre Venezie*, May 1932.

57. Biennale di Venezia, *Le Esposizioni internazionali d'arte, 1895–1995: artisti, mostre, partecipazioni nazionali, premi* (Venice: Electa, 1996), 189–90, 239.

58. SPDCO, 524260, 8 September 1935, Yoï Maraini to Mussolini; 1 February 1937, Antonio Maraini to Mussolini's office.

59. SPDCO, 524260, 31 July 1934, Maraini to Sebastiani.

60. Mario Corsi, *Il teatro all'aperto in Italia* (Milan: Rizzoli, 1939), ix.

61. *The Times*, 20 July 1934.

62. Ludovico Toeplitz, *Ciak a chi tocca* (Milan: Milano Nuova, 1964), 132.

63. *The Times*, 13 August 1932.

64. Flavia Paulon, *La dogaressa contestata: la favolosa storia della Mostra di Venezia dalle regine alla contestazione* (Venice: F. Paulon, 1971), 13–15.

65. *Il Gazzettino*, 29 August 1936.

66. Damerini, *Gli ultimi anni del Leone*, 276.

67. For a sensible introduction to the complex of messages given by the film festival, see Marla Stone, 'Challenging Cultural Categories: The Transformation of the Venice Biennale under Fascism', *Journal of Modern Italian Studies*, 4 (1999). After the war, the Mussolini prizes metamorphosised into the Leone d'Oro (Golden Lion), whereas the Volpi cups retained their name.

68. FO, 395/565/6/6/150, 23 August 1938, N. Kearney to N. Charles.

69. Francesco Bono, 'La mostra del cinema di Venezia: nascita e sviluppo nell'anteguerra (1932–1939)', *Storia contemporanea*, 22 (1991), 527.

70. Ibid., 520.

71. See, for example, AGG, busta 6, fasc. 35, 1 July 1930, Giuriati to Talamini.

72. Maurizio De Marco, *Il Gazzettino: storia di un quotidiano* (Venice: Marsilio, 1976), 99–102.

73. Renato Camurri, 'La classe politica nazionalfascista', in Mario Isnenghi and Stuart Woolf (eds), *Storia di Venezia: l'Ottocento e il Novecento* (Rome: Istituto dell'Enciclopedia Italiana, 2002), 1413–17; Giannantonio Paladini, *Uscire dall'isola: Venezia, risparmio privato e pubblica utilità, 1822–2002* (Bari: Laterza, 2003), 113. Pascolato's colleagues included Girolamo Marcello and Lodovico Foscari.

74. Rotary International, *Terza Conferenza regionale Europa–Africa–Asia Minore, Venezia, settembre 1935* (Venice: Zanetti, 1936), 11, 14, 29–32, 48–9, 89–90.
75. Paul Corner, *The Fascist Party and Popular Opinion in Mussolini's Italy* (Oxford University Press, 2012), 195.
76. Damerini, *Gli ultimi anni del Leone*, 81.
77. For images, see 'Il Duce a Venezia', *Le Tre Venezie*, August–September 1936, 251.
78. *Il Gazzettino*, 4 August 1936.
79. Mauro Mezzalira, 'Venezia anni trenta: il Comune, il partito fascista e le grandi opere', *Italia contemporanea*, 202 (1996), 63–5.
80. Alloway, *The Venice Biennale, 1895–1968: From Salon to Goldfish Bowl*, 193.
81. She went 'slumming' there in the summer of 1936. Axel Madsen, *Coco Chanel: A Biography* (London: Bloomsbury, 1990).
82. Josephine Ross (ed.), *Society in Vogue: The International Set between the Wars* (London: Condé Nast, 1992), 20.
83. *Il Gazzettino*, 15 July 1936.
84. *Il Gazzettino*, 18 September, 21 October 1936. Volpi received the businessmen enthusiastically.
85. DPP, busta 46, fasc. 3, 25 May 1934, report to Ministry of the Interior.
86. Silva Bon, *Gli Ebrei a Trieste* (Gorizia: Libreria Editrice Goriziana, 2000), 100, 215, 293. For further background, see Anna Millo, *Trieste, le Assicurazioni, l'Europa* (Milan: Franco Angeli, 2004).
87. Galeazzo Ciano, *Diary, 1937–1943*, ed. Renzo De Felice (London: Phoenix, 2002), 15.
88. *Il Gazzettino*, 24 December 1936.
89. Swimming pools were now favoured by Vivante on the grounds that other countries and other Italian cities, even Naples, already had them. See Raffaele Vivante, *Per la istituzione in Venezia di una piscina natatoria coperta* (Venice: Ateneo Veneto, 1937).
90. Mezzalira, 'Venezia anni trenta: il Comune, il partito fascista e le grandi opere', 58–65.
91. Camurri, 'La classe politica nazionalfascista', 1420.
92. Mezzalira, 'Venezia anni trenta: il Comune, il partito fascista e le grandi opere', 63.
93. Corner, *The Fascist Party and Popular Opinion in Mussolini's Italy*, 105.
94. Guido Marta, 'Amore di terra lontana: Raimondo Franchetti', *Le Tre Venezie*, September 1935, 454–8.
95. Carlo Franco, *Il liceo 'Raimondo Franchetti'* (Padua: Il Poligrafo, 2010), 21–2.
96. http://www.unive.it/nqcontent.cfm?a_id=60550 (accessed 18 February 2013).
97. Franco, *Il liceo 'Raimondo Franchetti'*, 24–45.
98. Ibid., 53.
99. DPP, busta 219, fasc. 1, 3 November 1939, report from Venice.
100. DPP, busta 200, 8 July 1939, report from Venice.
101. DPP, busta 220, 8 August 1939, report from Venice.
102. DPP, busta 220, 28 August 1939, report from Venice.
103. DPP, busta 220, 28 August 1939, two reports from Venice.
104. DPP, busta 220, 29 August, 1 September 1939, three reports from Venice.
105. *The Times*, 9 August 1939.
106. Pietro Orsi, '24 maggio 1915–24 maggio 1940', *Le Tre Venezie*, May 1940, 6.
107. *Il Gazzettino*, 7, 16 July 1940. Discipline also meant rejoicing in the availability of only one type of bread and rallying to expel from Piazza San Marco three women wearing slacks, deemed unseemly dress during a national crisis (2, 11 July 1940).
108. *Il Gazzettino*, 20 July 1940.
109. *Il Gazzettino*, 21 July 1940.
110. *Il Gazzettino*, 3 July 1940.
111. *Il Gazzettino*, 7 August 1940.
112. For the Istituto Luce newsreel of the event, see http://www.youtube.com/watch?v=4iAiPnd24ig (accessed 21 June 2013).
113. Giuseppe Volpi di Misurata, 'Premessa', *Le Tre Venezie*, July–August 1940, 6.
114. Antonio Maraini, 'Insegnamenti della Biennale', *Le Tre Venezie*, July–August 1940, 7–8.
115. *Il Gazzettino*, 24 August 1940.

116. *Il Gazzettino*, 2 September 1940.
117. *Il Gazzettino*, 13 September, 27 October 1940.
118. Gino Damerini, 'Il corso di Storia Veneta', *L'Ateneo Veneto*, May–June 1940, 232–5.
119. *Il Gazzettino*, 9 October 1940.
120. For background, see Alan Riding, *And the Show Went On: Cultural Life in Nazi-Occupied Paris* (London: Duckworth, 2012).

Chapter Seven: Venice, Nazi-fascist War and American peace, 1940–1948

1. *La Repubblica*, 12 November 2012.
2. For background, see Francesco Dal Co and Giuseppe Mazzariol (eds), *Carlo Scarpa: The Complete Works* (London: Electa, 1986); Richard Murphy, *Querini Stampalia Foundation: Carlo Scarpa* (London: Phaidon, 1993); Sergio Los, *Carlo Scarpa* (Cologne: Taschen, 2002).
3. *Rivista di Venezia*, 3, November–December 1957; http://capesaro.visitmuve.it/en/mostre-en/archivio-mostre-en/the-venetian-partisan-art-for-the-resistance/2011/07/838/la-storia–2/ (accessed 20 November 2012) has the image.
4. Maria Teresa Sega, 'Fragile come vita, solida come bronzo: la memoria della Resistenza e due monumenti alla Partigiana Veneta', in Maria Teresa Sega (ed.), *La partigiana veneta: arte e memoria della Resistenza* (Portogruaro: Edicola, 2004), 19.
5. Cesco Chinello, *Sindacato, Pci, movimenti negli anni sessanta: Porto Marghera–Venezia, 1955-1970*, 2 vols (Milan: Franco Angeli, 1996), 170.
6. Sega, 'Fragile come vita, solida come bronzo', 13–14.
7. Robert M. Edsel, *Saving Italy: The Race to Rescue a Nation's Treasures from the Nazis* (New York: W. W. Norton, 2013), 104.
8. Diego Valeri, *Guida sentimentale di Venezia* (Florence: Passigli, 1994); Diego Valeri, 'Elogio di Venezia', *Le Tre Venezie*, January 1940.
9. *Il Gazzettino*, 15 May 1941.
10. *L'Ateneo Veneto*, May–July 1941, editorial.
11. *Il Gazzettino*, 24 May 1941.
12. *Il Gazzettino*, 31 May, 2, 3 June, 24 August 1941.
13. *Il Gazzettino*, 24 June, 14, 21 July, 1, 18 August, 14, 15 September 1941.
14. *Il Gazzettino*, 15, 31 August, 10, 15 September 1941. Exhibiting at the festival were film makers from Bohemia, Belgium, Croatia, Denmark, Finland, Holland, Spain, Sweden, Switzerland, Romania, Slovakia, Turkey and Hungary, in addition, of course, to Italy and Germany.
15. Ministero delle Comunicazioni, Direzione Generale delle Poste e Telegrafi (ed.), *Il Fondaco dei tedeschi* (Venice: Zanetti, 1941).
16. Ten. Giacolone-Monaco, 'Le "sanzioni" cinque anni dopo', *L'Ateneo Veneto*, August–October 1941, 361–7.
17. *Il Gazzettino*, 17, 26 June 1941.
18. *Il Gazzettino*, 5, 24 July 1941.
19. *Il Gazzettino*, 26, 29 July, 6, 9, 21 August 1941.
20. *Il Gazzettino*, 18 September 1941.
21. Emilio Franzina and Ernesto Brunetta, 'La politica', in Emilio Franzina, *Venezia* (Bari: Laterza, 1986), 182.
22. N. Perissinotti, 'L'avvenire del porto di Venezia', *Le Tre Venezie*, January 1942.
23. *Il Gazzettino*, 22 October 1941.
24. Diego Valeri, 'La XXIII Biennale', *Le Tre Venezie*, August 1942.
25. *Il Gazzettino*, 2, 23 July 1942.
26. *Il Gazzettino*, 8 July 1942.
27. *Il Gazzettino*, 12 July 1942.
28. *Il Gazzettino*, 15 July 1942.
29. *Il Gazzettino*, 20, 27 July, 2 August, 11, 29 October 1942.
30. Giovanni Sbordone, Giorgio Crovato and Carlo Montanaro, *Via Garibaldi. La Regata Storica. I Cinema 'Peocéti'* (Padua: Il Poligrafo, 2005), 74.

31. *Il Gazzettino*, 30 August 1942.
32. *Il Gazzettino*, 11 August 1942.
33. Mario Nani Mocenigo, 'La Dalmazia Veneta', *L'Ateneo Veneto*, April–June 1942, 65–71.
34. SPDCO, 501101, 21 May 1941, Giovanni Marcello to Sebastiani.
35. Umberto Corrado, 'La Nuova Europa', *L'Ateneo Veneto*, July–September 1942, 162–7.
36. Simon Levis Sullam and Fabio Brusò, *Il Ghetto. Piazza Barche* (Padua: Il Poligrafo, 2008), 18.
37. DPP, busta 219, fasc. 2, 2 April 1942, report from Venice.
38. DPP, busta 219, fasc. 2, 6 November 1941, report from Venice.
39. *Il Gazzettino*, 13 February 1942.
40. *Il Gazzettino*, 7 July 1943.
41. *Il Gazzettino*, 5 June, 7, 10 July 1943.
42. Piero Calamandrei and Franco Calamandrei, *Una famiglia in guerra: lettere e scritti (1939–1956)*, ed. Alessandro Casellato (Bari: Laterza, 2008), 34.
43. ACS, Ministero dell'Interno, Direzione Generale di Pubblica Sicurezza, Divisione Affari Generali e Riservati, Segreteria del Capo della Polizia, 1940–3 (hereafter SCP), busta 1, 24 December 1940, *questore* Venice to Senise.
44. Emilio Franzina, 'Il fronte "interno" sulla laguna: Venezia in guerra (1938–1943)', in Mario Isnenghi and Stuart Woolf (eds), *Storia di Venezia: l'Ottocento e il Novecento* (Rome: Istituto dell'Enciclopedia Italiana, 2002), 1712.
45. SCP, busta 1, 4 February 1941, *questore* Venice to Senise.
46. SCP, busta 1, 18 February 1941, *questore* Venice to Senise.
47. SCP, busta 2, 4, 10, 31 March, 12, 19 April, and busta 3, 26 May 1941, all *questore* Venice to Senise.
48. SCP, busta 4, 4, 11 August 1941, *questore* Venice to Senise.
49. DPP, busta 219, fasc. 2, 24 August 1941, report from Venice.
50. DPP, busta 219, fasc. 2, 20 May 1942, report from Venice.
51. DPP, busta 219, fasc. 2, 26 May, 6 June 1942, reports from Venice.
52. SCP, busta 4, 11 August 1941, *questore* Venice to Senise.
53. See, for example, *Le Tre Venezie*, July–August 1940.
54. SCP, busta 5, 9 September 1941, *questore* Venice to Senise. The lavish dinner given for Pavolini at the closure of the festival was also widely resented (16 September 1941, *questore* Venice to Senise). The malfunctioning of state rationing remained a constant complaint of what the police identified as the 'petit bourgeois and popular classes'. See 22 September, 27 October 1941, *questore* Venice to Senise.
55. SCP, busta 7, 22 September 1942, *questore* Venice to Senise.
56. SCP, busta 7, 26 August, 2, 8 September 1942, *questore* Venice to Senise.
57. SCP, busta 8, 28 October, 11, 25 November 1942, *questore* Venice to Senise.
58. SCP, busta 9, 8 December 1942, *questore* Venice to Senise.
59. SCP, busta 9, 16, 23 December 1942, *questore* Venice to Senise.
60. SCP, busta 11, 27 February 1943, *questore* Venice to Senise. A final report before Mussolini's fall on 25 July 1943 had much the same emphases. See SCP, busta 12, 25 June 1943, *questore* Venice to Senise. A meeting between Hitler and Mussolini a week before the fall took place at a villa near Feltre owned by Achille Gaggia of the Volpi group.
61. SPDCO, 524260, 17 June 1943, memo, 6 July 1943, Maraini to De Cesare. ACS, Ministro dell'Interno, Direzione Generale di Pubblica Sicurezza, Ufficio Confino Politico, busta 612, 16 May 1943, prefect (Florence) to Ministry of the Interior. Influence paid in the end, however, as Fosco Maraini was released on 27 July 1943 (10 August 1943, Ministry of the Interior note).
62. Armando Gavagnin, *Vent'anni di resistenza al fascismo: ricordi e testimonianze* (Turin: Einaudi, 1957), 420–3.
63. *Il Gazzettino*, 26, 27, 28 July 1943. This restoration was also the theme of a special issue of *L'Ateneo Veneto*, April–June 1943.
64. *Il Gazzettino*, 4 August 1943.
65. Sandro Meccoli, *Viva Venezia* (Milan: Longanesi, 1985), 15.
66. Maurizio De Marco, *Il Gazzettino: storia di un quotidiano* (Venice: Marsilio, 1976), 110.

67. Sergio Romano, *Giuseppe Volpi: industria e finanza tra Giolitti e Mussolini* (Milan: Bompiani, 1979), 236.

68. Giannantonio Paladini, *Uscire dall'isola: Venezia, risparmio privato e pubblica utilità, 1822-2002* (Bari: Laterza, 2003), 162.

69. Giulio Bobbo, *Venezia in tempo di guerra, 1943-1945* (Padua: Il Poligrafo, 2005), 198.

70. ACS, Direzione Generale di Pubblica Sicurezza, Divisione Affari Generali e Riservati, Segreteria del Capo della Polizia RSI, 1943-5 (hereafter SCP RSI), busta 65, 31 December 1943, Special Inspector of Police report.

71. Arduino Cerutti, *Memorie* (Venice: Marsilio, 1980), 102.

72. SCP RSI, busta 65, 31 December 1943, Special Inspector of Police report.

73. Bobbo, *Venezia in tempo di guerra*, 156.

74. SCP RSI, busta 65, 30 January, 15 February 1944, Special Inspector of Police report.

75. SCP RSI, busta 65, 30 January, 15 April 1944, Special Inspector of Police report.

76. For further detail, see Bobbo, *Venezia in tempo di guerra*, 279-372.

77. See *Il Gazzettino*, 13, 17 September, 2, 7 October, 20 November, 25 December 1943, 24 February, 8, 21 April, 1, 11 June 1944.

78. *L'Ateneo Veneto*, January–December 1944, 77.

79. SPDCO, 102213, has an extensive file on his activities.

80. *Il Gazzettino*, 1 April 1944.

81. Renata Segre, *Gli ebrei a Venezia, 1938-1945: una comunità tra persecuzione e rinascita* (Venice: Il Cardo, 1995), 172.

82. For his speeches to his successive school classes, in which he married Italian patriotism with Zionism, see Adolfo Ottolenghi, *La scuola ebraica di Venezia attraverso la voce del suo Rabbino (1912-1944)*, ed. Elisabetta Ottolenghi (Venice: Filippi, 2012).

83. C. Cogo, 'Dalla Guerra ai nostri giorni', in Gianfranco Bettin, *Marghera: il quartiere urbano* (Biban di Carbonera (TV): Alcione, 2004), 72-4. For the school today, see, for example, the account of a serious theft there in *La Nuova Venezia*, 20 March 2013.

84. Carlo Franco, *Il liceo 'Raimondo Franchetti'* (Padua: Il Poligrafo, 2010), 61-6.

85. Bobbo, *Venezia in tempo di guerra*, 24.

86. Raffaele Liucci, 'Il '43-'45', in Isnenghi and Woolf (eds), *Storia di Venezia: l'Ottocento e il Novecento*, 1749.

87. Frank M. Snowden, *The Conquest of Malaria: Italy, 1900-1960* (New Haven and London: Yale University Press, 2006), 203-4.

88. Bobbo, *Venezia in tempo di guerra*, 369-71, 432-6.

89. Ibid., 327-31.

90. Liucci, 'Il '43-'45', 1744.

91. Ibid., 1745.

92. In July 1943, Utimperghe was complaining naively that his career had been slow to develop because of his long having remained a bachelor (for family reasons). See SPDCO, 518533. He had joined the party on 26 October 1922, but was yet another to have his membership backdated, in his case to 20 December 1920.

93. Bobbo, *Venezia in tempo di guerra*, 76-88.

94. Giulia Albanese and Marco Borghi (eds), *Memoria resistente: la lotta partigiana a Venezia nel ricordo dei protagonisti* (Portogruaro: Istituto veneziano per la storia della Resistenza e della società contemporanea, 2005), 34, 213.

95. Marco Borghi, *Tra Fascio Littorio e senso dello stato: funzionari, apparati, ministeri nella Repubblica sociale italiana (1943-1945)* (Venice: Istituto veneziano per la storia della Resistenza e della società contemporanea, 2001), 175.

96. Ibid., 123-4.

97. Liucci, 'Il '43-'45', 1750.

98. Bobbo, *Venezia in tempo di guerra*, 22.

99. Cf. the report along similar lines in ACS, Ministero dell'Interno, Direzione Generale di Pubblica Sicurezza, Divisione Affari Generali e Riservati RSI, 1943-5, 4 April 1944.

100. Stanis Ruinas, *Pioggia sulla Repubblica* (Rome: Corso, 1946), 21-4.

101. Maria Grazia Ciani and Maria Ida Biggi, *La spiaggia. Il Teatro La Fenice* (Padua: Il Poligrafo, 2006), 65-6.

102. Ruinas, *Pioggia sulla Repubblica*, 70–1.
103. Ibid., 201–5, 218.
104. Roberto Cuppone, *Il Teatro Goldoni* (Padua: Il Poligrafo, 2010), 44–9.
105. Cesco Chinello and Giulio Bobbo, *La Breda. Da Ca' Littoria a Ca' Matteotti* (Padua: Il Poligrafo, 2006), 58–9.
106. Bobbo, *Venezia in tempo di guerra*, 448–53.
107. Ibid., 170–3.
108. Giannantonio Paladini and Maurizio Reberschak (eds), *La resistenza nel Veneziano: la società veneziana tra fascismo, resistenza, repubblica*, 2 vols (Venice: Istituto Veneto per la storia della Resistenza, 1985), vol. 1, 466.
109. *The Times*, 12 May 1945.
110. Maurizio Reberschak, 'Dichiarazioni d'intenti: sindaci e programmi nel dopoguerra a Venezia (1945–1951)', in Bruno Bertoli (ed.), *Chiesa, società e stato a Venezia: miscellanea di studi in onore di Silvio Tramontin* (Venice: Studium Cattolico Veneziano, 1994), 263.
111. Silvio Tramontin, *Giovanni Ponti (1896–1961): una vita per la democrazia e per Venezia* (Venice: Comune di Venezia, 1983), 33–8.
112. Reberschak, 'Dichiarazioni d'intenti: sindaci e programmi nel dopoguerra a Venezia (1945–1951)', 240–1.
113. Cerutti, *Memorie*, 156–9.
114. John Berendt, *The City of Falling Angels* (New York: Penguin, 2005), 82.
115. See AGG, busta 7, fasc. 53, 26 June 1956, Giuriati to Aulo Barozzi.
116. Giovanni Giuriati, *Una fama usurpata: la proporzionale* (Rome: Edizioni di abc, [1954]), 7.
117. Alessandro Reberschegg, 'La Corte straordinaria di Venezia', *Venetica*, 12 (1998), 136–7.
118. Bobbo, *Venezia in tempo di guerra*, 448.
119. Cerutti, *Memorie*, 161.
120. Reberschegg, 'La Corte straordinaria di Venezia', 136.
121. Marco Borghi and Alessandro Reberschegg, *Fascisti alla sbarra: l'attività della Corte d'Assise Straordinaria di Venezia, 1945–1947* (Venice: Istituto veneziano per la storia della Resistenza e della società contemporanea, 1999), 82.
122. Ibid., 84.
123. Franco, *Il liceo 'Raimondo Franchetti'*, 66–74.
124. *L'Ateneo Veneto*, January–June 1945, 38–9.
125. Marco Battain, 'In memoria di Giuseppe Jona', *L'Ateneo Veneto*, January–June 1945, 51–8; July–December 1945, 141.
126. Ciani and Biggi, *La spiaggia. Il Teatro La Fenice*, 67–8.
127. Peggy Guggenheim, *Out of This Century: Confessions of an Art Addict* (London: Deutsch, 1980), 325–33, 379–81.
128. Philip Ziegler, *Diana Cooper* (London: Hamish Hamilton, 1981), 272.
129. Maurizio Reberschak, 'Venezia, dopoguerra: tra storia e memoria', in Maurizio Reberschak (ed.), *Venezia nel secondo dopoguerra* (Padua: Il Poligrafo, 1993), 26.
130. Giovanni Distefano and Giannantonio Paladini, *Storia di Venezia, 1797–1997*, 3 vols (Venice Lido: Supernova, 1997), vol. 3, 142–3.
131. Cesco Chinello, *Classe, movimento, organizzazione: le lotte operaie a Marghera/Venezia: I percorsi di una crisi, 1945–55* (Milan: Franco Angeli, 1984), 29, 71.
132. Ibid., 86, 123–4.
133. Raffaele Vivante, *I pianterreni inabitabili di Venezia, l'abitato di Mestre: nuove indagini sulle condizioni igieniche delle abitazioni del Comune* (Venice: Fantoni, 1948), 7–9.
134. ACS, Ministero dell'Interno, Direzione Generale di Pubblica Sicurezza, Divisione Affari Generali e Riservati, 1947–50 (hereafter DAGR), 1947–8, busta 20, 4 May 1948, prefect to Ministry of the Interior.
135. Giovanni Vian, *'La Voce di San Marco' (1946–1975)* (Padua: Il Poligrafo, 2007), 24.
136. DAGR, 1949, busta 9, 29 April 1949, Gargiulo to Ministry of the Interior.
137. Antonio Niero, *I patriarchi di Venezia da Lorenzo Giustiniani ai nostri giorni* (Venice: Studium Cattolico Veneziano, 1961), 218–21.

138. Mirella Vedovetto, 'Breda, marzo 1950: l'intervento del sindaco Giobatta Gianquinto: le cronache di Gianni Rodari', *Quaderni di storiAmestre*, 1 (2005), 12. For an official account of its failure, see DAGR, 1947–8, busta 20, 4 August 1948, prefect to Ministry of the Interior.
139. DAGR, 1947–8, busta 20, 7 May 1948, prefect to Ministry of the Interior.
140. DAGR, 1947–8, busta 20, 30 October 1948, prefect to Ministry of the Interior.
141. DAGR, 1947–8, busta 20, 30 November 1948, prefect to Ministry of the Interior.
142. DAGR, 1947–8, busta 20, 2 June 1948, prefect to Ministry of the Interior.

Chapter Eight: The many deaths of Post-war Venice, 1948–1978

1. Lavinia Cavalletti, *La dinastia Stucky, 1841–1941: storia del Molino di Venezia e della famiglia da Manin a Mussolini* (Venice: Studio LTL, 2011), 151–9, 173, 179.
2. Ibid., 208–10, 250.
3. http://www3.hilton.com/en/hotels/italy/hilton-molino-stucky-venice-VCEHIHI/index. html (accessed 6 December 2012).
4. Laura Cerasi and Michele Casarin, *Marghera. Sant'Elena* (Padua: Il Poligrafo, 2007), 13.
5. Jane Da Mosto et al., *The Venice Report: Demography, Tourism, Financing and Change of Use of Buildings* (Cambridge University Press, 2009), 13.
6. *La Repubblica*, 25 August 2006.
7. See, for example, DAGR, 1949, busta 9, 29 January, 15 October 1949, Gargiulo to Ministry of the Interior.
8. DAGR, 1949, busta 9, 29 April, 29 May, 29 August 1949, Gargiulo to Ministry of the Interior.
9. *Il Gazzettino*, 7 May 1957.
10. DAGR, 1950, busta 14, 28 December 1950, prefect to Ministry of the Interior.
11. DAGR, 1949, busta 9, 29 April 1949, Gargiulo to Ministry of the Interior.
12. DAGR, 1949, busta 9, 29 October 1949, Gargiulo to Ministry of the Interior.
13. Maria Teresa Sega and Nadia Maria Filippini, *Manifattura Tabacchi. Cotonificio Veneziano* (Padua: Il Poligrafo, 2008), 138–40.
14. *Il Gazzettino*, 2 March 1957.
15. *Il Gazzettino*, 1 March 1957.
16. Luciano Pes, 'Gli ultimi quarant'anni', in Mario Isnenghi and Stuart Woolf (eds), *Storia di Venezia: l'Ottocento e il Novecento* (Rome: Istituto dell'Enciclopedia Italiana, 2002), 2420.
17. Cesco Chinello and Giulio Bobbo, *La Breda. Da Ca' Littoria a Ca' Matteotti* (Padua: Il Poligrafo, 2006), 1.
18. Mirella Vedovetto, 'Breda, marzo 1950: l'intervento del sindaco Giobatta Gianquinto: le cronache di Gianni Rodari', *Quaderni di storiAmestre*, 1 (2005), 8.
19. Cesco Chinello, *Classe, movimento, organizzazione: le lotte operaie a Marghera/Venezia: i percorsi di una crisi, 1945–55* (Milan: Franco Angeli, 1984), 212, 241.
20. Ibid., 247–8.
21. Vedovetto, 'Breda, marzo 1950', 13.
22. DAGR, 1950, busta 14, 30 March, 28 April 1950, prefect to Ministry of the Interior.
23. Vedovetto, 'Breda, marzo 1950', 18.
24. Chinello, *Classe, movimento, organizzazione*, 284, 311.
25. Maurizio Reberschak, 'Venezia, dopoguerra tra storia e memoria', in Maurizio Reberschak (ed.), *Venezia nel secondo dopoguerra* (Padua: Il Poligrafo, 1993), 16. For a detailed story of worker politics over these decades, see Cesco Chinello, *Sindacato, Pci, movimenti negli anni sessanta: Porto Marghera–Venezia, 1955–1970*, 2 vols (Milan: Franco Angeli, 1996).
26. Fabrizio Fabbri, *Porto Marghera e la laguna di Venezia: vita, morte, miracoli* (Milan: Jaca Book, 2003), 43–4. The idea had been approved by *Il Gazzettino* as early as 1957. See the issue of 17 May.
27. Omar Favaro, 'Un cardellino in gabbia: fabbrica e lavoro nei primi anni Cinquanta a Porto Marghera', *Quaderni di storiAmestre*, 8 (2008), 13–15.

28. Chinello, *Sindacato, Pci, movimenti negli anni sessanta*, 113.
29. Gilda Zazzara, *Il Petrolchimico* (Padua: Il Poligrafo, 2009), 14–17.
30. Chinello, *Classe, movimento, organizzazione*, 439.
31. 'Una indagine campione sull'edilizia veneziana', *Rivista di Venezia*, n.s., 3, November–December 1957, has fuller detail. Cf. Leopoldo Pietragnoli and Maurizio Reberschak, 'Dalla ricostruzione al problema di Venezia', in Isnenghi and Woolf (eds), *Storia di Venezia: l'Ottocento e il Novecento*, 2245; Pes, 'Gli ultimi quarant'anni', 2410.
32. Margaret Plant, *Venice: Fragile City, 1797–1997* (New Haven and London: Yale University Press, 2002), has a useful English-language introduction to the cultural life of the post-Fascist city (after a notably garbled account of the Resistance; see 311–12).
33. DAGR, 1950, busta 14, 28 June, 29 July, 29 August 1950, prefect to Ministry of the Interior.
34. DAGR, 1950, busta 14, 28 June, 28 September 1950, prefect to Ministry of the Interior.
35. DAGR, 1950, busta 14, 29 October 1950, prefect to Ministry of the Interior.
36. DAGR, 1949, busta 9, 15 October 1949, Gargiulo to Ministry of the Interior.
37. http://www.aguideinvenice.com/en/venice-case-8-Report-on-tourism-in-Venice-December-2008.html (accessed 7 March 2013).
38. Maria Gabriella Dri, 'La società veneziana', in Reberschak (ed.), *Venezia nel secondo dopoguerra*, 45.
39. Luisa Bellina and Michele Gottardi, *Osterie. Il Venezia* (Padua: Il Poligrafo, 2006), 88.
40. Judith Martin, *No Vulgar Hotel: The Desire and Pursuit of Venice* (New York: W. W. Norton, 2007), 83.
41. Antonio Foscari, *Tumult and Order: Malcontenta, 1924–1939* (Zurich: Lars Müller, 2012), 200.
42. Nigel Dempster, *H.R.H. the Princess Margaret: A Life Unfulfilled* (London: Quartet, 1983), 59; Tim Heald, *Princess Margaret: A Life Unravelled* (London: Weidenfeld and Nicolson, 2007), 51–2.
43. Cecil Beaton, *Self-Portrait with Friends: The Selected Diaries of Cecil Beaton, 1926–1974* (London: Pimlico, 1979), 343–4. For a newsreel report of Countess Volpi's ball in 1952, see http://www.britishpathe.com/video/countess-volpi-ball (accessed 3 March 2013).
44. *The Times*, 5, 6, 7 January 1966. Cf. *Il Gazzettino*, 11 October 1966, on their 'zoo-ophile' intent.
45. *The Times*, 14 October 1971, 30 September 1975.
46. *The Times*, 23 August 1951.
47. *The Times*, 7 September 1949.
48. Nino Barbantini, *La fondazione Giorgio Cini nell'isola di S. Giorgio Maggiore* (Venice: C. Ferrari, 1951), 9.
49. Ibid., 16–20.
50. Sandro Meccoli, *Viva Venezia* (Milan: Longanesi, 1985), 17.
51. *The Times*, 14 July 1954.
52. Peter Hebblethwaite, *John XXIII: Pope of the Council* (London: G. Chapman, 1984), 287.
53. Silvio Tramontin, 'Il Cardinale Roncalli a Venezia', in Vittore Branca and Stefano Rosso-Mazzinghi (eds), *Angelo Giuseppe Roncalli dal patriarcato di Venezia alla cattedra di San Pietro* (Florence: Olschki, 1984), 38.
54. Vittore Branca, 'Angelo Giuseppe Roncalli per la cultura e nella cultura all'UNESCO e alla Fondazione Giorgio Cini', in ibid., 11.
55. Loris Francesco Capovilla (ed.), *Giovanni e Paolo, due Papi: saggio di corrispondenza (1925–1962)* (Rome: Studium, 1982), 63–4.
56. Antonio Niero, *I patriarchi di Venezia da Lorenzo Giustiniani ai nostri giorni* (Venice: Studium Cattolico Veneziano, 1961), 225.
57. Giancarlo Zizola, *The Utopia of Pope John XXIII* (Maryknoll, NY: Orbis, 1978), 216–17.
58. Ferruccio Carli, *Pio X e il suo tempo* (Florence: Adriano Salani, 1941), 232.
59. Zizola, *The Utopia of Pope John XXIII*, 321; Marco Roncalli, *Giovanni XXIII: la mia Venezia* (Venice: Canal e Stamperia, 2000), 84–5.
60. http://www.gesulavoratore.it/index.php?p=include/parrocchie (accessed 7 March 2013).

61. Giuseppe Alberigo, *Papa Giovanni (1881–1963)* (Bologna: Edizioni Dehoniane, 2000), 124.
62. *Il Gazzettino*, 14, 28 April 1959.
63. *Il Gazzettino*, 1 April 1959.
64. *Il Gazzettino*, 22 April 1959.
65. *Il Gazzettino*, 10 May 1959.
66. See generally *San Pio X a Venezia: celebrazioni e documenti, domenica 12 aprile–domenica 10 maggio 1959* ([Vatican City]: n.p., 1959).
67. Eugenio Bacchion, 'Due pontefici: Pio XII–Giovanni XXIII', *L'Ateneo Veneto*, July–December 1958, 11–20.
68. Antonio Niero, 'La questione dei plutei della Basilica di San Marco (documenti di un episodio tra pietà e liturgia)', in Branca and Rosso-Mazzinghi (eds), *Angelo Giuseppe Roncalli*, 105–6.
69. *Il Gazzettino*, 20 April 1957.
70. Niero, 'La questione dei plutei della Basilica di San Marco', 108–30.
71. Alberigo, *Papa Giovanni*, 115.
72. Zizola, *The Utopia of Pope John XXIII*, 220–1.
73. Wladimiro Dorigo, 'Introduzione al Piano di Venezia', *Rivista di Venezia*, n.s., 3, November–December 1957, 30–9.
74. Zizola, *The Utopia of Pope John XXIII*, 214.
75. See, for example, Giuseppe Samonà, 'Sacca Fisola: criterio per i nuovi quartieri', *Rivista di Venezia*, n.s., 3, November–December 1957, 51–61.
76. For the plan, see Plant, *Venice: Fragile City*, 349–51.
77. *The Times*, 23 April 1954. See also, for example, 16 October 1953, letter from Peter Quennell.
78. Foscari, *Tumult and Order*, 146.
79. For an introduction to Scarpa's work, see Richard Murphy, *Querini Stampalia Foundation: Carlo Scarpa* (London: Phaidon, 1993); Francesco Dal Co and Giuseppe Mazzariol (eds), *Carlo Scarpa: The Complete Works* (London: Electa, 1986). Visitors today can take a special tour of recent city buildings. See http://www.aguideinvenice. com/en/venice-itineraries–21-Contemporary-Architecture-in-Venice.html   (accessed 10 March 2013).
80. See   http://www.cislveneto.it/Rassegna-stampa-Veneto/Crolla-il-soffitto-negli-uffici-dell-.Enel.-E-accaduto-nella-sede-di-Rio-Novo-quando-i-dipendenti-non-erano-in-servizio (accessed 10 March 2013).
81. *Italia Nostra*, January–February 1961.
82. *Italia Nostra*, January–February 1964; Teresa Foscari Foscolo, 'La laguna di Venezia e le sue pertinenze demaniali non si toccano', *Italia Nostra*, March–April 1966; Ennio Gallo, 'Nuove minacce alla laguna di Venezia: strade "traslagunari"', *Italia Nostra*, May–June 1966.
83. *Italia Nostra*, special issue (*'Italia Nostra' difende Venezia*), [1956].
84. *Italia Nostra*, October–December 1962; *The Times*, 10 December 1962.
85. *Italia Nostra*, March–April 1962.
86. See, for example, Silvio Polli, 'I problemi di Venezia: sullo sprofondamento e sul fenomeno dell'acqua alta', *L'Ateneo Veneto*, July–December 1963, 1–10.
87. See, for example, *Il Gazzettino*, 5, 6, 7, 8 October 1966.
88. Alberto Toniolo, 'Ampliamento e sviluppo del porto di Venezia', *Italia Nostra*, March–May 1963.
89. Wladimiro Dorigo, 'I problemi di Venezia: il futuro assetto della vita culturale', *L'Ateneo Veneto*, July–December 1964.
90. Giorgio Bellavitis, 'La nuova sede della Cassa di Risparmio di Venezia', *Italia Nostra*, May–June 1966; Teresa Foscari Foscolo, 'Illegittima la licenza per la nuova sede della Cassa di Risparmio di Venezia?', *Italia Nostra*, May–June 1969.
91. See, for example, the special issue of *L'Ateneo Veneto*, 1966.
92. *Il Gazzettino*, 30 October 1966.
93. *Il Gazzettino*, 4 November 1966.

94. Giulio Obici, *Venice, How Long?* (Padua: Marsilio, 1967), 9.
95. *Il Gazzettino*, 3 November 1991.
96. Roberto Bianchin, *Acqua granda: il romanzo dell'alluvione* (Venice: Filippi, 1996), 52.
97. *Il Gazzettino*, 6 November 1966.
98. Obici, *Venice, How Long?*, 11–13. Cf. *Il Gazzettino*, 6 November 1966; the paper noted that four had died in the city and a further fifty-six in the province.
99. *Il Gazzettino*, 9, 11 November 1966.
100. *Il Gazzettino*, 6 November 1966.
101. Daniele Ceschin and Anna Scannapieco, *L'Archivio dei Frari. La Casa di Goldoni* (Padua: Il Poligrafo, 2005), 35.
102. *Il Gazzettino*, 11 November 1966. Cf. Piero Nardi, 'L'acqua alta a Venezia', *Nuova Antologia*, fasc. 1993, January 1967, 12.
103. *The Times*, 7, 9 November 1966.
104. *Il Gazzettino*, 8 November 1966.
105. FO, 371/189354/1701/2, 6 November 1966, J. Ward to the Foreign Office; *The Times*, 9 November 1966.
106. FO, 371/189354/1701/24, 15 December 1966, C. P. Scott (chargé in Rome) to the Foreign Office.
107. *Italia Nostra*, November–December 1966, editorial and Adalberto Minuzzi, 'Difendiamo Venezia dall'assalto del mare'.
108. Rotary Club di Venezia, *I problemi di Venezia/The Problems of Venice, 1960–1970* (Venice: Tipografia Commerciale, [1970]).
109. Vittorio Cini, 'Giuseppe Volpi e il cinquantennio di Porto Marghera', *L'Ateneo Veneto*, January–December 1967, 35–44.
110. Cini died on 18 September 1977, his fans mourning the closure of 'the last Renaissance house in Venice operating on the offer of hospitality "urbi et orbi"'. Meccoli, *Viva Venezia*, 11.
111. *The Times*, 10 November 1966.
112. See Ronald Shaw-Kennedy, *Art and Architecture in Venice: The Venice in Peril Guide* (London: Sidgwick and Jackson, 1972). It has a preface by Norwich. For the organisation's ongoing activities, see http://www.veniceinperil.org/projects (accessed 7 December 2013).
113. *The Times*, 21 January 1971.
114. *Italia Nostra*, January–February 1967.
115. UNESCO, *Rapporto su Venezia* (Milan: Mondadori, 1969).
116. Ennio Gallo, 'Continua la deturpazione della laguna di Venezia', *Italia Nostra*, May–June 1967.
117. *Italia Nostra*, July–August 1967.
118. Teresa Foscari Foscolo, 'Per salvaguardare la laguna di Venezia è necessario definirne lo status giuridico', *Italia Nostra*, March–April 1968.
119. Speech published in *Italia Nostra*, November–December 1970.
120. *Italia Nostra*, January 1971.
121. Giannandrea Mencini, *Il fronte per la difesa di Venezia e della laguna e le denunce di Indro Montanelli* (Venice Lido: Supernova, 2005), 21–4, 41–5.
122. Ibid., 23, 57.
123. Indro Montanelli, *Per Venezia*, ed. Nevio Casadio (Venice: Marsilio, 2010), 21, 25, 28. This republication includes a CD of the RAI TV programme of 1969.
124. Luigi Urettini, *Bruno Visentini* (Sommacampagna (VR): Cierre, 2005), 143.
125. Ibid., 126.
126. The volumes relevant to this book are Isnenghi and Woolf (eds), *Storia di Venezia: l'Ottocento e il Novecento*.
127. Bruno Visentini, 'La Fondazione Cini e la cultura italiana nel momento attuale', *Nuova Antologia*, fasc. 2115–17, March–May 1977, 492–3.
128. *Italia Nostra*, November–December 1970.
129. Wladimiro Dorigo, *Una laguna di chiacchiere: note a margine a 'tutto Montanelli a Venezia'* (Venice: n.p., 1972), 5–6.

130. Wladimiro Dorigo, *Battaglie urbanistiche: la pianificazione del territorio a Venezia e in Italia fra politica e cultura* (Sommacampagna (VR): Cierre, 2007), 352.

131. Guglielmo Zanelli, *Traghetti veneziani: la gondola al servizio della città* (Venice: Cicero, 2004), 35.

132. Eugenio Miozzi, *Venezia nei secoli: la città*, 2 vols (Venice: Libeccio, 1957). After the flood, he added another two volumes, with a similar but more urgent message: *Venezia nei secoli: la laguna* (Venice: Libeccio, 1968) and *Venezia nei secoli: il salvamento* (Venice: Libeccio, 1969).

133. Eugenio Miozzi, 'La verità sugli sprofondamenti di Venezia', *L'Ateneo Veneto*, January–December 1970, 109–20.

134. Eugenio Miozzi, 'Lo spopolamento di Venezia: cause e rimedi', *L'Ateneo Veneto*, January–December 1971, 277–86.

135. *Italia Nostra*, January 1972, editorial; see also 13, July–August 1971, editorial.

136. See, for example, *Italia Nostra*, August–September 1973. For a sustained foreign attack in *The Sunday Times*, see Stephen Fay and Phillip Knightley, *The Death of Venice* (London: Deutsch, 1976).

137. Zazzara, *Il Petrolchimico*, 27–8.

138. Ibid., 34–40.

139. Mario Moretti, *Brigate rosse: una storia italiana* (Milan: Mondadori, 2007), 58.

140. Zazzara, *Il Petrolchimico*, 64–8.

141. Ibid., 55–60.

142. Ignazio Musu, 'Venezia e la sua laguna: un problema di sviluppo sostenibile locale', in Ignazio Musu (ed.), *Venezia sostenibile: suggestioni dal futuro* (Bologna: Il Mulino, 1998), 18.

143. See http://informazioneveneta.blogspot.co.uk/2009/04/chiude-il-polo-industriale-di-marghera.html (accessed 13 March 2013).

144. Carlo Franco, *Il liceo 'Raimondo Franchetti'* (Padua: Il Poligrafo, 2010), 81.

145. Zazzara, *Il Petrolchimico*, 40.

146. Franco, *Il liceo 'Raimondo Franchetti'*, 98, 106–7.

147. Giovanni Distefano and Giannantonio Paladini, *Storia di Venezia, 1797–1997*, 3 vols (Venice Lido: Supernova, 1997), vol. 3, 194–7.

148. Chinello, *Sindacato, Pci, movimenti negli anni sessanta*, 573.

149. *The Times*, 19, 20, 22 June 1968.

150. Lawrence Alloway, *The Venice Biennale, 1895–1968: From Salon to Goldfish Bowl* (London: Faber and Faber, 1969), 24–6.

151. *The Times*, 8 August 1968.

152. Biennale di Venezia, *Spagna, 1936–1939: fotografie e informazione di guerra* (Venice: Marsilio, 1976).

153. See David Yallop, *In God's Name* (New York: Bantam, 1984).

154. Albino Luciani, *Illustrissimo: lettere al Patriarca* (Padua: Messaggero, 1976), 11–17, 31–7, 64, 113–18, 224, 283, 326–8.

155. For examples of Luciani's educational writings, see Albino Luciani, *Scuola di vita: antologie di testi sull'educazione*, ed. Natalino Bonazza (Venice: Marcianum, 2005).

Chapter Nine: Death postponed through globalised rebirth (and mass tourism)?

1. http://www.sanclementepalacevenice.com/it/ (accessed 18 March 2013).

2. Giovanna Cecconello, Carlo Giuliani and Michele Sgobba, *San Clemente: progetto per un'isola* (Venice: Cluva, 1980), 11–38.

3. Wiebke Willms, *San Clemente: storia di un'isola veneziana, uno dei primi manicomi femminili in Europa* (Venice: Centro Tedesco di Studi Veneziani, 1993), 23–4.

4. D. Casagrande, 'Cento anni di una istituzione manicomiale: problemi di riabilitazione e risocializzazione', in Cecconello, Giuliani and Sgobba, *San Clemente*, 51–4.

5. Willms, *San Clemente*, 24.

6. For her story, see Marco Zeni, *La moglie di Mussolini* (Trento: Effe e Erre, 2005).

7. Eugenio Miozzi, *Venezia nei secoli: la laguna* (Venice: Libeccio, 1968), 234–9.

8. For background, see Richard F. Mollica, 'From Antonio Gramsci to Franco Basaglia: The Theory and Practice of the Italian Psychiatric Reform', *International Journal of Mental Health*, 14 (1985), 22–41.

9. Nelli-Elena Vanzan Marchini, *San Servolo e Venezia: un'isola e la sua storia* (Sommacampagna (VR): Cierre, 2004), 131.

10. Lucio Strumendo, 'Premessa', in Mario Galzigna and Hrayr Terzian (eds), *L'Archivio della follia: il manicomio di San Servolo e la nascita di una fondazione: antologia di testi e documenti* (Venice: Marsilio, 1980), 9.

11. http://www.unive.it/nqcontent.cfm?a_id=44885 (accessed 18 March 2013). Cf. Venice International University, *Rapporto sulle attività/Report on Activities* (n.p., 2012).

12. For an account of stereotypes of Venice as a topic for advertisers, see Margaret Plant, *Venice: Fragile City, 1797–1997* (New Haven and London: Yale University Press, 2002), 419. She notes pigeons eating 'well-placed corn' letters that marked out the name 'Coca Cola' in the square.

13. Iain Fenlon, *Piazza San Marco* (London: Profile, 2010), 170–7.

14. *New York Times*, 13 September 2010.

15. *Il Gazzettino*, 14 September 2006.

16. *Il Gazzettino*, 15 September 2006.

17. Thomas F. Madden, *Venice: A New History* (New York: Viking, 2012), 6, 52, 279, 302.

18. Ibid., 340–1.

19. Ibid., 408. Madden omitted Cini entirely from his book and made only passing reference to Volpi (404–5), defining the latter as 'a brilliant businessman and native Venetian'. So, 'with a champion like Count Volpi, Venice prospered under Fascist management'.

20. *Il Gazzettino*, 6 April 1978.

21. *Il Gazzettino*, 15 May 1978.

22. *Il Gazzettino*, 17 May 1978.

23. *Il Gazzettino*, 20, 22 May 1978.

24. *Il Gazzettino*, 19 May 1978.

25. Giannandrea Mencini, *Venezia acqua e fuoco: la politica della 'salvaguardia' dall'alluvione del 1966 al rogo della Fenice* (Venice: Il Cardo, 1996), 54. Cf. *Il Gazzettino*, 10 March 1985.

26. Cesco Chinello, *Un barbaro veneziano: mezzo secolo da comunista* (Padua: Il Poligrafo, 2008), 142.

27. *Il Gazzettino*, 17 March 1985.

28. *Il Gazzettino*, 23 March 1985.

29. *Il Gazzettino*, 8 May 1985.

30. John Berendt, *The City of Falling Angels* (New York: Penguin, 2005), 207.

31. Mencini, *Venezia acqua e fuoco*, 68.

32. Stefano Boato, *Tessera City* (Venice: Corte del Fontego, 2011), 16.

33. *Il Gazzettino*, 10 September 2006.

34. Gianni De Michelis, *La lunga ombra di Yalta: la specificità della politica italiana: conversazione con Francesco Kostner* (Venice: Marsilio, 2003), 10.

35. Gianni De Michelis, *Dove andiamo a ballare questa sera? Guida a 250 discoteche italiane* (Milan: Mondadori, 1988), 135–67.

36. *Il Gazzettino*, 3, 4, 5, 6 May 1985. She did smile, the press reported, after her young sons flew in from London.

37. *Il Gazzettino*, 16 June 1985.

38. *Il Gazzettino*, 17 June 1985.

39. *Il Gazzettino*, 18 June 1985.

40. For a gentle exposure of the invention of tradition involved, see Silvio Tramontin, 'Il Redentore, il voto, il tempio, la festa', *L'Ateneo Veneto*, 1993.

41. *Il Gazzettino*, 6 July 1989.

42. *Il Gazzettino*, 8 July 1989.

43. *Il Gazzettino*, 15 July 1989.

44. *Il Gazzettino*, 9 July 1989.

45. *Il Gazzettino*, 11, 12 July 1989.

46. *Il Gazzettino*, 13 July 1989.
47. *Il Gazzettino*, 14 July 1989.
48. *Il Gazzettino*, 17 July 1989.
49. *Il Gazzettino*, 15 July 1989.
50. *Il Gazzettino*, 16, 17 July 1989.
51. *Il Gazzettino*, 18 July 1989.
52. *Il Gazzettino*, 17 July 1989.
53. Mencini, *Venezia acqua e fuoco*, 73–4.
54. *Il Gazzetttino*, 18, 19 July 1989.
55. *Il Gazzettino*, 20 July 1989.
56. *Il Gazzettino*, 11 November 1991.
57. *Il Gazzettino*, 14 November 1991.
58. *Il Gazzettino*, 3 November 1991.
59. Giuseppe De Rita, *Una città speciale: rapporto su Venezia* (Venice: Marsilio, 1993), 1–12. For a more general statement of his view that Italy was a country lacking a proper, productive bourgeoisie, see his *Intervista sulla borghesia in Italia*, ed. Antonio Galdo (Bari: Laterza, 1996).
60. De Rita, *Una città speciale*, 13, 18, 54.
61. Sophie Bowness and Clive Phillpot, *Britain at the Venice Biennale, 1895–1995* (London: The British Council, 1995), 9. Lavish commemorative volumes were inevitably published, notably Biennale di Venezia, *Le Esposizioni internazionali d'arte 1895–1995: artisti, mostre, partecipazioni nazionali, premi* (Venice: Electa, 1996).
62. Jean Clair in Biennale di Venezia, *46o Esposizione internazionale d'arte: Identity and Alterity: Figures of the body, 1895–1995* (Venice: Marsilio, 1995), unnumbered pages.
63. Giuseppe De Rita, 'Un progettista imprenditore per Venezia', in Aldo Bonomi (ed.), *Privatizzare Venezia: il progettista imprenditoriale* (Venice: Marsilio, 1995), 26.
64. Giovanni Cantagalli, 'Benetton Group', in ibid., 54–5.
65. Paola Somma, *Benettown: un ventennio di mecenatismo* (Venice: Corte del Fontego, 2011), 15.
66. Massimo Cacciari, 'Azione pubblica e azione privata per Venezia', in Bonomi (ed.), *Privatizzare Venezia*, 31–4. Cf., by contrast, his preface to Anna Renzini (ed.), *Nuove politiche per la residenza: ruolo e scelta del Comune in un quadro normativo rinnovato a livello nazionale* (Venice: Comune di Venezia, [1997]), 10, in which he was still fully convinced of the need for the Comune to back modern housing in the city.
67. There had been discussion of the problem for many years as part of a general debate about the pollution of the lagoon and other waters. See, notably, Giampietro Zucchetta, 'L'inquinamento della laguna di Venezia', *L'Ateneo Veneto*, 1983, 5–44; Giampietro Zucchetta, 'Determinazione dei metalli presenti nei sediment di canali e rii di Venezia', 91–109. See also G. Socal, 'Eutrofizzazione. Laguna veneta/Scarichi e approfondimento di canali fanno "fiorire" le alghe', *Italia Nostra*, July–August 1983.
68. *Il Gazzettino*, 30 January 1996.
69. *Il Gazzettino*, 30, 31 January 1996.
70. *Il Gazzettino*, 10 February 1996.
71. *Il Gazzettino*, 1 February 1996.
72. See Adalberto Signore and Alessandro Troncino, *Razza padana* (Milan: BUR, 2008), 39–49.
73. *Il Gazzettino*, 14, 16 September 1996.
74. *Il Gazzettino*, 17, 18 September 2006.
75. Francesco Jori, *Dalla Liga alla Lega: storia, movimento, protagonisti* (Venice: Marsilio, 2007), 43–5.
76. Ibid., ix.
77. Signore and Troncino, *Razza padana*, 87.
78. Jori, *Dalla Liga alla Lega*, 142–3.
79. *La Repubblica*, 26 February 2013.
80. Jori, *Dalla Liga alla Lega*, 144.
81. *La Nuova Venezia*, 29 March 2013.

82. *La Nuova Venezia*, 23 March 2014.

83. *Il Gazzettino*, 6 May 1997.

84. *Il Gazzettino*, 7, 8 May 1997.

85. Mario Isnenghi, 'Fine della Storia?', in Stefano Gasparri, Giovanni Levi and Pierandrea Moro (eds), *Venezia: itinerari per la storia della città* (Bologna: Il Mulino, 1997), 432.

86. Massimo Cacciari and Carlo Maria Martini, *Dialogo sulla solidarietà* (Rome: Lavoro, 1997), 4–5, 13–15, 45, 58.

87. Signore and Troncino, *Razza padana*, 106.

88. *Il Gazzettino*, 9, 10 May 1997.

89. *Il Gazzettino*, 9 May 1997.

90. *Il Gazzettino*, 10 May 1997.

91. Jori, *Dalla Liga alla Lega*, 110–11.

92. *Il Gazzettino*, 12 July 1997.

93. Laura Cerasi, *Perdonare Marghera: la città del lavoro nella memoria post-industriale* (Milan: Franco Angeli, 2007), 15–16, 107.

94. Fabrizio Fabbri, *Porto Marghera e la laguna di Venezia: vita, morte, miracoli* (Milan: Jaca Book, 2003), 157. See also a local report of Dioxin in fish and mussel stocks, *Il Gazzettino*, 4 September 1996.

95. Franco Mancuso, *Fronte del porto: Porto Marghera: la vicenda urbanistica* (Venice: Corte del Fontego, 2011), 31.

96. *La Nuova Venezia*, 28 March 2013.

97. Cerasi, *Perdonare Marghera*, 83. See also the moving photographic collection Gianfranco Bettin et al., *Venezia/Marghera/Mestre e ritorno: un viaggio quotidiano* (Venice: Marsilio, 2005).

98. For evidence of bickering among rich Americans, see Berendt, *The City of Falling Angels*.

99. Caroline A. Fletcher and Tom Spencer (eds), *Flooding and Environmental Challenges for Venice and Its Lagoon: State of Knowledge* (Cambridge University Press, 2005), xxiii. This book is an example of the admirably extensive research being directed at Venice and its lagoon.

100. Giovanni Distefano and Giannantonio Paladini, *Storia di Venezia, 1797–1997*, 3 vols (Venice Lido: Supernova, 1997), 209.

101. Alberto Vitucci, *Nel nome di Venezia: grandi opere e soliti nomi* (Venice: Corte del Fontego, 2012), 5–6.

102. Mencini, *Venezia acqua e fuoco*, 37, 91, 101.

103. For a critic, see Paolo Barbaro, *Venezia: l'anno del mare felice* (Bologna: Il Mulino, 1995), 76–9.

104. Mencini, *Venezia acqua e fuoco*, 65.

105. Edoardo Salzano, *La laguna di Venezia: il governo di un sistema complesso* (Venice: Corte del Fontego, 2011), 26–7, 31.

106. *Il Gazzettino*, 7 September 2006.

107. See http://www.lastampa.it/2013/10/12/italia/cronache/venezia-il-mose-degli-scandali-al-battesimo-dellacqua-alta-S7aBGGFDMDn6Vvp5jybjQI/pagina.html (accessed 11 December 2013).

108. Vitucci, *Nel nome di Venezia*, 14–17, 25–6.

109. *Leo*, August–October 2000.

110. Somma, *Benettown*, 5.

111. Ibid., 29.

112. Vitucci, *Nel nome di Venezia*, 31.

113. Donatella Calabi and Paolo Morchiello, *Il fontego dei Tedeschi: 'una piccola città in mezzo alla nostra'* (Venice: Corte del Fontego, 2012), 31–2.

114. Nelli-Elena Vanzan Marchini, *Il ponte di debole costituzione* (Venice: Corte del Fontego, 2011).

115. Paola Somma, *Imbonimenti: laguna, terra di conquista* (Venice: Corte del Fontego, 2012), 14–15.

116. Ibid., 17 (for an image of such a future, see 18–19).

117. Collegio degli ingegneri della provincia di Venezia, *Venezia: metropoli in cammino verso l'Europa* (Venice: Cartotecnica Veneziana, 1999), 7, 13–14.
118. Somma, *Imbonimenti*, 23–4.
119. *La Nuova Venezia*, 29 March 2013.
120. Mauro Cesco-Frare, 'La metropolitana a Venezia', *L'Ateneo Veneto*, January–June 1966, 123–5. Cf., later, Gianni Fabbri, *Venezia: quale modernità: idee per una città capitale* (Milan: Franco Angeli, 2005), 42–3. Fabbri was republishing essays that went back to the 1980s.
121. Giorgio Suppiej, 'L'autonomia amministrativa di Venezia e di Mestre: problema o pseudoproblema?', *L'Ateneo Veneto*, 1979, 29–35. For a critique, cf. Gianni Milner, 'A proposito di Venezia', *Italia Nostra*, December 1980.
122. Edoardo Salzano, *Lo scandalo del Lido: cultura e affari, turismo e cemento nell'isola di Aschenbach* (Venice: Corte del Fontego, 2011); cf. *Il Gazzettino*, 27 March 2013.
123. See Mario Dalla Costa, 'L'Arsenale di Venezia: osservazioni e proposte', *L'Ateneo Veneto*, 1987, 181–94.
124. See http://www.arsenaledivenezia.it/main/Default.aspx?page=128 (accessed 14 May 2013).
125. See Romano Chirivi, *L'Arsenale di Venezia: storia e obiettivi di un piano* (Venice: Marsilio, 1976), 11. The book came with an endorsing preface by Gianni De Michelis.
126. *Il Gazzettino*, 24 September 2006.
127. *La Nuova Venezia*, 5 April 2013.
128. Giannantonio Paladini, *Uscire dall'isola: Venezia, risparmio privato e pubblica utilità, 1822–2002* (Bari: Laterza, 2003), 213.
129. *La Nuova Venezia*, 30 October 2013. Cf. http://news.yahoo.com/controversial-bid-turn-venice-rubbish-island-fun-park–174525062.html;_ylt=A2KJ3CYFaHFS7xwAs PrQtDMD (accessed 1 November 2013).
130. Joanne M. Ferraro, *Venice: History of the Floating City* (Cambridge University Press, 2012), 213–14.
131. Polly Coles, *The Politics of Washing: Real Life in Venice* (London: Robert Hale, 2013), 15.
132. For an early such effort, see Pino Correnti, *Il Carnevale di Venezia* (Milan: Ecotour, 1968), 79.
133. Enrico Tantucci, *A che ora chiude Venezia? Breve guida alla disneylandizzazione della città* (Venice: Corte del Fontego, 2011), 7.
134. Isabella Scaramuzzi, 'L'offerta ospitale: caratteri strutturali e indicatori di qualità di luoghi', in Giuseppina Di Monte and Isabella Scaramuzzi (eds), *Una provincia ospitale: itinerari di ricerca sul sistema turistico veneziano* (Bologna: Il Mulino, 1996), 24.
135. Giuseppina Di Monte and Isabella Scaramuzzi, 'Gli ospiti della capitale: pernottanti ed escursionisti', in ibid., 179–80.
136. *Il Gazzettino*, 27 September 2006.
137. Paolo Lanapoppi, *Dear Tourist* (Venice: Corte del Fontego, 2012), 16–22, 28, 32.
138. Silvio Testa, *E le chiamano navi: il crocierismo fa boom in Laguna* (Venice: Corte del Fontego, 2011), 5–6.
139. Giannandrea Mencini, *Fermare l'onda: la secolare battaglia contro il moto ondoso* (Venice: Corte del Fontego, 2011), 35.
140. *La Repubblica*, 5 November 2013.
141. *Il Gazzettino*, 1 September 2006.
142. Bettin et al., *Venezia/Marghera/Mestre e ritorno*, 8.
143. An exception is the popular but usually anodyne crime writer Donna Leon. See her *Blood from a Stone* (London: Penguin, 2005).
144. *Il Gazzettino*, 6 September 2006.
145. *Il Gazzettino*, 29 September 2006.
146. *La Nuova Venezia*, 21 March 2013.
147. Ferdinando Sigona, 'Ethnography of the "Gypsy Problem" in Italy: The Case of Kosovo Roma and Ashkali in Florence and Venice' (unpublished Ph.D. thesis, Oxford Brookes University, 2009), 11.

148. For a general survey, see Stefania Bragato and Luciano Menetto (eds), *E per patria una lingua segreta: rom e sinti in provincia di Venezia* (Venice: Nuova Dimensione, 2007).
149. See, for example, *La Nuova Venezia*, 17, 31 May 2008, 20 March 2013.
150. Sigona, 'Ethnography of the "Gypsy Problem" in Italy', 222.
151. Robert C. Davis and Garry R. Marvin, *Venice, the Tourist Maze: A Cultural Critique of the World's Most Touristed City* (Berkeley: University of California Press, 2004), 58.
152. Suzanne H. Crowhurst Lennard, *The Venetian Campo: Ideal Setting for Social Life and Community* (Venice: Corte del Fontego, 2012), 13.

Conclusion

1. Robert C. Davis and Garry R. Marvin, *Venice, the Tourist Maze: A Cultural Critique of the World's Most Touristed City* (Berkeley: University of California Press, 2004), 2–4, 68.
2. Giorgio Agamben, *Dell'utilità e degli inconvenienti del vivere fra spettri* (Venice: Corte del Fontego, 2011), 5–9, 13.
3. See in this regard the play *Scenes from an Execution* (1990) by the British playwright Howard Barker, which was given a major revival in London in 2012. The play probes the meanings and representations of the Christian and Venetian victory at Lepanto in 1571.

Bibliography

Archival sources

Archivio Centrale dello Stato, Rome (ACS)

Carte Volpi
Fondo Agostino D'Adamo
Ministero dell'Interno, Direzione Generale della Sanità Pubblica, Atti amministrativi, 1882–1915
Ministero dell'Interno, Direzione Generale di Pubblica Sicurezza, Divisione Affari Generali e Riservati RSI, 1943–5
Ministero dell'Interno, Direzione Generale di Pubblica Sicurezza, Divisione Affari Generali e Riservati, 1947–50 (DAGR)
Ministero dell'Interno, Direzione Generale di Pubblica Sicurezza, Divisione Affari Generali e Riservati, Segreteria del Capo della Polizia, 1940–3 (SCP)
Ministero dell'Interno, Direzione Generale di Pubblica Sicurezza, Divisione Affari Generali e Riservati, Segreteria del Capo della Polizia RSI, 1943–5 (SCP RSI)
Ministero dell'Interno, Direzione Generale di Pubblica Sicurezza, Divisione Polizia Politica, 1927–44 (DPP)
Ministero dell'Interno, Direzione Generale di Pubblica Sicurezza, Ufficio Confino Politico, fascicoli personali
Segreteria particolare del Duce, Carteggio ordinario (SPDCO)
Segreteria particolare del Duce, Carteggio riservato

Archivio Storico della Camera dei Deputati, Rome

Archivio Giovanni Giuriati (AGG)

Public Record Office, London

Foreign Office (FO)

Newspapers and periodicals

L'Ateneo Veneto: rivista mensile di scienze, lettere ed arti
Il Bollettino della Camera di Commercio e Industria della Provincia di Venezia, 1921–9
Il Bollettino della Federazione Provinciale Fascista di Venezia, 1929–30
Il Gazzettino
L'Illustrazione Italiana
Italia Nostra

Leo: rivista di attualità e cultura dell'Azienda di Promozione Turistica a Venezia
New York City Venezia
Nuova Antologia
La Nuova Venezia
Rivista di Venezia
Rivista mensile della città di Venezia
Le Tre Venezie: rivista d'umanità, lettere ed arti

Further published sources

Abulafia, David, *The Great Sea: A Human History of the Mediterranean* (London: Allen Lane, 2011).

Ackroyd, Peter, *Venice: Pure City* (London: Chatto and Windus, 2009).

Agamben, Giorgio, *Dell'utilità e degli inconvenienti del vivere fra spettri* (Venice: Corte del Fontego, 2011).

Albanese, Giulia, *Alle origini del fascismo: la violenza politica a Venezia, 1919–1922* (Padua: Il Poligrafo, 2001).

Albanese, Giulia, *Pietro Marsich* (Sommacampagna (VR): Cierre, 2003).

Albanese, Giulia, and Marco Borghi (eds), *Memoria resistente: la lotta partigiana a Venezia nel ricordo dei protagonisti* (Portogruaro: Istituto veneziano per la storia della Resistenza e della società contemporanea, 2005).

Alberigo, Giuseppe, *Papa Giovanni (1881–1963)* (Bologna: Edizioni Dehoniane, 2000).

Alberti, Mario, *L'irredentismo senza romanticismi* (Como: Cavalleri, 1936).

Alberton, Angela Maria, *La sedia del Florian: tra i luoghi del dissenso e della cospirazione a Venezia in Risorgimento* (Venice: Corte del Fontego, 2011).

Aldrich, Robert, *The Seduction of the Mediterranean: Writing, Art and Homosexual Fantasy* (London: Routledge, 1993).

Alloway, Lawrence, *The Venice Biennale, 1895–1968: From Salon to Goldfish Bowl* (London: Faber and Faber, 1969).

Amodeo, Fabio, *Veneto: immagini del Novecento dall'archivio de 'Il Gazzettino'* (Padua: Federico Motta, 2000).

Andreolo, Aldo, and Elisabetta Borsetti, *Venice Remembers: The Faces, Lives and Works of the Venetians and non-Venetians Whom the City Has Wished to Commemorate in Marble* (Venice: Le Altane, 1999).

Angelini, Lucio, *Quel bruttocattivo di Papà Cacciari (dedicato a Massimo Cacciari, Sindaco di Venezia) dai 13 ai 31 anni* (Venice: Libri Molto Speciali, 1999).

Antongini, Tom, *D'Annunzio* (London: Heinemann, 1938).

Antonini, Debora, *Risorgimento a Venezia: impronte monumentali* (Venice: Corte del Fontego, 2012).

Associazione degli industriali nel 40° anniversario di Porto Marghera e del Rotary Club di Venezia nel 35° anniversario della sua fondazione (ed.), *Giuseppe Volpi: ricordi e testimonianze* (Venice: C. Ferrari, 1959).

Bacheler, Clementine, and Jessie Orr White, *The Nun of the Ca' Frollo: The Life and Letters of Henrietta Gardner Macy* (New York: William Farquhar Payson, 1931).

Balladelli, Mario, *Anita Mezzalira (1886–1962): una vita per la democrazia e per il socialismo* (Venice: Comune di Venezia, n.d.).

Banti, Alberto M., *La nazione del Risorgimento: parentela, santità e onore alle origini dell'Italia unita* (Turin: Einaudi, 2000).

Baratieri, Daniela, Mark Edele and Giuseppe Finaldi (eds), *Totalitarian Dictatorship: New Histories* (New York: Routledge, 2013).

Barbantini, Nino, *La fondazione Giorgio Cini nell'isola di S. Giorgio Maggiore* (Venice: C. Ferrari, 1951).

Barbaro, Paolo, *Venezia: l'anno del mare felice* (Bologna: Il Mulino, 1995).

Barbaro, Paolo, *Venice Revealed: An Intimate Portrait* (London: Souvenir, 2002).

Barbiani, Elia (ed.), *Edilizia popolare a Venezia: storie, politiche, realizzazioni per le Case Popolari della Provincia di Venezia* (Milan: Electa, 1983).

Barbiera, Raffaello, *Arride il sole: racconto dell'alta società straniera a Venezia nell'800* (Milan: Treves, 1929).

Barizza, Sergio, *Il Comune di Venezia, 1806–1946: l'istituzione, il territorio, guida-inventario dell'Archivio municipale* (Venice: Comune di Venezia, 1987).

Barnes, James Strachey, *Half a Life* (London: Eyre and Spottiswoode, 1937).

Barrès, Maurice, *Amori e dolori sacri: la mort de Venise* (Paris: Félix Juven, 1903).

Bassi, Elena, *La R. Accademia di Belle Arti di Venezia* (Florence: Le Monnier, 1941).

Bau, Alessandro, Antonio Marco Furio and Carlo Monaco, 'Il Veneto nei rapporti di Mussolini ai segretari federali (1930)', *Venetica*, 25 (2011).

Beaton, Cecil, *The Wandering Years: Diaries, 1922–1939* (London: Weidenfeld and Nicolson, 1961).

Beaton, Cecil, *Self-Portrait with Friends: The Selected Diaries of Cecil Beaton, 1926–1974*, ed. Richard Buckle (London: Pimlico, 1979).

Beaton, Cecil, *The Unexpurgated Beaton: The Cecil Beaton Diaries as They Were Written* (London: Weidenfeld and Nicolson, 2002).

Beaton, Cecil, *Beaton in the Sixties: The Cecil Beaton Diaries as They Were Written* (London: Weidenfeld and Nicolson, 2003).

Begley, Louis, and Anka Muhlstein, *Venice for Lovers* (London: Haus, 2005).

Bellavitis, Giorgio, *L'Arsenale di Venezia: storia di una grande struttura urbana* (Venice: Marsilio, 1983).

Bellavitis, Giorgio, and Giandomenico Romanelli, *Venezia* (Bari: Laterza, 1985).

Bellina, Anna Laura, and Michele Girardi, *La Fenice, 1792–1996: Theatre, Music and History* (Venice: Marsilio, 2003).

Bellina, Luisa, and Michele Gottardi, *Osterie. Il Venezia* (Padua: Il Poligrafo, 2006).

Beltramelli, Antonio, 'Venezia senza porpora (pagine di diario: 1916–1917)', *Nuova Antologia*, fasc. 1492, 16 May 1934.

Benadusi, Lorenzo, *Il nemico dell'uomo nuovo: l'omosessualità nell'esperimento totalitario fascista* (Milan: Feltrinelli, 2005).

Benatelli, Nicoletta, Gianni Favarato and Elisio Trevisan, *Processo a Marghera: l'inchiesta sul Petrolchimico, il CVM e la morte degli operai: storia di una tragedia umana e ambientale* (Portogruaro: Nuova Dimensione, 2002).

Benevolo, Leonardo, *Città in discussione: Venezia e Roma* (Bari: Laterza, 1979).

Berendt, John, *The City of Falling Angels* (New York: Penguin, 2005).

Bertarelli, Luigi Vittorio, *Guida d'Italia del Touring Club Italiano: Venezia Giulia e Dalmazia* (Milan: TCI, 1934).

Bertoli, Bruno (ed.), *La Chiesa di Venezia dalla Seconda Guerra Mondiale al Concilio* (Venice: Studium Cattolico Veneziano, 1994).

Bertoli, Bruno (ed.), *Chiesa, società e stato a Venezia: miscellanea di studi in onore di Silvio Tramontin* (Venice: Studium Cattolico Veneziano, 1994).

Bettin, Gianfranco, *Dove volano i leoni: fine secolo a Venezia* (Milan: Garzanti, 1991).

Bettin, Gianfranco, *Marghera: il quartiere urbano* (Biban di Carbonera (TV): Alcione, 2004).

Bettin, Gianfranco, et al., *Venezia/Marghera/Mestre e ritorno: un viaggio quotidiano* (Venice: Marsilio, 2005).

Bettiol, Nicola, *Feriti nell'animo: storie di soldati dai manicomi del Veneto, 1915–1918* (Treviso: ISTRESCO, 2008).

Bevilacqua, Piero, *Venezia e le sue acque: una metafora planetaria*, rev. edn (Rome: Donzelli, 1998).

Bianchi, Bruna, *Crescere in tempo di guerra: il lavoro e la protesta dei ragazzi in Italia, 1915–1918* (Venice: Cafoscariana, 1995).

Bianchi, Bruna, 'Venezia in guerra' (unpublished thesis, University of Venice Ca' Foscari, 2002).

Bianchin, Roberto, *Acqua granda: il romanzo dell'alluvione* (Venice: Filippi, 1996).

La Biblioteca Marciana nella sua nuova sede XXVII aprile MDCCCCV (Venice: Biblioteca Nazionale, 1905).

Biennale di Venezia, *Spagna, 1936–1939: fotografie e informazione di guerra* (Venice: Marsilio, 1976).

Biennale di Venezia, *46° Esposizione internazionale d'arte: Identity and Alterity: Figures of the Body, 1895-1995* (Venice: Marsilio, 1995).

Biennale di Venezia, *Le Esposizioni internazionali d'arte, 1895-1995: artisti, mostre, partecipazioni nazionali, premi* (Venice: Electa, 1996).

Biennale di Venezia, *Think with the Senses, Feel with the Mind: Art in the Present Tense: 52° Esposizione internazionale d'arte*, 3 vols (Venice: Marsilio, 2007).

Biggi, Maria Ida, and Giorgio Mangini, *Teatro Malibran: Venezia a San Giovanni Grisostomo* (Venice: Marsilio, 2001).

Black, Jeremy, *The British Abroad: The Grand Tour in the Eighteenth Century* (Stroud: Sutton, 2002).

Boato, Stefano, *Tessera City* (Venice: Corte del Fontego, 2011).

Bobbo, Giulio, *Venezia in tempo di guerra, 1943-1945* (Padua: Il Poligrafo, 2005).

Bognolo, Umberto, *Venezia eroica* (Rocca San Casciano: Cappelli, 1918).

Boito, Camillo, 'I restauri di San Marco', *Nuova Antologia*, fasc. 29, 15 December 1879.

Boito, Camillo, 'Venezia che scompare: Sant'Elena e Santa Marta', *Nuova Antologia*, fasc. 20, 15 October 1883.

Bon, Silva, *Gli Ebrei a Trieste* (Gorizia: Libreria Editrice Goriziana, 2000).

Bonfanti, Sicinio, *La Giudecca nella storia, nell'arte, nelle vite* (Venice: Libreria Emiliana, 1930).

Boni, Giacomo, *Il cosidetto sventramento: appunti di un veneziano* (Rome: Stabilmento Tipografico Italiano, 1887).

Boni, Giacomo, 'La torre di San Marco di Venezia', *Nuova Antologia*, fasc. 969, 1 May 1912.

Boni, Giacomo, 'Venezia e l'Adriatico', *Nuova Antologia*, fasc. 1131, 1 March 1919.

Boni, Giacomo, *Demagogia e parlamentarismo* (Rome: Eredi Mario Lupi, 1923).

Bono, Francesco, 'La mostra del cinema di Venezia: nascita e sviluppo nell'anteguerra (1932-1939)', *Storia contemporanea*, 22 (1991).

Bonomi, Aldo (ed.), *Privatizzare Venezia: il progettista imprenditoriale* (Venice: Marsilio, 1995).

Bonomi, Aldo, and Enzo Rullani, *Il capitalismo personale: vite al lavoro* (Turin: Einaudi, 2005).

Borghi, Marco, *Tra Fascio Littorio e senso dello stato: funzionari, apparati, ministeri nella Repubblica sociale italiana (1943-1945)* (Venice: Istituto veneziano per la storia della Resistenza e della società contemporanea, 2001).

Borghi, Marco, and Alessandro Reberschegg, *Fascisti alla sbarra: l'attività della Corte d'Assise Straordinaria di Venezia, 1945-1947* (Venice: Istituto veneziano per la storia della Resistenza e della società contemporanea, 1999).

Bosworth, R. J. B., 'The *Touring Club Italiano* and the Nationalization of the Italian Bourgeoisie', *European History Quarterly*, 27 (1997).

Bosworth, R. J. B., 'Tourist Planning in Fascist Italy and the Limits of a Totalitarian Culture', *Contemporary European History*, 6 (1997).

Bosworth, R. J. B., 'Venice between Fascism and International Tourism, 1911-45', *Modern Italy*, 4 (1999).

Bosworth, R. J. B., *Mussolini*, rev. edn (London: Bloomsbury, 2010).

Bowness, Sophie, and Clive Phillpot, *Britain at the Venice Biennale, 1895-1995* (London: The British Council, 1995).

Bradley, Alexander, *Ruskin and Italy* (Ann Arbor: University of Michigan Research Press, 1987).

Bragato, Stefania, and Luciano Menetto (eds), *E per patria una lingua segreta: rom e sinti in provincia di Venezia* (Venice: Nuova Dimensione, 2007).

Branca, Vittore, and Stefano Rosso-Mazzinghi (eds), *Angelo Giuseppe Roncalli dal patriarcato di Venezia alla cattedra di San Pietro* (Florence: Olschki, 1984).

Braudel, Fernand, and Folco Quilici, *Venezia: immagine di una città* (Bologna: Il Mulino, 1984).

Bregantin, Lisa, *Caduti nell'oblio: i soldati di Pontelongo scomparsi nella Grande Guerra* (Venice: Istituto veneziano per la storia della Resistenza e della società contemporanea, 2003).

Bregantin, Lisa, *Per non morire mai: la percezione della morte in guerra e il culto dei caduti nel primo conflitto mondiale* (Padua: il Poligrafo, 2010).

Bregantin, Lisa, Livio Fantina and Marco Mondini, *Venezia, Treviso e Padova nella Grande Guerra* (Treviso: ISTRESCO, 2008).

Bret, David, *Tallulah Bankhead: A Scandalous Life* (London: Robson, 1996).

Brown, Horatio F., *Venetian Studies* (London: Kegan Paul, Trench and Co., 1887).

Brown, Horatio F., *Life on the Lagoons* (London: Rivington, Percival and Co., 1894).

Brown, Horatio F., *In and around Venice* (London: Rivingtons, 1905).

Brunello, Piero, 'L'anarchico delle barche: notizie su Luciano Visentin, calzolaio (1898–1984)', *Quaderni di storiAmestre*, 2 (2005).

Brunetta, Gian Piero, *The History of Italian Cinema: A Guide to Italian Film from Its Origins to the Twenty-First Century* (Princeton University Press, 2009).

Bull, George, *Venice: The Most Triumphant City* (London: Folio Society, 1980).

Bush, John W., *Venetia Redeemed: Franco-Italian relations, 1864–1866* (Syracuse University Press, 1967).

Cacciari, Massimo, *Posthumous People: Vienna at the Turning Point* (Stanford University Press, 1996).

Cacciari, Massimo, and Carlo Maria Martini, *Dialogo sulla solidarietà* (Rome: Lavoro, 1997).

Calabi, Donatella, and Paolo Morchiello, *La piazza del Rialto: di tutto il mondo la più richissima parte* (Venice: Corte del Fontego, 2011).

Calabi, Donatella, and Paolo Morchiello, *Il fontego dei Tedeschi: 'una piccola città in mezzo alla nostra'* (Venice: Corte del Fontego, 2012).

Calabi, Donatella, and Paolo Morchiello, *Rialto: il ponte delle dispute* (Venice: Corte del Fontego, 2012).

Calamandrei, Piero, *Diario, 1939–1945*, ed. Giorgio Agosti, 2 vols (Florence: La Nuova Italia, 1982).

Calamandrei, Piero, and Franco Calamandrei, *Una famiglia in guerra: lettere e scritti (1939–1956)*, ed. Alessandro Casellato (Bari: Laterza, 2008).

Calimani, Riccardo, Giovannina Sullam Reinisch and Cesare Vivante, *Venice: Guide to the Synagogues, Museum and Cemetery* (Venice: Marsilio, 2000).

Callegari, Paola, and Valter Curzi (eds), *Venezia: la tutela per immagini: un caso esemplare dagli archivi della Fototeca Nazionale* (Bologna: Bononia University Press, 2005).

Camozza, Ugo, *Il Card. Pietro La Fontaine: patriarca di Venezia*, rev. edn (Venice: Studium Cattolico Veneziano, 1960).

Campbell, Gerald, *Of True Experience* (London: Hutchinson, n.d.).

Candida, Luigi, *Il porto di Venezia* (Naples: Memorie di Geografia Economica, 1950).

Cannistraro, Philip V., and Brian R. Sullivan, *Il Duce's Other Woman* (New York: W. Morrow, 1993).

Capovilla, Loris Francesco (ed.), *Giovanni e Paolo, due Papi: saggio di corrispondenza (1925–1962)* (Rome: Studium, 1982).

Carli, Ferruccio, *Pio X e il suo tempo* (Florence: Adriano Salani, 1941).

Carlyle, Thomas, *Gli eroi*, trans. Maria Pezzè Pascolato (Florence: G. Barbera, 1897).

Casarin, Michele, *Venezia Mestre, Mestre Venezia: luoghi, parole e percorsi di un'identità* (Venice: Istituto veneziano per la storia della Resistenza e della società contemporanea, 2002).

Casarin, Michele, and Giancarlo Scarpari, *Piazzale Roma. Il Lido di Venezia* (Padua: Il Poligrafo, 2005).

Casarini, Luigi, *Sulla origine, ingrandimento e decadenza del commercio di Venezia e sui mezzi che nella presente di lei situazione praticare potrebbonsi per impedirne la minacciata rovina: memoria* (Venice: Picotti, 1823).

Casati, L.A., 'La battaglia di Custoza', *Nuova Antologia*, fasc. 12, 31 December 1866.

Cassandro, Giovanni, 'Salviamo Venezia', *Nuova Antologia*, fasc. 2030, February 1970.

Castelfranco, Giorgio, 'La XXIX Biennale d'Arte a Venezia', *Nuova Antologia*, fasc. 1892, August 1958.

Castelli, A., and A. Fiorentino, *Manuale dell'albergatore* (Rome: F. Centenari, 1934).

Catalano, Franco, *Luigi Luzzatti: la figura e l'opera* (Milan: Banca Popolare di Milano, 1965).

Cavalletti, Lavinia, *La dinastia Stucky, 1841–1941: storia del Molino di Venezia e della famiglia da Manin a Mussolini* (Venice: Studio LTL, 2011).

Cecconello, Giovanna, Carlo Giuliani and Michele Sgobba, *San Clemente: progetto per un'isola* (Venice: Cluva, 1980).

Cerasi, Laura, *Perdonare Marghera: la città del lavoro nella memoria post-industriale* (Milan: Franco Angeli, 2007).

Cerasi, Laura, and Michele Casarin, *Marghera. Sant'Elena* (Padua: Il Poligrafo, 2007).

Cerutti, Arduino, *Memorie* (Venice: Marsilio, 1980).

Ceschin, Daniele, *La 'Voce' di Venezia: Antonio Fradeletto e l'organizzazione della cultura tra Otto e Novecento* (Padua: Il Poligrafo, 2001).

Ceschin, Daniele, *Gli esuli di Caporetto: i profughi in Italia durante la grande guerra* (Bari: Laterza, 2006).

Ceschin, Daniele, and Anna Scannapieco, *L'Archivio dei Frari. La Casa di Goldoni* (Padua: Il Poligrafo, 2005).

Chinello, Cesco, *Porto Marghera, 1902–1926: alle origini del 'problema di Venezia'* (Venice: Marsilio, 1979).

Chinello, Cesco, *Classe, movimento, organizzazione: le lotte operaie a Marghera/Venezia: i percorsi di una crisi, 1945–55* (Milan: Franco Angeli, 1984).

Chinello, Cesco, *Sindacato, Pci, movimenti negli anni sessanta: Porto Marghera–Venezia, 1955–1970*, 2 vols (Milan: Franco Angeli, 1996).

Chinello, Cesco, *Giovanni Tonetti, il 'conte rosso': contrasti di una vita e una militanza (1888–1970)* (Venice: Supernova, 1997).

Chinello, Cesco, *Un barbaro veneziano: mezzo secolo da comunista* (Padua: Il Poligrafo, 2008).

Chinello, Cesco, and Giulio Bobbo, *La Breda. Da Ca' Littoria a Ca' Matteotti* (Padua: Il Poligrafo, 2006).

Chirivi, Romano, *L'Arsenale di Venezia: storia e obiettivi di un piano* (Venice: Marsilio, 1976).

Ciacci, Leonardo, and Giovanni Ferracuti, *Abitare a Venezia negli anni '80* (Milan: Giuffrè, 1980).

Ciani, Maria Grazia, and Maria Ida Biggi, *La spiaggia. Il Teatro La Fenice* (Padua: Il Poligrafo, 2006).

Ciano, Galeazzo, *Diary, 1937–1943*, ed. Renzo De Felice (London: Phoenix, 2002).

Circolo Golf Venezia, *Sessantacinquesimo anniversario del Circolo* (Alberoni: Circolo Golf Venezia, 1995).

Clegg, Jeanne, *Ruskin and Venice* (London: Junction, 1981).

Coen Cagli, Enrico, *Il porto di Venezia* (Venice: La Poligrafica Italiana, 1925).

Cole, Toby (ed.), *Venice: A Portable Reader* (New York: Frontier, 1979).

Coles, Polly, *The Politics of Washing: Real Life in Venice* (London: Robert Hale, 2013).

Collegio degli ingegneri della provincia di Venezia, *Venezia: metropoli in cammino verso l'Europa* (Venice: Cartotecnica Veneziana, 1999).

Collier, Peter, *Proust and Venice* (Cambridge University Press, 1989).

Collotta, G., *Intorno alle questioni ferroviarie nei riguardi della provincia, della città e del porto di Venezia* (Venice: G. Antonello, 1873).

Comitato Regionale Veneto per la storia del Risorgimento italiano (ed.), *L'ultima dominazione austriaca e la liberazione del Veneto nel 1866: memorie di Filippo Nani Mocenigo, Ugo Botti, Carlo Combi, Antonino Di Prampero, Manlio Torquato Dazzi e Giuseppe Solitro* (Chioggia: Giulio Vianelli, 1916).

Comune di Venezia, *Le case economiche e popolari del Comune di Venezia* (Bergamo: Istituto Italiano d'Arti Grafiche, 1911).

Comune di Venezia, *Il campanile di San Marco riedificato: studi, ricerche, relazioni* (Venice: C. Ferrari, 1912).

Comune di Venezia, *MCMXV–MCMXVIII: Veneziani morti per la patria decorati al valore* (Venice: Umberto Bartoli, 1925).

Comune di Venezia, *Venezia* (Venice: Ufficio per il Turismo, 1938).

Comune di Venezia, *L'immagine e il mito di Venezia nel cinema* (Mirano (VE): Tonolo, 1983).

Consorzio Obbligatorio per il nuovo ampliamento del porto e della zona industriale di Venezia–Mestre, *Piano generale per la sistemazione della zona di cui alla legge 20 ottobre 1960 n. 1233* (Venice: n.p., [1961]).

Cooper, Diana, *The Light of Common Day: Autobiography* (London: Century, 1984).

Cooper, Diana, *The Rainbow Comes and Goes: Autobiography* (London: Century, 1984).

Coover, Robert, *Pinocchio in Venice* (London: Heinemann, 1991).

Corner, Paul, *The Fascist Party and Popular Opinion in Mussolini's Italy* (Oxford University Press, 2012).

Corni, Gustavo, 'L'occupazione austro-germanica del Veneto nel 1917–18: sindaci, preti, austriacanti e patrioti', *Rivista di storia contemporanea*, 18 (1989).

Correnti, Pino, *Il Carnevale di Venezia* (Milan: Ecotour, 1968).

Corsi, Mario, *Il teatro all'aperto in Italia* (Milan: Rizzoli, 1939).

Corti, Ernesto, *Lido di Venezia* (Venice: C. Ferrari, 1919).

Costantini, Massimo, 'Dal porto franco al porto industriale', in Alberto Tenenti and Ugo Tucci (eds), *Storia di Venezia: il mare* (Rome: Istituto della Enciclopedia Italiana, 1991).

Crawford, F. Marion, *Gleanings from Venetian History* (London: Macmillan, 1907).

Crouzet-Pavan, Elisabeth, *Venice Triumphant: The Horizons of a Myth* (Baltimore: Johns Hopkins University Press, 2002).

Crovato, Giorgio, and Maurizio Crovato, *Isole abbandonate della laguna: come'erano e come sono* (Padua: Liviana, 1978).

Cuppone, Roberto, *Il Teatro Goldoni* (Padua: Il Poligrafo, 2010).

Curiel, Roberta, and Bernard Dov Cooperman, *The Venetian Ghetto* (New York: Rizzoli, 1990).

Dainotto, Roberto M., 'The Gubbio Papers: Historic Centres in the Age of the Economic Miracle', *Journal of Modern Italian Studies*, 8 (2003).

Dal Co, Francesco, and Giuseppe Mazzariol (eds), *Carlo Scarpa: The Complete Works* (London: Electa, 1986).

Dalla Costa, Mario, *La basilica di San Marco e i restauri dell'Ottocento: le idee di E. Viollet-le-Duc, J. Ruskin e le 'Osservazioni' di A. P. Zorzi* (Venice: La Stamperia di Venezia, 1983).

Dall'Arche, Giuseppe, *Molo K Marghera: l'altra Venezia* (Vicenza: Terra Ferma, 2007).

Damerini, Gino, *Amor di Venezia* (Bologna: Zanichelli, 1920).

Damerini, Gino, *D'Annunzio a Venezia* (Venice: Marsilio, 1992).

Damerini, Gino, et al., *La gondola* (Venice: Nuova Editoriale, 1956).

Damerini, Gino, *L'isola e il cenobio di San Giorgio Maggiore* (Venice: Fondazione Giorgio Cini, 1959).

Damerini, Maria, *Gli ultimi anni del Leone: Venezia, 1929–1940* (Padua: Il Poligrafo, 1988).

Da Mosto, Jane, et al., *The Venice Report: Demography, Tourism, Financing and Change of Use of Buildings* (Cambridge University Press, 2009).

D'Annunzio, Gabriele, *Notturno* (Milan: Treves, 1921).

D'Annunzio, Gabriele, *The Flame* (London: Quartet, 1991).

Davis, James C., *A Venetian Family and Its Fortune, 1500–1900* (Philadelphia: American Philosophical Society, 1975).

Davis, Robert C., and Garry R. Marvin, *Venice, the Tourist Maze: A Cultural Critique of the World's Most Touristed City* (Berkeley: University of California Press, 2004).

De Angelis, R. M., 'Sulla XXXII Biennale Internazionale di Venezia', *Nuova Antologia*, fasc. 1963, July 1964.

De Angelis, R. M., 'La 33 Biennale Internazionale di Venezia', *Nuova Antologia*, fasc. 1987, July 1966.

De Benedetti, Michele, 'La X Esposizione Internazionale d'Arte a Venezia', *Nuova Antologia*, fasc. 970, 16 May 1912.

De Benedetti, Michele, 'La XI esposizione internazionale d'arte a Venezia', *Nuova Antologia*, fasc. 1026, 16 September 1914.

De Benedetti, Michele, 'La XIII Esposizione Internazionale d'Arte a Venezia', *Nuova Antologia*, fasc. 1206, 16 June 1922.

De Biasi, Mario, 'La Deputazione di storia patria e le terre irredente dopo il primo conflitto mondiale', *Archivio Veneto*, 151 (1998).

De Biasi, Mario, 'La casa di Daniele Manin e la deputazione di storia patria per le Venezie', *Archivio Veneto*, 176 (2005).

De Blasi, Marlena, *A Thousand Days in Venice: An Unexpected Romance* (Sydney: Allen and Unwin, 2003).

Debray, Régis, *Against Venice* (London: Pushkin, 2002).

De Grazia, Victoria, *Irresistible Empire: America's Advance through Twentieth-Century Europe* (Cambridge, MA: Belknap, 2005).

Deleuse, Margherita, 'Maria Pezzè Pascolato: commemorazione tenuta il 26 marzo 1933 nella Sala Maggiore dell'Ateneo Veneto dalla Fascista Margherita Deleuse, Vice Fiduciario prov. del Fascio femminile di Venezia' (printed pamphlet held in the Biblioteca Marciana, Venice).

De Marco, Maurizio, *Il Gazzettino: storia di un quotidiano* (Venice: Marsilio, 1976).

De Michelis, Gianni, *Dove andiamo a ballare questa sera? Guida a 250 discoteche italiane* (Milan: Mondadori, 1988).

De Michelis, Gianni, *Oggi è domani* (Pomezia: PGS, n.d.).

De Michelis, Gianni, *La lunga ombra di Yalta: la specificità della politica italiana: conversazione con Francesco Kostner* (Venice: Marsilio, 2003).

De Osma, Guillermo, *Fortuny: The Life and Work of Mariano Fortuny* (London: Aurum, 1994).

De Rita, Giuseppe, *Una città speciale: rapporto su Venezia* (Venice: Marsilio, 1993).

De Rita, Giuseppe, *Intervista sulla borghesia in Italia*, ed. Antonio Galdo (Bari: Laterza, 1996).

Di Monte, Giuseppina, and Isabella Scaramuzzi (eds), *Una provincia ospitale: itinerari di ricerca sul sistema turistico veneziano* (Bologna: Il Mulino, 1996).

Distefano, Giovanni (ed.), *Atlante storico di Venezia* (Venice Lido: Supernova, 2008).

Distefano, Giovanni, and Giannantonio Paladini, *Storia di Venezia, 1797–1997*, 3 vols (Venice Lido: Supernova, 1997).

Donaglio, Monica, *Un esponente dell'élite liberale: Pompeo Molmenti politico e storico di Venezia* (Venice: Istituto Veneto di Scienze, Lettere ed Arti, 2004).

Donatelli, Plinio, *La casa a Venezia nell'opera del suo istituto* (Rome: Stabilimento Poligrafico per l'Amministrazione dello Stato, 1928).

Doody, Margaret, *Tropic of Venice* (Philadelphia: University of Pennsylvania Press, 2007).

Dorigo, Wladimiro, 'Impegno a confronto per la "nuova sinistra"', *Quaderni di lavoro politico*, 2 (1968).

Dorigo, Wladimiro, *Una laguna di chiacchiere: note a margine a 'tutto Montanelli a Venezia'* (Venice: n.p., 1972).

Dorigo, Wladimiro, *Una legge contro Venezia: natura, storia, interessi nella questione della città e della laguna* (Rome: Officina, 1973).

Dorigo, Wladimiro, *Venezia romanica: la formazione della città medioevale fino all'età gotica*, 2 vols (Sommacampagna (VR): Cierre, 2006).

Dorigo, Wladimiro, *Battaglie urbanistiche: la pianificazione del territorio a Venezia e in Italia fra politica e cultura* (Sommacampagna (VR): Cierre, 2007).

Eden, Frederic, *A Garden in Venice* (London: G. Newnes, 1903).

Edwards, Anne, *Throne of Gold: The Lives of the Aga Khans* (London: HarperCollins, 1996).

Ercolani, Antonella (ed.), *Carteggio D'Annunzio–Gravina (1915–1924)* (Rome: Bonacci, 1993).

Ermacora, Matteo, 'Assistance and Surveillance: War Refugees in Italy, 1914–1918', *Contemporary European History*, 16 (2007).

Errera, Alberto, *Storia e statistica delle industrie venete* (Venice: Giuseppe Antonelli, 1870).

Evans, R. H., *Life in a Venetian Community* (University of Notre Dame Press, 1976).

Fabbri, Elisabetta, *La Fenice: splendidezza di ornamenti e dorature* (Rome: De Luca, 2004).

Fabbri, Fabrizio, *Porto Marghera e la laguna di Venezia: vita, morte, miracoli* (Milan: Jaca Book, 2003).

Fabbri, Gianni, *Venezia: quale modernità: idee per una città capitale* (Milan: Franco Angeli, 2005).

Facco de Lagarda, Ugo, *Morte all'impiraperle* (Venice: Evi, 1967).

Fambri, Paulo, 'L'avvenire di Venezia', *Nuova Antologia*, fasc. 9, 1 May 1878.

Favaro, Omar, 'Un cardellino in gabbia: fabbrica e lavoro nei primi anni Cinquanta a Porto Marghera', *Quaderni di storiAmestre*, 8 (2008).

Fay, Stephen, and Phillip Knightley, *The Death of Venice* (London: Deutsch, 1976).

Federazione delle Casse di Risparmio delle Venezie, *Cenni sull'attività della Federazione nell'anno 1930* (Venice: Giovanni Magrini, 1931).

Federici, Girolamo, *Portuali a Venezia: cinquant'anni di storia del porto, 1945–1995* (Venice: Il Cardo, 1996).

Federzoni, Luigi, *La Dalmazia che aspetta* (Bologna: Zanichelli, 1915).

Federzoni, Luigi, *1927: Diario di un ministro del fascismo*, ed. A. Macchi (Florence: Passigli, 1993).

Feest, Christian F. (ed.), *Indians and Europe: An Interdisciplinary Collection of Essays* (Aachen: Rader, 1987).

Fenlon, Iain, *Piazza San Marco* (London: Profile, 2010).

Ferrara, Luciana, 'La XXVIII Biennale di Venezia', *Nuova Antologia*, fasc. 1867, July 1956.

Ferraro, Joanne M., *Venice: History of the Floating City* (Cambridge University Press, 2012).

Ferris, Kate, *Everyday Life in Fascist Venice, 1929–1940* (Houndmills: Palgrave Macmillan, 2012).

Filippini, Nadia Maria, *Maria Pezzè Pascolato* (Sommacampagna (VR): Cierre, 2004).

Filippini, Nadia Maria, and Tiziana Plebani (eds), *La scoperta dell'infanzia: cura, educazione e rappresentazione: Venezia, 1750–1930* (Venice: Marsilio, 1999).

Fleming, George [Julia Constance Fletcher], *Little Stories about Women* (London: Grant Richards, 1897).

Fletcher, Caroline A., and Tom Spencer (eds), *Flooding and Environmental Challenges for Venice and Its Lagoon: State of Knowledge* (Cambridge University Press, 2005).

Fontanella, Aristide, *Saggio sulla utilità e sulla opportunità di costruire a Venezia una Società di Navigazione coll'Egitto e i principali Porti del Levante in armonia colla prossima apertura dell'Istmo di Suez e cogli ordini del giorno 13 giugno 1867 e 25 giugno 1868 al Parlamento e 10 luglio successivo al Senato* (Venice: n.p., 1869).

Foot, John, *Italy's Divided Memory* (Houndmills: Palgrave Macmillan, 2009).

Fortis, Umberto (ed.), *Venezia ebraica: atti delle prime giornate di studio sull'ebraismo veneziano (Venezia 1976–1980)* (Rome: Carucci, 1979).

Foscari, Antonio, *Tumult and Order: Malcontenta, 1924–1939* (Zurich: Lars Müller, 2012).

Foscari, Piero, *Il porto di Venezia nel problema adriatico* (Venice: F. Garzia, 1904).

Foscari, Piero, *Nel cinquantenario della liberazione del Veneto* (Rome: L'Italiana, 1916).

Foscari, Piero, *Dopo cinquant'anni della liberazione del Veneto dal dominio austriaco* (Venice: Libreria Editrice Nazionalista, 1917).

Foscari, Piero, *Per il più largo dominio di Venezia: la città e il porto* (Milan: Treves, 1917).

Foscari, Piero, *Per l'Italia più grande: scritti e discorsi*, ed. T. Sillani (Rome: Edizioni della Rassegna Italiana*, 1928).

Fozzati, Luigi, *Sotto Venezia* (Venice: Corte del Fontego, 2011).

Fradeletto, Antonio, *Il precursore: conferenza* (Milan: Treves, 1915).

Fradeletto, Antonio, *I martiri nostri* (Milan: Treves, 1918).

Fradeletto, Antonio, *La missione di Venezia di fronte all'Austria* (Venice: C. Ferrari, 1926).

Fradeletto, Antonio, 'Venezia antica e Italia moderna', *Nuova Antologia*, fasc. 1356, 16 September 1928.

Francesconi, Daniele, *La questione delle ceneri di Daniele Manin nella Basilica di S. Marco: osservazioni* (Venice: Tipografia del *Tempo*, 1868).

Franco, Carlo, *La libreria 'Toletta'* (Padua: Il Poligrafo, 2006).

Franco, Carlo, *Il liceo 'Raimondo Franchetti'* (Padua: Il Poligrafo, 2010).

Franzina, Emilio (ed.), *Venezia* (Bari: Laterza, 1986).

Freely, John, *Strolling through Venice: The Definitive Walking Guidebook to 'La Serenissima'* (London: I. B. Tauris, 2008).

Freud, Sigmund, *The Interpretation of Dreams*, ed. James Strachey (Harmondsworth: Penguin, 1976).

Gagliardi, Tommaso, *L'industria turistica ed alberghiera in Italia* (Vicenza: Arti Grafiche delle Venezie, 1959).

Galzigna, Mario, and Hrayr Terzian (eds), *L'Archivio della follia: il manicomio di San Servolo e la nascita di una fondazione: antologia di testi e documenti* (Venice: Marsilio, 1980).

Gambuzzi, Loredana, *Venezia come simbolo: l'archetipo della grande madre* (Venice: Helvetia, n.d.).

Gaspari, Oscar, *L'emigrazione veneta nell'Agro Pontino durante il periodo fascista* (Brescia: Morcelliana, 1985).

Gasparri, Stefano, Giovanni Levi and Pierandrea Moro (eds), *Venezia: itinerari per la storia della città* (Bologna: Il Mulino, 1997).

Gattinoni, Gregorio, *Il campanile di San Marco: monografia storica* (Venice: G. Fabbris, 1910).

Gavagnin, Armando, *Vent'anni di resistenza al fascismo: ricordi e testimonianze* (Turin: Einaudi, 1957).

Gavagnin, Francesco, *Sulle abitazioni dei poveri: lettere al compilatore* (Venice: Tipografia della *Gazzetta*, 1866).

Geltmayer, Ty, *Tired of Living: Suicide in Italy from National Unification to World War I, 1860-1915* (New York: P. Lang, 2002).

Ginsborg, Paul, *Daniele Manin and the Venetian Revolution of 1848-9* (Cambridge University Press, 1979).

Gioannini, Marco, and Giulio Massobrio, *Custoza 1866: la via italiana alla sconfitta* (Milan: Rizzoli, 2003).

Giordano, Davide, *Conferenze di chirurgia in tempo di guerra fatte agli Ufficiali Medici nello Spedale Militare Principale di Venezia, Febbraio–Marzo 1917* (Turin: Editrice Torinese, 1917).

Giordano, Davide, *Pietro d'Abano* (Genoa: Marsano, 1928).

Giuriati, Domenico, *Memoire d'emigrazione* (Milan: Treves, 1897).

Giuriati, Domenico (ed.), *Duecento lettere inedite di Giuseppe Mazzini con proemio e note* (Turin: L. Roux, 1887).

Giuriati, Giovanni, *La vigilia (gennaio 1913-maggio 1915)* (Milan: Mondadori, 1930).

Giuriati, Giovanni, *Con D'Annunzio e Millo in difesa dell'Adriatico* (Florence: Sansoni, 1954).

Giuriati, Giovanni, *Una fama usurpata: la proporzionale* (Rome: Edizioni di abc, [1954]).

Giuriati, Giovanni, *La parabola di Mussolini nei ricordi di un gerarca*, ed. Emilio Gentile (Bari: Laterza, 1981).

Giuriati, Giovanni (jun.), *Il porto di Venezia: aspetti e problemi della sua rinascita* (Venice: C. Ferrari, 1924).

Golf Club di Venezia, *Regolamento ed etichetta del gioco* (Venice: n.p., n.d.).

Golf Club di Venezia, *Statuto* (Venice: n.p., 1957).

Goy, Richard J., *Venice: An Architectural Guide* (New Haven and London: Yale University Press, 2010).

Grano, Amedeo, *Vivere a Venezia* (Spinea (VE): Helvetia Servizio, 2001).

Grasso, Franco (ed.), *Girolamo Li Causi e la sua azione per la Sicilia* (Palermo: Libri Siciliani, 1966).

Gray, Ezio Maria, *La bella guerra* (Florence: Bemporad, 1912).

Gray, Ezio Maria, *Il Belgio sotto la spada tedesca* (Florence: A. Beltrami, [1915]).

Gray, Ezio Maria, *Germania in Italia* (Milan: Ravà, 1915).

Gray, Ezio Maria, *L'invasione tedesca in Italia (professori, commercianti, spie)* (Florence: Bemporad, [1915]).

Gray, Ezio Maria, *The Bloodless War* (London: Hutchinson, 1917).

Gray, Ezio Maria, *Venezia in armi* (Milan: Treves, 1917).

Grundy, Milton, *Venice: An Anthology Guide* (London: Lund Humphries, 1971).

Gruppo Consiliare Lega Veneta Repubblica, *Veneto: un popolo sovrano verso l'Europa: atti del Convegno di Studi* (Padua: Crivellaro Pasquale, 1999).

Guasco, Alberto, *Cattolici e fascisti: la Santa Sede e la politica italiana all'alba del regime (1919-1925)* (Bologna: Il Mulino, 2013).

Guerri, Giordano Bruno, *Filippo Tommaso Marinetti: invenzioni, avventure e passioni di un rivoluzionario* (Milan: Mondadori, 2009).

Guggenheim, Peggy, *Out of This Century: Confessions of an Art Addict* (London: Deutsch, 1980).

Guiton, Shirley, *No Magic Eden* (London: H. Hamilton, 1972).

Guiton, Shirley, *A World by Itself: Tradition and Change in the Venetian Lagoon* (London: H. Hamilton, 1977).

Gundle, Stephen, *Bellissima: Feminine Beauty and the Idea of Italy* (New Haven: Yale University Press, 2007).

Guzzi, Virgilio, 'La XXXI Biennale di Venezia', *Nuova Antologia*, fasc. 1940, August 1962.

Hales, E. E. Y., *Pope John and His Revolution* (London: Eyre and Spottiswoode, 1965).

Hare, Augustus J. C., *Cities of Northern Italy*, vol. 2: *Venice, Ferrara, Piacenza, Parma, Modena and Bologna* (London: G. Allen, n.d.).

Hare, Augustus J. C., and St Clair Baddeley, *Venice* (London: G. Allen, 1904).

Healey, Ben, *Last Ferry from the Lido* (London: Robert Hale, 1981).

Hebblethwaite, Peter, *John XXIII: Pope of the Council* (London: G. Chapman, 1984).

Hemingway, Ernest, *Across the River and into the Trees* (London: J. Cape, 1950).

Hemingway, Ernest, *A Farewell to Arms* (New York: Bantam, 1976).

Hibbert, Christopher, *Venice: The Biography of a City* (New York: W. W. Norton, 1989).

Hill, Reginald, *Another Death in Venice* (London: The Crime Club, 1976).

Hoare, Philip, *Noël Coward: A Biography* (London: Sinclair-Stevenson, 1995).

Horodowich, Elizabeth, *A Brief History of Venice: A New History of the City and Its People* (London: Constable and Robinson, 2009).

Howells, William D., *Venetian Life* (Leipzig: Bernard Tauchnitz, 1883).

Hughes, Hetty Meyric (ed.), *Venice: A Collection of the Poetry of Place* (London: Eland, 2006).

Hughes-Hallett, Lucy, *The Pike: Gabriele D'Annunzio, Poet, Seducer and Preacher of War* (London: Fourth Estate, 2013).

Hutton, Edward, *Venice and Venetia* (London: Methuen, 1911).

Hutton, Edward, *The Pageant of Venice* (London: John Lane, The Bodley Head, 1922).

Iorga, Nicolae, *La Romania alla Biennale di Venezia, 1938* (n.p., n.d.).

Isman, Fabio, *Venezia, fabbrica della cultura tra istituzioni ed eventi* (Venice: Marsilio, 2000).

Isnenghi, Mario, 'D'Annunzio e l'ideologia della venezianità', *Rivista di storia contemporanea*, 19 (1990).

Isnenghi, Mario (ed.), *Il diario di Letizia (1866)* (Verona: Novacharta, 2004).

Isnenghi, Mario, and Silvio Lanaro (eds), *La Democrazia Cristiana dal fascismo al 18 aprile: movimento cattolico e Democrazia Cristiana nel Veneto, 1945–1948* (Venice: Marsilio, 1978).

Isnenghi, Mario, and Stuart Woolf (eds), *Storia di Venezia: l'Ottocento e il Novecento* (Rome: Istituto dell'Enciclopedia Italiana, 2002).

Isnenghi, Mario, Filippo Maria Paladini and Giovanni Sbordone, *Il Liceo Convitto Marco Foscarini. Canottieri e remiere. La Camera del Lavoro* (Padua: Il Poligrafo, 2005).

Jachec, Nancy, *Politics and Painting at the Venice Biennale, 1948–64: Italy and the Idea of Europe* (Manchester University Press, 2007).

James, Henry, *The Aspern Papers* (London: Penguin, 1994).

James, Henry, *Letters from Palazzo Barbaro*, ed. Rosella Mamoli Zorzi (London: Pushkin, 1998).

James, Henry, *The Wings of the Dove* (London: Mandarin, 1998).

Jesurum, Michelangelo, *Cenni storici e statistici sull'industria dei merletti* (Venice: Marco Visentini, 1873).

Jori, Francesco, *Dalla Liga alla Lega: storia, movimento, protagonisti* (Venice: Marsilio, 2007).

Julier, Jürgen, *Il Molino Stucky a Venezia* (Venice: Centro Tedesco di Studi Veneziani, 1978).

Keates, Jonathan, *The Siege of Venice* (London: Chatto and Windus, 2005).

Lamin, Bill, *Letters from the Trenches: A Soldier of the Great War* (London: Michael O'Mara, 2009).

Lanapoppi, Paolo, *Dear Tourist* (Venice: Corte del Fontego, 2012).

Lanaro, Guido, 'Il popolo delle pignatte: storia del Presidio permanente No Dal Molin (2005–2009)', *Quaderni di StoriAmestre*, 10 (2009–10).

Lanaro, Silvio, 'Intorno ai cattolici veneti e alle elezioni amministrative (1872–1889)', *Archivio Veneto*, 93 (1971).

Lanaro, Silvio (ed.), *Il Veneto* (Turin: Einaudi, 1984).

Lane, Frederic C., *Venice and History: The Collected Papers* (Baltimore: Johns Hopkins Press, 1966).

Laven, David, *Venice and Venetia under the Habsburgs, 1815–1835* (Oxford University Press, 2002).

Laven, David and Laura Parker, 'Foreign rule? Transnational, national, and local perspectives on Venice and Venetia within the "multinational empire"', *Modern Italy*, 19, 2014.

Lee, Vernon, *The Enchanted Woods and Other Essays on the Genius of Places* (London: John Lane, The Bodley Head, 1905).

Lega Navale Italiana, *The Adriatic Avenged: Apotheosis of Nazario Sauro* (Rome: Lega Navale, 1917).

Lennard, Suzanne H. Crowhurst, *The Venetian Campo: Ideal Setting for Social Life and Community* (Venice: Corte del Fontego, 2012).

Leon, Donna, *Acqua alta* (London: Pan Macmillan, 1996).

Leon, Donna, *Blood from a Stone* (London: Penguin, 2005).

Leon, Donna, *About Face* (London: Arrow, 2009).

Leon, Donna, *Death at the Fenice* (London: Arrow, 2009).

Leon, Donna, *A Question of Belief* (London: Heinemann, 2010).

Leoni, Carlo, *Cronaca segreta de' miei tempi*, ed. Giuseppe Toffanin (Cittadella (PD): Rebellato, 1976).

Levi, M. R. (ed.), *I bagni marini sulla spiaggia del Lido per i poveri scrofolosi di Venezia nell'estate 1868: relazione del Comitato Promotore e proposta dell'erezione di un ospizio marino veneto* (Venice: G. Antonelli, 1868).

Levis Sullam, Simon, *Una comunità immaginata: gli ebrei a Venezia (1900–1938)* (Milan: Unicopli, 2001).

Levis Sullam, Simon, and Fabio Brusò, *Il Ghetto. Piazza Barche* (Padua: Il Poligrafo, 2008).

Li Causi, Girolamo, *Il lungo cammino: autobiografia 1906–1944* (Rome: Riuniti, 1974).

Littlewood, Ian, *Venice: A Literary Companion* (London: John Murray, 1991).

Lombroso, Cesare, 'Perché fu grande Venezia?', *Nuova Antologia*, fasc. 647, 1 December 1898.

Los, Sergio, *Carlo Scarpa* (Cologne: Taschen, 2002).

Lucas, E. V., *A Wanderer in Venice* (London: Methuen, 1914).

Luciani, Albino, *Illustrissimi: lettere al Patriarca* (Padua: Messaggero, 1976).

Luciani, Albino, *Scuola di vita: antologie di testi sull'educazione*, ed. Natalino Bonazza (Venice: Marcianum, 2005).

Lutyens, Mary (ed.), *Effie in Venice: Unpublished Letters of Mrs John Ruskin Written from Venice between 1849–1852* (London: John Murray, 1965).

Luzzatti, Luigi, 'La politica economica e finanziaria di Venezia', *Nuova Antologia*, fasc. 1214, 16 October 1922.

Luzzatti, Luigi, *Memorie*, 3 vols (Milan: Istituto centrale delle Banche Popolari italiane, 1966).

Luzzatto, Aldo (ed.), *La comunità ebraica di Venezia e il suo antico cimitero*, vol. 1 (Milan: Il Polifilo, 2000).

McBrien, William, *Cole Porter: The Definitive Biography* (London: HarperCollins, 1999).

McCarthy, Mary, *Venice Observed* (London: Heinemann, 1961).

Macgregor, James H. S., *Venice from the Ground Up* (Cambridge, MA: Harvard University Press, 2006).

Mack Smith, Denis, *Victor Emanuel, Cavour, and the Risorgimento* (Oxford University Press, 1971).

McNeill, William H., *Venice: The Hinge of Europe* (University of Chicago Press, 1974).

Madden, Thomas F., *Venice: A New History* (New York: Viking, 2012).

Madsen, Axel, *Coco Chanel: A Biography* (London: Bloomsbury, 1990).

Mancuso, Franco, *Costruire sull'acqua: le sorprendenti soluzioni adottate per far nascere e crescere Venezia* (Venice: Corte del Fontego, 2011).

Mancuso, Franco, *Fronte del porto: Porto Marghera: la vicenda urbanistica* (Venice: Corte del Fontego, 2011).

Manfroni, Alvise, 'Attraverso la laguna – il tunnel subacqueo Venezia-Lido', *Nuova Antologia*, fasc. 974, 16 July 1912.

Mann, Katia, *Unwritten Memories*, ed. Elisabeth Plessen and Michael Mann (London: Deutsch, 1973).

Mann, Thomas, *Death in Venice* (Penguin: Harmondsworth, 1955).

Maraini, Yoï, *In a Grain of Sand* (London: Collins, 1922).

Maranesi, Lorenzo, *Giovanni Someda e il suo tempo (30 maggio 1901–31 marzo 1978)* (Venice: Istituto di Scienze, Lettere ed Arti, 2004).

Marcello, Girolamo, 'Contro la tassa di successione – Per la conservazione dei monumenti e degli oggetti d'arte – Per Venezia', *Discorso al Senato pronuciato 5 giugno 1931* (Rome: Tipografia del Senato, 1931).

Marcello, Girolamo, 'Sulle condizioni di Venezia', *Discorso al Senato pronunciato il 15 dicembre 1933* (Rome: Tipografia del Senato, 1933).

Marchesi, Vincenzo, *Settant'anni di storia politica di Venezia (1798–1866)* (Turin: L. Roux, [1894]).

Maretto, Paolo, *La casa veneziana nella storia della città dalle origini all'Ottocento* (Venice: Marsilio, 1986).

Margetson, Stella, *The Long Party: High Society in the Twenties and Thirties* (Farnborough: Saxon House, 1974).

Mariani, Filippo, Francesco Stocco and Giorgio Crovato, *La reinvenzione di Venezia: tradizioni cittadine negli anni ruggenti* (Padua: Il Poligrafo, 2007).

Mariano, Emilio, *Gino Damerini: cittadino dell'altra Venezia* (Venice: Fondazione Giorgio Cini, [1968]).

Mariano, Emilio (ed.), *D'Annunzio a Venezia* (Rome: Lucarini, 1991).

Marqusee, Michael (ed.), *Venice: An Illustrated Anthology* (London: Conran Octopus, 1988).

Martin, Judith, *No Vulgar Hotel: The Desire and Pursuit of Venice* (New York: W. W. Norton, 2007).

Massola, Umberto, and Girolamo Li Causi, *Gli scioperi, 1943–1944: la classe operaia in lotta contro il fascismo e l'occupante* (Rome: Società Editrice L'Unità, 1945).

Matsumoto-Best, Saho, 'The Art of Diplomacy: British Diplomats and the Collection of Italian Renaissance paintings, 1851–1917', in Markus Mösslang and Torsten Riotte (eds), *The Diplomats' World: A Cultural History of Diplomacy, 1815–1914* (Oxford University Press, 2008).

Matvejević, Predag, *L'altra Venezia* (Milan: Garzanti, 2003).

Maxwell, Elsa, *I Married the World* (London: Heinemann, 1955).

Meccoli, Sandro, *Viva Venezia* (Milan: Longanesi, 1985).

Mencini, Giannandrea, *Venezia acqua e fuoco: la politica della 'salvaguardia' dall'alluvione del 1966 al rogo della Fenice* (Venice: Il Cardo, 1996).

Mencini, Giannandrea, *Il fronte per la difesa di Venezia e della laguna e le denunce di Indro Montanelli* (Venice Lido: Supernova, 2005).

Mencini, Giannandrea, *Fermare l'onda: la secolare battaglia contro il moto ondoso* (Venice: Corte del Fontego, 2011).

Meneghello, Luigi, *The Outlaws* (London: Michael Joseph, 1967).

Meneghini, Francesco, *Delle abitazioni dei poveri: considerazioni pratiche* (Venice: Antonio Clementi, 1866).

Mezzalira, Mauro, 'Venezia anni trenta: il Comune, il partito fascista e le grandi opere', *Italia contemporanea*, 202 (1996).

Miani, Mariapia, Daniele Resini and Francesca Lamon, *L'arte dei maestri vetrai di Murano* (Dosson (TV): Matteo, 1984).

Middlemas, Keith, *Pursuit of Pleasure: High Society in the 1900s* (London: Gordon and Cremonesi, 1977).

Millo, Anna, *Trieste, le Assicurazioni, l'Europa* (Milan: Franco Angeli, 2004).

Ministero delle Comunicazioni, Direzione Generale delle Poste e Telegrafi (ed.), *Il Fondaco dei tedeschi* (Venice: Zanetti, 1941).

Minniti, Fortunato, *Il Piave* (Bologna: Il Mulino, 2000).

Miozzi, Eugenio, *Venezia nei secoli: la città*, 2 vols (Venice: Libeccio, 1957).

Miozzi, Eugenio, *Venezia nei secoli: la laguna* (Venice: Libeccio, 1968).

Miozzi, Eugenio, *Venezia nei secoli: il salvamento* (Venice: Libeccio, 1969).

Miserocchi, Manlio, 'I vent'anni della Mostra cinematografica a Venezia', *Nuova Antologia*, fasc. 1823, November 1952.

Missori, Mario, *Governi, alte cariche dello stato e prefetti del Regno d'Italia* (Rome: Ministero dell'Interno, 1973).

Mollica, Richard F., 'From Antonio Gramsci to Franco Basaglia: The Theory and Practice of the Italian Psychiatric Reform', *International Journal of Mental Health*, 14 (1985).

Molmenti, Pompeo, *Vecchie storie* (Venice: F. Ongania, 1882).

Molmenti, Pompeo, 'Delendae Venetiae', *Nuova Antologia*, fasc. 3, 1 February 1887.

Molmenti, Pompeo, *Venezia calunniata: discorso* (Venice: Fratelli Visentini, 1894).

Molmenti, Pompeo, 'Un nuovo ponte sulla laguna di Venezia', *Nuova Antologia*, fasc. 630, 1 March 1898.

Molmenti, Pompeo, 'Per i monumenti veneziani', *Nuova Antologia*, fasc. 744, 16 December 1902.

Molmenti, Pompeo, 'Il Lido di Venezia', *Nuova Antologia*, fasc. 912, 16 December 1909.

Molmenti, Pompeo, 'Venezia e i barbari', *Nuova Antologia*, fasc. 1054, 16 December 1915.

Molmenti, Pompeo, *I nemici di Venezia: polemiche raccolte ed annotate da Elio Zorzi* (Bologna: Zanichelli, 1924).

Molmenti, Pompeo, *Venice* (London: The Medici Society, 1926).

Molmenti, Pompeo, and Dario Mantovani, *Le isole della laguna veneta* (Bergamo: Istituto Italiano d'Arti Grafiche, 1925).

Montanelli, Indro, *Per Venezia*, ed. Nevio Casadio (Venice: Marsilio, 2010).

Montanelli, Indro, Giuseppe Samonà and Francesco Valcanover, *Venezia caduta e salvezza* (Florence: Sansoni, 1970).

Monti, Antonio, *Il Conte Luigi Torelli: il Risorgimento italiano studiato attraverso una nobile vita* (Milan: R. Istituto Lombardo di Scienze e Lettere, 1931).

Monzali, Luciano, *The Italians of Dalmatia: From Italian Unification to World War I* (University of Toronto Press, 2009).

Moorehead, Alan, *The Villa Diana: Travels in Post-War Italy* (New York: Charles Scribner's Sons, 1951).

Morand, Paul, *Venices* (London: Pushkin, 2002).

Morgan, Philip, '"The Trash Who Are Obstacles in Our Way": The Italian Fascist Party at the Point of Totalitarian Lift-Off, 1930–31', *English Historical Review*, 127 (2012).

Moro, Pierandrea (ed.), *Il piano di attacco austriaco contro Venezia con le schede della storia e lo stato attuale delle fortificazioni veneziane* (Venice: Marsilio, 2001).

Morris, James, *Venice* (London: Faber and Faber, 1960).

Morris, Jan, *The Venetian Empire: A Sea Voyage* (London: Faber and Faber, 1980).

Mosca, Oreste, *Volpi di Misurata* (Rome: Pinciana, 1928).

Moscarda, Giorgio, *Venezia nel 1930* (Venice: Tip. Società M. S. Fra Compositori, 1898).

Moschetti, Andrea, *I danni ai monumenti e alle opere d'arte delle Venezie nella guerra mondiale MCMXV–MCMXVIII*, rev. edn (Venice: C. Ferrari, 1932).

'Il movimento dei forestieri e la guerra', *Nuova Antologia*, fasc. 1052, 16 November 1915.

Murphy, Richard, *Querini Stampalia Foundation: Carlo Scarpa* (London: Phaidon, 1993).

Musatti, Cesare, *Dello insegnamento dell'igiene specialmente per le classi operaie: lezione popolare tenuta al Veneto Ateneo nel dicembre 1874* (Venice: Grimaldo, 1875).

Musolino, Giovanni, *The Basilica of St Mark in Venice* (Venice: F. Ongania, 1956).

Musu, Ignazio (ed.), *Venezia sostenibile: suggestioni dal futuro* (Bologna: Il Mulino, 1998).

Nani Mocenigo, Mario, *L'Arsenale di Venezia* (Rome: Ministero della Marina, 1938).

Nardi, Piero, 'L'acqua alta a Venezia', *Nuova Antologia*, fasc. 1993, January 1967.

Nasalli Rocca, Amedeo, *Memorie di un prefetto* (Rome: Mediterranea, 1946).

Niero, Antonio, *I patriarchi di Venezia da Lorenzo Giustiniani ai nostri giorni* (Venice: Studium Cattolico Veneziano, 1961).

Norwich, John Julius, *A History of Venice* (New York: A. A. Knopf, 1982).

Norwich, John Julius (ed.), *Venice: A Traveller's Companion* (London: Constable, 1990).

Norwich, John Julius, *Paradise of Cities: Venice in the Nineteenth Century* (New York: Vintage, 2004).

Obici, Giulio, *Venice, How Long?* (Padua: Marsilio, 1967).

Odenigo, Armando, *Piero Foscari: una vita esemplare* (Rocca San Casciano: Cappelli, 1959).

Okey, Thomas, *The Story of Venice* (London: J. M. Dent, 1928).

Okey, Thomas, *A Basketful of Memories: An Autobiographical Sketch* (London: J. M. Dent, 1930).

Olsberg, Nicholas, et al., *Carlo Scarpa Architect: Intervening with History* (New York: Monicelli, 1999).

O'Neill, Michael, Mark Sandy and Sarah Wotton (eds), *Venice and the Cultural Imagination: 'This Strange Dream upon the Water'* (London: Pickering and Chatto, 2012).

Oppo, Cipriano E., 'La XXVI Esposizione di Venezia: le retrospettive che contano', *Nuova Antologia*, fasc. 1821, September 1952.

Oppo, Cipriano E., 'Italiani e stranieri alla XXVI Biennale', *Nuova Antologia*, fasc. 1823, November 1952.

Ori, Alessandro, *La febbre tifoide a Venezia* (Venice: Libreria Emiliana, 1933).

Orio, Marco, *A S. E. Benito Mussolini, genio providenzialmente devoto alla grandezza della Terza Italia, questa petitizione per l'Arsenale di Venezia* (Venice: n.p., 1934).

Ottokar, Nicola, *Venezia: cenni di storia e di cultura veneziane* (Florence: La Nuova Italia, 1941).

Ottolenghi, Adolfo, *La scuola ebraica di Venezia attraverso la voce del suo Rabbino (1912-1944)*, ed. Elisabetta Ottolenghi (Venice: Filippi, 2012).

Ottolenghi, G., *La camorra nell'industria veneziana: opuscolo dedicato a S. E. il Ministro Zanardelli* (Venice: n.p., 1887).

Paget, Walburga, *Scenes and Memories* (London: Smith, Elder and Co., 1912).

Paladini, Filippo Maria, *Arsenale e Museo Storico Navale di Venezia: mare, lavoro e uso pubblico della storia* (Padua: Il Poligrafo, 2008).

Paladini, Giannantonio, 'Momenti ed aspetti della lotta politica e sociale a Venezia (1870-1874)', *Risorgimento Veneto*, 1 (1972).

Paladini, Giannantonio, *Uscire dall'isola: Venezia, risparmio privato e pubblica utilità, 1822-2002* (Bari: Laterza, 2003).

Paladini, Giannantonio, and Maurizio Reberschak (eds), *La resistenza nel Veneziano: la società veneziana tra fascismo, resistenza, repubblica*, 2 vols (Venice: Istituto Veneto per la storia della Resistenza, 1985).

Paladini, Vinicio, *Arte nella Russia dei Soviets: il padiglione dell'URSS a Venezia* (Rome: Edizioni di 'la bilancia', 1925).

Le Palais Dandalo à Venise (Venice: G. Zanetti, [1922]).

Papadopoli, Angelo, *Della necessità di un nuovo indirizzo nella pubblica beneficenza in Venezia* (Venice: Marco Visentini, 1871).

Papadopoli, Nicolò, *Le monete anonime di Venezia dal 1472 al 1605* (Milan: L. F. Cogliati, 1871).

Pascolo, Sergio, *Abitando Venezia* (Venice: Corte del Fontego, 2012).

Passarella Sartorelli, Lina (ed.), *Maria Pezzè Pascolato: notizie raccolte da un gruppo di amici* (Florence: Le Monnier, 1935).

Pasternak, Boris, *Safe Conduct: An Early Autobiography and Other Works* (London: Elek, 1959).

Patassini, Domenico (ed.), *Contaminazione, rischio e stigma: bonifica a Porto Marghera* (Venice: Marsilio, 2011).

Paulon, Flavia, *La dogaressa contestata: la favolosa storia della Mostra di Venezia dalle regine alla contestazione* (Venice: F. Paulon, 1971).

Peli, Santo, 'Le concentrazioni industriali nell'economia di guerra: il caso di Porto Marghera', *Studi storici*, 16 (1975).

Pemble, John, *The Mediterranean Passion: Victorians and Edwardians in the South* (Oxford: Clarendon, 1987).

Pemble, John, *Venice Rediscovered* (Oxford University Press, 1996).

Pertot, Gianfranco, *Venice: Extraordinary Maintenance* (London: Paul Halberton, 2004).

Petri, Rolf, *La zona industriale di Marghera, 1919–1939: un'analisi quantitativa dello sviluppo tra le due guerre* (Venice: Centro Tedesco di Studi Veneziani, 1985).

Petri, Rolf, 'Acqua contro carbone: elettrochimica e indipendenza energetica italiana negli anni trenta', *Italia contemporanea*, 168 (1987).

Pezzè Pascolato, Maria, 'Fasci femminili', *Gerarchia*, 12 (1932).

Picchini, Luigi, *Tentati suicidi e suicidi con particolare riguardo alla città di Venezia* (Venice: Sorteni, 1933).

Picchini, Luigi, *Venezia contro la bestemmia e il turpiloquio* (Venice: Libreria Emiliana, 1937).

[Picciolo, Angelo (ed.)], *La rinascita della Tripolitania: memorie e studi sui quattro anni di governo del Conte Giuseppe Volpi di Misurata* (Milan: Mondadori, 1926).

Pignatti Morano, Carlo, *La vita di Nazario Sauro ed il martirio dell'eroe* (Milan: Treves, 1922).

Pilot, A., *Antichi alberghi veneziani* (Venice: Zanetti, n.d.).

Piva, Francesco, *Lotte contadine e origini del fascismo, Padova–Venezia: 1919–1922* (Venice: Marsilio, 1977).

Piva, Francesco, *Contadini in fabbrica: Marghera, 1920–1945* (Rome: Lavoro, 1991).

Piva, Francesco, and Giuseppe Tattara (eds), *I primi operai di Marghera: mercato, reclutamento, occupazione, 1917–1940* (Venice: Marsilio, 1983).

Plant, Margaret, *Venice: Fragile City, 1797–1997* (New Haven and London: Yale University Press, 2002).

Pomoni, Luciano, *Il Dovere Nazionale: i nazionalisti veneziani alla conquista della piazza (1908–1915)* (Padua: Il Poligrafo, 1998).

Pratt, Hugo, *Corto Maltese: favola di Venezia* (Milan: Rizzoli and Lizard, 2010).

Provincia di Venezia (ed.), *Immagine di popolo e organizzazione del consenso in Italia negli anni trenta e quaranta* (Venice: Marsilio, 1979).

Querini, Patrizia, *Immagini nello specchio: l'altra Venezia* (Cittadella (PD): Biblos, 2008).

Quill, Sarah (ed.), *Ruskin's Venice: The Stones Rediscovered* (Aldershot: Ashgate, 2000).

Racinaro, Roberto, *Sul partito democratico: opinioni a confronto* (Naples: Guida, 2007).

Radnor, Helen, Countess-Dowager of, *From a Great-Grandmother's Armchair* (London: Marshall, n.d.).

Ragg, Laura M., *Crises in Venetian History* (London: Methuen, 1928).

Ragg, Lonsdale, and Laura M. Ragg, *Things Seen in Venice* (London: Seeley, Service and Co., 1912).

Rapex, Raffaele, *L'affermazione della sovranità italiana in Tripolitania: governatorato del Conte Giuseppe Volpi (1921–1925)* (Tientsin: Chilhi Press, 1937).

Reato, Danilo, *Venice: Places and History* (Vercelli: White Star, 1996).

Reato, Danilo (ed.), *Florian, un caffè, la città* (Venice: Filippi, 1986).

Reato, Ermenegildo, *Pensiero e azione sociale dei cattolici vicentini e veneti dalla 'Rerum Novarum' al Fascismo (1891–1922)* (Vicenza: Nuovo Progetto, 1991).

Reberschak, Maurizio, 'Stampa periodica e opinione pubblica a Venezia durante i quarantacinque giorni (25 luglio–8 settembre 1943)', *Archivio Veneto*, 94 (1971).

Reberschak, Maurizio, 'Epurazioni: giustizia straordinaria, giustizia politica', *Venetica*, 12 (1998).

Reberschak, Maurizio (ed.), *Venezia nel secondo dopoguerra* (Padua: il Poligrafo, 1993).

Reberschegg, Alessandro, 'La Corte straordinaria di Venezia', *Venetica*, 12 (1998).

Redford, Bruce, *Venice and the Grand Tour* (New Haven: Yale University Press, 1996).

Redman, Tim, *Ezra Pound and Italian Fascism* (Cambridge University Press, 1991).

Régnier, Henri de, 'Sur l'altana ou la vie vénitienne', *Revue des deux mondes*, 97 (1927).

Renzini, Anna (ed.), *Nuove politiche per la residenza: ruolo e scelta del Comune in un quadro normativo rinnovato a livello nazionale* (Venice: Comune di Venezia, [1997]).

Resini, Daniele (ed.), *Cent'anni a Venezia: la Camera del Lavoro, 1892–1992* (Venice: Il Cardo, 1992).

Resini, Daniele, and Myriam Zerbi (eds), *Venezia tra Ottocento e Novecento nelle fotografie di Tomaso Filippi* (Rome: Palombi, 2013).

Robertson, Bruce (ed.), *Sargent and Italy* (Princeton University Press, 2008).

Rodd, James Rennell, *Social and Diplomatic Memories*, 3 vols (London: Edward Arnold, 1922–5).

Roeck, Bernd, *Florence, 1900: The Quest for Arcadia* (New Haven: Yale University Press, 2004).

Rolfe, Frederick, *The Desire and Pursuit of the Whole: A Romance of Modern Venice* (Oxford University Press, 1984).

Romanelli, Giandomenico (ed.), *Venice and the Biennale: itineraries of taste* (Monza: Fabbri editori, 1995).

Romano, Sergio, *Giuseppe Volpi: industria e finanza tra Giolitti e Mussolini* (Milan: Bompiani, 1979).

Romeo, Rosario, *L'Italia unita e la prima guerra mondiale* (Bari: Laterza, 1978).

Roncalli, Marco, *Giovanni XXIII: la mia Venezia* (Venice: Canal e Stamperia, 2000).

Ross, Josephine (ed.), *Society in Vogue: The International Set between the Wars* (London: Condé Nast, 1992).

Rossi-Osmida, Gabriele, *1872–1972: cento anni di sport a Venezia* (Venice: n.p., 1971).

Rotary Club di Venezia, *I problemi di Venezia/The Problems of Venice, 1960–1970* (Venice: Tipografia Commerciale, [1970]).

Rotary International, *Terza Conferenza regionale Europa–Africa–Asia Minore, Venezia, settembre 1935* (Venice: Zanetti, 1936).

Roth, Cecil, *Gli ebrei in Venezia* (Rome: P. Cremonese, 1933).

Ruinas, Stanis, *Pioggia sulla Repubblica* (Rome: Corso, 1946).

Rumor, Mario, *I Democratici Cristiani per il rinnovamento dello stato, per lo sviluppo della democrazia, per la libertà e per la pace* (Rome: Cinque Lune, 1968).

Rumor, Mario, *Memorie (1943–1970)*, ed. Ermenegildo Reato and Francesco Malgeri (Vicenza: Neri Pozza, 1991).

Ruskin, John, *The Stones of Venice*, vol. 1: *The Foundations* (London: Smith, Elder and Co., 1851).

Ruskin, John, *The Stones of Venice*, vol. 2: *The Sea-Stories* (London: Smith, Elder and Co., 1853).

Ruskin, John, *The Stones of Venice*, vol. 3: *The Fall* (London: Smith, Elder and Co., 1853).

Ryersson, Scot D., and Michael Orlando Yaccarino, *Infinite Variety: The Life and Legend of the Marchesa Casati* (London: Pimlico, 2000).

Saikia, Robin, *The Venice Lido: A Blue Guide Travel Monograph* (London: Somerset, 2011).

Salbe, Giampaolo, *Storia dei trasporti pubblici di Venezia–Mestre–Lido* (Cortona: Calosci, 1985).

Salzano, Edoardo, *Ma dove vivi? La città raccontata* (Venice: Corte del Fontego, 2007).

Salzano, Edoardo, *La laguna di Venezia: il governo di un sistema complesso* (Venice: Corte del Fontego, 2011).

Salzano, Edoardo, *Lo scandalo del Lido: cultura e affari, turismo e cemento nell'isola di Aschenbach* (Venice: Corte del Fontego, 2011).

Sammartini, Tudy, *Venezia from the Bell Towers* (London: Merrell, 2002).

San Pio X a Venezia: celebrazioni e documenti, domenica 12 aprile–domenica 10 maggio 1959 ([Vatican City]: n.p., 1959).

Sarazani, Fabrizio, *L'ultimo doge: vita di Giuseppe Volpi di Misurata* (Milan: Edizioni del Borghese, 1972).

Sarfatti, Margherita, 'La XV Biennale: forestieri a Venezia', *Nuova Antologia*, fasc. 1300, 16 May 1926.

Sarfatti, Margherita, 'Architettura, teatro e mostra dell'ottocento a Venezia', *Nuova Antologia*, fasc. 1351, 1 July 1928.

Sarto, Giuseppe (Pope Pius X), *Le pastorali del periodo veneziano (1894–1898)*, ed. Antonio Niero (Asolo: Quaderni della Fondazione Giuseppe Sarto, 2, [1991]).

Sarto, Giuseppe (Pope Pius X), *Le pastorali del periodo veneziano (1899–1903)*, ed. Antonio Niero (Asolo: Quaderni della Fondazione Giuseppe Sarto, 3, [1991]).

Sbordone, Giovanni, *Nella Repubblica di Santa Margherita: storie di un campo veneziano nel primo Novecento* (Venice: Istituto veneziano per la storia della Resistenza e della società contemporanea, 2003).

Sbordone, Giovanni, *La Camera del Lavoro* (Padua: Il Poligrafo, 2005).

Sbordone, Giovanni, Giorgio Crovato and Carlo Montanaro, *Via Garibaldi. La Regata Storica. I Cinema 'Peocéti'* (Padua: Il Poligrafo, 2005).

Scano, Luigi, *Venezia: terra e acqua* (Rome: Edizioni delle Autonomie, 1985).

Scarabello, Giovanni, *Il martirio di Venezia durante la grande guerra e l'opera di difesa della Marina italiana*, 2 vols (Venice: Tipografia del *Gazzettino Illustrato*, 1933).

Sega, Maria Teresa (ed.), *La partigiana veneta: arte e memoria della Resistenza* (Portogruaro: Edicola, 2004).

Sega, Maria Teresa, and Nadia Maria Filippini, *Manifattura Tabacchi. Cotonificio Veneziano* (Padua: Il Poligrafo, 2008).

Segre, Renata, *Gli ebrei a Venezia, 1938–1945: una comunità tra persecuzione e rinascita* (Venice: Il Cardo, 1995).

Sepeda, Toni, *Brunetti's Venice: Walks with the City's Best-Loved Detective* (New York: Grove, 2008).

Shaw-Kennedy, Ronald, *Art and Architecture in Venice: The Venice in Peril Guide* (London: Sidgwick and Jackson, 1972).

Sheehy, Helen, *Eleonora Duse: A Biography* (New York: A. A. Knopf, 2003).

Signore, Adalberto, and Alessandro Troncino, *Razza padana* (Milan: BUR, 2008).

Sigona, Ferdinando, 'Ethnography of the "Gypsy Problem" in Italy: The Case of Kosovo Roma and Ashkali in Florence and Venice' (unpublished Ph.D. thesis, Oxford Brookes University, 2009).

Sindacato Nazionale Fascista Belle Arti (ed.), *L'ordinamento sindacale fascista delle belle arti* (Rome: CFAP, 1939).

Sitwell, Osbert, *Winters of Content and Other Discursions on Mediterranean Art and Travel* (London: Duckworth, 1950).

Snowden, Frank M., *Naples in the Time of Cholera, 1884–1911* (Cambridge University Press, 1995).

Snowden, Frank M., *The Conquest of Malaria: Italy, 1900–1960* (New Haven and London: Yale University Press, 2006).

Somers Cocks, Anna, 'The Coming Death of Venice', *New York Review of Books*, 20 June 2013.

Somma, Paola, *Benettown: un ventennio di mecenatismo* (Venice: Corte del Fontego, 2011).

Somma, Paola, *Imbonimenti: laguna, terra di conquista* (Venice: Corte del Fontego, 2012).

Sorcinelli, Paolo 'Che pazzia affidarsi al mare! Per una storia del turismo balneare sull'Adriatico', *Il Risorgimento*, 45 (1993).

[Spadolini, Giovanni], 'Il dramma dell'alluvione', *Nuova Antologia*, fasc. 1992, December 1966.

Sponza, Lucio, 'L'onore e la legge: un dramma d'onore a Venezia (1924)', *Quaderni di stori-Amestre*, 9 (2009).

Sprigge, Sylvia, *The Lagoon of Venice: Its Islands, Life and Communication* (London: Max Parrish, 1961).

Statuto della Società di Mutuo Soccorso fra camerieri, caffettieri, cuochi ed interpreti addetti agli alberghi in Venezia (Venice: Tipografia Istituto Coletti, 1885).

Stone, Marla, 'Challenging Cultural Categories: The Transformation of the Venice Biennale under Fascism', *Journal of Modern Italian Studies*, 4 (1999).

Sully, James, *Italian Travel Sketches* (London: Constable, 1912).

Symons, Alphonse J. A., *The Search for Corvo* (Harmondsworth: Penguin, 1934).

Talenti, Achille, *Come si crea una nuova città: il Lido di Venezia: la storia, la cronaca, la statistica* (Padua: Angelo Draghi, 1921).

Tamaro, Attilio, *L'Adriatico – Golfo d'Italia: l'italianità di Trieste* (Milan: Treves, 1915).

Tamborra, Angelo, 'The Rise of Italian Industry and the Balkans (1900–1914)', *Journal of European Economic History*, 3 (1974).

Tanner, Tony, *Venice Desired* (Oxford: Blackwell, 1992).

Tantucci, Enrico, *A che ora chiude Venezia? Breve guida alla disneylandizzazione della città* (Venice: Corte del Fontego, 2011).

[Tassini, Giuseppe ('G. Nissati')], *Aneddoti storici veneziani* (Venice: Libreria Filippi, 1965).

Taylor, Richard, and Claus Melchior (eds), *Ezra Pound and Europe* (Amsterdam: Rodopi, 1993).

Testa, Silvio, *E le chiamano navi: il crocierismo fa boom in Laguna* (Venice: Corte del Fontego, 2011).

Thompson, Mark, *The White War: Life and Death on the Italian Front, 1915–1918* (London: Faber and Faber, 2010).

Toeplitz, Ludovico, *Il banchiere: al tempo in cui nacque, crebbe, e fiorì la Banca Commerciale Italiana* (Milan: Milano Nuova, 1963).

Toeplitz, Ludovico, *Ciak a chi tocca* (Milan: Milano Nuova, 1964).

Torelli, Luigi, *Le condizioni della provincia e della città di Venezia nel 1867* (Venice: Tipografia della *Gazzetta*, 1867).

Torelli, Luigi, *Descrizione di Porto Said, del Canale Marittimo e di Suez* (Venice: Giuseppe Antonelli, 1869).

Torelli, Luigi, *L'eucalyptus a Roma: memorie* (Rome: Tipografia dell'*Opinione*, 1879).

Tramontin, Silvio, 'Il fascismo nel "Diario" del card. La Fontaine', *Storia contemporanea*, 1 (1970).

Tramontin, Silvio, 'Patriarca e cattolici veneziani di fronte al Partito Popolare Italiano', *Storia contemporanea*, 4 (1973).

Tramontin, Silvio, *Cattolici, popolari e fascisti nel Veneto* (Rome: Cinque Lune, 1975).

Tramontin, Silvio, 'I Veneziani e la preparazione del primo congresso cattolico italiano', *Archivio Veneto*, 108 (1977).

Tramontin, Silvio, *San Zaccaria* (Venice: Luigi Salvagno, 1980).

Tramontin, Silvio, *Giovanni Ponti (1896–1961): una vita per la democrazia e per Venezia* (Venice: Comune di Venezia, 1983).

Tramontin, Silvio, *Il Cardinale Roncalli a Venezia* (Florence: Olschki, 1984).

Tramontin, Silvio, 'Il Cardinale Pietro La Fontaine, patriarca di Venezia, e il suo tempo', *Archivio Veneto*, 129 (1987).

Tramontin, Silvio (ed.), *Patriarcato di Venezia* (Padua: Gregoriana Libreria, 1991).

Tramontin, Silvio (ed.), *La chiesa di Venezia nel primo Novecento* (Venice: Studium Cattolico Veneziano, 1995).

Trentin, Silvio, *Dieci anni di fascismo totalitario in Italia: dall'istituzione del Tribunale speciale alla proclamazione dell'Impero (1926–1936)* (Rome: Riuniti, 1975).

Trevelyan, George Macaulay, *Scenes from Italy's War* (London: T. C. and E. C. Jack, 1919).

Trevelyan, George Macaulay, *Manin and the Venetian Revolution of 1848* (London: Longmans, Green and Co., 1923).

Treves, Anna, 'Anni di Guerra, anni di svolta: il turismo italiano durante la prima guerra mondiale', in Giorgio Botta (ed.), *Studi geografici sul paesaggio* (Milan: Cisalpino-Goliardica, 1989).

Twain, Mark, *The Innocents Abroad* (London: Collins, n.d.).

UNESCO, *Rapporto su Venezia* (Milan: Mondadori, 1969).

Unrau, John, *Ruskin and St Mark's* (London: Thames and Hudson, 1984).

Urettini, Luigi, *Bruno Visentini* (Sommacampagna (VR): Cierre, 2005).

Valeri, Diego, *Guida sentimentale di Venezia* (Florence: Passigli, 1994).

Vanzan Marchini, Nelli-Elena, *San Servolo e Venezia: un'isola e la sua storia* (Sommacampagna (VR): Cierre, 2004).

Vanzan Marchini, Nelli-Elena, *Il ponte di debole costituzione* (Venice: Corte del Fontego, 2011).

Vanzan Marchini, Nelli-Elena (ed.), *La memoria della salute: Venezia e il suo ospedale dal XVI al XX secolo* (Venice: Arsenale Editrice, 1985).

Varè, Daniele, *Ghosts of the Rialto* (London: John Murray, 1956).

Vedovetto, Mirella, 'Breda, marzo 1950: l'intervento del sindaco Giobatta Gianquinto: le cronache di Gianni Rodari', *Quaderni di storiAmestre*, 1 (2005).

Venezia restaurata, 1966-1986: la campagna dell'UNESCO e l'opera delle organizzazioni private (Venice: Electa, 1986).

Venice International University, *Rapporto sulle attività/Report on Activities* (n.p., 2012).

Venice under the Yoke of France and Austria with Memoirs of the Courts, Governments, and People of Italy: Presenting a Faithful Picture of Her Present Conditions by a Lady of Rank (London: G. and W. B. Whittaker, 1824).

Vian, Agostino, *Giambattista Paganuzzi: la vita e l'opera* (Rome: Edizioni di Presenza, 1950).

Vian, Giovanni, *Sposa e pastore: oltre vent'anni di chiesa veneziana (1978-2000)* (Gorle (BG): Servitium, 2001).

Vian, Giovanni, *'La Voce di San Marco' (1946-1975)* (Padua: Il Poligrafo, 2007).

Vicentini, Raffaele A., *Il movimento fascista veneto attraverso il diario di uno squadrista* (Venice: Zanetti, [1934]).

Vidal, Gore, *Vidal in Venice* (London: Weidenfeld and Nicolson, 1985).

Villari, Luigi, 'Luigi Luzzatti', in Hector Bolitho (ed.), *Twelve Jews* (London: Rich and Cowan, 1934).

Visentini, Bruno, 'La Fondazione Cini e la cultura italiana nel momento attuale', *Nuova Antologia*, fasc. 2115-17, March–May 1977.

Vittadini, Maria Rosa, *Fare a meno dell'acqua: arrivare a Venezia annullando la Laguna?* (Venice: Corte del Fontego, 2012).

Vitucci, Alberto, *Nel nome di Venezia: grandi opere e soliti nomi* (Venice: Corte del Fontego, 2012).

Vivante, Angelo, *Irredentismo adriatico* (Florence: Parenti, 1912).

Vivante, Raffaele, *La malaria in Venezia* (Turin: Fratelli Pozzo, 1902).

Vivante, Raffaele, *Il problema delle abitazioni in Venezia* (Venice: C. Ferrari, 1910).

Vivante, Raffaele, *La lotta contro la tubercolosi in Venezia* (Milan: Stucchi, Ceretti, 1915).

Vivante, Raffaele, 'La difficoltà della lotta legislativa contro l'alcoolismo e la propaganda antialcoolica nelle scuole elementari di Venezia', *Rivista mensile della città di Venezia*, 3 (1924).

Vivante, Raffaele, *Nuovo contributo allo studio del problema delle abitazioni in Venezia* (Venice: F. Garzia, 1935).

Vivante, Raffaele, *Per la istituzione in Venezia di una piscina natatoria coperta* (Venice: Ateneo Veneto, 1937).

Vivante, Raffaele, *I pianterreni inabitabili di Venezia, l'abitato di Mestre: nuove indagini sulle condizioni igieniche delle abitazioni del Comune* (Venice: Fantoni, 1948).

Vivian, Giannarosa, 'Per riva e per marina: Pellestrina raccontata dalle zie', *Quaderni di storiAmestre*, 7 (2007).

'Volframo', 'Teatri ed Arti', *Nuova Antologia*, fasc. 735, 1 August 1902.

Volpi di Misurata, Giuseppe, 'Italy's financial policy', *International Conciliation*, 234 (1927).

Volpi di Misurata, Giuseppe, 'La Repubblica di Venezia e i suoi ambasciatori', *Nuova Antologia*, fasc. 1334, 16 October 1927.

Volpi di Misurata, Giuseppe, *Finanza fascista: Anno VII* (Rome: Libreria del Littorio, 1929).

Volpi di Misurata, Giuseppe, *Economic Progress of Fascist Italy* (Rome: Usila, 1937).

Volpi di Misurata, Giuseppe, 'Ricordi e orizzonti balcanici', *Rassegna di politica internazionale*, 4 (1937).

Volpi di Misurata, Giuseppe, *Venezia antica e moderna* (Rome: Atena, 1939).

Wawro, Geoffrey, *The Austro-Prussian War: Austria's War with Prussia and Italy in 1866* (Cambridge University Press, 1996).

Webster, Richard A., *Industrial Imperialism in Italy, 1908-1915* (Berkeley: University of California Press, 1975).

Wells, H. G., *War and the Future: Italy, France and Britain at War* (London: Cassell, 1917).

Whyte, William, *Oxford Jackson: Architecture, Education, Status and Style, 1835-1924* (Oxford University Press, 2006).

Wiel, Alethea, *Venice* (New York: T. Fisher Unwin, 1894).

Wiel, Alethea, *The Navy of Venice* (London: John Murray, 1910).

Willms, Wiebke, *San Clemente: storia di un'isola veneziana, uno dei primi manicomi femminili in Europa* (Venice: Centro Tedesco di Studi Veneziani, 1993).

Winterson, Jeanette, *The Passion* (London: Bloomsbury, 1987).

Woodhouse, John, *Gabriele D'Annunzio: Defiant Archangel* (Oxford: Clarendon, 1998).

Zanelli, Guglielmo, *Traghetti veneziani: la gondola al servizio della città* (Venice: Cicero, 2004).

Zazzara, Gilda, *Il Petrolchimico* (Padua: Il Poligrafo, 2009).

Ziegler, Philip, *Diana Cooper* (London: Hamish Hamilton, 1981).

Zilotto, Pietro, *L'ubriachezza: discorso tenuto agli uditori di Medicina legale nello spedale civile generale di Venezia* (Venice: Locatelli, 1866).

Zizola, Giancarlo, *The Utopia of Pope John XXIII* (Maryknoll, NY: Orbis, 1978).

Zorzi, Alvise, *Venezia scomparsa*, vol. 1: *Storia di una secolare degradazione* (Milan: Electa, 1977).

Zorzi, Alvise, *Venezia scomparsa*, vol. 2: *Repertorio degli edifici veneziani distrutti, alterati o manomessi* (Milan: Electa, 1977).

Zorzi, Alvise, *Venezia austriaca, 1798–1866* (Bari: Laterza, 1985).

Zorzi, Alvise, *Venezia ritrovata, 1895–1939* (Milan: Mondadori, 2001).

Zorzi, Elio, 'I restauri della Basilica di San Marco', *Nuova Antologia*, fasc. 1343, 1 March 1928.

Zorzi, Elio, 'Il ponte del Littorio sulla Laguna', *Nuova Antologia*, fasc. 1469, 1 June 1933.

Zorzi, Elio, *Osterie veneziane* (Venice: Filippi, 1967).

Zorzi, Ettore, *A S. A. R. il Principe Umberto* (Venice: n.p., 1914).

Acknowledgements

For those English-speaking historians of my generation and their predecessors, a telling question is often where did you first enter Italy. Was it Turin? Milan? Genoa? Naples? Sicily? Or even Rome? In my case, however, it was none of the above. Rather, in August 1967, Michal and I crossed the border in the Julian Alps at Tarvisio and pushed south towards the Adriatic. We were driving a battered van of inadequate English mechanical design. Surviving on my less than lavish Commonwealth scholarship grant, we were given to pulling off the road where we happened to be and to sleeping in the back. Our first Italian night we spent near Gemona (soon to be battered by the Friuli earthquake of 1976); our second at Grado on the coast. En route we had slaked some of my passion for Edward Gibbon by surveying the remains of Aquileia and, that evening, we paddled in a tepid Adriatic while biting into luscious local peaches whose ample juices ran down our bodies. Somewhere in our minds, we knew that we had found a place that was not identical to Cambridge, England or Sydney, Australia.

The next day, we moved quickly to the west and actually paid to camp at Mestre. There was time that afternoon to go into Venice, to gawp in our capacity as the most naïve of day-trippers. What I best remember is a retreat in a vaporetto up the Grand Canal towards midnight. By then, a summer thunderstorm was wrecking tents in our camping ground but not afflicting our van. Lightening flashed across the celebrated palaces that we were passing. A wind swirled. Rain hammered down. The ferry leaked mightily and everyone in it talked and complained, roaring as loudly inside as the thunder burst outside. Cambridge had seemed to us Australians a place of deference, decorum and silence. Venice was not. One day trip and our lives were being entangled with Italy in a way that, to our delight, we have never escaped.

As I have already noted in my last book, *Whispering City: Rome and its Histories*, it was Rome not Venice that thereafter became our most accustomed venue in Italy. The archives were there. However, we never forgot Venice. In 1981 we returned there as a family, living on the Lido in a flat on the Via Dardanelli (for Australians, could Gallipoli be far away)? Our children crossed the lagoon each day to a school in Campo San Luca. When passage was closed by frequent strikes, it was quickly re-opened by a speedier, more modern and more expensive ferry called *Il Pirata*.

In so far as our absorption of local culture was concerned, eleven-year old Edmund distinguished himself at Carnevale by going to the fancy dress party in Piazza San Marco as a Standa supermarket bag, a choice which some locals found puzzling. Michal wrote a children's story about a short-sighted monster who lived in the canal, consuming the black plastic garbage bags that Venetians threw into it, a happy relationship until a visiting American ambassador ventured out in a black gondola that was sadly confused with the rubbish.[1] Mary of all of us, perhaps, was most entranced by the place and, in recent years, we have spent wonderful days there with her, Anthony and their daughters, Ella and Sophia, by now ready to be a little Venetian on their own parts.

Our sojourn in 1981 confirmed Venice as a place that we would always try to visit on our recurrent trips to Italy. Our choice was helped by Venetian friends, notably Giovanni Minelli (to whom this book is dedicated) and our children's teacher, Suzanna Miles; Giovanni and Suzanna became an item that year of our stay. Back in Australia, Gino Rizzo, a Venetian who travelled further than Marco Polo, was Sydney's professor of Italian and, for some years, I had been his deputy on the Frederick May Foundation for Italian Studies, learning much about Italy, Rizzo and Venice in the process.[2] My Venice also had by then acquired an extra dimension through friendship with two Triestine boys, Fabio Malusà, who stayed at home, and Gianfranco Cresciani, who moved to Sydney and became the leading historian of Italian migration to Australia. Malusà and Cresciani may be Triestines of some definition but each has a Venice inscribed in his soul. Minelli, Miles, the Rizzos, Cresciani and Malusà all acted as prompts for me to write this book.

I have other debts aplenty. Christopher Duggan, my sometime colleague at Reading University, read much of the manuscript and always managed to combine counsel and encouragement. Lucio Sponza, another wandering

---

[1] Michal Bosworth, 'Garbage Guts' in Peter and Barbara Holland (eds), *Summer Shorts* 2 (Fremantle Arts Centre Press, 1994).
[2] For its history, see G. Cresciani and B. Mascitelli (eds), *Italy and Australia: An Asymmetrical Relationship* (Ballarat: Connor Court Publishing, 2014).

Venetian who spends much of each year at home, was another to proffer stimulus and hospitality. While I was entering that time of life Australian historian Manning Clark loved to moralise over as the years of the sere and the yellow leaf, I was rejuvenated by my Senior Research Fellowship at Jesus College, Oxford. In such asylum from the rigours of contemporary neoliberal fretting of the teaching university, can any historian have ever been so lucky? Great company, great scholarship. A morning at home writing. Then a time with Jesus. It is the perfect formula for a man who has racked up three score years and ten but not yet lost the zest to write and argue.

Equally pleasurable has been my renewed relationship with Yale University Press. I launched the idea of the book with Heather McCallum (after approval from my agent, Clare Alexander) and have thereafter enjoyed her regular endorsement. Rachael Lonsdale has been adept in tracing photographs that we needed to add to those snapped by Michal on our various trips to the city. Tami Halliday has dotted the i's and crossed the t's of book production with aplomb. Laura Davey was the perfect sub-editor, precise and perspicacious.

Research on Venice was also scarcely burdensome, when I went off to work at the Marciana or the Querini Stampalia or the various libraries and archives of Rome where I am an ancient devotee. Back in Oxford, the Bodleian, fifteen minutes walk from my new home, is also a wondrous repository of all sorts of reading matter that you might not expect it to be. Amid its staff, Michael Athanson acted as a sure guide to map production, while Emma Slayton expertly drew those charts that appear in the text.

Enough, enough. My curriculum vitae as a historian from 20,000 kilometres away whose life course has always overcome, and ever more overcomes, such tyranny of distance must seem all but Martian to many of my Italian subjects. But it is mine and I am glad of it. And, in conclusion, *nota bene* to all who sourly deride every day tripper to Venice, I, too, began that way. Therefore it is all the greater pleasure to have argued in the pages that have preceded this acknowledgement that tourists of whatever kind are yet another form of history-bearing Venetian.

Index